J.M. BARRIE
&
THE LOST BOYS

The Love Story
that Gave Birth
to Peter Pan

ANDREW BIRKIN

RESEARCH:
ANDREW BIRKIN
SHARON GOODE

Clarkson N. Potter, Inc., Publishers, New York

Distributed by Crown Publishers, Inc.

First published in Great Britain 1979
by Constable and Company Ltd
10 Orange Street London WC2H7EG

Copyright © 1979 by Andrew Birkin
and Laurentic Film Productions Ltd

First published in the United States of America 1979
by Clarkson N. Potter, Inc./Publishers
One Park Avenue
New York, N.Y. 10016

Printed in the United States of America
Published simultaneously in Canada
by General Publishing Company Ltd

Library of Congress Cataloging in Publication Data

Birkin, Andrew.
    J. M. Barrie: Peter Pan and the lost boys.

    1. Barrie, James Matthew, Sir, bart., 1860–
1937—Biography. 2. Authors, English—19th
century—Biography.
PR4076.B5 1979   828'.9'1209 [B]   79-14571
ISBN 0-517-53873-3

J. M. Barrie and the Lost Boys

"TO DIE WILL BE AN AWFULLY BIG ADVENTURE?"

To my Mother

Into my heart an air that kills
   From yon far country blows:
What are those blue remembered hills,
   What spires, what farms are those?

That is the land of lost content,
   I see it shining plain,
The happy highways where I went
   And cannot come again.

        A. E. Housman

Contents

'You're old, but you're not grown up.
You're one of us.'

Alexander Puttnam, aged 11

Introduction   'May God blast any one who writes a biography of me' warned J. M. Barrie in one of his last notebooks. The curse, scrawled across the page like the hieroglyphics on an Egyptian tomb, seems as good a reason as any to state at the outset that this is not a biography of Barrie; nor is it a critical assessment of his works; nor a psychological dissection of his mind – 'an attempt to dig up the dead and twist a finger in their sockets', as he put it. It is, rather, a love story told through the words and images of the *dramatis personae* concerned. Unlike *The Lost Boys*, a trilogy I wrote for BBC television, this is a documentary account, and I have tried to limit my role to that of an editor, allowing the letters, diaries, notebooks, interviews, photographs, and Barrie's own works, to unfold the narrative with a minimum of editorial interference. There is, of course, no such thing as a totally objective documentary, for were I to withhold my opinion throughout, a degree of subjectivity would still be evidenced by what I had chosen to include or omit. Indeed, my selection of material has not been particularly objective: I have quoted certain items of questionable merit simply because they appealed to me, while other things of more possible value have been discarded.

Much of the material here has never appeared before in print, with one main exception: Barrie's novels and plays. I make no apology for this, since his works – many of them long out of print – are inextricably bound up with his own private world. Moreover I am fond of them. It has become fashionable to dismiss Barrie as being sentimental or 'whimsical'; neither adjective describes him fully, a fact recognized by contemporary critics who were obliged to resort to such neologisms as 'Barrieish', 'Barriesque', and 'J.-M.-Barrieness'. When Barrie died in 1937, *The Daily Telegraph* wrote of him, 'A romantic, indeed, he never was. . . . Whether one liked his work or not, he owed nothing to anybody or any school. . . . He was not so much a great artist – though the sanest critic knew he was that, too – as a man who could see visions.' I hope this book may prompt some to rediscover those visions for themselves.

Notwithstanding my own evident partiality for Barrie's writing, I have endeavoured to leave this account tolerably free of opinion and judgement. It is not a scholarly work, though I have striven to ensure the accuracy of its content, and have supplied references for sources not identified in the text.

Many people have provided documents, reminiscences, and helpful advice. In particular I should like to thank Michael Asquith; Elisabeth Bergner; Lord Boothby; Isabella Bruce; Clive Burt; Theodora Calvert; Sir Roger Chance; Jeremy Clutterbuck; Patrick Crocker; George Llewelyn Davies Jnr; Geraldine Llewelyn Davies; Peter Llewelyn Davies Jnr; Ruthven Llewelyn Davies; W. A. Darlington; Norma Douglas Henry; Janet Dunbar;

Sebastian Earl; Carl Michael Emyers; Diana Farr; Dr Michael
Finlay; Dr Morris Fraser; Roger Lancelyn Green; Anthony Hall;
Mary Hill; Eiluned and Medina Lewis; Joan Ling; the late Johnny
Mackay; Sir John Masterman; Major and Mrs John Mathias; Angela
and Daphne du Maurier; Doreen Nisbet; Mark Oliver; the Dowager
Lady Ponsonby; Sir James Pitman; Foy Quiller-Couch; Pia
Hewlett; Mary and Anne Mackail; Sir Peter Scott; Her Grace the
Duchess of Sutherland; Margaret Ogilvy Sweeten; Julian
Vinogradoff; Joan Waldegrave.

I must also record my thanks to the many institutions which have
given access to material. By far the most vital source has been the
Walter Beinecke Collection – the largest Barrie collection in
existence – housed in the Beinecke Rare Book and Manuscript
Library at Yale University. Marjorie Wynne and her staff have
provided a constant stream of xeroxes, photographs and microfilm,
often at panic notice, and their help and enthusiasm throughout the
long period of research has been invaluable. The National Trust for
Scotland has shown equal courtesy, and I am much indebted to Olga
Bennell and her staff at the Trust's Barrie Birthplace, Kirriemuir, for
their assistance and hospitality. Additional acknowledgements are
due to the Academy of Motion Picture Arts and Sciences (Los
Angeles), the Bodleian Library, the BBC, the British Film Institute,
British Movietone News, the British Library, the British Theatre
Museum, Colindale Newspaper Library, Dumfries Academy,
Edinburgh University, EMI – Pathé News, Eton College, Glasgow
University, the Houghton Library (Harvard University), the
University of Illinois, Kensington & Chelsea Public Library, the
Lillie Library (Indiana University), the National Film Archives,
New York Public Library, Norland Place School, Oxford Uni-
versity, Radlett Public Library, the Royal Commission on Historical
Manuscripts, the Royal Collection at Windsor Castle, the University
of Southern California, St Andrews University, Texas University,
and the Victoria and Albert Museum. The many publishers who
have given permission to quote copyright material are acknowledged
in the Select Bibliography at the end of the book. I am particularly
beholden to the generosity of the Barrie Estate for permission to
quote so extensively from Barrie's unpublished notebooks, letters,
and other writings; to the Great Ormond Street Hospital, who
control the copyright of all works that fall into the category of *The
Peter Pan Gift*; to Barrie's principal publishers: Hodder &
Stoughton Ltd in England, Charles Scribner's Sons in the U.S.A.;
and to the Llewelyn Davies family, for permission both to quote
from unpublished family papers, and to reproduce photographs from
various family albums.

On a more personal level, I should like to thank all those concerned with the BBC television production of *The Lost Boys*, particularly my producer Louis Marks and director Rodney Bennett who tolerated trials and tribulations above and beyond the call of duty; Jane Annakin and the William Morris Agency, whose services have amounted to unregistered charity; my copy-editor and fellow-pedant, Herbert Rees; Frank Dunn for his comprehensive index; my long-suffering publishers; Linda Siefert; Gary Smith and Dwight Hemion; Mia Farrow; Bruce Robinson; Colin Rogers; my sister Linda, who restored a number of photographs to their former glory; Peter Lodge and the National Westminster Bank, without whose support there would have been no *Lost Boys*; David Puttnam and his family: Patsy, Debbie, and especially Sacha, my technical advisor on boyhood and unwitting author of the best lines in the script; Nicholas Borton, Paul Spurrier and Alexander Buss, who supplemented Sacha's contribution with ideas of their own; Ian Holm, for bringing Barrie miraculously to life, his wife Bridget, who undertook most of the photographic labour of this book, and their son Barnaby, who earned himself a small fortune playing the young George Llewelyn Davies, and a larger one correcting galley proofs at a shilling a mistake; and finally my own family, for being a constant source of encouragement and offering me much valuable advice.

Two acknowledgements remain, though the term does scant justice to the debt of gratitude I owe them. Sharon Goode, my co-researcher, has devoted three years of her spare time to *The Lost Boys*, both television and book, and much of the content is solely due to her diligence, perseverance and skill; moreover, her efficiency and organization has more than compensated for my own failings in those fields. But even her efforts, not to mention my own, would have been wasted had it not been for the full co-operation and assistance of Nicholas Llewelyn Davies throughout this enterprise. I am reluctant to praise his contribution too fully, since an element of coercion may be suspected. When Sharon Goode first tracked him down in 1975, he wrote to her, 'I am certainly ready to help in any way I can, but I must warn you that I am entirely devoted to Barrie's memory, by which I mean that you will hear little but praise from me.' Nico has been true to his word. Knowing that I was a scriptwriter, he no doubt suspected that I was after a 'good story' – which I was – and that truth might take second place to dramatic licence – which it did, frequently, until he cajoled me back onto the right path; but never under pressure. As principal copyright holder of his family's letters and papers, he had every right to ask for script approval. He didn't, so I gave it to him. That he made no use of it almost led me to suspect that he had consigned the finished script to the waste-paper basket unread (and at 540 daunting pages I wouldn't have blamed him); but I then received a letter from him telling me that he had sent, under separate cover, 'a few notes of things that aren't quite accurate, but they don't amount to much, so of course disregard them if you want'. By the next post arrived a large package containing the few notes: four dozen sheets of closely written comments, each one relating to some factual error in the script. Subsequent drafts were subjected to the same treatment, and at the beginning of rehearsals Nico journeyed up to the BBC with his wife, Mary, to spend an afternoon fielding a barrage of questions from both cast and production team. A similar process of involvement took place on the book; answering questions (with over two hundred letters), making suggestions and checking proofs, but again without restraint. This may not seem particularly remarkable, until one considers the amount of speculation that has arisen in the last decade over Barrie's sexuality. Several psychiatrists have classified him as a paedophile, while a number of critics and viewers jumped to the same conclusion on watching *The Lost Boys*. It would seem that sexual categories, like so many judgements, lie in the eye of the beholder, and some readers will inevitably behold similar ambiguities in this book. As Barrie's sole surviving adopted son, perhaps Nico is better placed than most for determining the truth; and so, while thanking him profoundly for having allowed me to trespass so freely on his past and present, I give him the last word: 'Of all the men I have ever known, Barrie was the wittiest, and the best company. He was also the least interested in sex. He was a darling man. He was an innocent; which is why he could write *Peter Pan*.'

On April 5th, 1960, a middle-aged publisher, Peter Llewelyn Davies, left the Royal Court Hotel, London, crossed Sloane Square, walked down into the local underground station and threw himself beneath an on-coming train. Eight days later a Coroner's Jury returned a verdict of 'suicide while the balance of his mind was disturbed'.

Peter Davies had been a leading figure in the London publishing world since 1926, when he founded his own publishing house, Peter Davies Ltd. Compton Mackenzie called him 'an artist among publishers', and Herbert van Thal, writing in *The Times*, described his death as 'an irreparable loss to the publishing trade, for here was a personality, witty, astringent, with a brilliant and remarkable knowledge of literature, and withal he possessed a deep and kindly understanding of his fellow men'.

Apart from the tributes of friends and colleagues, the death of a publisher would normally warrant little more than a tidy obituary in the better-class newspapers. That his death made front-page news around the world was not due to Peter Davies, publisher, but to his namesake, Peter Pan.

'BARRIE'S PETER PAN KILLED BY A LONDON SUBWAY TRAIN' announced *The New York Times*, while Fleet Street seized upon the evident irony implicit in the story: 'THE BOY WHO NEVER GREW UP IS DEAD' . . . 'PETER PAN STOOD ALONE TO DIE' . . . 'PETER PAN'S DEATH LEAP' . . . 'PETER PAN COMMITS SUICIDE' . . . 'THE TRAGEDY OF PETER PAN'. The *Daily Express* informed its readers:

Peter Llewelyn Davies at Barrie's funeral in 1937

'Until he died at 68* Peter Davies was Peter Pan. He was the Little Boy Who Never Grew Up; the boy who believed in fairies. The name was the gift to him of playwright Sir James Barrie and Peter Davies hated it all his life. But he was never allowed to forget it until, as a shy, retiring publisher, he fell to his death on Tuesday night.'

Despite the inaccuracies, the article was correct in one respect: the mass media never allowed Peter Davies to forget his namesake, and it was little wonder that he came to loathe his association with what he once referred to as 'that terrible masterpiece'. Nor were his four brothers immune to the same treatment. Every time George, Jack, Peter, Michael or Nico made news, however insignificant, Peter Pan took the headlines – whether it was George in 1914: 'PETER PAN ENLISTS', Michael in 1919: 'PETER PAN FINED FOR SPEEDING', Nico in 1926: 'PETER PAN GETS MARRIED', or Peter, on the birth of Peter Davies Ltd: 'PETER PAN BECOMES PUBLISHER':

'Mr Peter Davies, the publisher, was as shy as the boy who inspired Pan when a "Daily Express" representative called on him yesterday.

*He was actually 63.

He would speak about his first book, but not a word would he utter about Peter Pan. "Please forget that," he said, and his lips seemed to say, "I'm grown up now, you know."'

But was Peter Davies the real Peter Pan? Barrie claimed that he was an amalgam of all five Davies boys: 'I made Peter by rubbing the five of you violently together, as savages with two sticks produce a flame. That is all he is, the spark I got from you.' Certainly the Five had a profound influence on Peter's creation—as indeed that creation and his creator had on each of them—but they were as much the inspiration for the Lost Boys and the Darling family as they were for Peter Pan.

The real genesis of the Boy Who Would Not Grow Up had begun almost one hundred years prior to Peter's death in 1960, in the little Scottish weaving town of Kirriemuir, where James Matthew Barrie was born on May 9th, 1860.

1

'On the day I was born we bought six hair-bottomed chairs, and in our little house it was an event', wrote Barrie in *Margaret Ogilvy*,[1] a portrait of his mother and his own boyhood. Certainly his birth caused little stir in a family that already numbered two boys and four girls, but the implied poverty was an affectation adopted by Barrie in later life. His father, David Barrie, was a hand-loom weaver of more than average means, and the dominant priority in the Barrie household was one of fierce educational ambition rather than a struggle for survival. By the time James Barrie was six, that ambition had been partly realized. Alexander Barrie, the eldest son, had graduated from Aberdeen University with first-class honours in Classics, and had opened his own private school in Lanarkshire. The second son, David, was thirteen, and showed every sign of emulating Alexander's achievements; moreover he was tall, athletic, handsome and charming, the Golden Boy of his mother's eye. Margaret Ogilvy (who had retained her maiden name in accordance with an old Scots custom) was the driving force of the family, and all her hopes were focused on the aspiration that David would one day become a Minister. The six-year-old James was, by comparison, something of a disappointment. He showed no particular academic promise, nor did he possess his brother's looks. He was small for his age, rather squat, with a head too large for his body. In short, the runt of the family.

Until he was six, James Barrie lived in the shadow of David. But in January 1867, David was killed in a skating accident on the eve of his fourteenth birthday. Barrie was too young to remember the tragedy with any clarity, his chief memory being that of playing with his younger sister Maggie under the table on which stood David's coffin.

Barrie aged 6

Barrie's birthplace: Lilybank in the Tenements, Kirriemuir. The wash-house in foreground was the theatre of Barrie's first play, written and performed at the age of 7. It was also, according to his Dedication to *Peter Pan*, 'the original of the little house the Lost Boys built in the Never Land for Wendy'

For his mother, however, it was a catastrophe beyond belief, and one from which she never fully recovered. 'She was always delicate from that hour, and for many months she was very ill', wrote Barrie in *Margaret Ogilvy*. 'I peeped in many times at the door and then went to the stair and sat on it and sobbed.' Barrie's elder sister, Jane Ann, was quick to perceive the damaging effect that Margaret Ogilvy's protracted grief was having on her youngest son:

'This sister told me to go ben to my mother and say to her that she still had another boy. I went ben excitedly, but the room was dark, and when I heard the door shut and no sound come from the bed I was afraid, and I stood still. I suppose I was breathing hard, or perhaps I was crying, for after a time I heard a listless voice that had never been listless before say, "Is that you?" I think the tone hurt me, for I made no answer, and then the voice said more anxiously "Is that you?" again. I thought it was the dead boy she was speaking to, and I said in a little lonely voice, "No, it's no' him, it's just me." Then I heard a cry, and my mother turned in bed, and though it was dark I knew that she was holding out her arms.

(left) Margaret Ogilvy in 1871
(right) Barrie aged 9

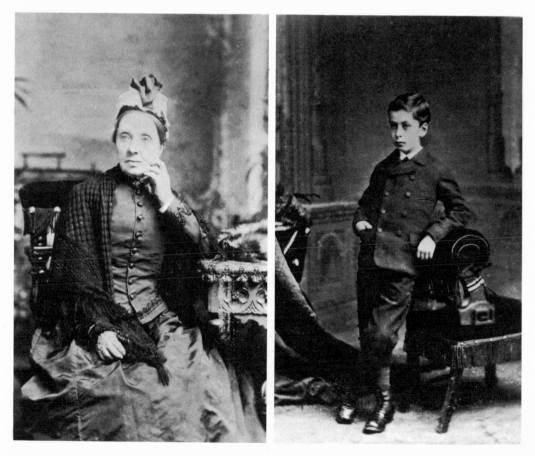

'After that I sat a great deal in her bed trying to make her forget him. . . . At first, they say, I was often jealous, stopping her fond memories with the cry, "Do you mind nothing about me?" but that did not last; its place was taken by an intense desire . . . to become so like him that even my mother should not see the difference, and many and artful were the questions I put to that end. Then I practised in secret, but after a whole week had passed I was still rather like myself. He had such a cheery way of whistling, she had told me, it had always brightened her at her work to hear him whistling, and when he whistled he stood with his legs apart, and his hands in the pockets of his knickerbockers. I decided to trust to this, so one day after I had learned his whistle (every boy of enterprise invents a whistle of his own) from boys who had been his comrades, I secretly put on a suit of his clothes . . . and thus disguised I slipped, unknown to the others, into my mother's room. Quaking, I doubt not, yet so pleased, I stood still until she saw me, and then—how it must have hurt her! "Listen!" I cried in a glow of triumph, and I stretched my legs wide apart and plunged my hands into the pockets of my knickerbockers, and began to whistle.

'She lived twenty-nine years after his death . . . But I had not made her forget the bit of her that was dead; in those nine-and-twenty years he was not removed one day farther from her. Many a time she fell asleep speaking to him, and even while she slept her lips moved and she smiled as if he had come back to her, and when she woke he might vanish so suddenly that she started up bewildered and looked about her, and then said slowly, "My David's dead!" or perhaps he remained long enough to whisper why he must leave her now, and then she lay silent with filmy eyes. When I became a man . . . he was still a boy of thirteen.'

If Margaret Ogilvy drew a measure of comfort from the notion that David, in dying a boy, would remain a boy for ever, Barrie drew inspiration. It would be another thirty-three years before that inspiration emerged in the shape of Peter Pan, but here was the germ, rooted in his mind and soul from the age of six.

When not acting out the role of his dead brother, Barrie would invent other parts for himself. Some were performed in amateur theatricals in his mother's wash-house; others in real life:

'When I was a very small boy, another as small was woeful because he could not join in our rough play lest he damaged the "mourning blacks" in which he was attired. So I nobly exchanged clothing with him for an hour, and in mine he disported forgetfully while I sat on a stone in his and lamented with tears, though I knew not for whom.'[2]

It was this same vicarious curiosity, this 'devouring desire to try on other folk's feelings as if they were so many suits of clothes',[3] that led the young James Barrie to question his mother about her own girlhood. 'Those innumerable talks with her made her youth as vivid to me as my own, and so much more quaint, for, to a child, the oddest of things, and the most richly coloured picture-book, is that his mother was once a child also.' Margaret Ogilvy had a captive audience of one as she unfolded the picture-book of her own childhood: 'She was eight when her mother's death made her mistress of the house and mother to her little brother, and from that time she scrubbed and mended and baked and sewed, . . . then [rushed] out in a fit of childishness to play dumps or palaulays with others of her age.'

A hand-loom weaver. The bunches of thread above the loom were known as 'thrums', which Barrie later adopted as his pseudonym for Kirriemuir

The story of Margaret Ogilvy's childhood expanded into other stories, told to her as a small girl: tales of the weaving community before the Industrial Revolution, of a Scotland long vanished and coloured by her memory. Many of these stories concerned the Auld Lichts, or Old Lights, a religious sect to which Margaret Ogilvy had belonged before her marriage. These tales, or Idylls, never failed to fire Barrie's imagination, and were, at a later date, to provide him with much of the source material for his articles and 'Thrums' novels. But it was the image of the substitute mother that was to take the deepest root: the memory of his own mother as a little girl, refashioned and remoulded into numerous heroines, epitomized as Wendy mothering the Lost Boys and Peter Pan in the Neverland. In *Margaret Ogilvy*, Barrie admitted with pride that 'I soon grow tired of writing tales unless I can see a little girl, of whom my mother has told me, wandering confidently through the pages. Such a grip has her memory of her girlhood had upon me since I was a boy of six.'

Barrie's sense of rejection and inferiority, suffered while in the shadow of David, was largely dispelled by his younger sister Maggie. She worshipped him, and her unswerving loyalty and devotion helped to restore in him a measure of self-confidence. Barrie's father, on the other hand, appears to have had little influence on his son's character and development. He is scarcely mentioned in any of Barrie's autobiographical writings, beyond a cursory reference to him in *Margaret Ogilvy* as 'a man I am very proud to be able to call my father', and it was left to his mother to fire the boy with an enthusiasm for literature:

Barrie's father, David Barrie, in about 1871

'We read many books together when I was a boy, "Robinson Crusoe" being the first (and the second), and the "Arabian Nights" should have been the next, for we got it out of the library (a penny for three days), but on discovering that they were nights when we had paid for knights we sent that volume packing, and I have curled my lips at it ever since. . . . Besides reading every book we could hire or borrow I also bought one now and again, and while buying (it was the occupation of weeks) I read, standing at the counter, most of the other books in the shop, which is perhaps the most exquisite way of reading.'

Barrie also subscribed to various 'Penny Dreadfuls'—the forerunners of adventure comics—which were, like the later Neverland, 'not large and sprawly . . . with tedious distances between one adventure and another, but nicely crammed'.[4] In addition to the staple diet of blood and thunder, pirates and desert islands, the penny comics contained serial characters, including a young girl who sold water-cress and bore a striking resemblance to 'that little girl, of whom my mother has told me'—the young Margaret Ogilvy:

'This romantic little creature took such hold of my imagination that I cannot eat water-cress even now without emotion. I lay in bed wondering what she would be up to in the next number; I have lost trout because when they nibbled my mind was wandering with her; my early life was embittered by her not arriving regularly on the first of the month. I know not whether it was owing to her loitering on the way one month to an extent flesh and blood could not bear, or because we had exhausted the penny library, but on a day I conceived a glorious idea, or it was put into my head by my mother, then desirous of making progress with her new clouty hearthrug. The notion was nothing short of this, why should I not write the tales myself? I did write them—in the garret—but they by no means helped her to get on with her work, for when I finished a chapter I bounded downstairs to read it to her, and so short were the chapters, so ready was the pen, that I was back with the new manuscript before another clout had been added to the rug. . . . They were all tales of adventure (happiest is he who writes of adventure), no characters were allowed within if I knew their like in the flesh, the scene lay in unknown parts, desert islands, enchanted gardens, with knights (none of your nights) on black chargers, and round the first corner a lady selling water-cress. . . . From the day on which I first tasted blood in the garret my mind was made up; there could be no hum-dreadful-drum profession for me; literature was my game.'

Barrie aged 14 at Dumfries Academy

At the age of thirteen, Barrie 'put the literary calling to bed for a time, having gone to a school where cricket and football were more esteemed'. His childhood was over. In *Margaret Ogilvy* he wrote:

'The horror of my boyhood was that I knew a time would come when I also must give up the games, and how it was to be done I saw not

7

(this agony still returns to me in dreams, when I catch myself playing marbles, and look on with cold displeasure); I felt that I must continue playing in secret.'

For a man seemingly convinced that the end of boyhood is the end of life worth living—'nothing that happens after we are twelve matters very much'—it comes as something of a surprise to find that he recalled his five years spent at Dumfries Academy as being the happiest of his life. But Barrie had Found a Way; moreover, there was no need for him to play in secret, for on the very first day at school he met another boy who shared his own appetite for high adventure. The boy's name, according to the school register, was Stuart Gordon:

'But that wasn't the name he was known by at school. He came up and asked me my name. I told him. It didn't seem to please him. He said, "I'll call you Sixteen String Jack." I asked his name, and he said it was Dare Devil Dick.'[5]

Dare Devil Dick was one of the characters in the 'Penny Dreadful' comics so familiar to Barrie, a boy who had run away to sea and become a pirate. Gordon invited him to join his own pirate crew, and Barrie readily accepted:

'... when the shades of night began to fall, certain young mathematicians shed their triangles, crept up walls and down trees, and became pirates in a sort of Odyssey that was long afterwards to become the play of *Peter Pan*. For our escapades in a certain Dumfries garden, which is enchanted land to me, were certainly the genesis of that nefarious work. We lived in the tree-tops, on coconuts attached thereto, and that were in a bad condition; we were buccaneers and I kept the log-book of our depredations, an eerie journal, without a triangle in it to mar the beauty of its page. That log-book I trust is no longer extant, though I should like one last look at it, to see if Captain Hook is in it.'[6]

A 'certain Dumfries garden': Moat Brae, by the river Nith

Although Barrie was soon to develop an almost legendary shyness and reserve, there were few signs of this during his years at Dumfries. He quickly became immersed in school life, playing football for the Dumfries Academy XI, taking part in monthly recitations, the Debating Society, fishing expeditions and frequent visits to the local theatre:

'The theatre in Dumfries ... was the first I ever entered; so it is the one I liked best. I entered many times in my school days, and always

An early piece of Barrie journalism, contributed to the Dumfries Academy's school magazine, 'The Clown', edited by Wellwood Anderson

tried to get the end seat in the front row of the pit, which was also the front row of the house, as there were no stalls. I sat there to get rid of stage illusion and watch what the performers were doing in the wings. . . . Such doings led inevitably to the forming of a dramatic club at school for which I wrote my first play, "Bandelero the Bandit". No page of it remains, but though it played for less than half an hour it contained all the most striking scenes that boy had lapped up from his corner seat, and had one character (played by same boy) who was a combination of his favourite characters in fiction.'[7]

In later life, Barrie often lamented that he had never written anything shocking, daring or harmful. His first dramatic effort, 'Bandelero the Bandit', was considered all of these by a clergyman who denounced it in the columns of a local newspaper as being a grossly immoral play. Barrie was, not unnaturally, delighted by the clergyman's attack, and he and his accomplice, Wellwood Anderson, wrote off to Sir Henry Irving and other theatrical personalities of the day, enlisting their support in the cause of the Dramatic Club. The splendour of the clergyman's vitriol, which ran to several columns, was only slightly marred by the newspaper's dramatic critic, who reviewed the play in more sober terms:

'Two awful villains, Gamp and Benshaw, were characters in Barrie's play "Bandelero the Bandit". They were no worse, and no better, than the average stage villain of the "penny plain and tuppence coloured" variety and were probably based on Deadwood Dick, Spring-Heeled Jack, a Fenimore Cooper pirate, or the cruel robbers of the Babes in the Wood. Presumably this was the "grossly immoral play" referred to by the accusing person.'[8]

Nevertheless Barrie had scored a hit, and the ensuing controversy, which was taken up by several London newspapers, turned him into a celebrity at school. At any rate among the boys. Girls, however, were another matter. Dumfries Academy was co-educational, and in his earlier days there Barrie had received a prize of special distinction: 'It was awarded by the girls of the school by plebiscite, to the boy who had the sweetest smile in the school. The tragic thing was that my smile disappeared that day and has never been seen since.'[9] But as he grew older, the girls turned their attentions and affections elsewhere. Barrie recorded his sense of failure in one of his early notebooks:[10]

—The boys write on walls, &c, name of boy & girl, coupling them together. As never did it to me I wrote my own with girl's name.
—Ashamed at being small enough to travel half ticket by rail.

At seventeen, Barrie was barely five foot—and had stopped growing. He had not yet begun to shave. He was still a boy. For the moment this did not greatly matter: there were plenty of other boys, even if they were a few years younger than himself. One in particular left a lasting impression: James McMillan, a 'thin, frightened-looking boy, poorly clad and frail',[11] who was, like David, to attain the unattainable by dying young. A quarter of a century later, Barrie recalled McMillan in a speech given to the students at his old school:

'He was the greatest boy that ever sat on the forms of the old Dumfries Academy. I don't mean merely as a scholar, though in scholarship he was of another world from the rest of us; so he shone, pale star that he was, when he went to Glasgow University and afterwards to Oxford, until—someone turned out that light. He was too poor, was that brave little adventurer. I think that explains it all. The other boys felt that there was something winged about him, just as I did. He couldn't play games, and yet we all accepted him as our wonder one. . . . What was it about James McMillan that has stayed with me for so many years, and can still touch me to the quick? I felt, when we were boys, that he was—a Presence, and I feel it still.'[12]

Barrie courted McMillan's friendship, and the two boys became comrades. Together they would go for long walks in the neighbouring countryside, seeking out their hero, Thomas Carlyle, or set out on expeditions where 'we became backwoodsmen, and left our mark on what we agreed were primeval forests'.[13] But their favourite haunt was a ruined keep up in the hills:

'It [was] a spot heavy with romance, as indeed is all that favoured land. There we talked poetry, and fame, and the clash of arms and poor dead things said to escape back into the world for that horrid hour when day and night, their gaolers, are in the grip. . . . One day we wrote something about ourselves in cryptogram and hid it in a crevice in the ruin, agreeing to have another look for it when we were men. So when I was a man I dug for it and found it, having then quite forgotten what it said. But before putting it back I spelt it out. It gave our names and ages, and said that McMillan and I had begun to write a story of school life, "by Didymus". . . . School life is not what a boy usually takes as the subject of his first book, and I think there was something rather pathetic in the choice. It was as if we knew already that the next best thing to being boys is to write about them. Some day, perhaps, that book will be finished, but I must practise for a long time on men first. Men are so much easier to write about than boys.'[14]

Your most esteemed virtue	Modesty.
Your highest characteristic in man	Sense.
Your highest characteristic in woman	Silence!???
Your happiest employment	Composition. Singing hymns.
Your greatest misery	Shirt-buttons. (Clean Sheets on a cold night)
Your pet flower and colour	The rose: red.
Your favourite novelist	Sir Walter Scott.
Your most admired poet	Shakespeare.
Your favourite opera and artist	Never seen one.
Your favourite historical hero	Sir William Wallace.
Your favourite historical heroine	Joan of Arc.
Your favourite hero in fiction	Cooper's "Pathfinder."
Your favourite heroine in fiction	Cordelia in "King Lear."
Your luxurious ambrosia and nectar	Sponge-cakes and Lemonade.
Your most loveable name	Minnie (Jemima Jane!).
Your pet antipathy	The Academy bell.
What peculiarity can you most tolerate?	That of giving presents.
Your favourite amusement	Fishing. Private Theatricals.
At what age should a man marry?	Dot-age.
At what age should a woman marry?	Any time between 18 and 60.
Do you believe in love at first sight?	Yes, if the object is in the pastry line.
Do you believe in marrying for love and working for money?	Not if you have a rope handy.
Were you ever in love? and if so, how often?	Yes: every time I pass a sweetie shop.
Your favourite proverb	"Be aisy, an' if ye canna be, aisy, be as aisy as ye can."
Your age next birthday	Decimal 64. Find cube root for answer.
My confession	James M. Barrie.

Barrie's entry in a Querist's Album, given to him by Margaret Ogilvy for his 17th birthday. In *The Greenwood Hat* (1930) he recalled, 'In my schooldays I wrote the most beautiful copperplate. . . . It went, I think, not gradually with over-writing, but suddenly, like my smile.'

In 1878, at the age of eighteen, Barrie left Dumfries Academy and returned home to Kirriemuir with the intention of becoming a writer. But his parents had other plans. Margaret Ogilvy impressed upon him that David would have gone to University, had he lived. Reluctantly, Barrie complied with his mother's wishes and matriculated at Edinburgh. However, his instincts were right. University was not the place for him, and it was a somewhat desolating experience in a city that held no family and few friends. A fellow student, Robert Galloway, later recalled him as being 'exceedingly shy and diffident, and I do not remember ever to have seen him either enter or leave a classroom with any companion. . . . Nor did he, I think, connect himself with any of the debating societies of the College—at least I never saw him at any. Yet I remember him distinctly—a sallow-faced, round-shouldered, slight, somewhat delicate-looking figure, who quietly went in and out amongst us, attracting but little observation, but himself observing all and measuring up men and treasuring up impressions.'[15]

Barrie was indeed treasuring up impressions—in his notebook:

—Men can't get together without talking filth.
—He is very young looking—trial of his life that he is always thought a boy.
—Far finer and nobler things in the world than loving a girl & getting her.
—Greatest horror—dream I am married—wake up shrieking.
—Grow up & have to give up marbles—awful thought.
—Want to stop everybody in street & ask if they've read 'The Coral Island'. Feel sorry for if not.
—Want to go into shop & buy brooch for child, but don't dare.

If Dumfries had been the happiest period of his life, Edinburgh was the loneliest. He was a man among men; and yet he was not a man. As he later wrote vicariously in *The Wedding Guest*, 'I lived too much in my art, and my solitary thoughts. I shrank from men's free talk of women, and yet when I left them it was to brood of the things they spoke of; theirs was a healthier life than mine.' His attempts to cultivate the opposite sex met with similar failure. Mocking himself (in the third person, as 'Anon'), Barrie afterwards wrote:

'Did Anon ever hear ladies discussing him for the briefest moment in a train or anywhere else? Alas, his trouble was that ladies did not discuss him. . . . I remember (I should think I do) that it was his habit to get into corners. In time the jades put this down to a shrinking modesty, but that was a mistake; it was all owing to a profound dejection about his want of allure. They were right, those ladies in the train; "quite harmless" summed him up, however he may have writhed (or be writhing still). . . . If they would dislike him or fear him it would be something, but it is crushing to be just harmless. . . . In short, Mr Anon, that man of secret sorrows, found it useless to love, because, after a look at the length and breadth of him, none would listen.'[16]

None, that is, except children. His brother Alexander had married in 1877, and Barrie now had two young nieces, whom he visited whenever he could. They were not puzzled by him, as many of his contemporaries were puzzled, and while he was in their company, he ceased to be a puzzle to himself. He felt safe with them, alive with them, at one with them.

In 1882, Barrie was able to return home to Kirriemuir with the letters M.A. after his name. But if the intervening years at University had brought about an increasing shyness, they had not dimmed his determination to become a writer:

'It was not highly thought of by those who wished me well. I remember being asked by two maiden ladies, about the time I left the university, what I was to be, and when I replied brazenly, "An author", they flung up their hands, and one exclaimed reproachfully, "And you an M.A.!" My mother's views at first were not dissimilar; for long she took mine jestingly as something I would grow out of, and afterwards they hurt her so that I tried to give them up. To be a Minister—that she thought was among the fairest prospects.'

Barrie as an M.A.

It was Barrie's sister, Jane Ann, who was instrumental in securing him his first literary opportunity. She saw an advertisement in *The Scotsman* for a leader-writer on an English provincial newspaper, the *Nottingham Journal*, and showed it to him. He duly applied, and was offered the post at the seemingly enormous salary of three pounds a week.

One of Barrie's tasks in preparing for his M.A. at Edinburgh had been to write essays on topics of surpassing boredom and make them both convincing and readable. His duties on the *Nottingham Journal* required him to perform a similar feat with the humdrum subjects handed him by his Editor. Whether it was 'English Blank Verse', 'Roses', 'The Leafy Month' or 'My Umbrella', Barrie's approach was invariably the same: enter the mind of another for the space of a column, adopt the standpoint least expected by the reader, then proceed to inject into the affair as much cynicism and laconic humour as his spirits could muster. These techniques were soon to become his literary hallmarks, though presently they would be tempered, and in the opinions of some marred, by two other idiosyncratic characteristics: sentiment and 'whimsy'. Their absence from his writing at this stage was no accident: Barrie himself was only too well aware of the sentimental streak in him, and his intellect fought against it.

Not all of his articles were on topics beyond his sphere of interest. Cricket was already making an appearance; so too were the theatre and amateur theatricals. A third subject had also found its way into the anonymous columns of the *Nottingham Journal*: boys. His first article on the breed was a typical piece of cynicism, entitled 'Pretty Boys':

'Pretty boys are pretty in all circumstances, and this one would look as exquisitely delightful on the floor as when genteelly standing, in his nice little velvet suit with his sweet back to the fireplace, but think of the horror and indignation of his proud and loving mother. . . . When you leave the house, the pretty boy trips politely to the door and . . . holds up his pretty mouth for a pretty kiss. If you wish to continue on visiting terms with his mother you do everything he wishes; if you are determined to remain a man whatever be the consequences, you slap his pretty cheeks very hard while the mother gazes aghast and the father looks another way, admiring your pluck and wishing he had the courage to go and do likewise. It would, on the whole, be a mistake to kill the child outright, because, for one thing, he may grow out of his velvet suit in time and insist on having his hair cut, and, again, the blame does not attach to him nearly so much as to his mother.'[17]

Strath View, the Barries' home in Kirriemuir from 1872

It would appear that Barrie's provincial readers were not altogether amused by his sense of humour: at any rate his employment on the newspaper was short-lived, and by the end of October 1884 he was back in Kirriemuir—without a job. He had never regarded Nottingham as anything more than a stepping-stone towards Fleet Street journalism, and he now bombarded various London publications with unsolicited articles. One of these, entitled 'An Auld Licht Community', was based on some of Margaret Ogilvy's anecdotes about the Kirriemuir of her childhood. The *St James's Gazette* published it on November 17th, 1884, and Barrie quickly followed it with another article on a different theme, having assumed he had exhausted the subject of the Auld Lichts. It came back by return of post with a reject slip attached; the *Gazette*'s editor, Frederick Greenwood, softened the blow by adding a note of his own: 'I liked that Scotch thing—any more of those?'[18] Barrie consulted his mother, and soon 'An Auld Licht Funeral' was on its way to Greenwood, followed in rapid succession by 'An Auld Licht Courtship', 'An Auld Licht Scandal' and 'An Auld Licht Wedding'. Spurred on by Greenwood's enthusiasm, Barrie decided it was time to make his assault on London:

Auld Licht gossips

'I wrote and asked the editor [Greenwood] if I should come to London, and he said No, so I went, laden with charges from my mother to walk in the middle of the street, . . . never to venture forth after sunset, and always to lock up everything (I who could never lock up anything, except my heart in company). . . . London, which she never saw, was to her a monster that licked up country youths as they stepped from the train; there were the garrets in which they sat abject, and the park seats where they passed the night. . . . I daresay that when night comes, this Hyde Park which is so gay by day, is

haunted by the ghosts of many mothers, who run, wild-eyed, from seat to seat, looking for their sons.'

Before leaving Kirriemuir, Barrie took the precaution of sending Greenwood another offering, though it was a somewhat risky venture, since the article, 'The Rooks Begin to Build', had nothing to do with his mother's Auld Licht stories. Without waiting for a response, he packed his all-purpose university box and caught the night train to London. In *The Greenwood Hat*, Barrie described himself in hindsight:

'Let us survey our hero': Barrie in 1886, aged 26

'Let us survey our hero as he sits awake in a corner of his railway compartment. . . . He is gauche and inarticulate, and as thin as a pencil but not so long (and is going to be thinner). Expression, an uncomfortable blank. . . . Manners, full of nails like his boots. Ladies have decided that he is of no account, and he already knows this and has private anguish thereanent. Hates sentiment as a slave may hate his master. Only asset, except a pecuniary one, is a certain grimness about not being beaten. . . . The baggage of our hero . . . consisted of a powerful square wooden box. . . . Having reached London for the great adventure, he was hauling this box to the left-luggage shed at St. Pancras when his eyes fell upon what was to him the most warming sight in literature. It was the placard of the "St. James's Gazette" of the previous evening with printed on it in noble letters "The Rooks begin to Build". In other dazzling words, having been a minute or so in London, he had made two guineas. Forty-five years having elapsed since this event, the romance of my life, I myself can now regard it with comparative calm, but I still hold that it was almost as if Greenwood had met me at the station.'

'The most precious possession I ever had [was] my joy in hard work. I do not know when it came to me—not very early, because I was an idler at school, and read all the wrong books at college. But I fell in love with hard work one fine May morning. . . . I found her waiting for me at a London station [and] she marched with me all the way to Bloomsbury. . . . Hard work, more than any woman in the world, is the one who stands up best for her man.'[1]

For once, this was no exaggeration. Hard work took Barrie's mind off his increasing bouts of depression, when he would 'lie awake busy with the problems of my personality'.[2] Moreover it was sheer hard work that took him, within the space of three years, to the top of his profession. By 1887 he was contributing articles to virtually every prestigious publication in the country, including W. E. Henley's influential *National Observer* in the select company of Thomas Hardy, Rudyard Kipling, H. G. Wells and W. B. Yeats.

But journalism was only a stepping-stone; literature was still his game, and in 1888 he tried his hand at his first novel, *Better Dead*. The title was somewhat apt, and Barrie, who had it published at his own expense, lost £25 to experience. The book was cool, witty and satirical, but, like his articles for the *Nottingham Journal*, it was too sophisticated for the general reader. He had written it from his head, not from his heart—indeed one reviewer went so far as to suggest that the novel was a collaboration between Bernard Shaw and Oscar Wilde. Undaunted, Barrie collected together his old articles from the *St James's Gazette* on the Auld Lichts, and offered them in book form to Hodder and Stoughton, who cautiously agreed to publish it. When *Auld Licht Idylls* appeared on the bookstalls in April 1888, it was greeted with a chorus of praise from reviewers and public alike, while its sequel, *A Window in Thrums*, put Barrie among the authors and Thrums among the places which the reading public knew better than their own homes. Thrums was, of course, the Kirriemuir of Margaret Ogilvy's childhood, as were many of the stories and characters. But the style in which they were told was unique to Barrie. After years of repressing his sentimental streak, he had at last allowed it to blend with his intellect and humour. This sentiment had a reverse side, a form of genial sadism. As *The Times* later observed, Barrie could be 'as hard as nails, as cruel as the grave, as cynical as the Fiend. . . . The cruelty in him came of his intellectual vision; the tenderness came of his warm, trusting, but painfully sensitive heart.' The results repelled a number of readers, while others, particularly in Scotland, were indignant at the way in which Barrie chose to portray his fellow countrymen in the Thrums novels. The critic George Blake wrote: 'It is perhaps the most puzzling thing about Barrie from first to last that the expert toucher of emotions, the

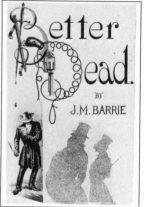

Barrie's first novel. When asked his opinion of it in later years, Barrie's reply was the title

(*right*) A 'Souvenir of Thrums': picture postcards such as this were commonplace in Kirriemuir during the 1890s, marketed for literary tourists hunting out the scenes of the Thrums novels

(*right*) Barrie writing *The Little Minister* at Strath View in 1890. The little minister of the title is Gavin Ogilvy: '"It's a pity I'm so little, mother," he said with a sigh. "You're no' what I would call a particularly long man," Margaret said, "but you're just the height I like." . . . Though even Margaret was not aware of it, Gavin's shortness had grieved him all his life.'

KIRRIEMUIR.

A SOUVENIR OF THRUMS.

THE HIGH STREET.

A WINDOW IN THRUMS.

AULD LIGHT MANSE.

We shall be delighted to
take tea with you & your mother
We mean to come together
about 5 o'clock.

weaver of charmingly whimsical webs, the delight of the nurseries, had in all his dealings as a writer with such topics as death and sepulture and grief and suffering the way of a sadist.'[3]

Barrie's third Thrums novel, *The Little Minister*, appeared in 1891 and was hailed as 'A Book of Genius' in a front-page review by the *National Observer*. The book's success was not limited to Great Britain: in New York alone, five publishers brought out their own pirated editions, and sales throughout the British Empire turned it into an international best-seller. If Barrie had lost a few of his more intellectual admirers, he had gained a world-wide readership that would remain solidly behind him for over half a century. Nor was his following restricted to the common man; Barrie's boyhood hero, Robert Louis Stevenson, wrote to Henry James from his island retreat in the South Pacific:

'Hurry up with another book of stories. I am now reduced to two of my contemporaries, you and Barrie—O, and Kipling—you and Barrie and Kipling are now my Muses Three. And with Kipling, as you know, there are reservations to be made. . . . But Barrie is a beauty, the *Little Minister* and *The Window in Thrums*, eh? Stuff in that young man; but he must see and not be too funny. Genius in him, but there's a journalist at his elbow—there's the risk.'[4]

Stevenson later wrote to Barrie in person:

'I am proud to think you are a Scotchman . . . and please do not think when I thus seem to bracket myself with you, that I am wholly blinded with vanity. . . . I am a capable artist; but it begins to look to me as if you are a man of genius.'[5]

Barrie's friendship with Stevenson was restricted to a lengthy correspondence, but his increasing fame brought him into close contact and friendship with a number of other writers, despite his somewhat cultivated reputation for shyness and inaccessibility. Closest of all were George Meredith and Thomas Hardy:

Barrie and George Meredith

'The most satisfactory thing in my little literary history is that the two whom as writers I have most admired became the two whom as men I have most loved. Hardy I first met at a club in Piccadilly, where he had asked me to lunch. It is a club where they afterwards adjourn to the smoking-room and talk for a breathless hour or two about style. Hardy's small contribution made no mark, but I thought how interesting that the only man among you who doesn't know all about style and a good deal more is the only man among you who has got a style.'[6]

In 1890, Barrie recruited some of his friends into his own cricket club, the Allahakbars (Arabic for 'Heaven help us!'), afterwards changed with complimentary intentions to the Allahakbarries. He soon found, however, that the more distinguished as authors his men were, the worse they played. Over the years, the Allahakbarries increased their reputation, if not their skill, and sometime members included Conan Doyle, Will Meredith, Charles Turley Smith, A. E. W. Mason and P. G. Wodehouse.

Barrie's circle of friends had also expanded to include the children of many of his associates: Sir Arthur Quiller-Couch's son Bevil, W. Robertson Nicoll's two children, and W. E. Henley's daughter Margaret, who christened Barrie 'my Friendy', but because she couldn't pronounce her *r*'s, it came out as 'my Wendy'—a non-existent name at that time. Meanwhile his young nieces in Scotland now had two brothers, Charlie and Willie. Charlie was exceptionally good-looking and intelligent, which appealed to Barrie; he was also extremely destructive and anarchistic, which appealed to him even more. His younger brother Willie was well-mannered, obedient and polite—a very conventional affair compared to Charlie, and consequently a rather dull companion. Unlike Kingsley, Carroll and Wordsworth, Barrie rarely perceived children as trailing clouds of glory; he saw them as 'gay and innocent and heartless'[7] creatures, inspired as much by the devil as by God. He exulted in their contradictions: their wayward appetites, their lack of morals, their conceit, their ingratitude, their cruelty, juxtaposed with gaiety, warmth, tenderness, and the sudden floods of emotion that come without warning and are as soon forgotten. Their unpredictable nature was a source of constant fascination and delight to him. Barrie knew exactly how to win a boy's affection: flatter his insatiable ego, treat him as an equal, and play him at his own game. When Charlie teased and flirted, his uncle would respond with the same tactics; when he hurt his feelings, Barrie would hurt back with equal relish.

Never one to waste good copy, Barrie turned his young nephews into bread and butter on several occasions. In *My Lady Nicotine*, a novel extolling the joys of smoking, Charlie appears thinly disguised as Primus, a wily nephew who steals his uncle's cigarettes and smokes them with a friend in Kensington Gardens. On another occasion, a visit from his nephew became the basis of an article in the distinguished *Edinburgh Evening Dispatch*, entitled 'Peterkin: A Marvel of Nature':

'Peterkin will be six years old by and by. . . . Circumstances have allowed me, his uncle, to see a good deal of Peterkin lately, and though we are now far parted, he has left an impression behind. . . .

'Peterkin and I first realised that we were no common persons three

Two Allahakbarries: Barrie (in straw hat) and Bernard Partridge

Margaret Henley, who died at the age of 6. Her cloak was later copied for Wendy, the name she invented

weeks ago. His hammer, which has a habit of flying from his hand and making straight for any brittle article in its neighbourhood (when Peterkin immediately disappears), alighted on my head one evening. Then I arose in my wrath and addressed Peterkin in these words:–

' "You thundering curmudgeon, get out of this, or I'll kick you round the room."

'Peterkin bolted, and I heard him clattering up the stairs. . . .

'I returned to my work, and by and by Peterkin walked in with a look of importance on his face such as I had not seen since he first got hold of the hammer. I left him severely alone, but every time I looked up his eye was on me. He came and stood by my side, offering himself mutely for slaughter. Then he sat down on a chair by the fire, and presently I discovered that he was crying.

' "What is the matter now?" I demanded fiercely.

' "You said you would kick me round the room," he moaned.

' "Well, I won't do it," I said, "if you are a good boy."

' "But you said you would do it."

' "You don't mean that you want it?"

' "Ay, I want it. You said you would do't."

'Wondering, I arose and kicked him.

' "Is that the way?" he cried in rapture.

' "That's the way," I said, returning to my chair.

' "But," he complained, "you said you would kick me right round the room."

'I got up again, and made a point of kicking him round the room.

' "Kick harder!" he shouted, and so I kicked him into the lobby.

'However desirous of gratifying Peterkin, I could not be always kicking him . . . and for the sake of peace I bribed quietness from him with the promise that I would kick him hard at eight o'clock. He now spent much of his valuable time gazing at the lobby clock, and counting the ticks—each of which he fondly believed meant a minute. . . .

'Most people keep their distance from me, regarding me as morose and unsociable; but Peterkin thought he had found the key to me, and was convinced that I would not kick him so heartily if I did not consider him rather nice. He said that eight o'clock was longer in coming round than any other time of the day, and he frequently offered me chocolate to kick him in advance. . . .

'He also thoroughly enjoys being tied with strings that leave their mark on him for days.

'To-day Peterkin departed for his own home, in grief to a certain extent, but, on the whole, gladly. The fact is that he was burning to tell his various friends how I kicked him. . . .

'Last night Peterkin drew from me a promise to get up early this morning and kick him just fearfully. Astonishing as it seems to

Charlie Barrie, the original of Peterkin

myself, I would nowadays do anything in my power to oblige Peterkin, and at this moment I am confident he is black and blue. I turned him upside down six times as an extra farewell, swept the floor with his head, and doubled him up by flinging books at his waistcoat. He is, therefore, off in high spirits.

'I told Peterkin that I would be glad to get rid of him; but the house has been very solemn since he left. At eight o'clock I felt quite strange and out of sorts, and at nine I was looking sadly at his hammer. In dark corners I trip over marbles that he has forgotten, and now and again my feet discover the cushions which he has left lying about in odd places. The lobby is deserted without any Peterkin waiting for eight p.m., and the clock, which used to strike eight differently from the other hours, has ceased to have any personal interest in the time of day.'[8]

   *   *   *

'Six feet three inches . . . If I had really grown to this it would have made a great difference in my life. I would not have bothered turning out reels of printed matter. My one aim would have been to become a favourite of the ladies which between you and me has always been my sorrowful ambition. The things I could have said to them if my legs had been longer. Read that with a bitter cry . . .'[9]

In his younger days, Barrie went a good way towards fulfilling that aim, particularly with pretty young actresses. As early as 1883, while working as a journalist in Nottingham, he fell for an actress called Minnie Palmer, who was appearing on tour in the local theatre. He was too shy to introduce himself without some pretext, so he quickly wrote her a one-act farce, *Caught Napping*, and took it round to her dressing-room; but when he came face to face with Minnie, he was overcome with nerves and could barely utter a word. Both the play and the author were turned down.

Although Barrie's early years in London were mainly occupied in journalism and his first novels, his interest in the theatre—and in actresses—had not diminished. In 1891 he collaborated with Marriott Watson on *Richard Savage*, in which another actress friend, Phyllis Broughton, appeared in its one and only performance. Two months later, Barrie tried his dramatic hand again with a parody on Ibsen's *Hedda Gabler*, entitled *Ibsen's Ghost*. The *Illustrated London News*, in reviewing the one-act play, noted that the author 'is the most kindly and pungent satirist. He does not hit out hard and fell his antagonist. He dances round him, and digs him in the ribs.'

Ibsen's Ghost provided Barrie with his first critical stage success, albeit a minor one. It also allowed him to worship from afar yet another young actress, Irene Vanbrugh, who was to star in many of his subsequent plays. But once again their relationship amounted to little more than a mild flirtation. Several biographers, and numerous psychiatrists, have laid the blame for Barrie's inhibitions at his mother's feet, suggesting that she was excessively prudish and repressive in her views on sex. Certainly she was a religious woman, as were most of her Victorian contemporaries, but there is little to suggest that she was unduly puritanical. The Thrums novels abound in irreligious humour and amoral detail, yet there is no evidence to indicate that his mother was offended by them—indeed, she was exceedingly proud of her son's achievements.

What, then, held him back? There is no certain answer, but there are possible clues in his notebooks. These entries were usually written in the third person, often relating to a character in a proposed article or novel:

Caricature of Irene Vanbrugh as Thea in *Ibsen's Ghost*

—Bashful with women . . . He always wanted to kiss pretty girls tho' manner made him stiff with them—His reserve—How far his shyness is the real cause of all his weakness, got on with so few people that had to make much of the few. Thus missed flirting days of boyhood & they came later when he knew the world.
—He never has contact with a woman—If he had this might have made him exult less in making women love him.
—Had he even a genuine deep feeling that wasn't merely sentiment? Was he capable of it? Perhaps not.
—Perhaps the curse of his life that he never 'had a woman'.

Irene Vanbrugh was again given the leading role in Barrie's second play, *Walker, London,* which went into rehearsal in the spring of 1892 under the direction of the actor-manager J. L. Toole, who had staged *Ibsen's Ghost.* The play was a light-weight comedy about an impostor posing as a man of substance. The cast called for a second leading lady, and Toole gave the part to one of the actresses in his company. But Barrie was dissatisfied. He asked his cricketing friend Jerome K. Jerome if he could suggest someone who was 'young, beautiful, quite charming, a genius for preference, and able to flirt'.[10] Jerome put forward Mary Ansell, an actress who ran her own touring company, but who was in London at the time, resting between engagements. Barrie went to meet her, and was once again swept off his feet. Without consulting Toole, he not only offered her the part, but promised her a higher fee than Irene Vanbrugh. Mary Ansell was delighted, Toole furious, Irene Vanbrugh indignant. But Barrie was adamant: 'Miss Ansell plays the par–r–t,' he growled. In her autobiography, Irene Vanbrugh later wrote: 'Mary Ansell . . . was delightful and extremely pretty. I acknowledge this now more freely

Mary Ansell in an unidentified role

Mary Ansell 'peering over her fur collar'

than I did at the time because I was jealous of her success; especially as the author was in love with her.'

In reviewing *Walker, London*, the critics were as enthusiastic about J. M. Barrie the Playwright as their literary counterparts were about J. M. Barrie the Novelist. *The Times* predicted: 'Like Rousseau, Mr Barrie may flatter himself that as no one has anticipated him, so he will have no imitator.' Mary Ansell's performance was not singled out for special praise, but she had her consolation; to a young but not particularly talented actress, J. M. Barrie made an attractive proposition. The fact that he was not much over five foot didn't concern Mary: she was barely five foot herself. Barrie had always enjoyed the company of pretty actresses, and though Mary was no scintillating conversationalist, she was intelligent, albeit rather provincial, and had a keen perception of Barrie's dour sense of humour—an essential prerequisite in any relationship with or understanding of him. Many of his contemporaries found his erratic moods quite impossible to gauge. He could be exhilarating company when he wanted to be, witty and alive with conversation, yet at other times he would grace a dinner-table with the silence of the grave. Barrie himself gave no clues as to his mood. He rarely smiled, yet was for ever poking fun at everything that lay closest to his heart. But when to laugh with him, and when to sympathize, when to take him seriously and when to ignore him? Navigating his humour could be a hazardous affair.

Barrie's notebooks for the spring and summer of 1892 are crammed with observations about himself and Mary Ansell, ostensibly for a novel under the working title of 'The Sentimentalist':

—This sentimentalist wants to make girl love him, bullies and orders her (this does it) yet doesn't want to marry.

—Such a man if an author, wd be studying his love affair for book. Even while proposing, the thought of how it wd *read* wd go thro' him.

—Literary man can't dislike any one he gets copy out of.

—First, her independence, 2nd hates herself at feeling it go, 3rd proud to be his slave—Their talk of this—his pride in making her say she is his slave & he her master.

—*Love Scenes*—Her abandonment of self to him—asking 'Do you love me' &c. Bursts of fondling him. 'How I give myself away by showing how I love you—why am I so ridiculous &c. Yet I like to show I am yr slave—tho' my idea formerly of how things in love shd be was just the reverse.'

—She pretends doesn't want to marry him—really this cause of her doubts—she can't be sure he loves her.

—Her way of peering over her fur collar.

—Her ordering clothes for him, &c.—Motherly feelings.

—The girl when won't do what he tells her to do (knowing it wrong—he treating her like child) lies on floor with head on chair, twisting about in woe. . . . She makes him say he is her slave—then impulsively cries it is she who is his—she wants him to say he is because she knows he isn't. 'I shd hate you really to be my slave—oh, say again that you *are*!'

—His feelings of repentance after making her act as slave to him.

—If she an actress, shd he not be a dramatist?

—His kindliness (weak), he feels for her & keeps the thing going on because doesn't want to make her miserable.

—The man reflecting in his own mind as to whether he shd marry her—pros and cons—his pleasures in mild love with many girls to which his position has at last given him an entrance, they admire his work so much—He feels absolutely that married life wd be insupportable & putting it to himself sees that he has many good points & ought not to give his future over to misery.

—He writes great book or play on this love affair of his, & the papers gush over its noble sentiment, &c, discuss the hero also, who is drawn unsparingly from himself, tho' they don't know this.

While Mary Ansell and *Walker, London* continued to play to packed houses, Barrie slipped away to visit his friend Arthur Quiller-Couch ('Q.') at Fowey in Cornwall. Sir Henry Irving had commissioned him to write a comedy for the Lyceum, and he liked to bounce ideas with Q.; he also relished the company of Q.'s three-year-old son, Bevil— 'my favourite boy in the wide wide world'. With Miss Ansell still on his mind, Barrie started to work on an idea about a Bookworm, which was to end up as *The Professor's Love Story*:

Barrie and Margaret Ogilvy in 1893

—*BKWM* [Bookworm] First act in writer's London study. Sister in Scotland. He is in woe, can't work, gets doctor who at first thinks it is a malady, then sees he is in love. Horror of Bookworm. 'With whom?' He has no idea, and doctor (who guesses it is A) won't tell. Alarm of Bookworm, change of life &c, packs to go off to sister in Scotland to fly from this woman, whoever she is.

Barrie himself went up to Scotland a week later—to visit his sister Maggie, who was engaged to a friend of the family, the Rev. James Winter. Barrie was particularly fond of this younger sister, with whom he had once hidden under the table that bore the coffin of his brother David: 'No one could understand me much who did not know what she has been to me all her life.'[11] Maggie was to be married at the end of May, so Barrie stayed with his parents in Kirriemuir until the wedding.

Both sides of Barrie's family were fiercely independent, and despite his new-found wealth, they would accept little from him; it was only after a good deal of persuasion that Margaret Ogilvy agreed to have a servant in the house, and even then she continued to do most of the work herself. But wedding presents were different, and Maggie's fiancé was happy to accept the gift of a horse from her brother. While preparations for the wedding continued, Barrie resumed his notes on the Bookworm:

—B[ookworm] realises he has been leading a selfish life engrossed in own work, &c, & not playing citizen's part in world.
—Doctor maintains . . . that B's marrying wd be the remaking of him—he has got so sunk in books, they'll drown him, he'll become a parchment, a mummy.
—Doctor says a sister can never be like a wife . . . Realising love better than books & fame.
—Strange after loved one's death to see papers again & see all world crying out ag[ain]st pinpricks—as we ourselves did but the other day, & will do again.

This last note was entered on Barrie's 32nd birthday, after a telegram had arrived announcing that James Winter had been flung from his horse and killed. Maggie responded to the tragedy as her mother had done to the news of David's death: she took to her bed and refused to be comforted. Barrie was overcome with guilt; the horse had been his wedding present. He sat with his sister in her darkened room, brooding over the tragedy. But the journalist was ever at his elbow:

—*Novel*. After death, a character (à la Maggie) talks beautiful resignation, &c. Yet what is the feeling at heart? A kicking at the awfulness? A bitterness? Work this out in novel, showing how almost no one in these cir[cumstances] gets at other's real feelings. Each conceals from the other.

A few days later, the wedding guests invited to attend James Winter's marriage attended his funeral; but his bride remained in the darkened room, wrapped in her grief, with Barrie at her side. He had written a four-page open letter, to be read out at the funeral service, explaining his sister's absence: 'She has not physical strength to be with you just now in body, but she is with you in spirit, and God is near her, and she is not afraid. . . . God chose his own way, and took her Jim, her dear young minister, and she says, God's will be done.'[12] Not content to limit his audience to the graveside mourners, Barrie proceeded to send this uncharacteristic piece of mawkishness to the *British Weekly* and the *Pall Mall Gazette*, both of whom published it in full. Perhaps it was done in an effort to comfort Maggie, who, unlike her brother, held deep religious beliefs. Barrie's truer feelings were reserved for the privacy of his notebook:

—A stone on road in memorial of the fatal accident might have awful words carried on it as—

> Here was killed so & so,
> Brave gallant man,
> Knocked out of the world
> by God
> While doing his duty.
> Left by his God to die
> in a ditch.
> God is love.

In the heat of the tragedy, Barrie had somewhat rashly promised to look after Maggie for the rest of her life. He was devoted to his sister, but nevertheless Maggie was a woman whose company was best enjoyed in small doses, and it must have come as something of a relief to him when she announced her engagement to her dead fiancé's brother, Willie Winter, in the following year. This too found its way into his notebook as grist for a possible story:

—*Club Window Book*. Girl's lover to whom about to be married dies. Her mother instrumental in getting her to marry another man. Yet in end it is seen secretly mother thinks daughter shd have remained virgin to old love & herself feels has shamed herself before old love's memory.

Barrie's engagement to Mary Ansell was now being confidently predicted in most of London's society magazines and gossip columns, but Barrie declined either to confirm or deny the rumours. He was caught in a cross-fire of conflicting emotions. On the one hand he was 'in love' with Mary—as much as he felt he was ever likely to be with a woman—and she was certainly in love with him. On the other hand he knew full well that he was temperamentally unsuited to married life. As early as 1887 he had contributed an article in black-comedy vein to the *Edinburgh Evening Dispatch* entitled 'My Ghastly Dream':

'When this horrid nightmare got hold of me, and how, I cannot say, but it has made me the most unfortunate of men.

'In my early boyhood it was a sheet that tried to choke me in the night. At school it was my awful bed-fellow with whom I wrestled nightly while all the other boys in the dormitory slept with their consciences at rest. It had assumed shape at that time: leering, but

> My dear beloved
> Jamie my heart
> keeps blessing and
> thanking you
> but in love no words
> can say, and especially your
> present th my heart fails
> words, for my last
> birthday gift.
> My dear beloved
> son God bless you

> and prosper you
> are a precious God
> given son to me
> the light of my eyes.
> and my darling
> Maggie is safe
> with God and
> you till we
> meet
> your loving
> mother

Margaret Ogilvy's only surviving letter to her son. They corresponded almost daily, and in *Margaret Ogilvy* Barrie wrote, 'My thousand letters that she so carefully preserved, always sleeping with the last beneath the sheet, where one was found when she died – they are the only writing of mine of which I shall ever boast'

fatally fascinating; it was never the same, yet always recognisable. One of the horrors of my dream was that I knew how it would come each time, and from where. I do not recall it in my childhood, but they tell me that, asleep in my cot, I would fling my arms about wildly as if fighting a ghost. It would thus seem that my nightmare was with me even then, though perhaps only as a shapeless mass that a too lively imagination was soon to resolve into a woman. My weird dream never varies now. Always I see myself being married, and then I wake up with the scream of a lost soul, clammy and shivering. . . .

'My ghastly nightmare always begins in the same way. I seem to know that I have gone to bed, and then I see myself slowly wakening up in a misty world. As I realise where I am the mist dissolves; and the heavy shapeless mass that weighed upon me in the night time when I was a boy, assumes the form of a woman, beautiful and cruel, with a bridal veil over her face. When I see her she is still a long way off, but she approaches rapidly. I cower in a corner till she glides into the room and beckons me to follow her. . . . Her power is mesmeric, for when she beckons I rise and follow her, shivering, but obedient. We seem to sail as the crow flies to the church which I attended as a child, and there everyone is waiting for us. . . .

'One hideous night she came for me in a cart. I was seized hold of by invisible hands and flung into it. A horrible fear possessed me that I was being taken away to be hanged, and I struggled to escape. . . . My hands were bound together with iron chains, and as soon as I snapped them a little boy with wings forged another pair. Many a time when awake I have seen pictures of that little boy generally with arrows in his hands, one of which he is firing at some man or woman. In pictures he looks like a cherub who has over-eaten himself, but, ah, how terribly disfigured he is in my dreams! He is lean and haggard now, grown out of his clothes, and a very spirit of malignity. She drives the cart, laughing horribly as we draw nearer and nearer the church, while he sits behind me and occasionally jags me with an arrow. When I cry out in pain she turns and smiles upon him, and he laughs in gay response.'[13]

Mary Ansell at the time of her marriage

This hauntingly vivid premonition hardly boded well for marital bliss; yet despite his better judgement Barrie proposed to Mary Ansell, and she accepted. In his notebook he wrote:

—Morning after engagement, a startling thing to waken up & remember you're tied for life.

Barrie travelled up to Kirriemuir to break the news to his mother, but on his arrival he was almost immediately struck down with pleurisy and pneumonia, which left him with a permanent cough for the rest of his life. His illness was of national concern while his life hung in the balance. Mary Ansell quit the cast of *Walker, London*, and headed north to nurse her fiancé back to health. If Margaret Ogilvy harboured any doubts about her son marrying an actress, they were now swept aside by the spectacle of Mary's love and devotion. On July 1st, Barrie was able to write to Quiller-Couch:

'My lungs are quite right again, and I have only to pick up strength now. Miss Ansell, who has an extraordinary stock of untrustworthy information on diseases of the human frame, knows all about quinsy and says she can sympathise in full. Yes, it is all true though it was in the papers. . . . We have worked hard to get married unbeknown to the lady journalists but vainly. In about a week it will be,—up here, so that we can go off together straight away, she to take charge. We go across the channel first for a month and fully mean to come your way soon thereafter.'

A rather different account of the prelude to the marriage was given by Hilaire Belloc's sister, the writer Marie Belloc Lowndes, in a letter to Mrs Thomas Hardy dated June 21st, 1937—two days after Barrie's death:

'I was very intimate with a young woman, now long dead, who was Mary Ansell's beloved friend. As of course you know, all that about her nursing Barrie is rubbish. She refused to marry him many times. Then he fell ill at Kirriemuir, and his mother telegraphed to Mary who came and they were married on what was supposed to be his deathbed. He told all this to Mrs Oliphant who told me and my mother, just after she had seen him.'

Whatever the truth, Mary Ansell accepted James Matthew Barrie as her husband on Monday July 9th, 1894. The ceremony was a simple affair, performed by a local minister in his parents' home, according to Scottish custom. After it was over, the newly-married couple left for their honeymoon in Switzerland. The ubiquitous notebooks went with them. Two days before the wedding, Barrie had jotted down in one of them:

—Our love has brought me nothing but misery.
—Boy all nerves. 'You are very ignorant.'
—How? Must we instruct you in the mysteries of love-making?

Barrie at the time of his marriage

In rounding off an interview with the 'bewitchingly flirtatious' Miss Mary Ansell, the *Sketch* noted that Barrie had 'not long ago declared to an American interviewer that he quite intended to marry, if only to have the convenience of using his wife's hair-pins to clean his pipes'.[1] The truth of the jest soon became apparent to Mary, and she later confided to Hilda Trevelyan that the honeymoon had been a shock to her. She did not elaborate, but Barrie's Swiss notebook makes an oblique reference to his dilemma:

—*Scene in Play. Wife*—Have you given me up? Have nothing to do with me? *Husband* calmly kind, no passion &c. (*à la self*)

While in Lucerne, Mary embarked on what was to become a lifelong passion: her love for dogs. She saw a litter of St Bernard puppies in a pet-shop window, and Barrie bought her one as a wedding present. She later wrote in *Dogs and Men*:

'Perhaps my love for dogs, in the beginning, was a sort of mother-love. Porthos was a baby when I first saw him: a fat little round young thing. The dearest of all in a lovely litter of St Bernards, away there in Switzerland. My heart burnt hot for love of him. . . .

'I have never been really happy with people. Some constraint tightens me up when I am with them. They seem so inside themselves, so unwilling to reveal their real selves. I am always asking for something they won't give me; I try to pierce into their reserves; sometimes I feel I am succeeding, but they close in again, and I am left outside.

'But with animals it is different. An animal is so helplessly itself. . . . I become one with them. I, too, become helplessly myself. They never withhold themselves from me as men withhold themselves. When the dogs loved me, they did it without forethought or afterthought, because they couldn't help it. But men didn't love me unless they wanted to; unless I fitted in with their idea of me. The dogs didn't have an idea of me. They just loved me—me—me—with passion and warmth, without thinking about it.

'I only loved clever men. And clever men, it seems to me, are made up of reserves. It is out of their reserves they bring their clever things.

'You think they will one day open their reserves, and that you will be the favoured one who is admitted to the cupboards where they keep their cleverness. But that is an illusion. The reserves of men are as helpless as a dog's lack of reserve is helpless. A man had to be clever, really clever, to please me. And I loved my dogs so passionately because they could never, never be clever in that way. They could never be complicated as the men were complicated.'

Although Porthos had been a wedding present to Mary, Barrie soon won the dog's affection for himself. The method of capture held good for both dogs and children:

'[Porthos] passionately loved his master. He really loved him more than he did me. It was a case of Mary and Martha. I gave him medicine, and kept him clean, and generally looked after him, but his master played with him. And he was a genius at games. They had fearful wrestling matches. These went on until both were exhausted. And they ran races, in and out of the rooms, up and down the stairs, out of the front door, in by the back, over and over and over again.... When it was all over I went round collecting the debris.'[2]

And Barrie went back to the silence of his study. He once told a correspondent that the 'taking of myriads of notes first has always been my way, and occupied me longer than the actual writing'.[3] For the past five years he had been filling notebooks with notes for a novel provisionally entitled 'The Sentimentalist'. Most of these notes concerned the adult life of the central character, Tommy Sandys, which inevitably related to his own. He had already decided to make Tommy a writer, and his intention had been to write a single book about the adult Tommy under the title *Sentimental Tommy*. But as he set to work on the actual text, he found himself becoming increasingly preoccupied with Tommy's childhood. He later explained in the introduction to the American edition:

'This is not in the smallest degree the book I meant it to be. Tommy ran away with the author. When we meet a man who interests us, and is perhaps something of an enigma, we may fall a-wondering what sort of boyhood he had; and so it is with writers who become inquisitive about their own creations. It was Sentimental Tommy the man that I intended to write here; I had thought him out as carefully as was possible to me; but when I sat down to make a start I felt that I could not really know him at one and twenty unless I could picture him at fifteen, and one's character is so fixed at fifteen that I saw I must go farther back for him, and so I journeyed to his childhood. Even then I meant merely to summarize his early days, but I was loath to leave him, or perhaps it was he who was loath to grow up.'

The major part of the novel explores Tommy's character against a setting of boyhood episodes and adventures. Tommy is a boy who is in love with himself. He is a born actor, who 'passes between dreams and reality as through tissue-paper' and has the faculty of 'stepping into other people's shoes and remaining there until he became someone else'. There is little that is 'sentimental' about Tommy in

Porthos, named after the St Bernard in George du Maurier's novel *Peter Ibbetson*

Notebook entry for 'The Sentimentalist', slightly smaller than actual size. The second paragraph reads: 'Treat man really loving, yet not wanting to marry – effect on woman (M.A.)' Presumably 'M.A.' refers to Mary Ansell

the sense of mawkish; Barrie used the word in its artistic meaning of sympathetic insight. It is Tommy's schoolmaster, Cathro, who brands him 'Sentimental Tommy', for reasons explained to one of Tommy's adult admirers:

' "Tommy Sandys has taken from me the most precious possession a teacher can have—my sense of humour." '

' "He strikes me as having a considerable sense of humour himself." '

' "Well, he may, Mr McLean, for he has gone off with all mine. . . . But I think I like your young friend worst when he is deadly serious. He is constantly playing some new part—playing is hardly the word though, for into each part he puts an earnestness that cheats even himself, until he takes to another. I suppose you want me to give you some idea of his character, and I could tell you what it is at any particular moment; but it changes, sir, I do assure you, almost as quickly as the circus-rider flings off his layers of waistcoats. A single puff of wind blows him from one character to another, and he may be noble and vicious, and a tyrant and a slave, and hard as granite and melting as butter in the sun, all in one forenoon. All you can be sure of is that whatever he is he will be it in excess. . . . Sometimes his emotion masters him completely, at other times he can step aside, as it were, and take an approving look at it. That is a characteristic of him, and not the least maddening one. . . . He baffles me; one day I think him a perfect numbskull, and the next he makes such a show of the small drop of scholarship he has that I'm not sure but what he may be a genius." '

' "That sounds better. Does he study hard?" '

' "Study! He is the most careless whelp that ever— . . . I don't think he could study, in the big meaning of the word. I daresay I'm wrong, but I have a feeling that whatever knowledge that boy acquires he will dig out of himself. There is something inside him, or so I think at times, that is his master, and rebels against book-learning. No, I can't tell what it is; when we know that, we shall know the real Tommy." ' '

Although *Sentimental Tommy* was to be largely based on his own boyhood in Kirriemuir, Barrie found that the companionship of a real boy helped to bring the memories swinging back. Such a boy was Arthur Quiller-Couch's son, Bevil. Barrie wrote to 'Q.' on November 7th: 'Being at present without any home in particular, liking your quarter of the world, eager to see yourselves, and itching to smash that there boy, we propose a descent on Fowey.' Barrie duly descended on the Quiller-Couches in December, bringing with him his wife, his dog, his notebooks—and his camera. This camera had

Title page and two photographs of Bevil Quiller-Couch ('The Pippa') and Porthos from 'The Pippa & Porthos'

- *The Pippa* -

- & -

- *Porthos* -

Jan. 1895

Dedicated to Mrs Quiller-Couch
(without her permission)
The Literary Matter by J. M. Barrie
The drudgery by Mary Barrie

been bought in Switzerland, and it was now put to use on New Year's Day 1895, to record the exploits of Bevil (nicknamed 'The Pippa') and Porthos. He later compiled twenty-four of the photographs into a hand-written story for Bevil, entitled 'The Pippa & Porthos' – 'Dedicated to Mrs Quiller-Couch (without her permission). The Literary Matter by J. M. Barrie. The drudgery by Mary Barrie.'[4]

By early March, the Barries were back in London and moving into their first house, 133 Gloucester Road—one of the capital's more hideous examples of late Victorian architecture. There was, however, a consolation. Kensington Gardens was only a short distance from the house, and its proximity afforded Porthos the luxury of a daily walk.

133 Gloucester Road, South Kensington

The Gardens were wild territory in those days, a rustic sanctuary from the bustle and roar of London's horse-drawn traffic. Sheep grazed in the long grass, wildfowl inhabited the inlets along the edge of the Serpentine lake and the island in its middle. Barrie and his wife could wander undisturbed for hours if they wished, with only Porthos for company. But the Broad Walk was another matter. 'All perambulators lead to the Kensington Gardens' wrote Barrie in *The Little White Bird*, and between the hours of two and four the Broad Walk became the domain of that vanished race, nursemaids. Here they would congregate every afternoon, busily airing their views on the business of babies, while their elder charges raced hoops or sailed boats on the near-by Round Pond.

Portrait of Barrie by William Nicholson

Kensington Gardens and the Round Pond in 1897. In *The Little White Bird*, Barrie wrote, 'There are men who sail boats on the Round Pond, such big boats that they bring them in barrows, and sometimes in perambulators, and then the baby has to walk. . . . But the sweetest craft that slips her moorings in the Round Pond is what is called a stick-boat, because she is rather like a stick until she is in the water and you are holding the string. Then as you walk round, pulling her, you see little men running about her deck, and sails rise magically and catch the breeze, and you put in on dirty nights at snug harbours which are unknown to the lordly yachts. . . . You are a solitary boy while all this is taking place, for two boys together cannot adventure far upon the Round Pond, and though you may talk to yourself throughout the voyage, . . . you know not, when it is time to go home, where you have been or what swelled your sails; your treasure-trove is all locked away in your hold, so to speak, which will be opened, perhaps, by another little boy many years afterwards.'

The Barries and Porthos soon became familiar figures to the regular patrons of the Gardens. They made an incongruous spectacle: Barrie minute, in a bowler hat and an overcoat several sizes too big for him, accompanied by his cough, his pipe, his minute wife and their vast St Bernard, who had a habit of standing on his hind legs and dwarfing them both. Porthos and Barrie could perform a number of tricks and games together, from simple hide-and-seek to a full-blooded boxing match. Sometimes smaller children ran screaming from the noble Porthos, which horrified their nursemaids, distressed Mary Barrie, and on the whole left her husband smiling. Like many childless women, Mary adored all children, and wanted to be loved by them. Barrie, on the other hand, feigned indifference to the breed. He could afford to; he had total confidence in his ability to fascinate any child he cared to ensnare.

The Barries decided to spend their first wedding anniversary in Switzerland again, but before going, they paid their regular visit north to Kirriemuir. Although weak and frail, Margaret Ogilvy seemed to be in reasonable health; Barrie's elder sister, Jane Ann, had long ago sacrificed her own ambitions so that she might nurse their mother in her old age. The manuscript of *Sentimental Tommy* was at last finished, and Barrie read the story to his mother, as he had done with all his stories.

The book appears to have met with her full approval and he now began to make notes for an introduction, requested by his American publisher, Charles Scribner. Since there could be no disguising that the book was about his boyhood, he decided that the introduction should be about his mother. Sitting by her bedside, Barrie started to jot down his observations of her:

—*Mother*. Her love for her father—In old age she thinks she is young again, & he is alive. She thinks her son (self) is him, & he pretends he is, & says the kind of things her father wd have said, & she is happy— yet it is pathetic to think that she has forgotten son who has been so good to her. The whole thing a proof how the people & events of our own childhood impress us. As we die, all else vanishes, & we use the words (like mother) that we have not used for sixty years & see the old furniture & faces & seem to live the old life.
—Her thoughts on death—secret feelings, wistful $\frac{1}{2}$ afraid, wandering mind, 'Is this my bed?' 'Is that you? You're my son, aren't you?' Using words of childhood.

Despite the ominous ring evident in these notes, Barrie felt it safe to leave Kirriemuir and travel to Switzerland with Mary. 'I had been gone a fortnight when the telegram was put into my hands. I had got a letter from my sister, a few hours before, saying that all was well at home. The telegram said in five words that she [Jane Ann] had died suddenly the previous night. There was no mention of my mother, and I was three days' journey from home. The news I got on reaching London was this: my mother did not understand that her daughter was dead, and they were waiting for me to tell her.'[5]

At about the same time as the Barries were catching the night train to Kirriemuir, Margaret Ogilvy was drifting about her home, vaguely intimating that she knew her daughter was dead. More than once she whispered eagerly, 'Is that you, David?', then asked that she might hold the old robe in which all her children had been christened. 'It was brought to her, and she unfolded it with trembling, exultant hands, and when she had made sure that it was still of virgin fairness her old arms went round it adoringly, and upon her face there was the ineffable mysterious glow of motherhood.'[6]

By the time Barrie arrived the next morning, Margaret Ogilvy had been dead for twelve hours. She was buried with Jane Ann in the same grave that held her beloved son David. The date was September 6th, 1895—Margaret Ogilvy's seventy-sixth birthday.

Margaret Ogilvy's grave

Two weeks later Barrie was back in London, writing to his friend W. E. Henley, whose own daughter Margaret had died some months before at the age of six:

133 Gloucester Road, S.W.
17 Sept '95.

My dear Henley,
   It is all as you say. My mother died full of years and honours, and the debt of nature was paid with the simplicity in which she always lived. She was always the glory of my life, and now I sit thinking and thinking, but I cannot think of one little thing I cd have done for her that was left undone. That leaves me with a kind of gladness even now. What saddens me most is the loss of my sister, who had given a whole life's devotion to her.
   It is very pathetic to me, your visit to that little grave. I shall go there too some day. She flits thro' the opening of my story, which is now in America.*
                              Yours ever,
                              J. M. Barrie.

*The 'flitting through' refers to Margaret Henley's brief appearance in *Sentimental Tommy* as Reddy, a child-friend of Tommy's, who dies at the age of six.

The frontispiece to *Margaret Ogilvy*

In reviewing *A Window in Thrums*, *The Scotsman* had observed that Barrie was 'a man who could make copy out of the bones of his grandmother'. No one knew this better than Barrie himself. In *When A Man's Single*, a semi-autobiographical account of his journalist days, he wrote: 'My God!... I would write an article, I think, on my mother's coffin.' He was now poised to do just that. The introduction to *Sentimental Tommy* about his mother had grown beyond the scope of a preface, and he decided to expand it into a full-length book: '*Margaret Ogilvy*, by her son, J. M. Barrie'. It was, in every sense, an extra-ordinary book, a memoir of an unknown woman, which revealed far more about the author than it did about her. It was a first of its kind, and it caught the public's imagination like a whirlwind when it appeared on the bookstalls in December 1896. The *British Weekly* review took up the whole of its front page: '*Margaret Ogilvy* is a book which it is almost sacrilegious to criticise. . . . It stands unmatched in literature as an idyll of the divinest of human feelings—a mother's love. . . . This is Mr Barrie's finest and noblest book. . . . It has been so written that no book of the generation is so likely to outlive us all as this.'

The praise was not universal. Many Scottish critics felt that family privacy had been violated, while Barrie's own family—in particular his elder brother Alexander—alleged that Barrie had exaggerated his humble origins, fabricated a number of incidents, and portrayed Margaret Ogilvy as a 'simple-minded' woman. The literary critic George Blake later echoed their indignation in *Barrie and the Kailyard School*:

'One may very well wonder why *Margaret Ogilvy* was ever written, except for private circulation, but Barrie threw the portrait of his mother into the whirlpool of commerce: in cold fact, cashing in on his own popularity. Not many men would deliberately expose their own domestic affairs in this fashion, but Barrie was one of the few; and we can only conclude that commercial success, after a chilly boyhood, had turned his head. On the other hand, it is difficult to determine whether or not *Margaret Ogilvy* is true to the facts of the woman's life.

'You never know where you are with Barrie. He could lie like a trooper to get the wanted, decisive effect; he made a world to suit his own fancy. For all his reputation for the understanding of women and children, we have to deal here with what seems to be a case of refined sadism.'

Whether *Margaret Ogilvy* is true to the facts of the woman's life is largely a matter of speculation; Barrie was writing as an artist, not as an historian, and the result was a portrait of a relationship, not an objective biography. If the facts are in doubt (and they have never been seriously challenged), one essential truth pervades every page: that Barrie's lifelong quest for the Land of Lost Content, which so often seemed to manifest itself in his affinity with children, was no nostalgic desire to return to his own boyhood. It was, rather, a craving to experience a childhood he had never personally known: the childhood of Margaret Ogilvy. The book concludes:

'And now I am left without them [Margaret Ogilvy and Jane Ann], I trust my memory will ever go back to those happy days, not to rush through them, but dallying here and there, even as my mother wanders through my books. And if I also live to a time when age must dim my mind and the past comes sweeping back like the shades of night over the bare road of the present it will not, I believe, be my youth I shall see but hers, not a boy clinging to his mother's skirt and crying, "Wait till I'm a man, and you'll lie on feathers," but a little girl in a magenta frock and a white pinafore, who comes toward me through the long parks, singing to herself, and carrying her father's dinner in a flagon.'

* * *

In September 1896, while awaiting the publication of *Margaret Ogilvy*, the Barries made their first trip to America in the company of the *British Weekly*'s editor, W. Robertson Nicoll—'one of the few men I think I could travel with without wanting to push him over a cliff'.[7] The trip had been arranged by Barrie's newly acquired theatrical agent, Addison Bright, with a view to engineering a meeting between his client and the legendary Broadway producer, Charles Frohman. Barrie had half-completed a stage adaptation of his novel, *The Little Minister*, and Bright knew that Frohman was looking for a suitable vehicle for his latest discovery, a young actress named Maude Adams. Barrie had misgivings about the enterprise— 'when a man dramatises his troubles begin';[8] moreover the female role of Babbie was infinitely inferior to the title role of the Little Minister. Bright knew of Barrie's reservations; but he also knew his client's susceptibility to pretty young actresses, particularly when viewed across the footlights. Maude Adams was appearing in *Rosemary* at Frohman's Empire Theater, and Bright arranged for a box to be placed at Barrie's disposal for his first night in New York. He declined the box, and instead sat in the back row with Mary. Within minutes of Maude Adams's appearance on stage, Barrie turned to his wife and announced, 'Behold, my Babbie.'

Barrie's enthusiasm for Charles Frohman was no less than his admiration for Maude Adams. The two men were exact contemporaries; both had sprung from humble origins and conquered

Maude Adams

Charles Frohman, known to some as the Beaming Buddha of Broadway

their chosen professions; both men worshipped mothers and children, yet both were childless themselves. Barrie later described Frohman as 'the man who never broke his word':

'His energy . . . was like a force of nature, so that if he had ever "retired" from the work he loved (a thing incredible) companies might have been formed . . . for exploiting the vitality of this Niagara of a man. They could have lit a city with it.

'He loved his schemes. They were a succession of many-colored romances to him, and were issued to the world not without the accompaniment of the drum, but you would never find him saying anything of himself. He pushed them in front of him, always taking care that they were big enough to hide him. . . . A sense of humor sat with him through every vicissitude like a faithful consort. . . . I have never known any one more modest and no one quite so shy. . . . Because we were the two shyest men in the world, we got on so well and understood each other so perfectly.'[9]

Little wonder that, with so much in common, these two men joined forces and formed such a close, lasting and profitable relationship. Barrie later claimed to have had only one real quarrel with Frohman—'but it lasted all the sixteen years I knew him. He wanted me to be a playwright and I wanted to be a novelist.'[10] Although Frohman was soon to have his way, Barrie continued, for the time being, to be both. He returned to England, finished the dramatization of *The Little Minister*, then set to work on the sequel to *Sentimental Tommy – Tommy and Grizel*. This novel, Barrie's longest—and, in the opinion of many critics, his finest—work, was to become over the next four years the repository for all his innermost thoughts and feelings. It was to prove not so much a labour of love as a labour of ruthless self-analysis and self-criticism. In his notebook he had vowed: '*T & G*. This book to contain what ordinary biographies omit.' Barrie was true to his pledge. No one reading the book, either then or now, could be left in any doubt that the central character of Tommy was once again drawn from himself, but this time unsparingly so. The storyline continues from where *Sentimental Tommy* ended. Tommy has left Scotland and come to London, where he becomes a fashionable writer. His childhood friend, Grizel, is now a grown woman, with a woman's passions, but Tommy has remained a boy at heart. He is still Sentimental Tommy. Like his creator, Tommy uses his sentimentalism—'escapism' would be a better word—to full advantage in his writings, but in his relationship with Grizel it ultimately leads to emotional ruin. It remains one of the more extraordinary facets of Barrie's highly complex personality that he could lay bare his own private anguish on the printed page, could

Gareth Hughes as Tommy Sandys and Mary McAvey as Grizel in Paramount's 1921 film, *Sentimental Tommy*

analyse the failure of his marriage even as it was failing, without any apparent restraint or inhibition:

' "Grizel, I seem to be different from all other men; there seems to be some curse upon me. I want to love you, . . . you are the only woman I ever wanted to love, but apparently I can't. I have decided to go on with this thing because it seems best for you, but is it? . . . I think I love you in my own way, but I thought I loved you in their way, and it is the only way that counts in this world of theirs. It does not seem to be my world. . . ."

'If we could love by trying, no one would ever have been more loved than Grizel. . . . He knew it was tragic that such love as hers should be given to him; but what more could he do than he was doing? Ah, if only it could have been a world of boys and girls! . . . He could not make himself anew. They say we can do it, so I suppose he did not try hard enough. But God knows how hard he tried.

'He went on trying. In those first days [of marriage] she sometimes asked him, "Did you do it out of love or was it pity only?" And he always said it was love. He said it adoringly. He told her all that love meant to him, and it meant everything that he thought Grizel would like it to mean. . . . They had a honeymoon by the sea . . ., Tommy trying to become a lover by taking thought, and Grizel not letting on that it could not be done in that way. . . . He was a boy only. She knew that, despite all he had gone through, he was still a boy. And boys cannot love. Oh, is it not cruel to ask a boy to love? . . . He did not love her. "Not as I love him," she said to herself. "Not as married people ought to love, but in the other way he loves me dearly." By the other way she meant that he loved her as he loved Elspeth [his sister], and loved them both just as he had loved them when all three played in the den. He was a boy who could not grow up. . . . He gave her all his affection, but his passion, like an outlaw, had ever to hunt alone.'

Whatever Mary's thoughts might have been as she read her husband's work, they have not been recorded. Much of the original text was deleted before it went to press, possibly at her instigation. One such deletion appears on the last page of the manuscript (the deleted sentence in italics):

'She lived so long after Tommy that she was almost a middle-aged woman when she died. *What God will find hardest to forgive in him, I think, is that Grizel never had a child.*'[11]

After three years of marriage, the Barries were still childless. Mary desperately wanted to have children, yet was left with little alternative but to direct her maternal instincts towards Porthos. For

George. 'I could forgive him everything' wrote Barrie of George in *The Little White Bird* – 'Save his youth'. (JMB) *

Barrie, however, there was a very real alternative: other people's children. To his close circle of child friends he now added the writer Maurice Hewlett's two children, Cecco and Pia. The Hewletts lived near Kensington Gardens, and the four-year-old Cecco often accompanied him on his walks with Porthos. Presently two other boys made Barrie's acquaintance: a spectacularly attractive five-year-old named George and his four-year-old brother Jack. The pair wore blue blouses and bright red tam-o'-shanters, and took regular walks in Kensington Gardens in the company of their nurse, Mary, and their baby brother Peter—still in his perambulator. George was a remarkably forthright individual, and he made it his business to cultivate Barrie's friendship. To him he was not J. M. Barrie the celebrated writer, but a small man with a cough who could wiggle his ears and perform magic feats with his eyebrows. Moreover he seemed to be singularly well-informed on the subject of cricket, fairies, murders, pirates, hangings, desert islands and verbs that take the dative. George had never met anyone quite like him; he was old, but he was not grown up. He was one of them. His unpredictable moods made him all the more intriguing. Some days he would be in the giving vein, and could be relied upon to tell an endless supply of stories, while at other times he would be steeped in silence. These silences, so disconcerting to his wife, who invariably took them personally, were accepted by George as an integral part of his character. Like most children, he was far too arrogant and self-centred to take offence. Another child friend of Barrie's at this time was eight-year-old Pamela Maude, whose father, the actor Cyril Maude, had just begun rehearsing *The Little Minister* in the title role. Pamela later recalled the spell that Barrie cast over her as a child:

'He was a tiny man, and he had a pale face and large eyes with shadows round them. We only stayed with him once, in Scotland, but he had always been in our lives. . . . Our parents called him "Jimmy". He was unlike anyone we had ever met, or would meet in the future. He looked fragile, but he was strong when he wrestled with Porthos, his St Bernard dog. . . .

'Mr Barrie talked a great deal about cricket and wanted Margery [her sister] to like it and to be boyish, but the next moment he was telling us about fairies as though he knew all about them. He was made of silences, but we did not find these strange; they were so much part of him that they expressed him more than anything he could say.

' "Jimmy didn't say *one word* the whole of lunch," we heard Mam say to our father, . . . but it seemed to us that his silences spoke loudly. . . . We came to look on Mr Barrie as our friend; he did not

*Photographs known to have been taken by Barrie are indicated thus.

seem to belong to the theatre like other playwrights; when he and our parents talked together he told jokes that had nothing to do with the play, and he looked shy with the actors and actresses. He and Papa liked to talk about fishing. We never saw him without his pipe. . . .

'Mrs Barrie was lovely, . . . but we could not feel at ease with her. She did not talk to us and she never smiled when we were with her. Mr Barrie did not talk and she did not smile, and yet he was our companion. When we were away from him he seemed to be with us; he was more present than our parents or Mrs Barrie who were beside us.

'In the evening, when the strange morning light had begun to change, Mr Barrie held out a hand to each of us in silence, and we slipped our own into his and walked, still silently, into the beechwood. We shuffled our feet through leaves and listened, with Mr Barrie, for sudden sound, made by birds and rabbits. One evening we saw a pea-pod lying in the hollow of a great tree-trunk, and we brought it to Mr Barrie. There, inside, was a tiny letter, folded inside the pod, that a fairy had written. Mr Barrie said he could read fairy writing and read it to us. We received several more, in pea-pods, before the end of our visit.'[12]

Barrie had known many children, but none of them so captivated him as the boy in the red tam-o'-shanter. George seemed to combine all the finest qualities of boyhood in rare abundance. 'There never was a cockier boy', he later wrote of him in *The Little White Bird*, a fictional account of his relationship with George, in which the boy is thinly disguised as 'David':

George: 'He strikes a hundred gallant poses in a day' (JMB)

'It is difficult to believe that he walks to the Kensington Gardens; he always seems to have alighted there: and were I to scatter crumbs I opine he would come and peck. . . . He strikes a hundred gallant poses in a day; when he tumbles, which is often, he comes to the ground like a Greek god. . . . One day I had been over-friendly to another boy, and, after enduring it for some time David up and struck him. It was exactly as Porthos does when I favour other dogs . . . so I knew its meaning at once; it was David's first public intimation that he knew I belonged to him.

'[His nurse] scolded him for striking that boy, and made him stand in disgrace at the corner of a seat in the Broad Walk. The seat at the corner of which David stood suffering for love of me is the one nearest to the Round Pond to persons coming from the north. . . .

'I returned to David, and asked him in a low voice whether he would give me a kiss. He shook his head about six times, and I was in despair. Then the smile came, and I knew that he was teasing me only. He now nodded his head about six times.

'This was the prettiest of all his exploits.'

Barrie was rarely accompanied by his wife on these afternoon strolls through Kensington Gardens. He preferred to walk alone with Porthos, meeting up with George and Jack for another round of stories before retiring to a shady bench by the Round Pond to continue his work on *Tommy and Grizel*:

'Poor Tommy! he was still a boy, he was ever a boy, trying sometimes, as now, to be a man, [but] always when he looked round he ran back to his boyhood as if he saw it holding out its arms to him and inviting him to come back and play. He was so fond of being a boy that he could not grow up. In a younger world, where there were only boys and girls, he might have been a gallant figure. . . . Oh, who by striving could make himself a boy again as Tommy could! I tell you he was always irresistible then. What is genius? It is the power to be a boy again at will. When I think of him flinging off the years and whistling childhood back, . . . when to recall him in those wild moods is to myself to grasp for a moment at the dear dead days that were so much the best, I cannot wonder that Grizel loved him. I am his slave myself, I see that all that was wrong with Tommy was that he could not always be a boy.'

Barrie rehearsing Winifred Emery as Babbie in *The Little Minister*

On September 27th, 1897, Maude Adams opened in *The Little Minister* at Frohman's Empire Theater, New York. Despite cautious reviews, the play ran for over three hundred performances, breaking all Broadway records. The London production was due to open in November, with Pamela Maude's parents playing the leads — Cyril Maude as Gavin Ogilvy (the Little Minister of the title), and his wife Winifred Emery as the gypsy girl Babbie. Barrie attended every rehearsal, and once again fell in love across the footlights with his leading lady. He made a habit of paying Winifred lavish compliments from the wings, despite the presence on stage of her husband (who was also the producer) and of his own wife sitting in the otherwise empty stalls. Mary Barrie's acting career now consisted largely of disguising her feelings in front of others; if Barrie wished to flirt with his leading lady, she was not going to make an issue of it. She understood her husband's sentimental weakness for pretty young actresses; she also knew, for the most bitter and private of reasons, the limitations of a sentimentalist's ardour.

Maude Adams as Babbie in *The Little Minister*

Mary came out of retirement briefly to play Babbie in a copyright performance of the play.* The American writer Richard Harding Davis happened to be present, and was asked to play Babbie's father. He gave an account of the somewhat bizarre performance in a letter home:

'Mrs Barrie played the gypsy and danced most of the time, which she said was her conception of the part as it was in the book. Her husband explained that this was a play and not a book, but she did not care and danced on and off. She played my daughter [Babbie], and I had a great scene in which I cursed her, which got rounds of applause. Lady Lewis's daughters in beautiful Paquin dresses played Scotch lassies, and giggled in all the sad parts. . . . At one time there were five men on the stage all talking Scotch dialects and imitating Irving at the same time. It was a truly remarkable performance.'[13]

One of Barrie's favourite photographs of himself

By December 1897, Barrie's name as a playwright was established on both sides of the Atlantic. Despite his avowed dislike of social events, he was in a celebratory mood, and accepted an invitation to Sir George and Lady Lewis's New Year's Eve dinner party — an annual event, considered to be one of the highlights of the season. Sir George was the most distinguished society lawyer of his day (his clientele included the Prince of Wales), and it was his two daughters

---

*A copyright performance was a preliminary performance of a new play, prior to its theatrical opening, designed to protect the author's dramatic rights. The performance was usually acted by the cast in front of a 'witness' audience of friends.

who had taken part in the copyright performance of *The Little Minister*. The dinner party was for seventy-two persons, consisting mainly of fashionable actors and actresses, artists, musicians, writers, lawyers and politicians.

The event turned out to be less tedious than Barrie had expected, for he found himself seated next to 'the most beautiful creature he had ever seen'[14] — Mrs Arthur Llewelyn Davies, the wife of a young barrister. She had a tip-tilted nose, wide-spaced grey eyes, black hair and a crooked smile. She seemed to say very little, and was more interested in secreting the after-dinner sweets into her silk reticule than in the conversation around her. Barrie became intrigued, and asked her who the sweets were for. 'For Peter', she replied, as if it were the most natural thing in the world. On further inquiry he learned that she had formerly been Miss Sylvia Jocelyn du Maurier, sister of the actor Gerald du Maurier and daughter of George du Maurier — author of *Peter Ibbetson* and *Trilby*. A conversation developed, Barrie telling her that he had named his dog Porthos after the St Bernard, Porthos, in her father's novel *Peter Ibbetson*; she in turn told him that she had named her youngest son Peter, the beneficiary of the sweets, after Peter Ibbetson himself. It emerged that she had two other sons, George and Jack, the eldest being named after her father.

Gradually the penny dropped. She was talking to the man with the cough who could wiggle his ears, while he had come face to face with the mother of the boy in the bright red tam-o'-shanter.

Sylvia Llewelyn Davies (JMB)

'There never was a simpler happier family until the coming of Peter Pan,' wrote Barrie in *Peter and Wendy*. Doubtless he was well aware that, in describing the Darling family thus, he was alluding, with shades of perverse humour, to his own intrusion into the lives of the Llewelyn Davies family, on whom the Darlings were to be based.

Sylvia's husband Arthur, later caricatured as Mr Darling, was the second son of the Reverend John Llewelyn Davies, himself a brilliant scholar and theologian, President of the Union at Cambridge University, Honorary Chaplain to the Queen, a Radical of the Broad Church party, and a lifelong supporter of workers' rights, trade-unionism, and women's suffrage. His reputation was such that he was widely expected to be offered a bishopric, and might well have reached the highest pinnacle of the ecclesiastical hierarchy had he not chosen to deliver in Queen Victoria's presence a blistering attack on Imperialism from the pulpit at Windsor. The Queen was outraged, and her Prime Minister, Gladstone, took some relish in seeing the Reverend John transferred to the remoter regions of Westmorland. Nevertheless, as Rector of Kirkby Lonsdale he continued to air his radical views, both from the pulpit and in print. In his spare time he mountaineered the local heights (in 1858 he had been the first man to scale the Dom, the highest mountain in Switzerland), frequently broke the ice on his daily swim, made an authoritative translation of Plato's *Republic*, and fathered six boys and a girl. His sister, Emily, in addition to founding Girton College, Cambridge, had been one of the original petitioners for women's suffrage, and in 1883 his daughter Margaret, Arthur's elder sister, become a founder member of the Women's Co-operative Guild, editing their magazine and organizing campaigns from an office in the vicarage. There was soon so much activity there that the gardener's wheelbarrow had to be enlisted to carry all the reports, petitions and circulars to the post; indeed, had it not been for the tempering influence of Arthur's mother, Mary, the country vicarage might well have been mistaken by their staid Victorian neighbours for a den of subversive revolutionaries. Mary Crompton had married the Reverend John Llewelyn Davies in 1859, and, while not exactly an atheist, she is said to have not attended a single sermon delivered by her husband in their thirty-six years of married life. Despite this, or perhaps because of it, they remained devoted to one another. What the Reverend John provided for his family in intellectual stimulation, Mary balanced with a presiding sense of grace and humour. Her seven children adored her, and on the last day of their holidays would follow her from room to room as she did their packing, unable to bear being out of her sight for an instant.

It was in this formidable but invigorating atmosphere that Arthur grew up. He and his five brothers were encouraged to emulate their

The Reverend John Llewelyn Davies outside Kirkby Lonsdale Vicarage

Mary Crompton in her early thirties, from the painting by Sir William Blake Richmond

Arthur Llewelyn Davies in 1890

George and Emma du Maurier with their daughter May, photographed by Julia Cameron

father's scholastic achievements, and all but one obtained scholarships in public school and university. By 1891 Arthur had been called to the Bar, and was able to account for himself in the following terms to the Council of Legal Education:

My Lords and Gentlemen,

I beg to offer myself as a Candidate for an Assistant Readership in English Law.

I was born in February, 1863, and was educated at Marlborough (where I obtained Foundation, Junior, and Senior Scholarships and a School Exhibition) and Trinity College, Cambridge (of which I was Minor and Foundation Scholar) and was placed in the First Class of the Classical Tripos in June, 1884.

Since that time I have obtained the Lebas Essay Prize (Cambridge University) in 1884, an Inns of Court Studentship in 1886, the First Whewell International Law Scholarship (Cambridge University) in 1887, and an Inner Temple Pupil Scholarship in Common Law in 1889.

For a year (1886–7) I was an Assistant Master at Eton College, and I have had a good deal of other experience of various kinds of teaching.

ARTHUR LLEWELYN DAVIES

Arthur first met Sylvia du Maurier at a dinner party in 1889. According to the artist H. J. Ford, an eyewitness, the young lawyer found himself sitting next to a woman of extraordinary grace, beauty and charm, who 'displayed liberally the most beautiful neck, shoulders and bosom to the admiring world, . . . and I dimly perceived that his fate was sealed. A few weeks later, the engagement of Arthur Ll. D. was announced to Sylvia du M.'[1] The engagement came as something of a surprise to their friends, for although Arthur and Sylvia made a spectacularly handsome couple, their families had virtually nothing in common. In contrast to the Spartan austerity of the Llewelyn Davies family, the du Mauriers epitomized the gaiety and Bohemian frivolity of the 'nineties. At about the same time as Arthur's father was being ordained, Sylvia's father was leading the dissipated life of an impoverished art student in Paris. Despite his stylish surname, George du Maurier's only connection with the aristocracy lay in the Duke of York's bed, which his grandmother, Mary Anne Clarke, had graced on and off from 1801 to 1804 as mistress to the Prince Regent's brother. After failing to enter the Sorbonne, George du Maurier left Paris for London, where in 1851 he married Emma Wightwick, the daughter of a Bond Street linen draper. His ambition to become an artist found a measure of fulfilment when he joined the staff of *Punch* in 1864, and over the next thirty years the name of du Maurier became a by-word for social lampoonery. He took particular pleasure in satirizing fashionable upper-class and middle-class life, and his cartoons, for which his five children were put to constant use as models, were responsible for creating a certain Philistine scorn towards artiness and that brand of earnest intellectualism reflected in the Llewelyn Davieses. Sylvia's brother-in-law, Charles Hoyer Millar, observed the great interest shown by 'the whole du Maurier family in the appearance of their friends and new people they met. . . . People in general were divided into good-looking, amusing, and bores. . . . One must never be *au sérieux* about anything. . . . The family in general had a rooted dislike to serious topics of any kind, at all events in the presence of each other.'[2]

Given their priorities, it was hardly surprising that the du Mauriers viewed Sylvia's engagement to Arthur with mixed feelings. The young man was unquestionably handsome, a point in his favour noted by George du Maurier in a letter to a friend: 'I will add—from my own aesthetic point of view—qu'il est joli garçon . . . j'ai toujours

George du Maurier frequently used his children (and their remarks) as inspiration for his contributions to *Punch*

DELICATE CONSIDERATION.

Mamma. "What a Din you're making, Chicks! What *are* you Playing at?"

Trixy. "O, Mamma, we're Playing at Railway Trains. I'm the Engine, and Guy's a First-Class Carriage, and Sylvia's a Second-Class Carriage, and May's a Third-Class Carriage, and Gerald, he's a Third-Class Carriage, too—that is, he's really only a *Truck*, you know, only you mustn't Tell him so, as it would Offend him!"

l'œil sur ma postérité!'[3] However, Emma du Maurier regarded her future son-in-law as too dry and serious a proposition for her gay and ebullient daughter; moreover he was evidently short of money, though his prospects as a barrister appeared promising. Sylvia's seventeen-year-old brother Gerald, a schoolboy at Harrow, was rather more generous in his enthusiasm:

> The Grove
> Harrow-on-the-Hill
> March 30th, 1890

My Darling Sylvia,

I am so sorry I haven't written to congratulate you, but I was 'struck all of a 'eap!' But I do congratulate you, fearfully, though I have never seen the charmer, I am sorry to say. . . .

I hope I get home in time to wish you goodbye to the heather of bonny Westmoreland. I am glad he is a 'barrister' because then he won't 'bar-sister'. O Lord!

> I remain, your loving brother,
> Gerald du Maurier.

The composer Sir Hubert Parry was an old friend of the Llewelyn Davies family, and his twelve-year-old daughter Dolly was staying at the vicarage a few days before Sylvia's arrival. She later wrote:

'When Arthur was engaged to Sylvia, I realised what it meant to Mrs Davies. I remember her telling us about it, and taking out of a cupboard in the drawing-room 2 photographs, saying "That is my sweet Sylvia." I was so fascinated by those photographs that I was always thinking whether I couldn't go to the cupboard and have another look.

'How romantic it is to think of Sylvia coming to Kirkby, to the outwardly severe-looking Georgian Rectory adjoining the graveyard on one side, and looking over the lovely Fells, where Mr Davies walked nearly every day. I like to think of Sylvia feeling the warmth within, and the love and sympathy she found in Arthur's mother. And Arthur's brothers, austere outwardly, felt, I feel sure, very soon the charm of this lovely sweet feminine creature. All the same, I feel it must have been a strange contrast to her easy-going, happy, more or less Bohemian home.'[4]

Sylvia wrote to Arthur's mother on her return to London:

15, Bayswater Terrace
April 15th [1890].

Dearest Mrs Davies,

    I feel I must just write a few lines to you, to thank you *with all my heart* for being so very kind and sweet to me. The journey to Kirkby was rather painful, but the sweetness at the end of it, and the dear ones waiting to meet me, was worth going through much, *much* more for. The recollection of my first visit to Kirkby will be very dear to me, and I shall never be able to thank you enough. I am very, very fond of you. I was, I think, the moment I saw you. . . .

Always affectionately yours,
Sylvia du Maurier.

Mary Llewelyn Davies replied the following day:

K.L., 16th April, '90

My dearest Sylvia,

    Thank you very much for your dear note and for all your loving words. It is delightful to think that your visit to us has established an intimacy and affection which will, I hope, go on always increasing.

    I have missed you so since you went away! It quite surprised me how you have got into my heart in so short a time! . . . After all I believe I shall not come to London just yet. . . . I am not sure that my chief disappointment (if there is any) is not seeing your dear face again. I want so to know you more, and to be with you ever so much! But there are some reasons why I am glad to stay on at home, in spite of my four days of solitude while his Reverence is having a fine gay time in town! . . .

    Now goodbye, darling. Write as often as you feel inclined. Kindest regards to yr. father and mother.

Your loving
Mary Ll.D.

Arthur and his mother in about 1891

Sylvia's strong bond of friendship and affection with Arthur's mother was to prove a very real comfort in the drawn-out period of engagement that followed, for it had been decided, probably at Emma du Maurier's insistence, that the couple should wait two full years before marriage in order to watch Arthur's progress at the Bar. It was through the help of George (later Sir George) Lewis that he obtained many of his early briefs; the eminent society solicitor was quick to perceive Arthur's ability at expressing himself with forceful clarity, together with his infinite capacity for hard work, and he confidently predicted that his protégé would one day rise to the top of his profession. But the legal ladder was a slow and weary climb, and Arthur knew that it would be many years before his labours began to reward him financially.

In October 1891, Sylvia and Arthur went to stay with the Parrys at their home at Rustington-on-Sea. Their 14-year-old daughter Dolly had begun to keep a long and detailed diary, in which she recorded her surprisingly perceptive observations:

'We have never seen such a pair of undemonstrative lovers as Sylvia and Arthur. They hardly ever speak to each other even when in a room by themselves. Sylvia is a delightful thing. I can't imagine her with Margaret [Llewelyn Davies] at all, with her love of pretty dresses and the stage; she is always dancing about the room. . . . Without being strictly speaking pretty, she has got one of the most delightful, brilliantly sparkling faces I have ever seen. Her nose turns round the corner—also turns right up. Her mouth is quite crooked . . . Her eyes are very pretty—hazel and very mischievous. She has pretty black fluffy hair: but her expression is what gives her that wonderful charm, and her low voice.'[5]

Sylvia, Arthur and George in 1893

In the following March, Arthur received a small windfall in the form of a legacy of £3,000 from his mother's brother, Charles Crompton. Sylvia had also begun to earn money by working with Mrs Nettleship, the celebrated theatrical dressmaker, making clothes for Ellen Terry. Their combined income came to little more than £400 a year, but Sylvia's father was able to add a small contribution from the modest profits derived from his first novel, *Peter Ibbetson*.

On August 15th, 1892, after two years of patient waiting, Arthur Llewelyn Davies was at last able to marry Sylvia du Maurier. They spent their honeymoon at Porthgwarra, in Cornwall, then returned to London and set up house at 18 Craven Terrace, Paddington, where their first son was born on July 20th of the following year. He was christened with one name only, George, after Sylvia's father. The event coincided with the publication of George du Maurier's second novel, *Trilby*, which all but eclipsed the family's pride over the birth of his grandson. As with *Peter Ibbetson*, the novel was drawn for the most part from du Maurier's recollections of his early life in Paris as an impoverished artist, but whereas *Peter Ibbetson* had caused only a modest stir, *Trilby* quickly became one of the biggest literary bonanzas of the century, heaping its bewildered author with such riches and fame that it positively distressed him. He found it all rather vulgar, and no amount of commercial success could compensate him for his rapidly failing eyesight.

In the summer of 1894, at about the same time as the newly-wed

Sylvia and Arthur

Barries were setting off for their honeymoon in Switzerland, Arthur and Sylvia again went to stay at Rustington. Sylvia was eight months pregnant with her second child, and this year they rented a Mill House near the Parrys' home. Dolly Parry wrote in her diary:

George

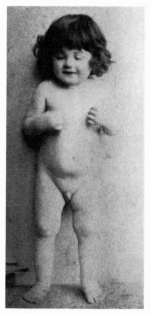

'Arthur and Sylvia came down to the Mill House for the summer which much delighted my heart: she is as sweet and dear as ever. They are very flourishing and content on £400 a year—but it is a miracle. ... I would rather marry her than anyone I know, she is so wonderfully fascinating and good. ... Mother's birthday, which we spent quietly with Sylvia to tea. Discussed cancer, and whether marriage was happy, and whether one would rather be born or not.'

The young couple returned to Craven Terrace, where their second son was born on September 11th. He was christened John, after Arthur's father, but was almost immediately nicknamed Jack. Mary Llewelyn Davies wrote to Sylvia from Kirkby Lonsdale:

K.L. Friday.

My Sylvia,
    No Mil [mother-in-law] ever got a dearer or sweeter letter than I did the other day! ... You tell me all so nicely, and I

Sylvia (JMB)

can so well fancy you lying in yr. blue bed, looking so delicious, and yr. two sons with you. Jack seems to make good progress—and never mind if you can't be all in all to him. It is better it should be so for your picking up your strength. . . .

Goodbye. I must not tire you, darling. I hope A's cold is better? I shall love to hug you and the 2 sons.

Bless you all!

M.

In February of the following year, Mary Llewelyn Davies died of a sudden heart-attack. Both Arthur and Sylvia were heartbroken by this first sorrow to cloud their blissfully happy lives. Dolly Parry wrote: 'When she died, I realised the depth of Sylvia's feeling for her—in fact, I don't think I ever came across a mother and a daughter-in-law so deeply attached. Sylvia could not talk about it.' A second bereavement followed swiftly upon the first: on October 8th, 1896, George du Maurier died at the early age of sixty. Sylvia's brother Gerald, who was playing a small part in the stage production of *Trilby*, had visited him a few days before his death. As he left the room, his father held out his hand and murmured, 'Si c'est la mort, ce n'est pas gai.'[6]

George du Maurier's ashes were interred in Hampstead Churchyard, the first in a long line of du Mauriers and Llewelyn Davieses who would eventually lie beside him. On his tombstone were written the last lines of *Trilby*:

A little trust that when we die
We reap our sowing! and so—good-bye!

*   *   *

By the beginning of 1897 it had become clear that the house in Craven Terrace was too small for a family that already consisted of two young boys—with another child on the way. The death of Sylvia's father had provided her with a very reasonable legacy, largely as a result of *Trilby*, and the recent death of one of Arthur's elderly aunts left him with the tail-end of a lease on a larger house in Notting Hill: 31 Kensington Park Gardens. The prospect of a third child also required the services of an under-nurse to supplement the efforts of the resident Nurse Woodward. Arthur's brother Maurice had recently dispensed with the services of a young under-nursemaid, Mary Hodgson. Mary's brother was a sidesman at the Reverend John Llewelyn Davies's church, and her family had long Kirkby Lonsdale connections. Arthur therefore wrote to her,

Mary Hodgson

53

George, Sylvia and Jack in 1895

offering her the post of under-nursemaid, and a few days later the twenty-two-year-old Mary Hodgson travelled south to London to take up her duties. Within a short space of time she had become exclusive nurse to the family, and proved to be worthy of the absolute trust Sylvia placed in her. From the outset she insisted that George and Jack addressed her as 'Mary'; to call her 'Nurse' was to incur her instant wrath. She brought to her role a measure of the traditional nanny, and walks in Kensington Gardens soon became a daily routine.

On February 25th, 1897, a third son was born to Sylvia and Arthur. He was named Peter, after *Peter Ibbetson*, but unlike George and Jack he was never christened. His parents decided that this was a choice he should be allowed to make for himself later on. Peter proved to be somewhat frailer than either of his two brothers. Dolly Parry wrote to him in later life, 'You were not nearly so strong as George or Jack. . . . You were pale and different, and the fact that you were not hearty for some years appealed to me.'[7]

Sylvia and Peter (JMB)

Sylvia continued her dressmaking with Mrs Nettleship, while at home she put her talent to practical account, making clothes for her-

Sylvia and George

self and her boys 'out of nothing and other people's mistakes',[8] as Barrie was to write of Mrs Darling. For Peter the scope was rather limited as he was still in his pram, but for George and Jack she created loose-fitting square-necked silk blouses, corduroy trousers and high-laced boots. One day, while clearing out an old chest of drawers, she found an ancient judicial robe of red velvet that had once belonged to Arthur's grandfather. Seeing no further use for it in its courtroom capacity, she cut it up and transformed the pieces into bright red tam-o'-shanters. Thus arrayed, George and Jack soon became a distinctive feature of Kensington Gardens, and could hardly fail to catch the attention of the little Scotsman out strolling with his dog.

Many of Arthur's briefs were now coming to him through the office of Sir George Lewis, and it was only natural that he and Sylvia should be invited to the Lewises' New Year's Eve dinner party on December 31st, 1897. 'If only I hadn't accepted that invitation to dine,' bemoans Mr Darling to his wife on returning from a dinner party to find that his children have flown away to the Neverland with Peter Pan. It was shortly to become Arthur's cry too.

George and Jack in 1897

15, Old Cavendish Street, W.
14 Aug. 1892.

Dear Miss du Maurier,

And so you are to be married tomorrow! And I shall not be present. You know why.

Please allow me to wish you great happiness in your married life. And at the same time I hope you will kindly accept the little wedding gift I am sending you . . . It reaches you somewhat late, but that is owing to circumstances too painful to go into.

With warmest wishes to you and Mr Davis,

Believe me, dear Miss du Maurier,

Yours sincerely,

J. M. Barrie.

P.S. To think that you don't know about Peterkin!

This 'characteristic whimsicality' (as Peter Llewelyn Davies later described it) is dated one day prior to Sylvia and Arthur's wedding date, the address being Barrie's at that time. It was, in fact, written some time in 1898, on the back of a piece of 133 Gloucester Road writing paper, and delivered to Sylvia by hand. The mis-spelling of 'Davies' was probably unintentional, but both the slip and the letter itself—not to mention the gift—must have proved mildly irritating to Arthur.

Sylvia (JMB)

Now that the ice had been broken, Barrie started seeing more of George and Jack, both at home and on their daily walks in Kensington Gardens. But it was George who won his closest affection, and their friendship soon started to blossom in the pages of Barrie's notebook:

George (JMB)

—George admires me as writer ∵ [= because] thinks I bind & print.
—George burying face not to show crying.
—Little White Bird book described to me by George.
—*L.W.B.* Telling George what love is . . . in answer to George's inquiries abt how to write a story.
—*L.W.B.* What George said while walking me round the Round Pond (abt what to have for his birthday—ship—greek armour—book &c)—I sneer.
—The queer pleasure it gives when George tells me to lace his shoes, &c.
—*L.W.B.* The boys disgrace one in shops by asking shopkeeper abt his most private affairs. Shopkeeper &c takes me for their father (I affect rage).

This was the key to their relationship: they were like father and son,

George, with Arthur and Jack in background (JMB)

George (JMB)

yet Barrie was spared the tiresome role of being the stern disciplinarian. He later elaborated on 'the particular pleasure this gives me' in *The Little White Bird*, disguising George as 'David':

'"Boy, you are uncommonly like your mother."

'To which David: "Is that why you are so kind to me?"

'I suppose I am kind to him, but if so it is not for love of his mother, but because he sometimes calls me father. On my honour . . . there is nothing more in it than that. I must not let him know this, for it would make him conscious, and so break the spell that binds him and me together. . . . He addresses me as father when he is in a hurry only, and never have I dared ask him to use the name. He says, "Come, father," with an accursed beautiful carelessness. So let it be, David, for a little while longer.

'I like to hear him say it in front of others, as in shops. When in shops he asks the salesman how much money he makes in a day, and which drawer he keeps it in, and why his hair is red, and does he like Achilles, of whom David has lately heard, and is so enamoured that he wants to die to meet him. At such times the shopkeepers accept me as his father, and I cannot explain the particular pleasure this gives me. I am always in two minds then, to linger that we may have more of it [or] to snatch him away before he volunteers the information, "He is not really my father."

'When David meets Achilles I know what will happen. The little boy will take the hero by the hand, call him father, and drag him away to some Round Pond.'

Just as *Tommy and Grizel* chronicled Barrie's failing marriage and his own inability to grow up, so *The Little White Bird* follows his relationship with George and his own profound yearnings for fatherhood—or, perhaps, motherhood. Like *Tommy*, the new novel would evolve slowly over the next four years before being published in 1902.

The book is narrated in the first person by Barrie, who thinly disguises himself as Captain W—, 'a gentle, whimsical, lonely old bachelor', who also happens to be a writer, given to long walks in Kensington Gardens with his St Bernard dog, Porthos. His unfulfilled ambition is to have had a son of his own, whom he would have called Timothy. He becomes involved with a needy young couple, acting as their anonymous benefactor when the opportunity arises. On the night their child is born, Captain W— meets the husband pacing the streets while his wife, Mary, is in labour. The husband assumes that the Captain is 'an outcast for a reason similar to his own, and I let his mistake pass, it seemed to matter so little and to draw us together so naturally'. Therefore when the father tells the

Captain that their baby is a son, he is obliged to pretend that he too now has a son — Timothy. Without ever revealing his true identity as their anonymous benefactor, the Captain continues to take a vicarious interest in the progress of their boy, David. One day he sees the mother about to sell her possessions to a pawnshop because she has no money with which to buy clothes for her child. The Captain contrives to meet the father, and blithely informs him that since his own son Timothy has recently died, he has no further use for Timothy's clothes. Barrie's style of narration up to this point has been one of dry, laconic humour, but in the following passage, in which he describes 'the last of Timothy', he quarries the depths of his own frustrated paternity to a degree that is almost embarrassing (to some even nauseating), and yet is such a cry from the heart that it all but transcends sentimentalism by its very sincerity:

George 'waiting for the dawn' (JMB)

George (JMB)

'Timothy's hold on life, as you may have apprehended, was ever of the slightest, and I suppose I always knew that he must soon revert to the obscure. He could never have penetrated into the open. It was no life for a boy.

'Yet now that his time had come, I was loth to see him go. I seem to remember carrying him that evening to the window with uncommon tenderness (following the setting sun that was to take him away), and telling him with not unnatural bitterness that he had got to leave me because another child was in need of all his pretty things; and as the sun, his true father, lapt him in his dancing arms, he sent his love to a lady of long ago whom he called by the sweetest of names, not knowing in his innocence that the little white birds are the birds that never have a mother. I wished (so had the phantasy of Timothy taken possession of me) that before he went he could have played once in the Kensington Gardens, and have ridden on the fallen trees, calling gloriously to me to look; that he could have sailed one paper galleon on the Round Pond; fain would I have had him chase one hoop a little way down the laughing avenues of childhood, where memory tells us we run but once, on a long summer day, emerging at the other end as men and women with all the fun to pay for; and I think (thus fancy wantons with me in these desolate chambers) he knew my longings, and said with a boy-like flush that the reason he never did these things was not that he was afraid, for he would have loved to do them all, but because he was not quite like other boys; and, so saying, he let go my finger and faded from before my eyes into another and golden ether; but I shall ever hold that had he been quite like other boys there would have been none braver than my Timothy.'

David's mother, Mary, is closely modelled on Sylvia. She guesses that Timothy was merely a figment of the Captain's imagination, and

George (JMB). In *The Little White Bird*, Barrie wrote 'I work very hard to retain that little boy's love; but I shall lose him soon; even now I am not what I was to him; in a year or two at longest, . . . [he] will grow out of me'.

that it is he who has been their mysterious benefactor. She sends him invitations, but he refuses to visit her unless David is first allowed to visit him alone in his chambers—without the disapproving presence of David's nurse, Irene (a somewhat caustic portrayal of Mary Hodgson). Mary agrees, and the Captain sets about winning the boy to himself: 'It was a scheme conceived in a flash, and ever since relentlessly pursued—to burrow under Mary's influence with the boy, expose her to him in all her vagaries, take him utterly from her and make him mine.' As David grows older, the Captain comes to look upon him as his own son. 'It would ill become me to attempt to describe this dear boy to you, for of course I know really nothing about children, so I shall say only this, that I thought him very like what Timothy would have been had he ever had a chance.' But despite his growing affection for David, the Captain feigns indifference towards the boy's mother. 'When Mary does anything that specially annoys me I send her an insulting letter. I once had a photograph taken of David being hanged on a tree. I sent her that. You can't think of all the subtle ways of grieving her I have.'

Unfortunately for Arthur, the real-life J. M. Barrie took precisely the opposite attitude towards George's mother. Far from declining invitations to visit her and the boys at 31 Kensington Park Gardens, he availed himself of every opportunity—regardless of whether an invitation had been extended or not. In the Davies family he had found what he had been searching for all his adult life—a beautiful woman who embodied motherhood, a brood of boys who epitomized boyhood—and he did not mean to let them go. What objection could Arthur offer to the intrusive little Scotsman? He knew well enough that he presented no threat to their marriage, that he was 'quite harmless'. Sylvia was devoted to Arthur, and in a curious way Barrie also found himself devoted to their mutual devotion. He could flatter Sylvia, even flirt with her, yet feel secure in the knowledge that she would never put him to the test.

While making notes for *The Little White Bird*, Barrie continued to toil away on *Tommy and Grizel*. He wrote to Quiller-Couch: 'Oh, that final "canter up the avenue". They [the publishers] should see the author belabouring the brute. I see the finish not so far off . . . but it cracked somewhere about the middle and needs a deal of sticking-plaster yet.'[1] Until now, Barrie had sketched the adult Grizel, Tommy's neglected wife, from his own wife. But the resulting portrait lacked charm. 'What *is* charm, exactly?' asks Alick in *What Every Woman Knows*. Barrie's reply was a succinct description of Sylvia Llewelyn Davies. 'Oh, it's—it's a sort of bloom on a woman. If you have it, you don't need to have anything else; and if you don't have it, it doesn't much matter what else you have.'

It is hard to decide which Mary Barrie found the more galling: to have Grizel based upon herself and her own private anguish, or to find her role as model usurped by Sylvia Llewelyn Davies. Whatever her feelings on the matter, she had little choice but to move aside; her husband had found his sticking-plaster:

—*T & G. Revise.* G's nose tiptilted (really more as if point cut off). She is square-shouldered—woman who will always look glorious as a mother, (so I think of her *now*, always so). A woman to confide in (no sex in this, we feel it in man or woman). All secrets of womanhood you feel behind these calm eyes & courage to face them. A woman to lean on in trouble.
—*Revise.* G's voice richness of contralto? like child's voice that has never known fear, boy's. Merry, infectious, cd soothe, be mothering.
—*Revise.* Grizel's crooked smile.
—*Grizel.* Trill in voice, gurgles like stream in gay hurry. Cooing voice.

Having decided to incorporate Sylvia into the character of Grizel, Barrie found it necessary to rewrite whole chapters at a time. One such chapter was almost entirely devoted to her description, under the title 'Grizel of the Crooked Smile':

Sylvia, from the portrait by Charles Furse

'When the winds of the day flushed her cheek she was beautiful, but it was a beauty that hid the mystery of her face; the sun made her merry, but she looked more noble when it had set, then her pallor shone with a soft radiant light, as though the mystery and sadness and serenity of the moon were in it. The full beauty of Grizel came out at night only, like the stars.

'I had made up my mind that when the time came to describe Grizel's mere outward appearance I should refuse her that word beautiful because of her tilted nose. . . . Her eyes at least were beautiful, they were unusually far apart, and let you look straight into them and never quivered, they were such clear, gray, searching eyes, they seemed always to be asking for the truth. And she had an adorable mouth . . . the essence of all that was characteristic and delicious about her seemed to have run to her mouth, so that to kiss Grizel on her crooked smile would have been to kiss the whole of her at once. . . . There were times when she looked like a boy. Her almost gallant bearing, the poise of her head, her noble frankness, they all had something in them of a princely boy who had never known fear.'

One of Bernard Partridge's illustrations from the American edition of *Tommy and Grizel*. Barrie confessed to not knowing what most of the characters looked like, but said he could be of some help when Partridge came to draw Grizel: 'Mrs Llewelyn Davies, whom she is meant to be a bit like, is willing to sit for you for this, and she has some idea of the dressing too'. The illustrations did not appear in the British edition, doubtless to spare Mary Barrie further loss of pride.

After an initial resentment towards Sylvia, Mary tried to win her friendship. Nor was she wholly unsuccessful. Sylvia could afford to be generous, and besides, the two women shared an interest in clothes and interior decoration. But Mary's character was altogether too pathetically flamboyant for Sylvia's taste: she would offer introductions to her famous husband (without her famous husband's permission), and talk loudly about his wealth (which displeased him even more); she would order writing-paper with her initials monogrammed thereon, and was in the habit of being singularly rude to shopkeepers and servants. Her frustration had turned her into a snob. 'I loathe snobbishness so much that I hate to write of it,'[2] commented Barrie to Quiller-Couch, though he himself was to have the accusation levelled against him in due course.

What Mary needed was some surrogate activity to which she could devote her energies. The Barries had never intended to live in London all the year round, and Mary therefore decided to look for a country house: a secluded retreat for her husband and herself, miles from the city—and the Davies family. Barrie made no objections; the search kept her occupied, and allowed him to get on with his own life.

George and Jack had now started day-school at Norland Place in Holland Park Road. Arthur would accompany them in the mornings on his way to the Temple, leaving Mary Hodgson to pick them up after lunch. Some days Barrie would meet them on their way home from school and take them off to Kensington Gardens. Although Sylvia had given her blessing to the affair, Mary Hodgson did not greatly approve of his intrusion. *She* was the boys' nurse, not Mr Barrie; how could she be expected to retain her authority over the boys when he so obviously gloried in their waywardness. Barrie was well aware of her hostility—indeed he exulted in it. He and George were companions, but Mary was a grown-up, an outsider. Naturally when George and Jack misbehaved, Barrie turned a blind eye; to have taken Mary's side would have been tantamount to a betrayal. Mary Hodgson's reactions to *The Little White Bird* are unrecorded, but she can have had little difficulty in recognizing the identity of David's nurse, Irene:

'I was now seeing David once at least every week, his mother, who remained culpably obtuse to my sinister design, having instructed Irene that I was to be allowed to share him with her, and we had become close friends, though the little nurse was ever a threatening shadow in the background. Irene, in short, did not improve with acquaintance. I found her to be high and mighty, chiefly, I think, because she now wore a nurse's cap with streamers, of which the little creature was ludicrously proud. She assumed the airs of an official person, and always talked as if generations of babies had passed through her hands. She was also extremely jealous, and had a way of signifying disapproval of my methods that led to many coldnesses

The Balloon Woman, a familiar sight outside the gates of Kensington Gardens. From *Peter Pan in Kensington Gardens* (1906) illustrated by Arthur Rackham

and even bickerings between us, which I now see to have been undignified. I brought the following accusations against her:–

'That she prated too much about right and wrong.

'That she was a martinet. . . .

'On the other hand, she accused me of spoiling him. . . .

'That I am not sufficiently severe with him, leaving the chiding of him for offences against myself to her in the hope that he will love her less and me more thereby. . . .

'Of not thinking of his future.

'Of never asking him where he expected to go if he did such things.

'Of telling him tales that had no moral application. . . .

'Of fibbing and corrupting youthful minds.'

Mary Hodgson

One of the 'tales that had no moral application' concerned George's baby brother Peter. According to Barrie, all children were birds once, and 'the reason there are bars on nursery windows and a tall fender by the fire is because [children] sometimes forget that they have no longer wings, and try to fly away through the window or up the chimney'. Peter, however, was still able to fly because his mother had forgotten to weigh him at birth. He therefore escaped through the unbarred window and flew back to Kensington Gardens:

'If you think he was the only baby who ever wanted to escape, it shows how completely you have forgotten your own young days. When David heard this story first he was quite certain that he had never tried to escape, but I told him to think back hard, pressing his hands to his temples, and when he had done this hard, and even harder, he distinctly remembered a youthful desire to return to the tree-tops, and with that memory came others, as that he had lain in bed planning to escape as soon as his mother was asleep, and how she had once caught him half way up the chimney. . . .

'Children in the bird stage are difficult to catch. David knows that many people have none, and his delight on a summer afternoon is to go with me to some spot in the Gardens where these unfortunates may be seen trying to catch one with small pieces of cake.'

Peter Pan as a baby (Rackham)

As the saga developed, an inherent defect in the story became evident. If Peter could fly, how was it that he remained singularly immobile in his perambulator? In order to solve the dilemma, a second Peter began to emerge, who soon became as real as his earthbound namesake. This second Peter was called Peter Pan, named after the Greek god who symbolized nature, paganism, and the amoral world. Whether this was a deliberate joke to provoke Mary Hodgson's preference for stories with a 'moral application', or merely an allusion to Peter's gay and heartless character, or a

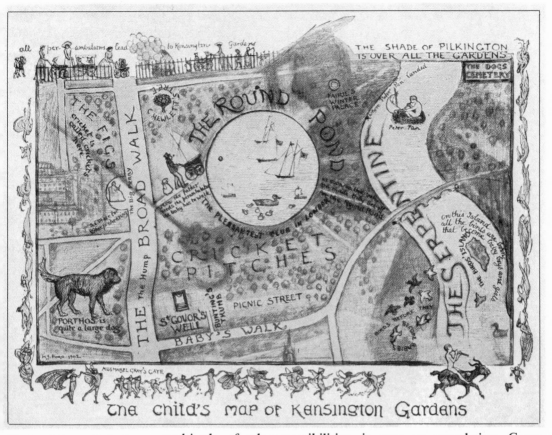

The child's Map of Kensington Gardens

The frontispiece to *The Little White Bird*. 'C. Hewlett's Tree' at top left is where Cecco lost a penny, went back to look for it after Lock-out Time and found threepence. 'Where Peter Pan landed' is now the site of the Peter Pan statue. 'The shade of Pilkington' celebrates Mr Wilkinson, headmaster of Wilkinson's private school in Orme Square, and precursor of Captain Hook

multitude of other possibilities, is open to speculation. Cecco Hewlett sometimes accompanied them in the Gardens, and his father, Maurice Hewlett, had just published a play entitled *Pan and the Young Shepherd*, which opened with the line, 'Boy, boy, wilt thou be a boy for ever?' This may have been a pure coincidence, but Barrie almost certainly knew of its existence, as he and Hewlett were close friends. Whatever the origins, Peter Pan soon became the topic of endless discussion between Barrie and George, recorded by Barrie in *The Little White Bird*:

'I ought to mention here that the following is our way with a story: First I tell it to him, and then he tells it to me, the understanding being that it is quite a different story; and then I retell it with his additions, and so we go on until no one could say whether it is more his story or mine. In this story of Peter Pan, for instance, the bald narrative and most of the moral reflections are mine, though not all, for this boy can be a stern moralist; but the interesting bits about the ways and customs of babies in the bird-stage are mostly re-miniscences of [his], recalled by pressing his hands to his temples and thinking hard.'

Having escaped from the nursery, Peter Pan, still believing himself to be a bird, returns to the island in the Serpentine from where he originated, presenting himself before the birds' potentate, Old Solomon Caw, for reinstatement. But Old Solomon points out the regrettable fact that Peter is no longer a bird but a human baby:

'"I suppose," said Peter huskily, "I suppose I can still fly?" . . .

'"Poor little half-and-half!" said Solomon, "you will never be able to fly again, not even on windy days. You must live here on the island always."

'"And never even go to the Kensington Gardens?" Peter asked tragically.

'"How could you get across?" said Solomon. He promised very kindly, however, to teach Peter as many of the bird ways as could be learned by one of such an awkward shape.

'"Then I shan't be exactly a human?" Peter asked.

'"No."

'"Nor exactly a bird?"

'"No."

'"What shall I be?"

'"You will be a Betwixt-and-Between," Solomon said, and certainly he was a wise old fellow, for that is exactly how it turned out.'

Peter Pan puts his case to Old Solomon Caw (Rackham)

Thus Peter Pan becomes an outlaw, living on the island in the Serpentine. Sometimes he rows across to Kensington Gardens in a bird's nest to watch real boys at play, or to join in adventures with the fairies after Lock-out Time. It is the fairies who teach him to fly without wings, and now and again he flies home to watch his mother weeping for her lost child, and is moved by her tears; but always the freedom of the Gardens calls him back. However, eventually he resolves to return home 'for ever and always', despite the fairies' pleas to stay:

Peter Pan rowing across the Serpentine (Rackham)

'He went in a hurry in the end, because he had dreamt that his mother was crying, and he knew what was the great thing she cried for, and that a hug from her splendid Peter would quickly make her to smile. Oh! he felt sure of it, and so he flew straight to the window, which was always to be open for him.

'But the window was closed, and there were iron bars on it, and peering inside he saw his mother sleeping peacefully with her arm round another little boy.

'Peter called, "Mother! mother!" but she heard him not; in vain he beat his little limbs against the iron bars. He had to fly back, sobbing, to the Gardens, and he never saw his [mother] again. What a glorious boy he had meant to be to her! Ah, Peter! we who have made the great mistake, how differently we should all act at the second

chance. But Solomon was right—there is no second chance, not for most of us. When we reach the window it is Lock-out Time. The iron bars are up for life.'

While the oral story of Peter Pan continued to evolve at a leisurely pace, Barrie utilized the bones of the idea in his revisions of *Tommy and Grizel*. In the following scene, Tommy Sandys is about to send his new manuscript to his publishers. He shows it to his wife, Grizel—who in this instance reflects Mary Barrie rather than Sylvia:

'She kissed the manuscript. "Wish it luck," he had begged of her; "you were always so fond of babies, and this is my baby." So Grizel kissed Tommy's baby, and then she turned away her face. . . . If he had not told her about his book it was because she did not and never could understand what compels a man to write one book, instead of another. "I had no say in the matter; the thing demanded of me that I should do it and I had to do it. Some must write from their own experience, they can make nothing of anything else; . . . I don't attempt to explain how I write, I hate to discuss it; all I know is that those who know how it should be done can never do it. . . . You have taken everything else, Grizel, surely you might leave me my books. . . . I must write. It is the only thing I can do. . . . Writing is the joy of my life . . . [and yet] if I could make a living at anything else I would give up writing altogether." . . .

Bedford's illustration of Peter Pan running through the woods of the Never Land

'"It was not that I did not love your books," she said, "but that I loved you more, and I thought they did you harm." . . .

'The new book, of course, was "The Wandering Child." I wonder whether any of you read it now. Your fathers and mothers thought a great deal of that slim volume, but it would make little stir in an age in which all the authors are trying who can say Damn loudest. It is but a reverie about a little boy who was lost. His parents find him in a wood singing joyfully to himself because he thinks he can now be a boy for ever; and he fears that if they catch him they will compel him to grow into a man, so he runs farther from them into the wood and is running still, singing to himself because he is always to be a boy. That is really all, but T. Sandys knew how to tell it. The moment he conceived the idea . . . he knew that it was the idea for him. He forgot at once that he did not really care for children. He said reverently to himself, "I can pull it off," and, as was always the way with him, the better he pulled it off the more he seemed to love them.

'"It is myself who is writing at last, Grizel," he said as he read it to her.

'She thought (and you can guess whether she was right) that it was the book he loved rather than the child. She thought (and you can guess again) that in a subtle way this book was his autobiography.'

On April 26th, 1899, Barrie strangled Tommy to death on an iron spike and wrote 'The End' across the 464th page of manuscript. It had been almost ten years since he had started making his first notes, and three years since the publication of its forerunner, *Sentimental Tommy*. The reading public had eagerly awaited its sequel, but they found *Tommy and Grizel* altogether too morbid and bitter, and despite a few enthusiastic notices the book had a poor reception. Barrie's account of The Boy Who *Couldn't* Grow Up had been a comparative failure.

*   *   *

In August 1899, the Davieses went down to Rustington for their annual holiday. Arthur's work at the Temple allowed him little time to see his sons, and he looked forward to spending the summer weeks alone with his family. There were no Parrys as neighbours this year, Dolly having married Arthur Ponsonby, a British attaché at Copenhagen, in 1898. However, there was no shortage of company; after a brief holiday in Germany, the Barries decided that they too would take the sea air throughout August, renting a house less than half a mile from the Davieses' mill cottage. George and Jack were delighted: it meant that they could spend whole days with Mr Barrie, not just the odd afternoon snatched now and then after school. The Peter Pan stories continued to develop; so too did an endless variety of games: Scottish games learnt by Barrie as a child — spyo, smuggle bools, kick-bonnety, peeries; games of his own invention, such as egg-cap and capey-dykey; and of course cricket, played between wickets improvised wherever he happened to be: trees in the park, chairs on the lawn, sand castles on the beach. Barrie had a natural flair for virtually any game that required a keen eye, whether it was billiards, croquet, or clock-golf, and his enthusiasm was soon shared by the boys.

George (JMB)

And Arthur played the perfect gentleman, remaining quietly in the background. In 1948, Peter Llewelyn Davies wrote to Mary Hodgson: 'It is clear enough that father didn't like him, at any rate in the early stages. Did J.M.B.'s entry into the scheme of things occasionally cause ill-feeling or quarrellings between mother and father?' Mary Hodgson replied, 'What was of value to the One had little or no value to the Other. Your father's attitude at all times was as "One Gentleman (in the *true* sense) to Another". Any difference of opinion was *never* made "Public Property" in the house. . . . The Barries were overwhelming (and found your mother's help, grace & beauty a great asset in meeting the right people, etc.) — aided by Mrs du Maurier — always ambitious for her favourite daughter. . . . The du Mauriers in a way stood in awe of your Father. There were times

Sylvia and Peter on the beach at Rustington in 1899 (JMB)

when he defied the lot — & stood alone — and his Wife stood by Him!' Despite the unspoken resentments, the holiday drifted along in a more or less care-free fashion. Sylvia wrote to Dolly at the British Legation in Copenhagen on August 8th:

Darling Dolly,

Your dear letters were a great joy, please write many more of them & sometimes in the midst of Kings & Queens, think a little of the poor barrister's wife at Sea Mill with all the winds of heaven blowing her about & a great many noisy but beloved sons jumping on her. . . .

Your friend George hurt his poor little finger badly yesterday — he got it pinched in a deck chair so hard that his little nail was wrenched off — He was very brave, but it was dreadful & I ached for him. I will send you a photograph of him quite soon — they are so good I think, but I haven't ordered any yet. . . .

Now dear Dolly I haven't any news—you know better than I how charming this little place is & how windy it is & how Sylvia goes in and out of the Mill cottage & looks after the 3 little boys with red caps, but when all is said & done Rustington can never be the same without *you*. . . .

I am,

your loving Sylvia

Jack, Sylvia and Peter on Rustington beach (JMB)

In sending this letter to Peter Davies in 1946, Dolly Ponsonby wrote:

'It conveys her so completely—at least to me. It recalls so visibly the Mill House, the sea, the wind and the little boys in red tam o'shanters. You were too young to remember it. It is too subtle to be conveyed in writing. But the calm and beauty of her, and her delicious whimsical sense of humour, sewing perhaps in a tiny cottage sitting-room with those rampageous boys tumbling about her—I shall never forget it.'

On November 25th, 1899, Sylvia celebrated her thirty-third birthday. Barrie gave her an amethyst necklace, set in gold, and inscribed with her middle name, 'To Jocelyn'. As she was normally known as Sylvia, Barrie adopted 'Jocelyn' as his own private pet-name for her. The necklace was accompanied by a card:

> To a Crooked Lady on her 33rd Birthday.
>
> At thirty-three she's twice as sweet
> As sweetest seventeen could be,
> At sixty-six I'm sure she'll beat
> The record made at thirty-three.
>
> So sure am I her crooked ways
> Will baffle Time and all his tricks,
> Impatiently I count the days
> Till Jocelyn shall be sixty-six.

Sylvia and Peter (JMB)

The Boer War had broken out in October, and Sylvia's elder brother Guy, a professional soldier, left for South Africa to command a Mounted Infantry company. But to his three young nephews, six thousand miles away, the war meant little more than shouting 'Kruger!' at old men with chin beards in Kensington Gardens. During one of their walks with Barrie, George noticed a pair of grey stones engraved 'W ST. M' and '13a P.P. 1841'. These were boundary stones, still in existence today, marking the various parish boundaries within Kensington Gardens. The initials on this particular pair marked the border between the Parish of Westminster St Mary's and the Parish of Paddington. George asked Barrie what they were for,

The Peter Pan 'gravestones' in Kensington Gardens (Rackham)

Sylvia (JMB)

and his explanation was somewhat more exotic. He told him that when Peter Pan found dead children in the Gardens after Lock-out Time, he would dig a grave and bury them, preferably in pairs, erecting a tombstone to mark the spot. The initials 'W ST. M' and 'P.P.' indicated the mortal remains of Walter Stephen Matthews and Phœbe Phelps, two babies who had fallen from their perambulators while their nurse was looking the other way. Evidently Peter Pan had quite an appetite for grave-digging, and was sometimes rather too quick with his spade—hence the profusion of gravestones in Kensington Gardens. Moreover, when children died—a common occurrence in Victorian days—Peter would 'sing gaily to them when the bell tolls',[3] dancing on their graves and playing riotously on his pipes to make them laugh; at other times he 'went part of the way with them, so that they should not be frightened'.[4] Their initial destiny was some unspecified after-life, later developed into the Never Never Land—a child's paradise, haven of the Lost Boys, abounding in pleasures designed to gratify a boy's appetite for blood. Such visions of delight led George to make the not unnatural declaration, 'To die will be an awfully big adventure!'

Sylvia was now expecting her fourth child, but to Barrie the event held all the novelty of a first-born. George, Jack and Peter had each to some extent been moulded before his arrival in their lives, but he would be able to share in the birth of this new child as if it were his own. It was hoped by Arthur that this newcomer would be a girl, and Barrie started to make notes for a story about an unborn child—Barbara:

—*Barbara*. Children chorus she's expected (excited) but not come yet tho' mother doing all kinds of things preparing for her—she's like ghost, there & not there—when she comes father in agony, says it may mean mother dying &c (mother recovers?). Story told for children as if of a real strange child they can't see yet (a child's ghost story in a sense. They discuss it—how children come, &c). The way she prepares children for new-comer (all their talk to me) pretend wants boy again—I send jeering messages—she wants girl (Barbara)—my White Bird a book, hers a baby. (His work is like babies to him—evidently he can't have babes).

—A mother dying when her child born—they pass each other in their dif[ferent] voyages (the one landing, the other setting sail)—seem to hail each other, all well—the only times we are confident, beginning & end.

—*Ghost Story* (Idea that ghosts shd be much more frightened at us than we at them). A young married woman dies—Haunts house to look after children—they grow up, age, &c—She always young—doesn't know them.

Barrie had already started working on the manuscript of *The Little White Bird*, and he did not have to wait long before finding a ready slot for these notes. When the narrator, Captain W—, meets the expectant father in the street, he comments to himself:

'Poor boy, his wife has quite forgotten him and his trumpery love. If she lives [through childbirth] she will come back to him, but if she dies, she will die triumphant and serene. Life and death, the child and the mother, are ever meeting as the one draws into harbour and the other sets sail. They exchange a bright "All's well," and pass on.

'But afterwards?

'The only ghosts, I believe, who creep into this world, are dead young mothers, returned to see how their children fare. There is no other inducement great enough to bring the departed back. They glide into the acquainted room when day and night, their jailers, are in the grip, and whisper, "How is it with you, my child?"

'What is saddest about ghosts is that they may not know their child. They expect him to be just as he was when they left him, and they are easily bewildered, and search for him from room to room, and hate the unknown boy he has become. Poor, passionate souls, they may even do him an injury. These are the ghosts that go wailing about old houses, and foolish wild stories are invented to explain what is all so pathetic and simple. . . . All our notions about ghosts are wrong. It is nothing so petty as lost wills or deeds of violence that brings them back, and we are not nearly so afraid of them as they are of us.'

Bird Island, on the Hyde Park side of the Serpentine, where 'all the birds are born that become baby boys and girls' (Rackham)

On June 16th, 1900, Sylvia gave birth to her fourth boy. Barrie wrote to her on the 21st:

My dear Jocelyn,

It is very sweet and kind of you to write me from the throne, which is what I take your present residence to be. He is a gorgeous boy, is Delight, which was your own original name for him in the far back days of last week or thereabouts when you used to hug Peter with such sudden vehemence that I am sure he wondered whether you were up to anything.

I don't see how we could have expected him to be a girl, you are so good at boys, and this you know is the age of specialists. And you were very very nearly being a boy yourself.

May he always be a dear delight to you and may all your dreams about all of them come true.

Ever yours,
J.M.B.

All the boys so far had been given names of special family significance, but for their fourth son Arthur and Sylvia had no particular namesake in mind. Like Peter, the new baby was not christened, and as with all the boys he was given only one name: Michael.

Michael and Sylvia (JMB)

Mary Barrie's search for a country retreat had at last yielded results. In April 1900, she found a house near Farnham in Surrey known as Black Lake Cottage. The house was almost entirely surrounded by a pine forest, with only a dusty, winding road to connect it with the outside world. On the far side of the road lay the Black Lake, hidden among the pines, while beyond it rose the crumbling ruins of Waverley Abbey.

Mary bought the cottage and set to work with a team of builders and gardeners, transforming it into a habitable country home, and by July the Allahakbarrie Cricket Team were able to forgather there for their annual match. Barrie's initial indifference to his wife's investment soon began to waver: she had thoughtfully converted one of the largest upstairs rooms into a private study for him, while the south lawn provided ample space for games of cricket and golf-croquet. Charles Frohman was an early visitor to Black Lake, ostensibly to discuss production details for *The Wedding Guest*, which was to be entrusted to his new London producer, Dion Boucicault. However, he spent most of his time playing golf-croquet or driving with Barrie to near-by Burpham, where the Davies family were on holiday. The play was due to open at the Garrick Theatre on September 27th, with H. B. Irving and Irene Vanbrugh's sister Violet in the leading roles. Barrie wrote to Sylvia on the 26th:

> My dear Jocelyn,
>   I am so glad you are coming tomorrow. The Box is Box 1 & is on the stalls floor on the audience's left hand. Stall is being sent to Arthur. I fully expect the men of the world to stamp on the thing, but never mind.
>
>   Yours,
>   J.M.B.

Black Lake Cottage

Barrie's expectations proved correct. Both audience and critics had assumed that this was to be another light-weight comedy in the style of *The Little Minister*, and were astonished and even shocked to find themselves confronted by a 'problem play' in the Ibsen mould, about an artist who is brought face to face with his ex-mistress and illegitimate child on his wedding day. *The Daily Telegraph* accused its author of 'unpleasantness, painfulness and doubtful morality', and suggested that the play advocated 'promiscuous seduction'. Only William Archer, a passionate Ibsenite, acclaimed the work, hailing Barrie as 'our new dramatist'.

Still smarting from the critics' attack on 'my bleeding and broken play',[1] Barrie returned to the safety of *The Little White Bird*. George was now seven, and had become his firm favourite among the boys, but the newly-arrived Michael had an instinctive appeal to him from

George aged 7 (JMB)

Peter, George and Jack in a
wheelbarrow (JMB)

George (JMB)

the moment of his birth: it was as if his imaginary Timothy had come
to life. And yet for all his romantic, sentimental side, Barrie was a
realist at heart, and the joy he experienced in George and Michael
was frequently soured by his frustration and yearnings for real
paternity—as the following episode in *The Little White Bird* makes
painfully clear, despite its humour:

'David and I had a tremendous adventure. It was this—he passed the
night with me. We had often talked of it as a possible thing, and at last
[his mother] consented to our having it.

'The adventure began with David's coming to me at the unwonted
hour of six p.m., carrying what looked like a packet of sandwiches, but
proved to be his requisites for the night done up in a neat paper
parcel. . . .

'We were to do all the important things precisely as they are done
every evening at his own home, and so I am in a puzzle to know how it
was such an adventure to David. But I have now said enough to show
you what an adventure it was to me. . . .

'At twenty-five past six I turned on the hot water in the bath, and
covertly swallowed a small glass of brandy. I then said, "Half-past
six; time for little boys to be in bed." I said it in the matter-of-fact

Sylvia and George in 1900 (JMB)

voice of one made free of the company of parents, as if I had said it often before, and would have to say it often again, and as if there was nothing particularly delicious to me in hearing myself say it. I tried to say it in that way.

'And David was deceived. To my exceeding joy he stamped his little foot, and was so naughty that, in gratitude, I gave him five minutes with a match-box. Matches, which he drops on the floor when lighted, are the greatest treat you can give David; indeed, I think his private heaven is a place with a roaring bonfire.

'Then I placed my hand carelessly on his shoulder, like one a trifle bored by the dull routine of putting my little boys to bed, and conducted him to the night nursery, which had lately been my private chamber. There was an extra bed in it tonight, very near my own, but differently shaped, and scarcely less conspicuous was the new mantleshelf ornament: a tumbler of milk, with a biscuit on top of it, and a chocolate riding on the biscuit. To enter the room without seeing the tumbler at once was impossible. I had tried it several times, and David saw and promptly did his frog business, the while, with an indescribable emotion, I produced a night-light from my pocket and planted it in a saucer on the washstand.

'David watched my preparations with distasteful levity, but anon made a noble amend by abruptly offering me his foot as if he had no longer use for it, and I knew by intuition that he expected me to take off his boots. I took them off with all the coolness of an old hand, and then I placed him on my knee and removed his blouse. This was a delightful experience, but I think I remained wonderfully calm until I came somewhat too suddenly to his little braces, which agitated me profoundly.

'I cannot proceed in public with the disrobing of David.

'Soon the night nursery was in darkness but for the glimmer from the night-light, and very still save when the door creaked as a man peered in at the little figure on the bed. However softly I opened the door, an inch at a time, his bright eyes turned to me at once.

'"Are you never to fall asleep, David?" I always said.

'"When are you coming to bed?" he always replied, very brave but in a whisper, as if he feared the bears and wolves might have him. When little boys are in bed there is nothing between them and bears and wolves but the night-light.

'I returned to my chair to think, and at last he fell asleep with his face to the wall, but even then I stood many times at the door, listening.

'Long after I had gone to bed a sudden silence filled the chamber, and I knew that David had awaked. I lay motionless, and, after what seemed a long time of waiting, a little far-away voice said in a cautious whisper, "Irene!"

'"You are sleeping with me to-night, you know, David," I said.

George 'on the idle hill of summer' (JMB)

75

'"I didn't know," he replied, a little troubled, but trying not to be a nuisance.

'I think he had nigh fallen asleep again when he stirred and said, "Is it going on now?"

'"What?"

'"The adventure."

'"Yes, David."

'Perhaps this disturbed him, for by and by I had to inquire, "You are not frightened, are you?"

'"Am I not?" he answered politely, and I knew his hand was groping in the darkness, so I put out mine and he held on tightly to one finger.

'"I am not frightened now," he whispered.

'"And there is nothing else you want?"

'"Is there not?" he again asked politely. "Are you sure there's not?" he added.

'"What can it be, David?"

'"I don't take up very much room," the far-away voice said.

'"Why, David," said I, sitting up; "do you want to come into my bed?"

'"Mother said I wasn't to want it unless you wanted it first," he squeaked.

'"It is what I have been wanting all the time," said I, and then without more ado the little white figure rose and flung itself at me. For the rest of the night he lay on me and across me, and sometimes his feet were at the bottom of the bed and sometimes on the pillow, but he always retained possession of my finger, and occasionally he woke me to say that he was sleeping with me. I had not a good night. I lay thinking.

'Of this little boy, who, in the midst of his play while I undressed him, had suddenly buried his head on my knees. . . .

'Of David's dripping little form in the bath, and how when I essayed to catch him he had slipped from my arms like a trout.

'Of how I had stood by the open door listening to his sweet breathing, had stood so long that I forgot his name and called him Timothy.'

*　　*　　*

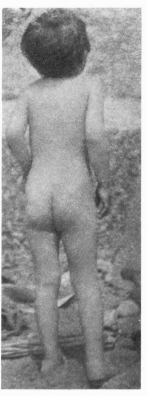

Peter (JMB)

133 Gloucester Road, S.W.
27 December 1900

My dear Couch,

To wish a merry Christmas time—to wish the same to thee and thine. From this you will see that I am writing a pantomime. We have been mad enough to be inveigled thereinto and the result will be on view at this address on January 7. Drawing-room turned into a Hall by magic. We much and deeply deplore that the Pippa cannot be present though he is now rather big. Our aim is to convulse the four year olds. . . .

Mary is at present trying on her fairy costume. She is a 'very-good-little-girl.' I tried on my trousers last night and have wanted to go into hiding ever since. Oh, that I had chosen the part of the Bear. . . . *I take off twelve waistcoats.*

Exit to rehearsal.

J.M.B.

The previous Christmas, Barrie had taken George and Jack to a pantomime of *The Babes in the Wood* at the Coronet Theatre in Notting Hill Gate. This year he decided to go one better and write them a pantomime himself. The result was 'The Greedy Dwarf', subtitled 'A moral tale' for Mary Hodgson's benefit, which received its first and last performance at 133 Gloucester Road on January 7th, 1901. The audience consisted of the Davies boys, their father, and numerous other children. As they entered the drawing-room, each was handed a programme, printed for the occasion and bearing a photograph of Peter as the author. The distinguished cast was headed by Sylvia as Prince Robin, A. E. W. Mason as Sleepyhead, Barrie himself as Cowardy Custard, Sylvia's brother Gerald as the Dwarf (his first appearance in a Barrie play), Meredith's son Will as the Policeman, Barrie's agent Arthur Addison Bright as the Bear, Mary Barrie as Brownie, and Porthos as the dog Chang. One of the children in the audience was Cyril Maude's daughter, Pamela:

Michael

'We were dressed in our party frocks and wrapped in white Shetland shawls and we drove to the house in the Gloucester Road, in a four-wheeler. . . . We went into a room near the front door which was crammed with children. It was quite dark and there was whispering around us. We were late: a play was about to begin. In the centre of the stage was an erection on which a horrible dwarf suddenly appeared, with a strong light on him. It was frightening but none of us cried—we were too excited. We saw the dim figures of the other children in the darkness, all of us staring at the dwarf who was really

Mr Gerald du Maurier. Mr Barrie was a schoolboy with a moustache and Mrs Barrie looked like a little girl, and happy. . . .

'It was not the same as watching the Drury Lane pantomime, but there was even better magic.'[2]

Another child in the audience was Barrie's future biographer, Denis Mackail, then aged nine:

'The children in front, only few of whom had ever seen a play at all, would never forget that afternoon. None of them, perhaps, would remember the plot, simple as it was and almost implicit in the programme; but to see grown-up people dressed up, and fighting each other, or being brave, or romantic, or funny; to know at least some of their faces, and yet to find them transformed like this—here was richness, and amazement, and silent joy. . . .

'Mrs Llewelyn Davies, modestly draped, and hardly attempting to act, smiled exquisitely at the onlookers with an air of bewildered apology. Mason put all his professional experience into the part of a comic sluggard. Barrie, the Bad Boy of the school, wearing a clubbed, corn-coloured wig—but retaining his moustache, so that some of the children found him almost as terrifying as the Dwarf—was of course unspeakably cowardly. His great scene was when he was challenged to fight, and delayed the proceedings by removing twelve waistcoats, one after another. .'. . Addison Bright was completely encased in a mask and dark-brown plush. . . . And Mrs. Barrie, as the Good Little Girl, looked remarkably pretty . . . and was a fairy-tale heroine from beginning to end.'[3]

The afternoon's entertainment put Barrie to some considerable expense, but this was more than compensated by the pleasure he derived in terrifying his young audience; moreover, he had gained valuable experience in determining their reactions and criticisms. After the play was over, the children were treated to a banquet of cakes and ice-cream, while Barrie jotted down his observations in his notebook:

—Babies Pantomime

1. Really Peter was the hero (not his mother). He youngest by day but terrifies brothers by night with tales—we adapt his tales.
2. 'That's my mother—she's 34.' [Jack's exclamation]
4. Sea of faces—mouths open.
8. Rage of Peter ·.· portrait [on programme] shows him in petticoats.
11. Dog exhausted & lying on sofa—trembling when curtain abt to go up.

◀ The
Greedy
Dwarf:
A moral tale

Portrait of the Author

133, Gloucester Road:
January 7, 1901:
at 3 p.m.

Peter in petticoats, used for the cover of 'The Greedy Dwarf'

The Allahakbarrie Cricket Club

Has the Honour to present

for the first and only time on any stage

an Entirely Amazing Moral Tale

entitled

The Greedy Dwarf

BY PETER PERKIN

Prince Robin Miss Sylvia du Maurier

Sleepyhead . . . Mr. Mason
Cowardy Custard . Mr. Barrie
Allahakbarrie . . Mr. Gerald du Maurier
Bruin, a Bear . . Mr. Bright
Policeman . . . Mr. Meredith
Chang, a Dog . . Mr. Porthos
Dame Trot . . Miss Priscilla Prunes

AND

Brownie . . Miss Mary Contrairy

SCENE   I. A Glade in the Forest
SCENE II. The Same Glade in Another Forest
SCENE III. The little Schoolhouse in the Wood
SCENE IV. The Horrible Home of the Greedy Dwarf

Chief of the Orchestra . . Mrs. Meredith

Enormous Engagement of

Miss Sylvia du Maurier

Who has been Brought Back from the
year 1892 in a Hansom to play

The Principled Boy

Have you never seen Mr. Bright as a Bear?
No? Then you have never seen him at Home

The School Scene
will contain

A Scathing Exposure

of

Our Educational System

Miss Mary Contrairy

will spell *Allahakbarrie* in
the last Act

The whole
to conclude
in

A Blaze of Glory

12. Children gazed intently—never smiled.

13. Their polite congratulations.

Ten days after the 'Greedy Dwarf' pantomime, Queen Victoria died – and George went back to Norland Place School for his last term. In May he would be starting at Wilkinson's preparatory school in Orme Square – presided over by the celebrated Mr Wilkinson. The school faced the northern stretch of Kensington Gardens, and Wilkinson was already a familiar sight to Barrie and George, marshalling his bevy of schoolboys into crocodile formation in the Broad Walk. He was an austere, imposing figure, with a long, pointed nose and a golden moustache; he was fond of referring to his pupils as blithering little fools, while they in turn dubbed him 'Milky'. A number of George's older friends were already going to Wilkinson's, and he eagerly awaited the summer when he would be joining them. It was therefore inevitable that sooner or later the glamorous headmaster would find his way into the expanding narrative of *The Little White Bird*:

'On attaining the age of eight, or thereabout, children fly away from the Gardens, and never come back. . . . Where the girls go to I know not, . . . but the boys have gone to Pilkington's. He is a man with a cane. You may not go to Pilkington's in knickerbockers made by your mother. . . . They must be real knickerbockers. It is his stern rule. Hence the fearful fascination of Pilkington's. . . .

'Abhorred shade! I know not what manner of man thou art in the flesh, sir, but figure thee bearded and blackavised, and of a lean, tortuous habit of body, that moves ever with a swish. . . . 'Tis fear of thee and thy gown and thy cane, which are part of thee, that makes the fairies to hide by day. . . . How much wiser they than the small boys who swim glamoured to thy crafty hook. Thou devastator of the Gardens, I know thee, Pilkington.

'I first heard of Pilkington from David, who had it from Oliver Bailey.

'This Oliver Bailey was one of the most dashing figures in the Gardens. . . . His not ignoble ambition seems always to have been to be wrecked upon an island . . . and it was perhaps inevitable that a boy with such an outlook should fascinate David. . . . The friendship of the two dated from this time; . . . he . . . walked hand in hand with him, and . . . it was already too late to break the spell of Oliver, David was top-heavy with pride in him; and, faith, I began to find myself very much in the cold, for Oliver was frankly bored by me, and even David seemed to think it would be convenient if I went and sat with Irene. Am I affecting to laugh? I was really distressed and lonely, and rather bitter; and how humble I became. . . . For years I had been fighting [his mother] for David, and had not wholly failed; . . . was I now to be knocked out so easily by a seven-year-old? I reconsidered my weapons, and I fought Oliver and beat him. . . .

'With wrecked islands I did it. I began in the most unpretentious way by telling them a story which might last an hour, and favoured by many an unexpected wind it lasted eighteen months. It started as the wreck of the simple Swiss family, . . . but soon a glorious inspiration of the night turned it into the wreck of David . . . and Oliver Bailey. At first it was what they were to do when they were wrecked, but imperceptibly it became what they had done. . . . As we walked in the Gardens I told them of the hut they had built; and they were inflated, but not surprised. . . .

'David was now firmly convinced that he had once been wrecked on an island, . . . [and] as I unfolded the story Oliver listened with an open knife in his hand, and David . . . wore a pirate-string round his waist. . . .

'Thus many months passed with no word of Pilkington, [but then] suddenly I heard the whir of his hated reel as he struck a fish. I remember that grim day with painful vividness; it was a wet day,

Maimie (the forerunner of Wendy) and her brother in *The Little White Bird*, drawn by Arthur Rackham. The boy's clothes were copied from George

George 'dressed for the kill' (JMB)

George aiming at Barrie's camera. An arrow later split Jack's lip (JMB)

Barrie and George

indeed I think it has rained for me more or less ever since. As soon as they joined me I saw from the manner of the two boys that they had something to communicate. Oliver nudged David and retired a few paces, whereupon David said to me solemnly:

' "Oliver is going to Pilkington's. . . . He has two jackets and two shirts and two knickerbockers, *all real ones*."

' "Well done, Oliver!" said I, but it was the wrong thing, . . . and . . . they disappeared behind the tree. Evidently they decided that the time for plain speaking was come, for now David announced bluntly —

' "He wants you not to call him Oliver any longer."

' "What shall I call him?"

' "Bailey."

' "But why?"

' "He's going to Pilkington's. And he can't play with us any more after next Saturday."

' "Why not?"

' "He's going to Pilkington's."

'So now I knew the law about the thing, and we moved on together, Oliver stretching himself consciously, and methought that even David walked with a sedater air.

' "David," said I, with a sinking, "are you going to Pilkington's?"

' "When I am eight," he replied.

' "And shan't I call you David then, and won't you play with me in the Gardens any more?"

'He looked at Bailey, and Bailey signalled him to be firm.

' "Oh no," said David cheerily.

'Thus sharply did I learn how much longer I was to have him. Strange that a little boy can give so much pain. I dropped his hand and walked on in silence, and presently I did my most churlish to hurt him by ending the story abruptly in a very cruel way. "Ten years have elapsed," said I, "since I last spoke, and our two heroes, now gay young men, are revisiting the wrecked island of their childhood. 'Did we wreck ourselves,' said one, 'or was there someone to help us?' And the other, who was the younger, replied, 'I think there was someone to help us, a man with a dog. I think he used to tell me stories in the Kensington Gardens, but I forget all about him; I don't remember even his name.' "

'This tame ending bored Bailey, and he drifted away from us, but David still walked by my side, and he was grown so quiet that I knew a storm was brewing. Suddenly he flashed lightning on me. "It's not true," he cried, "it's a lie!" He gripped my hand. "I shan't never forget you, father."

'Strange that a little boy can give so much pleasure.

'Yet I could go on. "You will forget, David, but there was once a boy who would have remembered."

' "Timothy?" said he at once. He thinks Timothy was a real boy, and he is very jealous of him. He turned his back to me, and stood alone and wept passionately, while I waited for him. You may be sure I begged his pardon, and made it all right with him, and had him laughing and happy again before I let him go. But nevertheless what I said was true. David is not my boy, and he will forget. But Timothy would have remembered.'

*   *   *

At Easter, Sylvia and Arthur took George, Jack and Peter down to the Isle of Wight for a short holiday, leaving Mary Hodgson in London to look after Michael, who had evidently been ill. Sylvia wrote to Mary every few days, anxious for news of him.

Hazlehurst,
Freshwater Bay.

(Please don't call me madam)   Good Friday morning.

My dear Mary,

We are here safe and sound and, considering the long journey, none the worse. . . . I am thinking of my little Michael all the time and longing to kiss him. . . . I can see him so well in his nursery. Mama wrote that she hadn't been very well, so I don't suppose she has been round. I hope she won't do too much. . . .

The boys are all well (G. and P. coughing slightly) and very happy, and get out in spite of the rain—you can imagine their shoes and all the changing! . . . I miss you very often, but we manage as well as we can. . . . I am longing to see my little Michael; it seems months since I had him in my arms. Kiss my little boy for me and whisper in his ear that I want him so much.

Sincerely yours,
Sylvia Llewelyn Davies.

George, Peter and Jack (JMB)

Mary Hodgson took a holiday herself in June, staying with her parents in Morecambe. Sylvia kept her informed of Michael's progress and of life at 31 Kensington Park Gardens:

'Little Michael is very well and has another tooth through at last—the other will be through soon I think. He has been wonderfully good. He had a few bad cries at first and clung to me and looked about for you which was pathetic, but considering everything he has been easy to soothe. He refuses to take any broth so I suppose I must cope with meat juice.

'Mr Davies and George came back on Wednesday and George thoroughly enjoyed himself. Jack was seedy for two days and afterwards Mr Barrie took him to spend an afternoon at Earl's Court. Peter wished to go too but I thought it would be wiser to let only one, so Peter is to go alone one day later on. . . . The weather here is very warm and they all have their thin combinations on, and Michael has his little drawers on and no petticoat at present.'

Michael, the age of the century in 1901

Sylvia wrote to Mary again on June 16th, Michael's first birthday, to make arrangements for the summer holidays: 'We have taken a charming cottage at Tilford, near Mr Barrie's, instead of Burpham. When you come back I will go down and settle about rooms. . . . Of course I shouldn't take more than 4 maids away to a cottage.' Peter Davies later commented in his family *Morgue*:*

' "4 maids to Tilford"! It's uncanny. . . . One has no notion of what Arthur's average income from the Bar may have been at this stage, but it certainly can't have been large. What made this enormous gang of servants possible was, I think, not only the almost non-existent taxation and the cheapness of servants themselves and of things in general, but also the simplicity of the way the family lived: hardly any drink (an occasional bottle of claret . . . and a glass of beer or so for Arthur), no car or carriage, practically no restaurants to eat and drink expensively in, . . . and no serious school bills. I think Arthur always had lunch at an A.B.C. for about 6d., and I take it Sylvia made most of her own lovely clothes.'

Sylvia, with Peter, Jack and George (standing), outside Tilford Cottage (JMB)

The cottage at Tilford was less than a five-minute walk along the dusty, winding road to Black Lake Cottage, where the Barries had taken up residence for the summer. Apart from the Allahakbarries' annual cricket match, Barrie had spent most of June and July writing Maude Adams's next vehicle, *Quality Street*, and by the time the Davieses arrived at Tilford at the end of July, he was posting off the finished manuscript to Frohman in New York. He was now able to devote all his energies to introducing the Davies boys to a world of pirates, Indians and 'wrecked islands': bloodthirsty sagas not merely described but enacted to the full in the 'haunted groves' of Black

*In 1945, Peter Llewelyn Davies began a compilation of numerous family letters and papers, linked with occasional comments of his own, into six unpublished volumes spanning the years 1874–1915, which he referred to wryly as the Family Mausoleum, or simply the *Morgue*. The Christian names of members of his family have been substituted throughout for his abbreviations.

Lake forest. The lake itself became a South Seas lagoon, the setting for numerous adventures in which an old punt was variously utilized as a long boat, a rakish pirate ship, and 'the ill-fated brig, *Anna Pink*'. Their escapades followed the approximate storyline of Barrie's favourite book as a boy, *The Coral Island*, in which Jack, Ralph and Peterkin are wrecked on a desert island. Porthos obliged his master by representing a whole host of characters, from the pirates' dog to a ferocious tiger in a papier-mâché mask, while Barrie created a role for himself as the pirate Captain Swarthy, a dark and sinister figure who displayed despicable cowardice in the face of his young antagonists, frequently forcing the four-year-old Peter to walk the plank into the murky waters of Black Lake. Fortunately the lake was only a few feet at its deepest, but on more than one occasion Sylvia and Arthur had to restrain the high degree of realism in the acting by disallowing the use of real arrows and long-bladed knives. Occasionally Barrie would step aside from the adventures and view them objectively, photographing the boys in action, or jotting down observations for use in *The Little White Bird* or his new play, *The Admirable Crichton*.

'What is genius? It is the power to be a boy again at will . . .' Denis Mackail observed that 'if Barrie is besotted with these boys and his

George, Jack and Peter at Black Lake in August 1901, setting off on their *Boy Castaway* adventures (JMB)

George, Jack and Peter in the Black Lake: 'It was a coral island glistening in the sun' (JMB)

Jack pointing out a vulture to George in the woods of Black Lake (JMB)

George and Jack outside their marooner's hut (JMB)

games, if sometimes his single-minded concentration on them is really a little excessive and alarming, no one again can stop him, and he is obviously so gloriously happy, too. And so kind. So funny. And only juggling with his own age.' Certainly Mary Barrie had no wish to stop him; on his own he habitually sank into black depression, but the boys brought him alive again, transforming him into a warm and witty companion, both for themselves and for Mary. Nor did Arthur attempt to break the spell; he had precious little in common with the man, but he no longer looked upon him as a rival. Just as Barrie commanded an area of affection entirely to himself, Arthur was equally confident of his family's need for the particular love and devotion that only he could provide. It was, perhaps, this mutual recognition of each other's territory that allowed the curious *ménage* to continue without serious disruption. A sign in the garden at Black Lake seemed to sum up the situation: PERSONS WHO COME TO STEAL THE FRUIT ARE REQUESTED NOT TO WALK ON THE FLOWER BEDS.

Although the world of fairies had been largely replaced by pirates and desert islands for George and Jack, there remained one who had faith in them, while the youngest still awaited initiation. The two elder boys therefore had to tolerate a certain amount of fairy nonsense for Peter's benefit, or stand idly by and watch Barrie hypnotize Michael with his 'famous manipulation of the eyebrows: . . . when the one was climbing my forehead the other descended it, like the two buckets in the well'.[4]

Throughout the long summer days of August, Barrie and the Davies boys were inseparable, and he decided to honour them by turning the photographs of their exploits into a book, as he had done for Bevil Quiller-Couch seven years before. However, this time he resolved to produce the book in an altogether grander fashion, commissioning Constable's to print the text and bind the photographs in the style of *The Coral Island*. He would have had little difficulty in finding a publisher for the finished product had he wished to do so, thereby recouping the cost of the enterprise, but he wanted it to be a private tribute. He therefore restricted the edition to two copies, one for the boys' father and one for himself, calling it *The Boy Castaways of Black Lake Island*:

Peter, aged four, 'wrote' in the Preface: 'I have still ... a vivid recollection of that strange and terrible summer, when we suffered experiences such as have probably never before been experienced by three brothers ... I should say that the work was in the first instance compiled as a record simply, at which we could whet our memories, and that it is now published for Michael's benefit. If it teaches him by example lessons in fortitude and manly endurance, we shall consider that we were not wrecked in vain.' *The Boy Castaways* was dedicated 'To Our Mother, in Cordial Recognition of her Efforts to Elevate us above the Brutes'.

In his Dedication* to *Peter Pan*, written over a quarter of a century later, Barrie described *The Boy Castaways* as 'a now melancholy volume, ... the literary record of that summer ... which is so much the best and the rarest of this author's works':

'It contains thirty-five illustrations and is bound in cloth with a picture stamped on the cover of the three eldest of you "setting out to be wrecked". This record is supposed to be edited by the youngest of the three, and I must have granted him that honour to make up for his being so often lifted bodily out of our adventures by his nurse, who kept breaking into them for the fell purpose of giving him a midday rest. Michael rested so much at this period that he was merely an honorary member of the band, waving his foot to you for luck when you set off with bow and arrow to shoot his dinner for him. ... The illustrations (full-paged) in *The Boy Castaways* are all photographs taken by myself; some of them indeed of phenomena that had to be invented afterwards, for you were always off doing the wrong things when I pressed the button. ...

'Though *The Boy Castaways* has sixteen chapter-headings, there is no other letterpress; an absence which possible purchasers might complain of, though there are surely worse ways of writing a book than this. These headings anticipate much of the play of *Peter Pan*. ... In *The Boy Castaways* Captain Hook has arrived but is called Captain Swarthy, and he seems from the pictures to have been a black man. This character, as you do not need to be told, is held by those in the know to be autobiographical. ...

'The dog in *The Boy Castaways* seems never to have been called Nana but was evidently in training for that post. ... There is ... a touching picture, a clear forecast of the Darling nursery, entitled "We trained the dog to watch over us while we slept." ... He was always willing to do any extra jobs, such as becoming the tiger in mask,

'We carried home the head and skin as trophies' (JMB)

*There are four different versions of the Dedication in existence: a first hand-written draft, a corrected typedraft, a corrected proof, and the final printed version. In all four versions, Barrie uses numbers to identify the boys instead of their names: No. 1 for George through No. 5 for Nico. Their names are reinstated here and subsequently for the convenience of the reader.

Two of Porthos's many roles: *(top)* as the pirate Swarthy's dog 'patrolling the island'; *(below)* playing a tiger in a papier-mâché mask: 'George found himself within four paces of a tiger . . . but missed' (JMB)

'Last night on the island' (JMB)

and when after a fierce engagement you carried home that mask in triumph, he joined in the procession proudly and never let on that the trophy had ever been part of him. . . .

'They do seem to be emerging out of our island, don't they, the little people of the play, all except that sly one, the chief figure, who draws farther and farther into the wood as we advance upon him? He so dislikes being tracked, as if there were something odd about him, that when he dies he means to get up and blow away the particle that will be his ashes.

'Wendy has not yet appeared, but she has been trying to come ever since that loyal nurse cast the humorous shadow of woman upon the scene and made us feel that it might be fun to let in a disturbing element. Perhaps she would have bored her way in at last whether we wanted her or not. . . . Was it the travail of hut-building that subsequently advised Peter to find a "home under the ground"? The bottle and mugs in that lurid picture, "Last night on the Island," seem to suggest that you had changed from Lost Boys into pirates, which was probably also a tendency of Peter [Pan]'s. . . . Even Tinker Bell had reached our island before we left it. It was one evening when we climbed the wood carrying Michael to show him what the trail was like by twilight. As our lanterns twinkled among the leaves Michael saw a twinkle stand still for a moment and he waved his foot gaily to it, thus creating Tink. . . .

'*The Boy Castaways* is a little battered and bent after the manner of those who shoulder burdens . . . I have said that it is the rarest of my printed works, as it must be, for the only edition was limited to two copies, of which one (there was always some devilry in any matter connected with Peter [Pan]) instantly lost itself in a railway carriage.'

The copy that euphemistically 'lost itself in a railway carriage' had been a present from Barrie to the boys' father. That Arthur should have been so strangely careless with it was, in Peter's opinion, 'doubtless his own way of commenting on the whole fantastic affair'.

(Right and overleaf): six full-page illustrations from the surviving copy of *The Boy Castaways*. Denis Mackail described the photographs in his 1941 biography, *The Story of J.M.B.*: 'The little boys look so happy, and intent, and absorbed in the magic which they only partly understood; and, somehow, also, so very, very far away'

THE BOY CASTAWAYS

OF BLACK LAKE ISLAND

BEING A RECORD OF THE TERRIBLE
ADVENTURES OF THE BROTHERS
DAVIES IN THE SUMMER OF 1901
FAITHFULLY SET FORTH BY

PETER LLEWELYN DAVIES

LONDON
Published by J. M. BARRIE
in the Gloucester Road
1901

The title page of *The Boy Castaways*

I. We set out to be wrecked.

III. We were the sole survivors of the ill-fated brig *Anna Pink*.

XIV. A last pipe before turning in.

XXII. We trained the dog to watch over us while we slept.

XXXI. We strung him up.

XXXV. We set sail for England, Home, and Wilkinson's.

'That strange and terrible summer' ended with the onset of September, and the Davieses set sail for London, Home and Wilkinson's—George to Wilkinson's for his second term, and the family to their new home at 23 Kensington Park Gardens, across the street from the smaller No. 31. Barrie stayed on at Black Lake for a few more weeks, working in the after-glow of his adventures with the boys, which he now turned to profitable account as further material for *The Little White Bird* and the castaway scenes in *The Admirable Crichton*. 'We were the sole survivors of the ill-fated brig *Anna Pink*' claimed George and Jack in the third photograph of *The Boy Castaways*; '*I* was the sole survivor of the ill-fated *Anna Pink*,' contradicted Captain W— in Chapter 23 of *The Little White Bird*, while Ernest stretched the exploitation still further in the original draft of *The Admirable Crichton* by proclaiming: 'Wrecked, wrecked, wrecked! ... We are the sole survivors of Lord Loam's steam yacht *Anna Pink*.'

On the other side of the Atlantic, Charles Frohman was launching Maude Adams in her second Barrie role as Phoebe Throssel, the heroine of *Quality Street*. Barrie wrote to Frohman on October 29th, 1901, 'to thank you most heartily for all the thought and care you have given to "Quality Street". I see it has been immense—and Miss Adams for the wonderful things she seems to be doing with Phoebe. She is a marvel.' The pleasure Barrie derived from his American success was somewhat marred by the death of his sister, Isabella—only two years older than himself. Sadder still was the demise of Porthos. After a summer of supreme exertions, the great hound gradually subsided into a state of lethargy. Mary Barrie later wrote, 'When it became impossible to have him any longer about the house, he was sent to that humane institution, the Dogs' Home at Battersea, and in the lethal chamber he was put peacefully to sleep. Buried with him were ... those first seven years of my married life.'[1]

At Christmas time, Barrie took the Davies boys to see a new production at the Vaudeville, *Bluebell in Fairyland*, which described itself as 'A Musical Dream Play' as distinct from a pantomime. The play starred Ellaline Terriss and her husband, Seymour Hicks, who had played opposite Mary Ansell in Barrie's first West End success, *Walker, London*. To the astonishment of most managers, *Bluebell in Fairyland* ran for nearly 300 performances, attracting a fanatical audience of children who saw the play again and again. The Davies boys were early enthusiasts, but the strongest impact was on Barrie. According to Denis Mackail, he 'talked about it, thought about it, and acted bits of it in more than one nursery. ... He was the crossing-sweeper—Hicks's part—he was Bluebell, the little flower-girl, and then, with special and overwhelming effect, he was the terrifying Sleepy King.' He immediately started making notes for

Porthos at Black Lake: 'The dog of a pirate had seen us' (JMB)

his own fairy play, though it would be many months before he found a peg on which to hang his ideas:

—*Fairy Play* Hero might be a poor boy of today with ordinary clothes, unhappy, &c, in Act 1.—Taken to Fairydom still in every-day clothes which are strange contrast to clothes worn by the people in fairydom—(à la Hans Xian Anderson)
—*Fairy Play* Characters might be carried thro' the air on sheets borne by birds.
—*Fairy Play* Alphabet biscuits, &c. George's anger—'You ate them instead of leaving me the G's.'
—*Fairy Play* What children like best is imitation of *real* boys & girls (not so much *comic* incidents).

Ellaline Terriss in *Bluebell in Fairyland*

After four years of gestation, *The Little White Bird* was finally completed in the summer of 1902. The Peter Pan saga had begun life as a single chapter within the main narrative, but it now ran to over a hundred pages, forming an elaborate book-within-a-book. The overall work, however, was still directed at adults, and Captain W—'s relationship with the boy David remained the dominant theme. Barrie later claimed that both story and title had been Sylvia's idea: he tried to persuade her to write it, she declined, so he wrote it himself. At the end of the novel, the Captain presents David's mother with the completed manuscript, telling her it is all about her 'little white bird'—the unborn child she has been expecting. When he asks for her opinion, she replies: 'How wrong you are in thinking this book is about me and mine, it is really all about Timothy.'

With the finished manuscript at last in the hands of his publishers, Barrie was able to forge his links with Kensington Gardens still closer by moving from 133 Gloucester Road to a small Regency house in the Bayswater Road, Leinster Corner, overlooking the northern stretches of the Gardens. The move also brought him considerably closer to the Davies family, and within a few yards of George's private school in Orme Square. Mary Barrie set to work with another team of builders and decorators, redesigning the new house, while her husband took up residence in an old stable at the end of the garden, which had already been converted into his study. No sooner had he settled himself back at his desk than news came from Scotland that his father had died at the age of eighty-seven after being struck down by a horse and cart. The Barries travelled up to Kirriemuir to watch him laid to rest beside Margaret Ogilvy, then invited the other members of his father's household—Barrie's elder sister Sara and his uncle, Doctor Ogilvy—down to Black Lake after the funeral. The gesture brought an oppressive layer of Scottish gloom to the

Leinster Corner

holiday cottage. His relatives felt ill-at-ease amid the comparative luxury, while Barrie found their tepid company a far cry from the savage days of the previous *Boy Castaways* summer. He affected warm devotion towards his family when they were north of the border, but here at Black Lake they seemed singularly out of context, and when they announced their intention of returning to Kirriemuir, little pressure was put on them to stay. They were replaced by the Davies family, and the gloom immediately lifted. Barrie emerged from his shell, and the woods were alive once more to the war-cries of pirates and Indians, the lake again transformed into a South Seas lagoon. But the adventures this year were subject to frequent interruptions. *Quality Street* had begun rehearsal at the Vaudeville, with Barrie's latest heroine, Ellaline Terriss, in the lead. Her husband, Seymour Hicks, had been given the part of the hero, Valentine Brown, and was also directing the proceedings, which frequently met with the author's displeasure as Hicks had the irritating habit of adding extra lines of his own. Barrie would have preferred to have had Dion Boucicault in charge, but he was busily occupied down the road at the Duke of York's Theatre, preparing *The Admirable Crichton* for presentation.

Quality Street opened on September 17th, 1902, and gathered the same adulatory reviews as it had received in New York. Six weeks later, *The Admirable Crichton* opened at the Duke of York's. Its story of a butler who, when wrecked on a desert island with his aristocratic employers, becomes ruler by 'natural selection', was seized upon as having great social significance. 'If ever a Problem Play was set before an audience *The Admirable Crichton* was one', wrote H. M. Walbrook in his study of Barrie's plays. 'No comedy of our time has set its beholders thinking so hard. In England and America, and even in Paris, it was hailed as one of the most penetrating dramatic social pamphlets of the day.' One critic went so far as to compare the play with the writings of Rousseau which had prepared the way for the French Revolution, while William Archer, the great social critic of his time, questioned whether Barrie was aware of the immensity of his attack upon the constituted social order of Great Britain. Amid the controversy aroused by *The Admirable Crichton*, Messrs Hodder and Stoughton published *The Little White Bird*. It would be hard to conceive of two such seemingly disparate creations from the same author appearing before the public in the same week, yet *The Times*, in reviewing both works, inadvertently put its finger on the common factor. '*The Admirable Crichton* . . . is signed "Barrie" over and over again,' observed A. B. Walkley in his 3,400-word review; 'hold it up to the light and you see "Barrie" in the watermark. . . . It deals with Rousseau's perpetual subject, "the return to nature". But it deals with that subject in a whimsical, pathetic, ironic, serious way which would

George and Jack at Black Lake: 'Deeper and deeper into those primeval forests' (JMB)

Gerald du Maurier as Ernest in *The Admirable Crichton*

have driven Rousseau crazy. Nevertheless it is as delightful a play as the English stage has produced in our generation.' The following day *The Times* book critic wrote:

'The peculiar quality of THE LITTLE WHITE BIRD ... is its J.-M.-Barrie-ness. Nobody else could have done it. ... The book is all Barrie-ness; whimsical, sentimental, profound, ridiculous Barrie-ness; utterly impossible, yet absolutely real, a fairy tower built on the eternal truth. To say what happens in it is to stultify one's praise for one of the most charming books ever written. ... To speak in sober earnest, this is one of the best things that Mr Barrie has written. From beginning to end it is a fantasy, of fairies, birds, old bachelors ... pretty young wives and their children—but especially their children. If a book exists which contains more knowledge and more love of children, we do not know it. To the [narrator] the smallest details of his adored David, his braces and his behaviour in the bath, are not too trivial to dwell on. ... In fine, here is an exquisite piece of work. To analyse its merits and defects ... would be to vivisect a fairy. Mr Barrie has given us the best of himself, and we can think of no higher praise.'

Irene Vanbrugh and Muriel Beaumont in *The Admirable Crichton*. Muriel Beaumont married her fellow castaway Gerald du Maurier at the end of the run

'The fairies of the Serpentine' (Rackham)

The secrets of Kensington Gardens were now well and truly out of the bag, and although the critic had assumed the book to be a fantasy from beginning to end, others knew better. George suddenly found himself the centre of attention at Wilkinson's—as did Wilkinson, caricatured as the infamous Pilkington—but despite a certain amount of teasing for his belief in fairies, he remained both proud of and loyal to his participation in the story. George was also aware that the book was a colossal best-seller, and that colossal best-sellers earn colossal sums for their authors—and extra pocket-money for their collaborators. Encouraged by George, Barrie began to think again about his fairy play. He noted down an idea that was a minor variation on the 'Wandering Child' story in *Tommy and Grizel*:

—*Play.* '*The Happy Boy*': Boy who can't grow up—runs away from pain & death—is caught *wild*. (*End* escapes)
—*Fairy Play.* Gerald [du Maurier] as the boy?
—*Fairy Play.* Important the mother treated from child's point of view—how mother scolds, wheedles, &c—scene in which children's behaviour to her wd tickle children because they recognise the truth of them.
—Ellaline [Terriss] their mother? Or Lena Ashwell? Or Mrs [Patrick] Campbell. Or Ellen Terry.
—Peter [Davies]: 'Mother, how did we get to know you?'
—Cd ghost mother (L.W.B.) work into this?

Sylvia's contribution to *The Little White Bird* had been almost as large as her son's, and Barrie's immediate reward was to take her off to Paris on a celebration trip. Arthur stayed at home, going about his business at the Temple and looking after the boys. He wrote to his father at Kirkby Lonsdale:

Sylvia at Black Lake (JMB)

> 2, Garden Court, Temple, E.C.
> Nov. 28, 1902.
>
> Dearest Father,
>   I don't know what your arrangements are for Christmas, nor if you are likely to have the Vicarage very full. I should like to come, if possible, bringing one boy or perhaps two. It is just possible that Sylvia may be induced to come too, but that is not likely. . . .
>   Sylvia is at present on a trip to Paris with her friends the Barries, by way of celebration of the huge success of Barrie's new plays and new book. The party is completed by another novelist, [A.E.W.] Mason, and they seem to be living in great splendour and enjoying themselves very much. They left on Monday and return tomorrow. Barrie's new book, The Little White Bird, is largely taken up with Kensington Gardens and our and similar children. There is a whole chapter devoted to Peter.
>   I was at the large Encyclopaedia Britannica dinner last week. . . . Bell of Marlborough was there, and professed indignation at my reminiscence that the Bishop of London was superannuated in the Lower Fifth.
>   My work is moderately prosperous but no more. . . .
>   Your affect. son,
>   A.Ll.D.

The reference to 'a whole chapter devoted to Peter' would seem to indicate that Arthur had only given the book a cursory glance, since the chapter to which he is referring is not about Peter, but his namesake, Peter Pan. Peter Davies observed in the *Morgue*:

'"*Her* friends the Barries" is a suggestive phrase; the Davieses and Barries had known one another now for some five years. Was Arthur a little put out by Sylvia's visit to Paris? . . . I think it pretty clear that Arthur was a shade vexed and thought it all rather a bore. On the other hand, how Sylvia must have enjoyed it, and why not? Paris meant something to her, and nothing, I think, to Arthur. And Jimmy was, in his own odd way, an excellent Parisian and most delightful of hosts, and it would have been hard to imagine a more satisfactory addition than Alfred Mason, a new and devoted admirer and one of

A joint letter from Barrie to Peter and Michael

> LEINSTER CORNER.
> LANCASTER GATE, W.
>
> 11 Mq. 1503
>
> Dear Petermikle,
>   i thank
> v 2 very much
> 4 your birth
> day presents
> and i hav
> putt your
> portraitgrafs
> on mi wall
> and yourselves
> in my hart and
> your honey lower
> down.
>   i am
> your frend
>   J. M. Barrie

April 23th 1903
16, ROYAL CRESCENT,
RAMSGATE.

Dear Mr Barrie

We are all comming back on Monday and we are longing to see you. We are having a very jolly et time at Ramsgate. We wish you were here. We spend most of our time on donkeys and the sands is when George and I

are riding donkeys. It makes four altogether. Uncle Gerald and Aunt Muriel are comming down on Sunday and Uncle Guy says they are always looking into each other's eyes. I hope you are enjoying yourself at BLACK-LAKE COTTAGE.

Is the new motor car finished yet. I've put Black Lake Cottage in capital letters because if you where-ever you are must be a very celebrated place. Mother has got rumertism in her shoulders I hope Clare Mackail

is better. Did you think Aunt Muriel looked beautiful at the wedding Mother said you were in the church. Father said you have got a topper! I didn't know it before

Your story-listener Jack Ll:-
Davies. P.S. I expect a letter

A letter to Barrie from Jack, aged eight, who was staying with his grandmother, Emma du Maurier, at Ramsgate. Gerald du Maurier had married Muriel Beaumont on April 11th. Clare Mackail was the sister of Denis Mackail, Barrie's 1941 biographer

the most romantically minded men of that day who put all beautiful women on a pedestal, and a most attractive, amusing and romantic figure himself. ... I have always, by the way, regarded [*The Little White Bird*] as being much more about George than about me. I can't say I like it, any more than, it would seem, Arthur did.'

Barrie soon found that the success of *The Little White Bird* had a number of unfortunate side effects. His walks in Kensington Gardens were now frequently spoilt by individuals accosting him for further information on the whereabouts of fairies and Peter Pan; moreover his celebrated 'love' of children led certain mothers to assume that he would instantly rhapsodize over their offspring. Such presumption invariably invoked the weariest of sighs and a paralysing lift of the eyebrow which rendered many a parent nonplussed. Barrie was singularly selective in his choice of friends, both adult and otherwise, and resented attempts to thrust any young whippersnapper into the path of his affections.

Porthos had been dead for over a year, and Mary Barrie decided to invest in another dog for company: a black and white Newfoundland named Luath. 'I became a child with him,' she wrote in *Dogs and Men*. 'We played ridiculous games together.... What races we ran in the Kensington Gardens!... Luath's proper place was the nursery. How happy he would have been if there had been one, full of gloriously noisy children!' Luath's happiness was assured the following summer, when the Davies family spent their third annual holiday with the Barries at Black Lake. He stepped into Porthos's role, joining in the *Castaway* games with Barrie and the boys as his predecessor had done, 'bringing hedgehogs to the hut in his mouth as offerings for our evening repasts'.[2]

Sylvia's friend Dolly Parry, now Dolly Ponsonby, had returned from Copenhagen with her husband, Arthur, and was living at near-by Shulbrede Priory in Hampshire:

'*Friday 21st Aug. 1903*. Sylvia, the Barrys [*sic*], Peter & Michael came in a motor car from Farnham to tea. Jim Barry with a child clinging to each hand at once went & sat in the dining room chimney corner.... Sylvia beautiful & satisfying, loving the house & appealing to "Jimmy" about it, while I tried to make myself pleasant to Mrs Barry—commonplace, 2nd rate & admirable. It is a strange ménage. It was very charming to see Michael give his hand to Jimmy as they walked down the garden path together & into the field. His devotion & genius-like understanding of children is beautiful & touching beyond words as he has none himself.'

Sylvia was now expecting her fifth child, and when Barrie returned to London at the end of August to begin rehearsals for his new play, *Little Mary*, the Davieses moved on to Rustington. Dolly Ponsonby's diary records a day spent on her father's yacht:

Sylvia (JMB)

'Sylvia looking divine, ... her beautiful sons more glorious than ever, ... splendidly full of courage and hope, swarming up the rigging like monkeys, and George, with the assistance of ropes, bathing off the boat though unable to swim.'

On another occasion the Ponsonbys motored over for dinner. Before going into the house, Dolly paused in the road to observe Arthur and Sylvia through the window:

Jack (JMB)

'The picture of them from the road through the open lamp-lit cottage window was the loveliest I ever saw. Arthur reading, with his Greek-coin profile, and Sylvia with her beautifully poised head and Empire hair, sewing in a gown of white and silver.'

Little Mary opened at Wyndham's Theatre on September 24th, 1903, and despite its 'rather silly' plot (as *The Times* commented) ran for over 200 performances. As usual, it contained a sprinkling of lines contributed by the boys, including a remark from Jack. When stuffing himself with cakes at tea, Sylvia had warned him, 'You'll be sick tomorrow.' 'I'll be sick tonight,' replied Jack cheerily, and went on stuffing. Barrie utilized the line, but when Jack heard it being used on stage, he felt his contribution entitled him to a share of the spoils. Barrie agreed to pay him a halfpenny a night during the run of the play, and drew up a document setting out the terms of their transaction:

> LEINSTER CORNER,
> LANCASTER GATE, W.
>
> Agreement this day, 6 Dec 1903 between J. M Barrie of Leinster Corner of the one part and John LL Davies of 23 Kensington Park Gardens of the other part. WHEREAS J. M Barrie (to be hereafter called the aforesaid) is part-author of a play named Little Mary, of which John LL Davies is part-author of the other part the aforesaid undertakes to pay to John LL Davies the sum (to be hereafter called the above-mentioned) the sum of one Halfpenny per diem during the run of the play.
>
> Signed
> J. M Barrie
> John Ll. Davies

Barrie's Agreement with Jack

Jack's contribution to *Little Mary* netted him a grand total of 8s. 8d., which caused a good deal of jealousy among his brothers. Barrie later wrote of them, 'You watched for my next play with peeled eyes, not for entertainment but lest it contained some chance witticism of yours that could be challenged as collaboration.'[3]

The boys did not have to wait long. On November 23rd, 1903, the day before the birth of Sylvia's fifth child, Barrie commenced work on the play that was to become *Peter Pan*, at present simply entitled 'Anon. A Play'. The opening scene, 'The Night Nursery of the Darling Family', in which Wendy and her two brothers play at

Opening page of the play that was to become *Peter Pan*, entitled 'Anon: A Play' and dated November 23rd 1903 – the eve of Nico's birth

Mothers and Fathers, bore a strong resemblance to a similar scene taking place at 23 Kensington Park Gardens, where doctors were standing by to deliver Sylvia's child. Mary Hodgson later wrote an account of 'The Night that Heralded Your Arrival' for the benefit of that child:

'Your father with a grim set face thought "Bed Time" might be earlier — . . . And one by one he took the four in turns to bid "Good Night" —somewhat disappointed. As G remarked "Why is father in a hurry?" . . . Quick on the spot —"Mother's got a Headache & isn't very well!" The hours dragged on & heavier grew your Father's step upon the stair. . . . Drs Bott & Rendell —up & down and restless as time wore on. No comfort to your father —outwardly the calmest of the three. At Dawn you came——How welcome, who shall say? Your father wan & weary to the Night Nursery came, announcing in glad tones —"This is a great day. I have a fifth son —and you a little brother." '[4]

ylvia and her fifth son, Nicholas, soon nick-named Nico or Nik-o)

It was mooted among the family that the new baby might be named Timothy, possibly at Sylvia's instigation. Arthur, not unnaturally, appears to have favoured other names (any name, one would imagine, but Timothy), and within two days of the birth he was writing to his sister Margaret suggesting Nicholas as a possibility:

> 2 Garden Court Temple.
> Nov 26, 1903.
>
> Dear Margaret,
>   Many thanks for your letter. Both Sylvia and the infant (Nicholas???) are doing very well, though S. will require great care for some time. We are much gratified by the size, vigour, maturity & unbaldness of the infant. He weighed 11 lb 3 oz at birth, a very unusual weight, & in face reminds us of the early George. George says he is not exactly pretty but looks agreeable & sensible. Michael gazes at him with wide eyes & Peter makes inarticulate noises at him. . . .
>   Yours affectly,
>   A.Ll.D.

Peter and Nico

Sylvia conceded the name Nicholas for her fifth son, who, like Peter and Michael, was not christened. She also began to yield to another of Arthur's wishes: a cherished ambition to move from London to the country. She wrote to Dolly Ponsonby in early January 1904:

> Beloved Dolly,
>   . . . My Nicholas is a dear creature, so fat & well —& very like George was at first —however they seem to alter every day. I am stronger now & longing to get up. Five sons, Dolly, think of it! We are thinking of living in the country now there are so many to bring up —perhaps at Berkhamsted which has a very good school & near my sister Trixie & not too far from London. We have heard of a nice old house, but of course we

can settle nothing till I am well enough to look about. . . . We often talk about you, you dear pretty Dolly. Write soon as I so enjoy hearing from you.

Your Sylvia.

Five boys and a resident staff of four made living at 23 Kensington Park Gardens a tight fit. Arthur's years of steady toil at the Bar had begun to pay their reward, but larger houses in London were beyond his means; moreover the prospect of educating five boys at boarding school was a formidable financial undertaking, even in those days. The 'nice old house' in Berkhamsted High Street—Egerton House—seemed to solve all problems. It was close to the station, which would allow Arthur to commute every day to London; it was large enough to accommodate an ever-expanding household; it had an excellent day school within walking distance of the house; it would provide the growing boys with clean country air; and it was twenty-five miles from J. M. Barrie's doorstep.

Nico

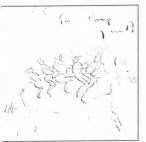

Postscript sketch by Barrie of
Sylvia and her five boys

Unaware of the Davies family's impending exodus, Barrie continued to work on his new play. In an early (unpublished) draft of the 1928 Dedication to *Peter Pan*, he wrote of the Davies boys: 'The play of Peter is streaky with you still, though none see this save you and I. A hundred acts must be left out, and you were in them all. . . . You never thought when you were at your brightest to claim the authorship of Peter. . . . You obviously have a better claim than most, and you could certainly trust to my remaining silent. . . . This dedication is no more than giving you back yourselves.' Barrie's generosity is perhaps overcharged, for although *Peter Pan* is indeed streaky with the Davies boys—and would become more so as he subjected it to constant annual revision—it is Barrie himself who pervades every character and situation to a degree unparalleled in all his other plays. The boys' very real contribution lay in their unwitting ability to sharpen his own memories and preoccupation with childhood which, when blended with the omnipotence of Margaret Ogilvy and the particular tragedy of his own being, produced the quintessence of all that lay deepest in his soul. Had he conceived *Peter Pan* at an earlier stage in his life, he would have doubtless tempered it with an excess of intellect; as it was, he allowed his heart to steer his pen, guided only by his practical and masterly knowledge of stagecraft, and as a result produced a play that was utterly different from anything yet known.

Barrie finished the first draft of his new play on March 1st, 1904. He was still undecided on a title, but had begun referring to it in his notebook as 'Peter & Wendy'. George was far from keen on Wendy's intrusion into the saga, but to Barrie she had become an element as integral as Peter Pan himself. He had promised Frohman that he would have a new vehicle ready for Maude Adams at the end of April, and he looked upon Wendy as that vehicle, while Peter, he assumed, would be played by a boy. He wrote to Maude Adams on April 18th, 1904:

> My dear Maudie,
>   I have written a play for children, which I don't suppose would be much use in America. She [Wendy] is rather a dear of a girl with ever so many children long before her hair is up and the boy is Peter Pan in a new world. I should like you to be the boy and the girl and most of the children and the pirate captain. I hope you are coming here before the summer is ended and I also hope I may have something to read you and tell you about. I can't get along without an idea that really holds me, but if I can get it how glad I shall be to be at work for little Maudie again.

Barrie's fears that the play might prove unacceptable to Frohman were not without justification. By contemporary standards, 'Peter & Wendy' read like a Barnum & Bailey circus extravaganza. Not only did the script require massive sets and a cast of over fifty – to include pirates, redskins, wolves, a lion, a jaguar, a crocodile, an eagle, an ostrich, a dog, and a 'living' fairy – but at least four of the cast were called upon to fly in highly complex movements. Aside from the mammoth cost of staging such a production, it was none too clear what sort of an audience Barrie had in mind. The story seemed to be aimed primarily at children, yet much of the dialogue was curiously sophisticated; there was a confusion of styles and moods: swashbuckling pirates juxtaposed with harlequins and columbines of the old pantomime tradition, burlesque and farce interlarded with heavy sentimentality, melodrama, and tragedy, while much of it appeared to consist of private jokes intelligible only to the author and the Davies family. Indeed the whole play seemed like self-indulgence on the grand scale, and as only Barrie could have written it, perhaps only Barrie might want to watch it. In Frohman's absence, Barrie took his play to the actor-manager Beerbohm Tree for consideration. Tree's elaborate and sumptuous productions at His Majesty's Theatre had earned him a considerable reputation for extravagance, and Barrie felt that he might put on 'Peter & Wendy' if Frohman turned it down. He read him the entire play, but Tree did not take kindly to it, and wrote to Frohman in America warning him: 'Barrie has gone out of his mind. . . . I am sorry to say it, but you ought to know it. He's just read me a play. He is going to read it to you, so I am warning you. I know I have not gone woozy in my mind, because I have tested myself since hearing the play; but Barrie must be mad.'[1]

Tree's reaction seemed ominous, and Barrie hurriedly extracted another play that he had written some months before, *Alice Sit-by-the-Fire*, in order to give himself bargaining power. When Frohman arrived from New York at the end of April, Barrie went to dine with him at the Garrick Club. He took both plays with him — *Alice Sit-by-the-Fire*, and 'Peter & Wendy', which he had retitled 'The Great White Father'. Their meeting was recounted by Frohman's biographers in *Charles Frohman: Manager and Man*:

'Barrie seemed nervous and ill at ease.

'"What's the matter?" said Charles.

'"Simply this," said Barrie. "You know I have an agreement to deliver you the manuscript of a play?"

'"Yes," said Frohman.

'"Well, I have it, all right," said Barrie, "but I am sure it will not be a commercial success. But it is a dream-child of mine, and I am so anxious to see it on the stage that I have written another play which I will be glad to give you and which will compensate you for any loss on the one I am so eager to see produced.'

' "Don't bother about that," said Frohman. "I will produce both plays." '

Frohman was true to his word. He found *Alice Sit-by-the-Fire* mildly amusing, and thought it would make a satisfactory vehicle for Ellen Terry. But 'The Great White Father' was something entirely different: he had never read anything quite like it, and the story went straight to his heart. He loved everything about the play except the title, which he suggested should be simply *Peter Pan*. The author welcomed the change; he also acceded to Frohman's second proposal: that Peter should be played by Maude Adams in America. Frohman had perceived at once that Peter Pan was the star role; besides, if Peter were played by a boy, then the ages of the other children would have to be scaled down in proportion, which in any event could not be under fourteen since English law prohibited the use of minors on stage after 9 p.m. Maude Adams was not available until the following summer, and Frohman was impatient to see the play produced. He therefore instructed his London manager, William Lestocq, to proceed at once with a West End production in time for Christmas. The decision required considerable courage, but then, as Bernard Shaw observed, Frohman was ever a gambler with his own money:

'There is a prevalent impression that Charles Frohman is a hard-headed American man of business who would not look at anything that is not likely to pay. On the contrary, he is the most wildly romantic and adventurous man of my acquaintance. As Charles XII became an excellent soldier because of his passion for putting himself in the way of being killed, so Charles Frohman became a famous manager through his passion for putting himself in the way of being ruined.'[2]

An impresario of less daring and vision might well have restricted his investment to a minimum, but this had never been Frohman's way. He gave instructions that Barrie was to have everything he wanted. 'No half-measures. Never mind the risk', wrote Denis Mackail in *The Story of J.M.B.* 'Never had [Frohman's] megalomania risen to greater heights. Never had this inspired little Jew been happier. And never, of course, had any author had quite such astounding luck.'

It was at this point that Arthur chose to move his family to Berkhamsted. Barrie's reaction is unrecorded, but it must have come as a bitter blow. For six years now he had looked upon the Davieses as his own family; hardly a week had gone by when he had not taken

Notebook entry for *Peter Pan* (actual size): 'Peter. Wendy, I'll each you. I'll show you how to mp on the wind's back, and en away we go – and if there e more winds than one they ss you about in the sky – they ng you miles & miles – but you ways fall soft on to another nd –and sometimes you go ashing through the tops of ees, scaring the owls – and if u meet a boy's kite in the air u shove your foot through it. he stars are giving a party night! Oh, Wendy, when you e sleeping in your silly bed, you ight be flying about with me ~~laying hide and seek with the ars!~~ saying funny things to the ars. Wind rustles) W'what was that? hat was the west wind whistling me. It is waiting outside to ke me back.' The proposed ialogue indicates Barrie's debt George MacDonald's *At the ack of the North Wind* (1870), n allegorical novel in which a oy discovers Heaven by flying ith the North Wind to a ountry very similar to Barrie's ever Land

them out to dinner or the theatre, visited their nursery, or merely strolled with one or more of the boys through Kensington Gardens. He had even moved house to be closer to them. And now they were leaving London – at the very moment when he thought he needed the boys most. In fact they had already played their part in Peter Pan's creation, but Barrie still regarded George as his sounding-board and technical adviser for the story. In the previous autumn he had been accorded the unique honour of being presented with his own personal key to the gates of Kensington Gardens, in recognition of the fame he had brought it in *The Little White Bird*. But what use was a key to the Gardens with no George?

Charles Frohman readily perceived how listless London would become for Barrie once the Davieses had gone. He therefore invited him over to Paris for a fortnight in June. Frohman's biographers recounted 'one of the great Frohman–Barrie adventures' that followed:

'Frohman was in Paris, and after much telegraphic insistence persuaded his friend to come over. . . . He wanted to give Barrie the time of his life.

'"What would a literary man like to do in Paris?" was the question he asked himself.

Charles Frohman

'In his usual generous way he planned the first night, for Barrie was to arrive in the afternoon. He was then [staying] at the Hôtel Meurice, . . . so he engaged a magnificent suite for his guest. He ordered a sumptuous dinner at the Café de Paris, bought a box at the Théâtre Français, and engaged a smart victoria for the evening.

'Barrie was dazed at the splendor of the Meurice suite, but he survived it. When Frohman spoke of the Café de Paris dinner he said he would rather dine quietly at the hotel, so the elaborate meal was given up.

'"Now what would you like to do this evening?" asked his host.

'"Are there any of those country fairs around here, where they have side shows and you can throw balls at things?" asked Barrie.

'Frohman, who had box seats for the most classic of all Continental theaters in his pocket, said:

'"Yes, there is one in Neuilly."

'"All right," said Barrie, "let's go there."

'"We'll drive out in a victoria," meekly suggested Frohman.

'"No," said Barrie, "I think it would be more fun to go on a 'bus."

'With the unused tickets for the Théâtre Français in his waistcoat, and the smart little victoria still waiting in front of the Meurice . . . the two friends started for the country fair, where they spent the whole evening throwing balls at what the French call "Aunt Sally". . . . When Frohman and Barrie returned to the Meurice that night they

P.S. from Barrie's 25 June 1904 letter to Peter: 'These are three of the knives'

had [won] fifty knives between them. . . . This was the simple and childlike way that these two men, each a genius in his own way, disported themselves on a holiday.'

Barrie wrote to the 7-year-old Peter Davies back in England:

> Hôtel Meurice,
> 228, Rue de Rivoli,
> Paris.
> 25 June 1904
>
> My dear Peter,
>   This is where we are holding out. One day we went to the fair and played at flinging rings on to pocket knives. If you get them on you get the knife. We have won eleven knives and if we go back we shall win some more. . . . I saw your mother at the corner of the Madeleine and in the Café de Paris and coming out of Paillard carrying a sardine in one hand and a handkerchief in the other. And in the Bois whom did I see but Michael Ll. D. strutting along with his girl. This was a few years afterwards. . . .
>   With my love to you all, I am,
>   Yours to command,
>   J.M.B.

Nicholson's 1904 portrait of Barrie

Barrie returned from Paris at the beginning of July and joined his wife down at Black Lake. There were no Davieses this summer – evidently Arthur felt that his sons would do better to settle into their new country home. On July 9th, 1904, James and Mary Barrie celebrated their Tin Wedding Anniversary: ten years of married life. The following day Barrie scrawled down a series of fragmentary notes, many of them so aggressively underlined that the pencil went through the page of his notebook:

—Tin Wedding in 10th Year.   July 10th, 1904.
Idea – Husband & wife story, scene caused by husband – evidently they don't get on well together – his fault – she violent – interrupted by visitors with Tin Wedding presents (He hasn't remembered it is their wedding day.) She immediately in woman's way sort of manner talks as if husband best in world – how he spoils her, &c, pretends grand present from him, &c. When they're gone, he remorseful & swears to make it happy day yet for her (thinks he's doing finely) then she shows true self – says can quarrel over little things . . . but not over the big things. Too late to talk of love & his giving it to her, she *no longer wants it.* Her own love for him has gone from her, spilt,

ended, &c. . . . She says he can have affairs with other women as he wills. They don't disturb her. *Do as he likes about that.* Wd like to go on pretending to people happy &c, less for his sake (he had thought it all so touching & *all for him*) as ∴ [= because] it's a woman's way, &c.

—He wishes cd do anything for her wedding day & she admits there's one thing he cd do. Sometimes for dif[ferent] reasons —as good mood or ∴ he's going off to dinner &c, leaving her, he paws her & he keeps up old custom of kissing her good night. She asks him not to do these things as her Tin Wedding gift. He consents, she goes off about business of house leaving him crushed. Curtain. . . .

—Audience probably think she is to be sweet long-suffering creature. Her parents, &c, all deceived by her now as always about their married life. She tells him she has borne for long & forgiven & forgiven, but love gone for a year & *he hasn't even seen it is gone*.

—She has scunner [= revulsion] of him over goodnight kiss & tells how feels at night coming on & has resorted to various artifices to escape kiss. . . . He points out she embraced him before friends – She how he little knows how horrible it was to her – Done to deceive. . . . He thinks she was generous to him in deceiving guests, but she tells him it wasn't generosity at all, but a woman's vanity.

—She says . . . I'm no grand figure of tragedy – not tall enough – too plain – hands too red – I'm just a woman who made a mistake (12 years ago), *Mary abt us.*

—She on the agonies of years of forgiveness, self-deceptions, clinging to straws, &c, & how all these have gone. Like stick in fire, flaming, red, with sparks, now black & cold.

—He says can't we pick up the pieces (of our love) & she says no – love not a broken jar but fine wine – contents spilt – *can't pick that up.*

*   *   *

William Nicholson's design for Captain Hook

When Charles Frohman first read *Peter Pan*, he is said to have been so entranced by it that he could not resist stopping his friends in the street and acting out the scenes. However, once rehearsals began at the Duke of York's in late October, a blanket of secrecy enveloped the proceedings. Few of the cast knew the title of the play, let alone the story, and most of the actors were given only those pages relevant to their parts. Frohman's decision that Peter should be played by Maude Adams in America meant that a girl would also have to play the part in the London production. Nina Boucicault was on hand, fresh from her success as Moira in *Little Mary*, and since her brother Dion ('Dot') had again been engaged as Producer ('Director' would be the modern term), the choice seemed ideal. John Crook was commissioned to write the music, and William Nicholson to design

'All children, except one, grow up': Nina Boucicault as the first Peter Pan

both costumes and sets. Ellaline Terriss had been Barrie's first choice for Wendy, but as she was expecting a baby, another candidate had to be found. A young actress named Hilda Trevelyan was playing Nina's former role of Moira in a touring production of *Little Mary*; Barrie went to see a performance, was duly impressed, and recommended her to Dion Boucicault. Hilda's nervous excitement at being offered a part in 'Mr. Barrie's new play', of which she had been told nothing, turned to nervous trepidation when she received her first rehearsal card: 'Rehearsal – 10.30 for Flying'.[3] Nor was her anxiety allayed when she arrived at the Duke of York's Theatre to be bluntly informed that she could not start work until her life had been insured.

Hilda Trevelyan as Wendy

George Kirby's Flying Ballet Company had been in operation since 1889, but the scope of his flying apparatus was limited to primitive aerial movements; moreover the harness was extremely bulky, and since it took several minutes to connect it to the flying wire, an actor was invariably attached to his ungainly umbilical cord throughout the scene in which he had to fly. While conceiving the play of *Peter Pan*, Barrie contacted George Kirby and asked him if he could produce a flying system that could overcome these restrictions. Kirby accepted the challenge, and invented a revolutionary harness that not only allowed for complex flight movements, but could also be connected and disengaged from the flying wire within a matter of seconds. Nevertheless it required great technical skill on the part of the flier, and the cast were subjected to a gruelling fortnight of instruction by Kirby. Hilda Trevelyan's first day of rehearsal consisted of lessons in the hazardous business of take-off and landing. If she voiced any complaint, Dion Boucicault would merely shake his head and say, 'Ah, but you haven't tried the Ship Scene yet.'[4] At the end of the first day of rehearsals, Boucicault summoned the cast for an announcement. 'I would like to swear you all to keep everything you see and hear in this play an absolute secret. Nothing must leak out as to what the play is about.'[5]

Gerald du Maurier as George Darling carrying Winifred Geoghegan as Michael Darling

However, a good deal of leakage had already taken place – not least via the Davies boys. One member of the cast had received a surfeit of inside information about *Peter Pan* long before the play had been written: Sylvia's brother, Gerald du Maurier. Seymour Hicks had originally been set to play Mr Darling and Captain Hook, but when his wife Ellaline Terriss became unavailable for Wendy, Barrie lost interest in Hicks and gave Gerald the twin roles instead. In Gerald's hands, the somewhat one-dimensional character of the scripted Hook began to expand in all directions, inspiring Barrie to make constant rewrites until the pirate captain came to fit the description given of him in the final version of the play: 'Cruelest jewel in that dark setting is HOOK himself, cadaverous and blackavised. . . . He is never more sinister than when he is most polite, and the elegance of his diction, the distinction of his demeanour, show him one of a different class from his crew, a solitary among uncultured companions.' Gerald's daughter, Daphne du Maurier, described her father's creation of Hook in *Gerald: A Portrait*:

Gerald du Maurier as Captain Hook and George Shelton as Smee

'Gerald *was* Hook; he was no dummy dressed from Simmons' in a Clarkson wig, ranting and roaring about the stage, a grotesque figure whom the modern child finds a little comic. He was a tragic and rather ghastly creation who knew no peace, and whose soul was in torment; a dark shadow; a sinister dream; a bogey of fear who lives perpetually in the grey recesses of every small boy's mind. All boys had their Hooks, as Barrie knew; he was the phantom who came by night and stole his way into their murky dreams. . . . And, because he had imagination and a spark of genius, Gerald made him alive.'

Wild rumours soon began to appear in print about the nature of Mr Barrie's eagerly awaited new play, and the Duke of York's management were obliged to recruit additional guards to stop enterprising journalists from sneaking into the theatre. Barrie dissuaded all but his closest friends from watching rehearsals, and even Mary Barrie's visits were infrequent, her husband rarely seeking her opinion nowadays. The only opinions he really cared for were twenty-five miles away in Berkhamsted. He wrote to Peter on November 3rd:

> Leinster Corner
> Lancaster Gate, W.

My dear Peter,
    Sometimes when I am walking in the Gardens with Luath
I see a vision and I cry, Hurray, there's Peter, and then
Luath barks joyously and we run to the vision and then it
turns out to be not Peter but just another boy, and then I cry
like a water cart and Luath hangs his sorrowful tail.
    Oh dear, how I wish you were here, and then it would be
London again.
> Goodbye.
> Write soon.
> Your loving
> godfather*
> J.M.B.

---

*Barrie was never formally godfather to any of the Davies boys, except Nico, who himself chose Barrie when he was christened at the age of fourteen. Peter and Michael remained unchristened.

Michael Darling (Winifred Geoghegan) riding Nana (Arthur Lupino), and (*right*) Barrie and Luath, whose coat was copied for Nana

While Luath's coat was being duplicated for the actor playing Nana, the Davies boys' clothes were copied for the Darling children and the Lost Boys. Barrie obtained a basketful from Sylvia, together with photographs and a sketch she had made of Michael – evidently from the shoulders downwards:

Leinster Corner
Lancaster Gate, W.
20 Nov, 1904.

My dear Jocelyn,

It seems almost profanation to turn your pretty ideas about babies to stage account, but I am giving the basketful of them to those people nevertheless, and the pictures too, and may they treat them with reverence. You know Michael so well that though you didn't dare trust yourself to drawing his head (you adore him so), the rest is so like him that he could be picked out as the king of the castle from among a million boys. He is so beautiful that the loveliest bit of him is almost as pretty as the plainest bit of his mother. . . .

    The boys will be burning such a lot of candles on the 25th [Sylvia's 38th birthday]! I think if they were to invite me I should have to go.

Your loving

J.M.B.

Michael in 1904, aged 4

When school ended in early December, Sylvia brought her boys up to London to visit *Peter Pan* in rehearsal. Barrie treated them like royalty, holding up the proceedings to let the boys fly about the stage, and introducing them to all concerned as being the real authors of the play. Their Uncle Gerald's first child, Angela, had been born earlier in the year, and Barrie celebrated her arrival by changing Wendy's third name to Angela. Further honours were extended to Michael: Alexander Darling became Michael Darling, with Nicholas added as a middle name so that all five boys should be represented among the *Dramatis Personae*.

    The success of the production, however, was by no means assured; indeed, quite the reverse: most of the company were expecting a mild disaster. According to Barrie, 'During the rehearsals of Peter [Pan] . . . a depressed man in overalls, carrying a mug of tea or a paint-box, used often to appear by my side in the shadowy stalls and say to me, "The gallery boys won't stand it." He then mysteriously faded away as if he were the theatre ghost.'[6] The cause for concern was not merely the bizarre nature of the play, so unlike anything that had ever been presented before; the opening night had been announced for December 22nd, but by mid-December the mechanical gear required for many of the special effects had not yet been installed, let alone rehearsed. Numerous elements from Barrie's original script had to be dropped at the eleventh hour. The 'living' fairy, now renamed Tinker Bell, was to have been achieved by means of an actress moving behind a giant reducing lens, but the complications were too great; so was the flying eagle that was meant to lift the pirate Smee from the deck of the ship by the seat of his trousers and carry him off across the auditorium on a trapeze wire. On December 21st, the night before the play was due to open, a mechanical lift collapsed, taking half the scenery with it. Dion Boucicault, who had worked himself almost to death, was forced to postpone the opening until the 27th. The scenery for the final Kensington Gardens scene was still not finished, and as the stage hands refused to work over the Christmas holiday, Barrie was obliged to think again. He too was dangerously overworked, and was suffering appalling headaches as a result. Nevertheless he repaired to an empty dressing-room, axed the final twenty-two pages of the

> [its laugh broke into a thousand pieces and they all went skipping about and that was its beginning of ~~fairies~~ _fairies_, and now whenever a new baby is born its first laugh becomes a fairy *

script, and spent most of Christmas Day rewriting what was by now the fifth revised ending.

Tuesday December 27th dawned clear and blue, but few of the *Peter Pan* company were up and about to see it. Most had limped home a few hours earlier after rehearsing all night, attempting to cover the interminable scenery changes with impromptu 'front-cloth' scenes hastily written the day before. Since several of the changes were taking anything from 15 to 20 minutes, Gerald was asked to pad out the time by amusing the audience with *ex tempore* impressions of Henry Irving – a somewhat incongruous interlude coming in the middle of a fairy play. Barrie was now quite convinced that Beerbohm Tree's estimation of his sanity had been accurate. 'The Greedy Dwarf' had been one thing, a hugely enjoyable amateur entertainment for children, but no more a contender for the West End stage than the Allahakbarries were for the Test Match. *Peter Pan*, however, was being staged before a highly sophisticated first-night audience, dressed up for the occasion and expecting to see a polished and professional play by one of the country's leading playwrights. 'Do you believe in fairies?' cries Peter Pan in his effort to save Tinker Bell. 'If you believe, wave your handkerchiefs and clap your hands!'[7] The prospect of a bleak, embarrassed silence did not bear thinking about, and at the last moment Barrie took steps to insure against such an eventuality by arranging with the musical director, John Crook, that if there was no response to Peter's plea, the orchestra should down instruments and clap.

In these inauspicious circumstances, the curtain finally rose on J. M. Barrie's dream-child, *Peter Pan, or The Boy Who Wouldn't Grow Up*. The time was 8.30 p.m. – 3.30 p.m. in New York State, where an anxious Charles Frohman was awaiting the verdict at his home in

Nina Boucicault's 1904 script of *Peter Pan*. Much of the dialogue was changed during rehearsals, and Peter's line on the origin of fairies appears to have been added as an afterthought

George Shelton as Smee, the non-conformist pirate

6

                    Peter! You know fairies!
Yes, but they are nearly all dead now. You see, Wendy, whenever
a baby laughs for the first time, a fairy is born, and so there
ought to be one fairy for every boy and girl.

                    Ought to be? Isn't there?
(Shakes head) You see children know such a lot now. They soon
don't believe in fairies, and every time a child says "I don't
believe in fairies" there is a fairy somewhere that falls down
dead.

                    Poor things!
There's only one fairy left now.

                         Only one!
(Restless) I can't think where she has gone to. (Calls)
Tinkerbell! Tink!

Nina Boucicault as Peter Pan, 'drunk with glory' after defeating Captain Hook: 'This conceit of Peter was one of his most fascinating qualities. To put it with brutal frankness, there never was a cockier boy.' (*Peter and Wendy*)

White Plains. He had more than just a fortune invested in the play: it had become an infatuation, an obsession. Plans were already under way for the American production, and if its London precursor could yield the merest glimmer of evidence that Tree's advice had been wrong, he was prepared to risk the whole enterprise all over again on Broadway, with Maude Adams in the title role. Frohman's ordeal as he awaited the news out at White Plains with his friend Paul Potter was later recounted by his biographers:

'It was a bitterly cold night, and a snow-storm was raging. Frohman's secretary in the office in New York had arranged to telephone the news of the play's reception which Lestocq [Frohman's London manager] was expected to cable from London. On account of the storm the message was delayed.

'Frohman was nervous. He kept on saying, "Will it never come?" His heart was bound up in the fortunes of this beloved fairy play. While he waited with Potter, Frohman acted out the whole play, getting down on all fours to illustrate the dog and crocodile. He told it as Wendy would have told it, for Wendy was one of his favorites. Finally at midnight the telephone-bell rang. Potter took down the receiver. Frohman jumped up from his chair, saying, eagerly, "What's the verdict?" Potter listened a moment, then turned, and with beaming face repeated Lestocq's cablegram:

PETER PAN ALL RIGHT. LOOKS LIKE A BIG SUCCESS.

'This was one of the happiest nights in Frohman's life.'

'Peter Pan all right' was an understatement characteristic of Lestocq, who, as Frohman's business manager, was primarily concerned with

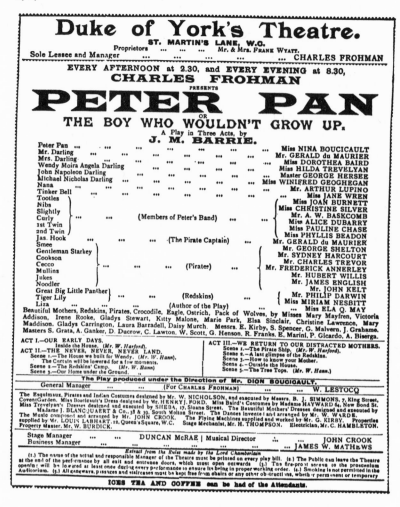

box-office takings. The cable intimated little of the thunderbolt that had struck the Duke of York's Theatre that night. For the past number of years, audiences had been subjected to a bombardment of 'problem plays', concerned with social criticism and steeped in gloom. Barrie himself had attempted such a play with *The Wedding Guest*, and since *Peter Pan* had been wrapped in secrecy from the outset, few had any idea of what the author had in store for them. When the curtain rose to reveal a dog preparing a small boy for his bath, it was greeted in stunned silence – followed by a gasp of astonished delight. For the rest of the evening the audience succumbed as one to Barrie's spell: the élite of London's society, with few children among them, emulated Sentimental Tommy by 'flinging off the years and whistling childhood back'. The audience were not the only ones to be taken unawares: the entire company, bleary-eyed and exhausted, were as astonished as anyone else by the reception they received. When Nina Boucicault turned to the distinguished gathering and begged their belief in fairies, the response was so overwhelming that she burst into tears.

Peter's character is a delicate balance between the mortal and the immortal in his being – 'Poor little half-and-half', Old Solomon Caw calls him in *The Little White Bird*. He is not a fairy, like Puck or Ariel, but 'a tragic boy', who seems to be perpetually engulfed by an immense sense of loneliness that stems from the mortal in him. Thousands of actresses have played Peter Pan, but, judging by contemporary evidence, few have caught his enigma with such exquisite perfection as did Nina Boucicault. Denis Mackail as a boy of twelve saw her performance:

'Miss Nina Boucicault as Peter Pan . . . The best, as no one has ever questioned, because of this haunting, eerie quality, this magic, and this sadness which is a kind of beauty too. Others will be more boyish, or more principal-boyish, or gayer and prettier, or more sinister and inhuman, or more ingeniously and painstakingly elfin. . . . But Miss Boucicault was the Peter of all Peters . . . She was unearthly but she was real. She obtruded neither sex nor sexlessness, which has so far beaten everyone else. Above all she had the touch of heart-breaking tragedy that is there in the story or fable from beginning to end; yet she never seemed to know it. . . . Barrie, lucky in so many of his actresses, was never luckier than here.'

The first night concluded with numerous curtain-calls, though inevitably there were a few dissenters to the general enthusiasm. The writer Anthony Hope found the sight of the Beautiful Mothers adopting the Lost Boys too much to stomach, and groaned aloud, 'Oh, for an hour of Herod!' while the musical-comedy impresario George Edwardes was heard to mutter, 'Well, if that's the sort of thing the public wants, I suppose we'll have to give it 'em.'[8] The critics, however, were more generous. *The Daily Telegraph* observed that the play was 'so true, so natural, so touching that it brought the audience to the writer's feet and held them captive there'. 'To our taste,' wrote A. B. Walkley in *The Times*, '*Peter Pan* is from beginning to end a thing of pure delight.' Beerbohm Tree's half-brother, Max Beerbohm, paid Barrie a perceptive though somewhat back-handed compliment in *The Saturday Review*:

'Undoubtedly, *Peter Pan* is the best thing [Barrie] has done – the thing most directly from within himself. Here, at last, we see his talent in its full maturity; for here he has stripped off from himself the last flimsy remnants of a pretence to maturity. . . .

'Mr Barrie is not that rare creature, a man of genius. He is something even more rare – a child who, by some divine grace, can

Nina Boucicault as Peter Pan. In her 1904 rehearsal script, Peter tells Mrs Darling 'Don't want to be useful. But I'll be good to the dead babies. I shall come and sing gaily to them when the bell tolls; and then they won't be frightened. I shall dance by their little graves and they will clap their hands to me and cry "Do it again, Peter, do it again", for they know I'm funny, and it's the funny things they like.'

Nina Boucicault and Hilda Trevelyan in the Tree Tops in the last scene of the play. Peter's command in the printed play, 'No one must ever touch me', was not added until 1928, at the request of Jean Forbes-Robertson

express through an artistic medium the childishness that is in him. . . . Mr Barrie has never grown up. He is still a child, absolutely. But some fairy once waved a wand over him, and changed him from a dear little boy into a dear little girl.'

Bernard Shaw went so far as to proclaim that *Peter Pan* was an artificial freak which missed its mark completely, and was 'foisted on children by the grown-ups'.[9] The play may have missed its mark on Shaw, but for the vast majority of children who trooped to see it, Barrie scored a bull's-eye on their aspirations. Peter Pan was the first of the pre-teen heroes: girls wanted to mother him, boys wanted to fight by his side, while the ambiguity of his sex stimulated a confusion of emotional responses. The play soon began to attract a hard-core following of matinée fanatics who occupied the front row of the stalls to hurl thimbles at Peter and abuse at Hook. Daphne du Maurier wrote of her father's performance:

'This man is mine!' Bedford's illustration from *Peter and Wendy* (1911)

'When Hook first paced his quarter-deck in the year of 1904, children were carried screaming from the stalls. . . . How he was hated, with his flourish, his poses, his dreaded diabolical smile! That ashen face, those blood-red lips, the long, dank, greasy curls; the sardonic laugh, the maniacal scream, the appalling courtesy of his gestures; . . . There was no peace in those days until the monster was destroyed, and the fight upon the pirate ship was a fight to the death.'[10]

Pre-eminent among Peter's fans were the boys who had started it all. After spending Christmas at Berkhamsted, they came up to London and went to the play with Barrie's friend, the writer E. V. Lucas, his wife Elizabeth, and their six-year-old daughter, Audrey. In 1939 Audrey recalled:

'I went . . . to the first matineé . . . with George, Jack, Peter, and Michael Llewelyn Davies (Nicholas being too young), and so imposing in size was our party that we drove to the theatre in one of those private buses which used to be hired by large families to take themselves and their luggage to railway stations. We sat in a box, in two more likely, and we loved the play . . . Hook had become one of us, the Jolly Roger had cast its spell, Smee was to become a household word, to fly a burning ambition. On the way home George demonstrated his excited approval by pretending to fall out of the bus.'[11]

The Davieses went back to Leinster Corner for tea, then returned home to the country, leaving the author alone with his wife. Barrie and Mary rarely communicated with each other these days, and any

J. M. Barrie in 1905

reflections that Barrie might have had on the triumph of *Peter Pan* were kept to himself. What was his mood, as he paced up and down his study, contemplating his success? Was he, like Frohman, elated? Perhaps his own description of Captain Hook best described him:

'Hook trod the deck in thought. O man unfathomable. It was his hour of triumph, . . . and knowing as we do how vain a tabernacle is man, could we be surprised if he [was] . . . bellied out by the winds of his success? But there was no elation in his gait, which kept pace with the action of his sombre mind. Hook was profoundly dejected. He was often thus when communing with himself . . . in the quietude of the night. It was because he was so terribly alone.'[12]

When Barrie wrote his Dedication to the five Davies boys in 1928, he expressed a further reason for his dejection:

'I suppose I always knew that I made Peter by rubbing the five of you violently together, as savages with two sticks produce a flame. I am sometimes asked who and what Peter is, but that is all he is, the spark I got from you.

'What a game we had of Peter before we clipped him small to make him fit the boards. He was the longest story on earth, and some of you were not born when that story began and yet were hefty figures before we all saw that the game was up. Do you remember a walled garden at Burpham, and the initiation thereat of Michael when he was six weeks old, and three of you grudged letting him in so young? Have you, Peter, forgotten Tilford, and your cry to the Gods, "Do I just kill one pirate all the time?" Do you remember Marooners' Hut in the haunted groves of Black Lake, and the St Bernard dog in a tiger's mask who so frequently attacked you, and the literary record of that summer, *The Boy Castaways*, which is so much the best and the rarest of this author's works? What was it that eventually made us give to the public in the thin form of a play that which had been woven for ourselves alone? Alas, I know what it was, I was losing my grip. One by one as you swung monkey-wise from branch to branch in the wood of make-believe you reached the tree of knowledge. Sometimes you swung back into the wood, as the unthinking may take a familiar road that no longer leads to home; or you perched ostentatiously on its boughs to please me, pretending that you still belonged; soon you knew it only as the vanished wood, for it vanishes if one needs to look for it. A time came when I saw that George, the most gallant of you all, ceased to believe that he was ploughing woods incarnadine, and with an apologetic eye for me derided the lingering faith of Jack; when even Peter questioned gloomily whether he did not really spend his nights in bed. There were still two who knew no better, but their day was dawning. In these circumstances, I suppose, was begun the writing of the play of Peter, so much the most insignificant part of him. That was a quarter of a century ago, and I clutch my brows in vain to remember whether it was a last desperate throw to retain the five of you for a little longer, or merely a cold decision to turn you into bread and butter. . . . You had played it until you tired of it and tossed it in the air and gored it and left it derelict in the mud and went on your way singing other songs; and then I stole back and sewed some of the gory fragments together with a pen-nib. . . . I talk of dedicating the play to you, but how can I prove it is mine? How ought I to act if some other hand thinks it worth while to contest the cold rights? Cold indeed they are to me now, and Peter is as far away in the woods as that laughter of yours in which he came into being long before he was caught and written down. . . . There is Peter still, but to me he lies sunk in that gay Black Lake.' [13]

9

By the spring of 1905, the Davies family had settled into a comfortable, almost idyllic existence at their new home in the country, Egerton House. Dolly Ponsonby went to visit them in February, writing in her diary:

'*Feb 13.* [1905] To Berkhampstead to stay with Sylvia & Arthur. They have a beautiful Elizabethan house in a street: the outlook is dreary, but nothing could be more perfect than the inside, especially for so large a family. There are huge nurseries & a schoolroom with mullioned windows which occupy the whole length of the rooms – odd-shaped bedrooms with beams & sloping floors – & all so charmingly done as only Sylvia can do things, with harmonious chintzes & lovely bits of Chippendale furniture. It seems very ideal – a cheap school where the elder boys go & a kindergarten for Michael. . . . Spent a happy day with Sylvia, who is as dear as ever she was. I like to see her at luncheon at the head of her long table in the beautiful Hall with its huge windows & great 16th century chimney piece – serving food to 4 beautiful boys who all have perfect manners & are most agreeable companions, especially George. Arthur came down in the evening, looking handsome and severe.'

Arthur and his five sons in 1905. l to r: Jack (aged 10), Michael (5), Peter (8), George (12); Nico (1) is in his father's arms. In *Peter and Wendy*, Barrie described Peter Pan's anguish as he gazed at the Darling family reunited after the children's adventures in the Never Land: 'There could not have been a lovelier sight; but there was none to see it except a strange boy who was staring in at the window. [Peter Pan] had ecstasies innumerable that other children can never know; but he was looking through the window at the one joy from which he must be for ever barred.'

Arthur was in no sense the typical Edwardian father of the Mr Darling variety. Dolly Ponsonby wrote of him, 'He was so tender and gentle with children that I never met one who feared him, in spite of his rather severe though wonderful looks.'[1] He never inflicted corporal punishment on his sons, and on the sole occasion when he was moved to curtail an excess of Jack's obstreperousness with a swift kick up his backside, he totally unmanned the boy by coming to him later in the day and apologizing for what he had done. In many ways, Arthur had a more parental instinct than Sylvia. Jack later gave his own wife the impression that 'Sylvia wore her children as other women wore pearls or fox-furs. They were beautiful children, but beautiful as a background to her beauty. If one of the boys was ill, it was never Sylvia who held their heads or took their temperatures – it was always Arthur who did that kind of thing.'[2] Dolly Ponsonby recalled a passing fragment of conversation indicative of their priorities. 'I remember a funny sort of conservatory through which you passed to go into the little garden – it was filled with plants and flowers by Sylvia. Mary [Hodgson] would put the prams there – and Sylvia said, "I do wish they wouldn't leave the prams here." And Arthur said, "I think the prams are more beautiful than the flowers." '[3]

Egerton House

Simplicity was one of Arthur's great virtues; considerable patience was another, for although he had put twenty-five miles between his family and Leinster Corner, Barrie had begun to make frequent visits to Egerton House. Nor was there any respite in his invitations to Sylvia and her boys. He had already taken Sylvia to Paris on several occasions, and at Easter 1905 he invited her to Dives, a fashionable resort on the Normandy coast. Arthur knew that Sylvia's character was more complex than his own. She had, in Peter's words, an 'innate and underlying tendency towards melancholy, a constant awareness of the *lacrimae rerum*',[4] counterbalanced by an appetite for luxury that Arthur neither shared nor could hope to satisfy. She once teased his sister Margaret's socialist principles by exclaiming, 'I should love to have money. I should like to have gold stays and a scented bed and *real* lace pillows!' Barrie was in a position to gratify those whims. Denis Mackail wrote, 'He was rich; in a way he was extraordinarily innocent; and if Sylvia Davies used him – which she was undoubtedly doing by this time – as a kind of extra nurse, extremely useful fairy-godmother, or sometimes even errand boy, it wasn't in her character to resist that amount of temptation. More, for her, never existed.' Mary Hodgson later told Peter, 'Your mother consented to go to France on condition that one or more of her boys should go with her. Your father was more than willing, where your mother's happiness was concerned.' Jack and Michael therefore accompanied Sylvia to Dives, where Barrie

Michael playing Romeo to Sylvia's Juliet at Dives (JMB)

Jack, Michael, Barrie and Sylvia at L'Hostellerie de Guillaume Le Conquérant, Dives, in April 1905

entertained them in his own inimitable style. He bought Michael a costume so that he could photograph him playing Romeo to Sylvia's Juliet on the balcony of their hotel, then in the evenings took Sylvia to the Casino at Trouville, observing in his notebook: 'Sylvia gambling – loses – gambles children.'

While Barrie was away in France, *Peter Pan* ended its first run at the Duke of York's to make way for *Alice Sit-by-the-Fire* and a one-act curtain-raiser, *Pantaloon*. *Alice* had been the play offered to Frohman as collateral against any losses incurred in staging *Peter Pan*. The outcome was the exact reverse. Despite Ellen Terry's fine performance, *Alice* barely survived its run, whereas the demand for *Peter Pan* was such that Frohman confidently announced that it would re-open the following December, with advance bookings commencing in May.

The prospect of a *Peter Pan* revival, in addition to the forthcoming American production, afforded Barrie the opportunity of revising the play, and he went down to Black Lake in early June to work on it. Mary Barrie had gone to France on a motoring trip with her friend Molly Muir, and although E. V. Lucas and his family were staying at the cottage, Barrie felt in need of a boy's company to spur his creativity. He therefore invited Sylvia and Michael to stay for a fortnight.

The Allahakbarries Cricket Team at Black Lake in 1905, with Michael as their mascot. Back row, l to r: Maurice Hewlett, Barrie, Harry Graham, E. V. Lucas. Front row: H. J. Ford, A. E. W. Mason, Charles Tennyson, C. Turley Smith

Michael was now approaching his fifth birthday, and was, in Peter's opinion, 'with his long curls just about at his most beautiful'. His mind still roamed freely in the wood of make-believe, which gave rise to a constant succession of nightmares that were to plague him throughout his boyhood. His cousin, Daphne du Maurier, remembered her own nanny telling her about these 'terrible nightmares. She told me that Michael used to wake up and think he could see strange people and things coming in through the window, which probably stemmed from Peter Pan.'⁵ Unlike George and Jack, Michael had been brought up to believe in Peter Pan as other children believe in Father Christmas. He knew that 'Uncle Jim' (as he had now begun to call Barrie) had written a play about Peter, and that the Peter in the play was an actress pretending to be a boy, but he also knew that there was a real Peter Pan, who sometimes visited the woods at Black Lake. Michael had been scarcely a year old during 'that strange and terrible summer' of 1901, and this was his first opportunity to explore for himself the haunted groves, primeval forests and South Seas lagoon of *The Boy Castaways*. Barrie had begun to fear that he might have lost his touch with children; in *Tommy and Grizel* he had written of a father in not dissimilar circumstances, who is about to introduce his son to the haunts of his own childhood:

Michael and Barrie on the lawn at Black Lake, July 1905

Michael at Black Lake (JMB)

'To-morrow he was to bring his boy to show him the old lair and other fondly remembered spots, to-night he must revisit them alone. So he set out blithely, but to his bewilderment he could not find the lair. It had not been a tiny hollow where muddy water gathered, he remembered an impregnable fortress full of men whose armour rattled as they came and went, so this could not be the lair. He had taken the wrong way to it, for the way was across a lagoon, up a deep-flowing river, then by horse till the rocky ledge terrified all four-footed things; no, up a grassy slope had never been the way. He came night after night trying different ways, but he could not find the golden ladder, though all the time he knew that the lair lay somewhere over there. . . . Then at last he said sadly to his boy, "I shall never be able to show you the lair, for I cannot find the way to it," and the boy was touched, and he said, "Take my hand, father, and I will lead you to the lair; I found the way long ago for myself."'

Barrie had originally planned to incorporate Black Lake into *Peter Pan*, featuring it as the setting for a mermaid's lagoon scene, but he had never got further than a few preliminary notes. The Lake was, in reality, little more than the 'tiny hollow where muddy water gathered', but with Michael providing the golden ladder, it once again became a South Seas lagoon, and Barrie set to work on a new

(*below*) Michael and Barrie
(*below right*) One of two surviving letters from Barrie to Michael. The remainder, numbering several thousands, were destroyed by Peter in 1952 because they were 'too much'

LEINSTER CORNER,
LANCASTER GATE. W

T CO 22·5091

YLRAED DEVOLOB.
LEAHCIM

EHT ESOR SI DER
ETT TELOIV EULB
YENOH SI TEEWS
DNA OS ERA UOY.

EIRRAB.M.J.

Act III for *Peter Pan*, in which Peter and Wendy are marooned on a
rock after an encounter with Captain Hook and his pirates. The tide
is rising and threatens to drown them both. Peter insists that Wendy
escapes by clinging to the tail of the kite; there is room for two, but
Peter, who is 'never one to choose the easy way', has a strange smile
about his face as he perceives the prospect of a new and tantalizing
adventure. The kite draws Wendy out of sight across the lagoon,
leaving Peter alone on the rock:

> *The waters are lapping over the rock now, and* PETER *knows that it will
> soon be submerged. Pale rays of light mingle with the moving clouds, and
> from the coral grottoes is to be heard a sound, at once the most musical
> and the most melancholy in the Never Land, the mermaids calling to the
> moon to rise.* PETER *is afraid at last, and a tremor runs through him, like
> a shudder passing over the lagoon; but on the lagoon one shudder follows
> another till there are hundreds of them, and he feels just the one. Next
> moment he is standing erect on the rock again.*
>
> PETER (*with that smile on his face and a drum beating in his breast as if he
> were a real boy at last*). To die will be an awfully big adventure.

*   *   *

On November 6th, 1905, *Peter Pan* opened in New York, with Maude
Adams in the title role. The American critics proved, as always, less
averse to Barrie's sentimentality than their British counterparts, and
the magazine *Outlook* welcomed the play 'like a breath of fresh air'.
Mark Twain wrote to Maude Adams: 'It is my belief that *Peter Pan* is
a great and refining and uplifting benefaction to this sordid and
money-mad age; and that the next best play is a long way behind it.'[6]
The American public embraced *Peter Pan* with a fervour that made
its London success seem almost trivial. It became the topic of much
earnest analysis and intellectual vivisection among adults: the play
was treated with a seriousness that mystified and amused its author –
every aspect of it was lapped up and swallowed whole, except
possibly its humour. The Never Land symbolized the New World,
while Peter Pan – the Great White Father – was seen to represent the
Spirit of Youth and Freedom, hailing the children of the Old World
to leave their antiquated nurseries and fly away to the Never Land of
Liberty. Audiences suddenly became 'nursery-conscious, fairy-
conscious, pirate-conscious' and, not least, 'Redskin-conscious',[7]
since Peter's intimacy with Tiger Lily and the Lost Boys' alliance
with the Red Indians was seen to have a special and meaningful
significance. Children, however, were oblivious to all these subtle
profundities: like their English peers, they contented themselves
with falling in love with Peter and pined to fly away with him and
indulge themselves in killing off pirates.

Michael by the shore (JMB)

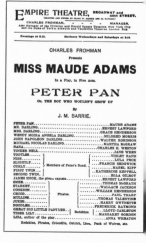

New York programme for *Peter
Pan*

Only a handful of lines were changed for the benefit of the American public: Hook's 'Down with King Edward!' became 'Down with the Stars and Stripes!', and the singing of 'Yankee Doodle' replaced 'God Save the King'. Peter's conceit at his victory over Hook took on an American flavour, and the Napoleonic tableau was expanded as a tribute to Frohman, who had a large bust of the Emperor in his New York office, and wore a Napoleonic ring:

(PETER, *now drunk with glory, pulls down the pirate flag and hoists his own – He marches about the deck in an ecstasy of glee*)

PETER. Oh, I'm a wonder!... Abe Lincoln, are you looking at me! Paul Jones, do you see me! (*He looks up for Abe, and down for Paul*) George Washington, what do you think? I'm the wonderfullest boy that ever was, and I don't say it in boasting, but just because I can't tell a lie!

(*The* BOYS *and* WENDY ... *with exclamations of admiration for him, almost worshipping him ...*)

WENDY. Oh, Peter, is there anything in the world you couldn't do?

PETER. There's nothing, nothing!

ALL. He's Napoleon – Napoleon!

PETER. That's who I am – Napoleon! He was little too!

After recording the longest single engagement in the history of the Empire Theater, Frohman toured Maude Adams in *Peter Pan* across the whole continent of North America. The play had become as a mission to him: he felt it his duty to bring Peter Pan into the life of every child in the country – not just in the large cities, but in remote outposts and 'one-horse towns' of what was then still the Wild West. It was a source of considerable satisfaction to the Davies boys to know that their own humble games of Red Indians, acted out in the comfortable woods of Black Lake, were being performed within the heart of real Indian Territory. For Maude Adams, the creation of Peter in America was no less a vocation than it was for Frohman, and over the next two decades her performance was witnessed by over two million people, from New Yorkers to the shattered populace of San Francisco (where the play opened ten days after the earthquake in 1906), from Southerners in Selma, Alabama, who took exception to Peter Pan's relationship with Tiger Lily, to Canadians in the frozen wastes of Northwest Territory. Frohman's biographers wrote: '*Peter Pan* ... became a nation-wide vogue. Children were named after [him]; articles of wearing-apparel were labeled with his now familiar title; the whole country talked and loved the unforgetable little character who now became not merely a stage figure, but ... the best beloved of all American children.'

While *Peter Pan* played to packed houses on Broadway, the first

Maude Adams (*right*) as Peter Pan

London revival began rehearsals in November 1905. For reasons that have never been made fully clear, Nina Boucicault was dropped from the cast, and replaced by the inferior Cecilia Loftus. Gerald du Maurier again played Mr Darling and Captain Hook, though he had begun to tire of the double role. His daughter Daphne wrote, 'Two performances a day was no joke, in a play that lasted nearly four hours, and playing to crowded houses of screaming, excited children was trying to the voice and to the temper. "There's only one thing I'd rather not be doing," said Gerald in a fit of irritation, "and that's sweeping the floors of a mortuary at a shilling a week." '[8]

Barrie invited Sylvia to Paris in the New Year, but she declined as both Michael and Nico were in bed with colds. He wrote to her on January 3rd, 1906:

> My Dearest Jocelyn,
>   As if I could be angry with you for caring for your children! I don't think it would have been the thing to leave them just now, and we can go to Paris any time.
>   I hope Nicholas is getting better and that Michael is obstreperous once again. How I love that boy. . . . Whenever they are able for P. Pan, it awaits them.
>   Your loving,
>   J.M.B.

Michael received a poem from Barrie a few days later:

A's any Asses that don't love my Mick,
B's what I fling at them, namely a Brick.
C's Combinations, with Michael inside,
D's Normandy's Dives where he once did reside.
E's Evian water, his favourite drink.
F is his Friend – who is that, do you think?
G stands for George, his elderly brother.
H for 14 and 2, that alarmed his mother.
I stands for Imp, which applies to the lot of you.
J is for Jack, who is sometimes too hot for you.
K is for Kads who don't do as you wish,
L's the eel caught at Dives when we went out to fish.
M's your dear Mary, who's always awake,
N's Nick, who's your sweet mother's smallest mistake.
O's the Oil you are told for to take like a man,
P stands for Peter, and Peter for Pan.
Q are the Questions Mick asks for to pose me,
R my Replies, which are vain, for he knows me.
S stands for Sylvia, Michael's delight,

Nico and Michael (JMB)

T is his Tu'penny when tucked in at night.
U is U silly who are reading this letter,
V is your Vanity, you couldn't do better.
W's old Wilk, who is still trouncing boys,
X is the X's sent Mick with his toys.
Y is the Yawns I give till we meet,
Z are the Zanies who are not at his feet.

J.M.B.

Michael's illness persisted throughout the early spring, and as he was unable to come up to London and see *Peter Pan*, Barrie and Frohman took *Peter Pan* to see him, complete with scenery and a special programme printed for the occasion:

'The performance [of *Peter Pan*] that is most vivid to me (and cannot be quite forgotten by you) is the one we presented to Michael in his bed. It was in the first or second year of Peter, and as Michael could not go to it, we took it to Michael, far away in the country, an array of vehicles almost as glorious as a travelling circus; the leading parts were played by the youngest children in the London company, and Michael, aged five, looked on solemnly from his bed and never smiled once. That was my only appearance in a professional performance, . . . and a copy of the special programme which I still have (my favourite programme of the play) shows that I was thought so meanly of that my name is printed in smaller letters than the others.'[9]

Peter gave a description of the play in a letter to his grandfather, the Reverend John Llewelyn Davies, who was going to be eighty the following day. Peter himself was celebrating his own ninth birthday:

Egerton House, Berkhamsted.
Feb. 25th [1906]

Dear Grandfather,
    I hope you will have a nice birthday, it is my birthday today, and although I am not quite so old as you, I hope to be soon. . . . Some actors and actresses from Peter Pan came down on Father's birthday in two large motor cars, to act the nursery. Peter Pan is about a boy [who] ran away from home the day he was born, and lived in the Never-never-never-Land. One day he came back to the house of some people called the Darlings, and in the night took away the three children away [*sic*]. The father was so sorry he had taken the dog, Nana, out of the room that he lived in the kennel. Then

one day they came back, and Wendy, the girl, was allowed
to go to Peter, every Spring cleaning.

Wishing you many happy returns of the day, from Peter.

P.S. I am sending you a programme of Peter Pan in
Michael's nursery.

Nico Davies wrote in 1975: 'There was never the remotest feeling
that Uncle Jim liked A better than B, though in due course we all
knew that George and Michael were The Ones – George because he
had started it all, and Michael . . . because he was the cleverest of us,
the most original, the potential genius. . . . I haven't the skill to
answer* about J.M.B. being 'in love' with George & Michael.
Roughly, yes – I would agree: he was in love with each of them: as he
was in love with my mother: when you come to Mary Ansell it's a
different 'feeling': . . . for myself, Peter & Jack at our different times
different again – nearer to normal deep affection.'

Barrie's letter to Peter on his ninth birthday was as affectionate as
usual:

25 Feb. 1906.

My dear Peter,

Hurrah for your birthday. Nine years ago the world was a
dreary blank. It was like the round of tissue paper the clown
holds up for the lady in the circus to leap through, and then
you came banging through it with a Houp-la! and we have
all been busy ever since.

I expect twenty years from now there will be a half
holiday given at the Berkhampstead School on the 25 of Feb.
because it is the birthday of the famous pupil, Mr (now Lieut-
General) Peter Davies, V.C.

I am to get a knife tomorrow to send you. I expect it will
draw blood before you lose it. If you are still on friendly terms
with Primus &c, give them my comps.

Your loving friend,
J.M.B.

It would be wrong to suppose that all Barrie's time and energy was
devoted to the Davies family. A glance at Denis Mackail's lengthy

*I had written to Nico asking him whether he felt that Barrie had been platonically in love with
George and Michael. In a later letter he wrote, 'I'm 200% certain there was never a desire to
kiss (other than the cheek!), though things obviously went through his mind – often producing
magic – which never go through the more ordinary minds of such as myself. . . . All I can say for
certain is that I . . . never heard one word or saw one glimmer of anything approaching
homosexuality or paedophilia: had he had either of these leanings in however slight a symptom
I would have been aware. He was an innocent – which is why he could write *Peter Pan*.'

George, aged 12, with his rabbit,
'Mr' (JMB)

(*right*) Programme specially
printed for PETER PAN in
Michael's Nursery. (*top right*)
Sylvia and Michael (JMB)

Peter (JMB)

PETER PAN

IN

MICHAEL'S

NURSERY.

February 20,
1906.

By COMMAND of
MICHAEL

Mr. CHARLES FROHMAN presents
Scenes from

. Peter Pan .

By J. M. BARRIE and ELA Q. MAY.

To be played in Michael's Nursery at

EGERTON HOUSE, BERKHAMSTED,

On Feb. 20th, 1906,

By the Growing Up Company,

From the Duke of New York's Theatre, London.

———

Peter Pan -	Miss WINIFRED GEOGHEGAN
	AND
Mr. Darling - - -	Master LESLIE OSWALD
	AND
Mrs. Darling - - -	Miss PHYLLIS BEADON
	AND
John Napoleon Darling -	Master HARRY DUFF
	AND
Michael Nicholas Darling	Miss GERALDINE WILSON
	AND
Nana - - - -	Master MARINI
	AND
Liza - - - -	Miss ALICE ROBINSON
	BUT
Wendy Moira Angela Darling	Miss ELA Q. MAY

Huge Engagement of
Winifred Geoghegan.

Delirious Engagement of
Phyllis Beadon,
the celebrated Mother.

The Management have the honour to announce
that Mr. J. M. BARRIE will be the Cabman.

Masters Duff, Oswald & Marini
will positively play.

Engagement Extraordinaire of
Geraldine Wilson
AND
Alice Robinson.

Stupendous Attraction of
Ela Q. May,
who will perform in her own play.
and
as
if
all
this
were
not
enough,

Pauline Chase,
The Twin.
The Twin.
The Twin.

biography shows that these early months of 1906 were, as ever, crammed with diverse activity: organizing a banquet in honour of Frederick Greenwood's seventy-fifth birthday; wooing the friendship of Captain Robert Falcon Scott, who had recently returned from his first Antarctic expedition; trying to protect his agent and friend, Arthur Addison Bright, from prosecution for misappropriating £28,000 of his clients' earnings – including £16,000 belonging to Barrie; following his fellow writer A. E. W. Mason on election campaigns (Mason was standing for election as Liberal M.P. for Coventry, and Barrie was noting down the tricks of the political trade for use in his next play, *What Every Woman Knows*); becoming godfather to one of the Lost Boys in the cast of *Peter Pan*, the American actress, Pauline Chase; organizing and subscribing to numerous charities (he was wealthy enough by now to be generous to the point of prodigality, helping virtually anyone who cared to plead a worthy case); accompanying his wife to her mother's funeral; writing a couple of one-act plays: *Josephine*, a political burlesque lampooning Joseph Chamberlain, and *Punch*, in which he satirized Bernard Shaw – both plays written, rehearsed, performed (and taken off) within the space of six weeks; corresponding with Frohman about the American production of *Alice Sit-by-the-Fire*, which was to star Ethel Barrymore; writing to Maude Adams – 'I feel sure you are the most entrancing little boy that ever was by sea or shore, and I hear of things you do in the part which are so absolutely what Peter did that it makes me gay. ... I *must* see you as Peter, and so, dear little Maudie, good-night';[10] and, in the same week, flirting by post with one of the most beautiful women in England, Her Grace the Duchess of Sutherland:

Pauline Chase as one of the Lost Boys (First Twin), doing her famous pillow dance. In 1906 she became Barrie's god-daughter and played Peter Pan annually until 1914

Dear Duchess,
    May I come to dinner on Thursday or Friday? I am dining beside a duchess on Sunday. I want to come very much either of these days. On Sunday I am dining with a duchess. I was away for the week-end at Berkhamsted, and next week-end I am dining with a duchess. I hope you are all well in your sphere of life. What ups and downs we have. For instance, next Sunday I am
                    Yours sincerely
                    J.M.B.

It was to prove the beginning of a long flirtation, not merely with Millicent, Duchess of Sutherland, but with the aristocracy as a whole, and was to earn him, from some, the label of a snob. For the moment, however, he retained his sense of humour and purpose, for though the dinner engagement was doubtless a pleasurable affair, Barrie was also measuring up Her Grace for future characterization in *What Every Woman Knows*.

Towards the end of May, Barrie once again invited Sylvia to Paris, and this time she accepted. Arthur wrote to his sister Margaret at Kirkby Lonsdale:

Margaret Llewelyn Davies, founder member of the Women's Co-operative Guild and close friend of Virginia Woolf

> Egerton House,
> Berkhamsted.
> May 26th, 1906.
>
> Dearest Margaret,
>   I had been hoping to manage a visit to Kirkby with Michael this Whitsuntide, to fit in with Sylvia's outing, but I am doomed to spend Whitsuntide less agreeably – in lying up for a small operation. I have a slight swelling in the side of the face, which is beyond the dentist's skill, and on his advice I consulted an expert in cheek and jaw. He is going to perform on Friday, and I shall stay at a nursing place till the following Tuesday. Probably the cause of the trouble is the root of an old dead tooth, possibly a minute fragment of a tooth long ago pulled out. . . . There is no ground for anxiety, but I can imagine pleasanter ways of spending money in June. . . . I expect to be more or less recovered after a week.
>   Sylvia will probably leave with her friends for Paris on Tuesday (June 5) if I am fit to be left. [*Margaret has scrawled her opinion in the margin*: 'I'm sure she won't!'] Crompton is kindly willing to come here on that day with me. . . .
>
> > Yours affectly,
> > A.Ll.D.

Sylvia's dilemma was resolved for her by Barrie's agent, Arthur Addison Bright, who had gone to Switzerland, telling his client that 'the mountain air would give him sleep'.[11] Faced with the humiliation of imminent prosecution, Bright shot himself, and Barrie was obliged to travel to Lucerne and identify the body. He blamed himself for the tragedy, believing that his own vagueness over money matters had been Bright's temptation – he had not even noticed the £16,000 missing until it was pointed out to him. He contributed a short obituary in *The Times* on June 1st, in which he described Bright as a man 'so beautiful and modest [in] nature that it may be said of him, he had never time to be much interested in himself he was so interested in his friends'. The irony was presumably unintentional.

On the same day, June 1st, Sylvia wrote to Arthur's sister Margaret telling her that 'Arthur seems pretty well and . . . I hope to get him home soon', but the following day Arthur was giving more ominous news:

12, Beaumont St., W.

June 2, 1906.

Dearest Margaret,

I am sorry to say that I have bad news. The swelling in my face turns out on investigation not to be an abscess, as was hoped, but a growth. It is of a very serious kind, called sarcoma, and requires a grave operation. . . . I am afraid it means removing half the upper jaw and palate. . . . Poor Sylvia! I have told her everything except the name of the disease and the details of the operation. She is brave and infinitely kind and dear. After the operation I shall be incapacitated for about 6 weeks, and unable to speak properly for 3 or 4 months – and there will always be an impediment in my speech. I think of our future and the boys.

We shall be very glad if you will come up on Monday and help us through this trying time – to me 'glad life's arrears of pain, darkness and toil.' My 43 years, and especially the last 14, leaves me no ground of complaint as to my life. But this needs fortitude. We both try our best.

My love to Father.

Your affect. brother,

A.Ll.D.

Dolly Ponsonby wrote in her diary:

'*Monday 4 June*. Got a letter from M.D. [Margaret Llewelyn Davies] to tell me the most *tragic* news about Arthur D. – That he has a terrible disease, sarcoma in the face, & will have to have part of his jaw & roof of his mouth removed – It is simply *unbelievable*! . . . That splendid, selfless, brave Arthur, who has slaved & worked all these years – to have his career absolutely changed if not *wrecked* by this – oh, it is *incomprehensible*!'

Barrie was in the midst of sorting out the chaos created by Bright's suicide when he heard the news of Arthur's impending operation. In *Tommy and Grizel* he had written, 'A burning house and Grizel among the flames, and he would have been the first on the ladder.' If ever Barrie had his chance to show Sylvia and Arthur what they and their boys meant to him, it was now. He immediately dropped everything, cancelled all other plans, assumed full responsibility for meeting the enormous medical fees involved in securing Arthur the

One of dozens of letters sent out by Barrie to Arthur's friends and colleagues. This one, to Sir Charles Dilke, reads: 'Dear Sir, Mr Arthur Llewelyn Davies has asked me to let a few friends know of his present condition. Only a week ago he knew that he was suffering from the disease called Sarcoma'. The letter continues for a further four pages, concluding 'He has been quite splendid all through this painful time.'

finest treatment available, then took up a more or less permanent vigil in his hospital room, performing any task or request that Sylvia and Arthur might ask of him, however menial or mundane. Before undergoing the operation, Arthur wrote to his father on June 4th: 'Barrie has been wonderful to us – we look on him as a brother.' Peter Davies commented in the family *Morgue*:

'J.M.B. stepped in to play the leading part; and played it in the grand manner. . . . I can sympathise in a way with the point of view that it was the last straw for Arthur that he should have had to accept charity from the strange little genius who had become such an increasing irritation to him in recent years. But on the whole I disagree. We don't really know how deep the irritation went; and even if it went deep, I am convinced that the kindness and devotion of which J.M.B. gave such overwhelming proof from now on, far more than outweighed all that, and that the money and promise of future financial responsibility he was so ready with – and with what charm and tact he must have overcome any resistance! – were an incalculable comfort to the doomed Arthur as well as to Sylvia in her anguish.'

Crompton, Arthur's younger brother, wrote to their father at Kirkby Lonsdale on June 8th, giving a report of the operation: 'They removed his cheek bone – apparently had intended to do so all along. . . . After coming round he is likely to be in some pain, and they will give him morphia as soon as possible. . . . His courage and serenity was so great that it gave others courage, I felt – and instead of requiring help he seemed able to give it.' Barrie telegraphed Arthur's father that evening – 'HE IS CONSCIOUS NOW AND SYLVIA SAT [AN] HOUR WITH HIM' – then stayed by his bedside through the night, reading him the newspaper or simply holding his hand. Arthur was unable to talk, his face being completely bandaged, but he managed to communicate with Barrie by making spidery notes:

Crompton Llewelyn Davies. Like his brother Theodore, who drowned in 1905, Crompton was one of the most remarkable men of his generation. 'He combined wit, passion, wisdom, scorn, gentleness, and integrity, in a degree that I have never known equalled' wrote Bertrand Russell in his *Autobiography*. 'In 1921 it was Crompton who drafted the treaty of peace that established Irish self-government, though this was never publicly known.'

Arthur's note of 'things I think about'

Among the things I think about

Michael going to school
Porthgwarra and S's blue dress
Burpham garden
Kirkby view across valley . . .
Jack bathing
Peter answering chaff
Nicholas in the garden
George always

While Arthur slept, Barrie made notes of his own:

—*The 1,000 Nightingales*. A hero who is dying. 'Poor devil, he'll be dead in six months' . . . He in his rooms awaiting end – schemes abandoned – still he's a man, dying a man. . . . Everything going splendidly for him (love &c) when audience hears of his doom.

—There's an ironical little God smiling at us. Favours – then gives twist of string & down we fall.

Arthur

10

A week after the operation, Arthur's bandages were removed from his face. When Gerald du Maurier visited the nursing home that evening, Sylvia broke down in the corridor outside Arthur's room, weeping on her brother's shoulder and crying, 'They've spoilt my darling's face.' [1] Dolly Ponsonby visited Arthur the following day, June 14th:

'Went to see Arthur Davies in a Nursing Home. . . . He looked very altered but with his usual determination insisted upon speaking in spite of having no roof to his mouth, or teeth, both of which he will have later. In spite of this I understood nearly everything he said. He tried to smile & made a remark as I left about my being beautiful in his old, dry, chaffy way; it was so pathetic. But to see Sylvia tending this poor maimed creature was something I shall never forget. She seemed a living emblem of love & tenderness & sorrow – Stroking his hair & his hand, & looking unutterable love at him & so beautiful – it seemed to have completed her. She broke down a little outside, & we talked about it, but she is brave, so brave – it was wonderful to see her. . . . Little Barrie was of course there, lurking in the background!'

Arthur wrote to Peter that evening:

'Mr Barrie is now sitting here with me reading the newspaper, and Mother has gone for a little drive in the motor with Mrs Barrie. Don't you think Mr Barrie is a very good friend to all of us? Goodbye now, my dear Peter and all my dear boys. I don't forget whose birthday it is on Saturday.'

Saturday's birthday was Michael's, and Arthur wrote to him from the nursing home:

My very dear birthday boy Michael,
    How I wish I could see you with my own eyes on your birthday, when you are really 6 years old. But I can only wish you many happy returns by a letter, and send you my dear love, and a pencil as a little birthday present for you. . . . Perhaps when I am well enough to come back you will take me to see some more cricket matches. I am going to have quite a long holiday, and shall be able to take you to school every morning. . . .
    Now goodbye my dearest 6 year old boy, and I hope you will have a very very very jolly birthday.
        From Your affectionate Father.

Sylvia also wrote to Michael:

For June the 16th,
My Michael's 6th birthday.

I am coming to see you & I will bring my present to you
my dear darling. I want so to tell you about father who is so
brave & you will be so proud that you are his little son.

I don't like being away from you on your dear birthday
but I shall see you in a few hours. Oh my little Michael
won't it be nice when we are all together again. Father *does
so want* to be back with his sons. He is sleeping now, & I am
being very still & writing this letter by his bed.

Mr Barrie is our fairy prince, much the best fairy prince
that was ever born because he is *real*.

Loving Mother

Last page of Sylvia's birthday
letter to Michael

Arthur wrote again to Michael on June 27th:

My dear Michael,

Here is my last letter of all before coming home to
Berkhamsted and my boys. We are coming all the way in Mr
Barrie's motor car, if it is fine, and we shall arrive in good
time for tea. I want very much to see your motor car and
Peter's stone roach, as well as Nicko's musical wheel-barrow.
And I wonder whether there will be any good songs to be
heard which I have never heard before. If there are it will be
altogether a fine homecoming for Mother and me. After tea
tomorrow you will take me carefully for a walk all round the
garden, and show me all the flowers which have come up
since we went away? . . .

Goodbye now, my dear boy. My love to all my boys, not
forgetting dear Nicko.

From your affectionate Father.

Michael and Nico in the walled
garden at Egerton House (JMB)

Arthur also wrote to his sister Margaret, who was staying at Egerton
House looking after the boys, asking her to send him the sole
surviving copy of *The Boy Castaways*. He had thought the book
rather a puerile extravagance at the time Barrie gave it to him –
indeed he had almost instantly lost his copy on a train – but now that
he was separated from his boys, the photographs brought him a
measure of comfort.

Sylvia had paved the way for Arthur's homecoming by repeatedly
asking Margaret to warn the boys of their father's 'poor face and
voice' – 'You will talk to the little boys and tell them how they can
help me and how they must listen well when he talks.' During the
course of the operation it had been necessary to remove the tear-duct

from Arthur's eye, with the result that he was unable to control the flow of tears – a somewhat harrowing sight for his boys, and one that he tried to hide by wearing a brown patch. A week after his return to Berkhamsted, Sylvia wrote to Margaret at Kirkby Lonsdale: 'He and I walked to the fields yesterday and watched George at cricket, and he was not too tired afterwards. . . . The little boys are really wonderfully good, and so far . . . all is well.' Arthur returned to London on July 5th to be measured for the artificial jaw that was to be fitted to facilitate his speech. Barrie wrote to Sylvia from Black Lake Cottage the same day:

> Dearest Jocelyn,
>   I am conceiving you both in London today and I fear Arthur is having a bad time. If they put something into his mouth what I am afraid of is that it may seem pretty right at the time and gradually become unendurable after he is home. . . . I seem so far away from you now, and feel that you are not so safe as when I am by. That is the feeling that makes you in your heart hate all of us who propose to take a few of the five away for a 'season' (as Jack puts it), and it is strange that I should feel so now about Arthur but I do. . . . It has been a terrible month to yourself, I had so hoped that Jocelyn would always be spared such a time. 'Sylvia in her blue dress.'
>   My love to Arthur and to his brown patch, and to dear Jocelyn.
> Your
J.M.B.

Peter commented in the *Morgue*: 'I am not sure that the ghastly plate, or artificial jaw, isn't the most dreadful element in the whole sad story. It must have been a nightmare, and so much seemed to depend on it, and it so soon became impossible to wear, as J.M.B. had foreseen.'

The annual Rustington holiday was spent at Cudlow House, which Emma du Maurier had rented for August. Whereas in previous years Barrie's presence at Rustington smacked of the uninvited guest, he was now accepted as an integral part of the family. Arthur no longer referred to him as 'Sylvia's friend' in his letters to Margaret, but as 'Jimmy'. He wrote to her on August 6th:

'We have had plenty of bathing, and the boys play endless cricket and lawn tennis in the garden. Just now we have an invasion by some friends of Jimmy's; Nicholson, an artist, and his family, one of them

Michael, dressed as Peter Pan, playing up to Barrie's Captain Hook

Michael, aged 6, dressed as Peter Pan and photographed by Barrie in July 1906

being of an age for George, and a large game of cricket is going on in the garden. . . . The sea has become thoroughly warm, and we all enjoy the water very much, except Sylvia, who has not yet completed her bathing costume.'

'Nicholson' was William Nicholson, who had designed the scenery and costumes for *Peter Pan*, and had brought with him a special Peter Pan costume requested by Barrie for Michael. The gift had an ulterior motive. Barrie had started to conceive vague notions of commissioning a statue of Peter Pan, and he wanted to give the prospective sculptor his own ideal vision of Peter on which to base the effigy. The result was a series of photographs of Michael, his eyes blazing with an energy that became entirely lost when translated into bronze six years later.

Dolly Ponsonby visited the Rustington household on August 17th, writing in her diary:

'Went to see Sylvia in the evening. She is an amazing creature, certainly beauty & charm could not go further, & now she is more beautiful with a touch of sadness in her face, & her wonderful blue garments. She talked so naturally of all her hopes & fears regarding Arthur, . . . [who] is more pathetic than he was – it gives one a terrible twinge to see him with his poor maimed face, & always escaping from people. Mr Barrie is always with him, a nurse to the children & an extraordinarily tactful & helpful companion to Sylvia & Arthur – though his moods like those of most genius types appear to be a little trying.'

Peter Davies wrote in his *Morgue*:

'The presence of J.M.B. at Cudlow House throughout these holidays was a queerish business, when you come to think of it: as odd a variation of the *ménage à trois* as ever there was, one would say. I think by now Arthur had surrendered utterly and was reconciled, for all sorts of reasons. But how strange the mentality of J.M.B., whose devotion to Sylvia seems to have thrived on her utter devotion to Arthur, as well as on his own admiration for him. It would be misleading to call his devotion more dog-like than man-like; there was too much understanding and perception in it – not to mention the element of masterfulness. And how about Mary Barrie meanwhile? I suspect that on the whole the state of affairs suited her well enough, and I say this in no disparaging sense.'

Arthur wrote to his sister Margaret on September 6th from Cudlow House:

Sylvia and Michael, who had a terror of water, though he fought to overcome it (JMB)

Fishing at Fortingal, August
1906. L to r: George, Jack,
Sylvia, Michael, Peter. Arthur is
standing in the background (JMB)

'We are just at the end of our stay here, having failed to get an extra week for which we asked. We have succumbed to an invitation to go to Scotland with Jimmy for the close of the holidays. First the scheme was to take George and Jack only, then we were unwilling to abandon Peter, and lastly Michael has, inevitably, been included. Nicholas so far remains out of the cast. We are to stay at a small village called Fortingal, in Glen Lyon, 2½ miles from Loch Tay among high mountains, . . . and surrounded by burns in which the boys will fish. They are all prodigiously excited at the prospect. . . . The holiday [at Rustington] has altogether been entirely successful.'

While in Scotland, Barrie received a letter from Captain Scott, telling him that he was thinking about another expedition to the Antarctic; he also asked Barrie if he knew of a boy who could fill a vacancy at Osborne Naval College. Barrie replied on September 6th:

My dear Scott,
    I know the right boy so well that it is as if I had been waiting for your letter. He is the second son of Mrs Llewelyn Davies [i.e. Jack] and so a grandson of du Maurier; from his earliest days he has seemed to all of us cut out for a sailor, he is really a fine intelligent quick boy with the open

143

fearless face that attracts at first sight and in view of the
future he already assumes a rolling gait. His people were
meaning to try and get him a nomination for the exams next
March (he is the right age) and so you can imagine how
grateful they are to you. Mrs Davies sends you such
messages that I decline to forward them. . . . Your invitation
[*to accompany Scott on a Naval manoeuvre*] is really the only
one I have had for years that I should much like to accept. I
can't, I mustn't, I have been doing practically nothing for so
long. But I know it means missing the thing I need most – to
get into a new life for a bit. . . . Altho', mind you, I would
still rather let everything else go hang and enrol for the
Antarctic. Everybody should do something once. I want to
know what it is really like to be alive. I should probably
double up the first day. So they say, but in my heart I beg to
inform you I am not so sure. I chuckle with joy to hear all
the old hankerings are coming back to you. I feel you have
got to go again, and I too keep an eye open for the man with
the dollars. It is one of the few things he can do with his
money that *can't* do harm. . . .

Sylvia and Jack, aged 11 (JMB)

> Yours ever,
> J. M. Barrie

Arthur wrote to Barrie on his return to Berkhamsted:

Dear Jimmy,
    You have done wonderful things for us since the beginning
of June – most, of course, during June and also in the last
week – but at Rustington also you made all the difference to
the success and pleasantness of the holiday. We all hope to
see you soon and often.
> Yours
> A.Ll.D.

Two days later, Arthur visited his specialist, Roughton, who
informed him that the tumour had spread to another part of his face,
but that no further operation would be possible. He wrote to
Margaret on September 18th:

'I asked how far off the end would be, but he could not say – perhaps 6
months or a year. . . . I have thought it best to tell poor Sylvia. . . .
She hardly realises what a support the boys will be to her as time goes
on. It is all very terrible for her. . . . Of course what I care about now
is to give her all the support I can, and also, if the worst comes, to
leave her with memories of the remaining time which will afterwards
be a comfort rather than an unhappiness. I myself have consolations

and even occasions of poignant happiness such as could not come to any man who had no wife and children. My burden is far less heavy than Sylvia's.'

Barrie was told the news, and wrote to Sylvia on September 20th:

> I mean to come down tomorrow: I may not be before seven
> or thereabout, as Mr Boucicault is pressing for a meeting in
> the afternoon [about *Peter Pan* rehearsals]. I shall bring a
> bag, and stay the night or not, just as you like. I am thinking
> of you and Arthur all the time. I am still full of hope.
>
> Your loving
J.M.B.

On the same day Arthur was writing to his father, who was now over eighty and in failing health himself:

Arthur's father, the Reverend John Llewelyn Davies, 1906

> Dearest Father,
>   Whatever may be in store for me, I hope I shall bear it as
> befits the son of a brave & wise man. I am troubled for
> myself, but much more for Sylvia. She is brave to a degree
> that I should have thought hardly possible, busy all day with
> endless activities & kindnesses for me & for the boys, & all
> the time the burden is almost heavier than she can bear.
> Besides her sympathy for me, she shrinks terribly from the
> loneliness after I am gone. She will have many good friends,
> but scarcely any one on whom she feels that she can really
> rely. I can see the end to what I may have to endure, but she
> at present seems to face the prospect of endless misery, &
> only sees that she must go on for the sake of the boys. I can
> foresee a not unhappy life for her in the future, with the boys
> growing up round her, but she cannot now see this. She &
> all the boys were never so desirable to me as now, & it is
> hard if I have to leave them. But whatever comes after death,
> whether anything or nothing, to die & leave them is not
> like what it would be if I were away from them in life,
> conscious that I could not see them or talk to them or help
> them.
>   Barrie's unfailing kindness & tact are a great support to
> us both. . . .
>
> Your affect. son,
A.Ll.D.

For a while it looked as though there had been a false alarm, and Arthur apologized to Margaret for 'having made a hullabaloo about nothing and having caused the family needless trouble'. Hope of an improvement was founded on faith in a new form of electrical treatment. The family clutched at the straw, and a semblance of normality returned; Barrie came down to Berkhamsted on Guy Fawkes Day, bringing box loads of fireworks for the boys. 'I shall have a good look at them before they are lighted,' wrote Sylvia to Margaret, 'Jimmy is sure to light them at the wrong end.' Michael also wrote to his aunt – his first surviving literary effort:

Nico, aged 3, at Egerton House (JMB)

> Dear Aunt Margaret, Uncle Maurice has been, and I have got an Acorn. and I am going to plant it, and I am going to plant a tulip bulb. and Mr Barrie has got a cold. and Jack has had a Football match and he did not win. and thank you for the Post cards, and I cant say the difficult word that Gandfather [sic] told me. from Michael with love from Nik-o.

But the optimism was short-lived. By late November, Arthur was telling his sister that the artificial jaw had become quite hopeless, and that he was now obliged to take morphia at night to ease his pain. Nevertheless he managed to write cheerfully on November 26th:

'We have been full of birthdays lately – Nicholas (aged 3) on Saturday, and Sylvia and also Smee [their dog], on Sunday. The boys got up a little acting of a humble sort. Michael much the best, though Jack also has some idea. Michael [aged six] reads to me regularly now, reversing our previous parts, and his reading is very clear and full of extraordinary spirit.'

Dolly Ponsonby's diary records the onset of the final phase in Arthur's suffering:

'*Dec 5th*. [1906] I left in the middle [of a dinner party] to go down to Berkhampstead where I spent the saddest most terrible night I can remember. Suffice it to say that Arthur Davies cannot live & told me so – but had not told Sylvia.
'*Friday 6th*. Returned to London after luncheon. It was awful having to leave him & I longed to go down on my knees to him & tell him I thought him the noblest most heroic being that ever lived – but it couldn't be & I had to persist in telling him he would live. Sylvia is an example too of everything a woman should be – Her *care* of him & of the children, her patience & lovingness & strength – there is no one like her.'

Peter Pan had now opened for its third London season, with Pauline Chase as the new Peter, and Arthur asked if Margaret could take the

Wendy (Hilda Trevelyan) and Peter Pan (Pauline Chase) on Marooners' Rock in the Never Land. 'The difference between [Peter] and the other boys . . . was that they knew it was make-believe, while to him make-believe and true were exactly the same thing.' (*Peter and Wendy*)

boys to see the play, though she personally disliked it. 'It would be dreadful if the children lost their pleasures', he told her in a conversation note. Like hundreds of other children, Michael wrote to Peter Pan afterwards:[2]

> Dear Peter Pan thank you very much For
> the Post Card you Gave me I am Longing
> For some more of them and I have sent
> you A picture of the Little House For
> you And Nik-o thinks he can fly But he
> Only tumbles about ~~his~~ he sends his Love.
> From MICHAEL

There was a second *Peter Pan* triumph this year: Barrie's publishers, Hodder and Stoughton, had extracted the Peter Pan chapters from *The Little White Bird* and published them separately as *Peter Pan in Kensington Gardens*, with fifty illustrations by Arthur Rackham. Barrie wanted to pay tribute to the Llewelyn Davies family by dedicating the book to them, but his complimentary gesture must have been somewhat painful to the dying Arthur:

TO SYLVIA AND ARTHUR LLEWELYN DAVIES
AND THEIR BOYS (MY BOYS)

Peter Davies wrote to Mary Hodgson in 1946: 'Would you say that, assuming father never really liked J.M.B., he nevertheless became much fonder of him towards the end, and was much comforted in his last months by the thought that J.M.B.'s money would be there to help mother and all of us after his death?' Mary replied, 'I understood that your Aunt Margaret had been asked by your Father – and could not see her way to accept the responsibility. That J.M.B. was put forward as being more than willing. Your Father acquiesced to the inevitable, with astounding Grace and Fortitude. It would help your Mother – and further than that he neither desired nor was *able* to go.' Jack, in later years, was of a similar opinion. He disagreed with Peter's conclusion that Arthur's gratitude to Barrie far outweighed his resentment: 'I couldn't at all agree that Father did anything but most cordially dislike the Bart. I felt again and again that his letters simply blazoned the fact that he was doing all he could, poor man, to put up a smoke screen and leave Mother a little less sad and try to show her he didn't grudge the Bart being hale and hearty and rich enough to take over the business. . . . I've no doubt at all he was thankful, but he was a proud man, and it must have been extraordinarily bitter for him. And altogether too soft and saintlike to like the little man as well.'

Mary Hodgson carrying Nico to bed (JMB)

Arthur was now unable to speak, and once again had to resort to making notes. Most of them represent fragmentary scraps of conversation, and were preserved after Arthur's death by his sister Margaret:

Barrie, George and Jack

—I think I've had the last of the quacks today. I do it because Sylvia may think afterwards I have not tried everything.
—I think it will be best for Sylvia to leave [Egerton House] as soon as possible & with George & Jack away, she will like to be in London I'm pretty sure – a small house in London. I can't talk about these things to her now – she doesn't like it. Her ways may not be quite understood by our family.
—George understands pretty well how serious it is. He does not know what to say & does not like to say nothing, but I expect he knows I understand. He is very understandable.
—*Dear* Jimmy.
—I just like to see you.
—I put all the burdens on you because you can help better than anyone.
—Perhaps better that none of them should see me afterwards? Impression so given never disappears – not the sort of impression one wishes to be permanent.
—Do write more things other than plays.

Peter Davies commented in his *Morgue*:

' "Do write more things other than plays." On the face of it a peculiar remark to address to J.M.B., and one which the world would be un-likely to endorse. He was at that time . . . the most praised as well as the most successful dramatist alive. But I think that, nevertheless, it was intended as a compliment, and may even have been accepted as one. I think that Arthur had heard so much that was wise and good and true said by that strange little Scotch genius, that he felt his plays, and indeed his writings generally, did less than justice to the brain that conceived them. The whimsicality that so many people have found intolerable in J.M.B.'s work and which was no doubt of the essence of his genius and primarily responsible for his achievements and success, was something almost beyond his control as soon as he had a pen or pencil in his hand. His conversation was often on a much higher plane, and doubtless rose to its highest in his talks with the dying Arthur.'

In another series of conversations notes, Arthur wrote to Margaret: 'Jimmy thinks George ought to be told everything.' Later he wrote, 'Told George – said probably, tho' always a chance. Asked him if he

would like to see Mr B[arrie] or me. Yes.' In Margaret's handwriting: 'Arthur said all had gone wrong – better talk to G[eorge] of
other things. . . . Death was the end of a glorious thing, Life. Life
would be nothing without death or the risk of it. Had never thought
death shd be a gloomy thing. Peter had seen this. How Michael and
he were discussing what gift they would like best. Michael said not to
die – but Peter saw it in the way Arthur did.'

Barrie went to Ireland with Frohman at the end of March 1907, for
the opening of *Peter Pan* in Dublin. He wrote to Sylvia on April 1st
from the Shelbourne Hotel:

> How I wish I could say to you that now I am going up to
> Arthur, it is the only thing I seem to want to do nowadays.
> He lies there like a wounded soldier and is the gallantest
> figure any of us is ever likely to see. I always had a passion
> for simplicity, and I feel sure now that there can be nothing
> very heroic or loveable without it. I hope you are taking your
> medicine and making faces at it, and I know your dear heart
> beats brave as ever. On Wednesday evening sometime you
> will see me minus my waistcoat and probably not well
> brushed.
>   Ever your loving
>   J.M.B.

Barrie returned to Berkhamsted and resumed his post at Arthur's
bedside. The dying man communicated with conversation notes,
telling him that he now suffered from nightmares:

Sylvia (JMB)

—Vague fancies . . . that I was going to have, or perhaps had had, an
infant. All this was vaguely connected with thirst and pain in my face.
—I'm quite happy. This last 6 months has been the happiest of my
life. I've received so much kindness. Bless my bones.
—It is in all the little things that character is shown. Anyone can face
the big things.
—[*After morphia*] This is the most blessed time in the day.
—Hurrah for Rustington and Fortingal!
—What have the boys been doing? I leave it entirely to you, subject
to Sylvia's wishes. He's been a wonderful son – you can always tell
him that.
—When you go, bring me Matthew Arnold – especially 'The Way of
Peace' . . . But don't bother this evening if difficult to find.
—I don't think anyone has ever done so much for me.
—Read this now, about the Child, Nurse & Death.
—Give me your hand.

Barrie's own notebook entries continued, prompted by his conversations with Arthur:

—*1,000 N's* Dying man's fears to friend that he may break down & blubber at end – weakness may master him. . . . His idea wd have liked to have children – to live on in them. Speaks to friend (a father) about great difference in dying if you have children (yourself living on) – if you haven't you go out completely.

—*Play. The Second Chance* on people being given a second chance – in first act they are shown at 6's & 7's wishing had done differently – if only had second chance (marriage, &c) – it is given them by supernatural means & we see how they make use of it – (or it is a dream). They might suddenly all go back 20 yrs. Shd they be aware while dreaming that this *is* a second chance & so try to avoid doing as before? Or shd they not know?*

—*Voices.* To an old man comes his mother, young & beautiful ∵ she died young, & they talk strangely of the promise & fulfilment. It takes her long to know *he* is her son – she is looking for the little boy she left behind.

—*Novel* on 'The Accursed Thing' – On everybody having one accursed vice to fight or yield to. Might have three young men all right but for this – the one physical, 2nd moral, 3rd mental. *Physical* – an illness. *Moral* – loose living. *Mental* – mind working to evil actions. To each the others' failings seem terrible, &c. All treated as diseases. Perhaps they shd overcome – or one do it wholly, one half & one fail.†

—*Character* who fails to develop normally, whose spirit remains young in an ageing body, constantly upset by the painful astonishment known to all of us when some outward proof suddenly jabs our inward conviction of perpetual youth.

—*Young Widow* whose husband instead of leaving it in will that if she marries she loses her money leaves it to the man she marries.

—*Play*: 'The Widow's Mite' (Little man's devotion to widow).

—*Death scene.* Character gathers them together for last words. Suddenly dies.

—*The Lovely Moment. Finest Dream in the World.* That it is early morning & I am out on a highland road – dew &c – it is time before I knew anything of sorrow pain or death. Everyone I have loved is still alive – it is the morning of life.

*   *   *

*This theme was eventually expanded into the play *Dear Brutus* (1917).
†The theme of the accursed thing first occurs in Chapter XXXV of *Tommy and Grizel*; Barrie developed it into a one-act play, 'The Accursed Thing' in 1908, but it was not performed until 1913, retitled *The Will*.

Michael in the sand at Ramsgate

All the boys except George were sent down to Ramsgate to stay with their grandmother, Emma du Maurier, for the Easter holidays. It was Arthur's last selfless gesture: he knew that he was dying, and he wanted his sons to be spared the anguish of the death-bed. He wrote the last letter of his life to Michael:

> Egerton House, Berkhamsted.
> April 15, 1907
>
> My dearest Michael
>
> My letters from my boys are indeed a pleasure to me when they arrive in the morning. I hope my boys are getting lots of happiness out of other people's kindness to them and their own kindness to other people every day. It would be fine to have a magic carpet and . . . [fly] to Ramsgate, and see what is going on. . . . I expect you are having plenty of fun and very fine weather, but that we are getting more flowers, especially primroses. My nurse is very good at finding primroses and violets.
>
> Your affectionate Father.

A few hours before Arthur's death, Sylvia wrote to Michael:

> 18 [April 1907]
>
> Darling son Michael,
>
> I hope your cold is not bad – get it quite well quickly for my sake.
>
> Here are some silkworm eggs from papa Gibbs [the local chemist] – I don't know what you do with them, but I've no doubt Mary [Hodgson] will know. . . . George is just going to Mr Timson to have his knickerbockers mended, but they look almost too bad to mend. What a pity it is that you all have to wear things – how much better if you could go about like Mowgli – then perhaps you would never have any colds.
>
> Goodbye now darling – write to me soon
> Mother

Peter Davies wrote:

'There is nothing more moving to me, or more admirable, in the whole of this melancholy record, than these two letters to Michael, the second written within a few hours of Arthur's death. . . . Nothing of the misery and despair Sylvia was racked with was allowed to reach her children. There is a stoicism in this which fully matches Arthur's. . . . It must have been very shortly after Michael received Sylvia's letter . . . that first Jack, and then I, was summoned to Grannie's bedroom ... and by her told the news, which she had perhaps just had by telegram. She told us very simply, without circumlocution or excessive emotion, sitting up in bed with (I think) a lace nightcap on; and I believe the meaning of her words penetrated pretty clearly to one's immature brain, though not of course their full and permanent significance. It was, as I remember it, a dull and windy day, and I recollect wandering up to the night nursery and staring out of the window for long minutes in vague wretchedness and gloom, at the grey sea and the distant Gull lightship. . . . "A boy's will is the wind's will", and as likely as not I was digging on the sands as usual next morning. But for the moment I think it was borne in on me that a disastrous thing had overcome us.'

Of the many tributes paid to Arthur after his death, perhaps the simplest and truest came from a close family friend, Eleanor Clough, who wrote: 'We used to think he was like a young warrior in an Italian picture. And now one knows that he was one.' Peter commented, 'I think Arthur's beauty was not less striking than Sylvia's, and, for my part, I confess that, much as I venerate all their other lovely qualities, it is the thought of their beauty which, more than anything else, brings the lump to my scrawny throat.'

Michael, Peter and Jack on
Ramsgate beach, April 1907

11

Egerton House,
Berkhamsted.
[May, 1907]

Dear Darling Dolly,

I think of you so often & I know how you love Arthur &
me & that helps me in my sorrow – You will love me always
won't you – & help me to live through the long long years.
How shall I do it I wonder – it seems so impossible. We
were so *utterly* & altogether happy & that happiness is the
most precious thing on earth. We were so young to part. I
must be terribly brave now & I know our boys will help me.
They only can keep me alive & I shall live for them and do
always what Arthur wd most like for them. How he loved us
all & he has been taken from us.

Kind Hugh Macnaghten – a dear friend of Arthur's – is
going to have George in his house at Eton in September. . . .
I *am* grateful to many many friends, & I will show it some
day I hope, but just now I am full of deadly pain & sorrow &
I often wonder I am alive. The little boys are loving &
thoughtful & I always sleep with my George now – & it
comforts, more than I can say, to touch him, & I feel Arthur
must know. He will live again in them I feel & that must be
my dear comfort till I go to him at last. We longed to grow
old together – oh my dear friend, it is all so utterly
impossible to understand. My Jack is at Osborne now &
writes happy letters to me – I am going to pay him a visit
when I am strong enough – I miss him very much – but they
have all got to be men & leave me & for Arthur's sake I must
fight that fight too. I shall come to London later on – we are
trying to let the house – it is too big for me & too full of pain
& sorrow. I think of him almost always now as he was before
the tragic illness & God gave him the finest face in the world.
Lovingly
Your Sylvia.

Dolly Ponsonby wrote to Peter Davies in 1946:

'Perhaps there were people who didn't know what [Sylvia's]
passionate devotion to your father was – I have neither before nor
since known such anguish as she suffered during his illness. She burst
out twice to me about it, but not more – words were inadequate to
both of us – and always her reserve about what she cared about was
very strong. She had an inner life of her own, which is what gave her
her great interest. I think I did know her as well as anybody – and I
know that many of her lesser friends merely saw the charming

vivacious lovely exterior, which is what she chose to show them. . . . I don't want to say that Sylvia was perfect. Perfection is dull, but she was perfect to me. . . . I loved her little feminine weaknesses, such as being frightened of going out in the dark. . . . I cannot think of any faults she had, unless it was that she would not answer letters – and enjoyed the admiration of men, naturally – while at the same time never apparently wanting to be the centre of a circle – which is very rare. She had some curiously old-fashioned virtues. She did not like one to criticize any one at all before the children. I remember her saying "Ssh" when I burst out with something about J.M.B. and Mary Barrie, who were staying at Rustington – looking at Michael, and I felt quite ashamed. . . . As I grew older, I realised that she was much more profound than as quite a young girl I had thought. Though so completely happy in her family, yet her sensitiveness and intuition did give her what I call an apprehensive imagination. She loved so much that she feared.'

'The ineffably tragic figure of Sylvia in her despair', with George at Egerton House (JMB)

Arthur had died leaving very little money. Both sides of the family knew that Barrie was more than willing and able to support Sylvia and her boys – in 1906 alone he had earned £44,000, and *Peter Pan* had grossed over half a million – but they felt that she would wish to remain independent. Unbeknown to her, Arthur's brother Maurice organized a whip round among his brothers and Arthur's colleagues at the Bar. The resulting collection was presented to Sylvia, who adamantly refused to accept a penny of it. She gave no reason, she merely requested that it be returned to the donors. There is no record of any precise commitment from Barrie either: possibly this too was initially declined, though, as Mackail observed, 'When Barrie had decided to give, he gave, and no one – unless they were literally superhuman – could hope to escape the gift.'

Shortly after Arthur's death, Sylvia wrote out a series of notes or 'Directions', later identified by Barrie as being 'Notes for a Will'. They are written in an urgent hand, on a block of drawing-paper, and appear to have been composed on impulse, ending in mid-sentence:

'I may die at any time but it's not likely to happen yet as I am strong I think on the whole. However in case it happens (& God forbid because of my precious boys) I will put down a few directions. I wonder if my dear kind Florence Gay [a close family friend] would care to make a home for them till they are out in the world (if she is still single) . . . she could always ask advice from Margaret & J.M.B. & Trixie & May & all the kind uncles – (also of course Mama if she is still alive). With dear Mary Hodgson, & I hope she will stay with them always (unless she marries) . . . I believe they will all be good brave men (seeing that they are Arthur's sons & understand how very very much they were beloved by him & Sylvia, his altogether faithful & loving wife). I hope they will marry & have children & live long & happily & be content to be poor if it should have to be . . . Also that they will realise that there is nothing so perfect as a true love match & in that no one was ever more blessed than their own mother. I hope that they will work hard, for to be idle is disastrous, that at play time (& everyone can play a little) I like to think of them doing so in a dear healthy honest way & bringing happiness to others as well as to themselves. . . . I should like all my dear one's love letters to me to be burnt unread . . . & lie with me & Arthur in the Hampstead churchyard close to that other dear grave. . . . Of one thing I am certain – that J. M. Barrie (the best friend in the whole world) will always be ready to advise out of his love for

Peter Davies commented:

'What would the next word or words have been if Sylvia had not stopped writing when she did? Jocelyn? My precious boys? . . . I think her attitude to him was a special and peculiar one, not very representative of her true self. Indeed, on reflection, I doubt if he brought out or even recognised (or wanted to) the true characteristics of anyone he made much of; he was such a fantasy-weaver that they ended by either playing up to him or clearing out. When he was strongly attracted by people, he wanted at once to own them and to be dominated by them, whichever their sex. The owning he was often able to manage for a time to a greater or less degree, with the help of his money, which made generosity an easy business for him (not that the rich are usually generous), plus his wit and charm and the aura of success and fame which surrounded him. The being dominated was more difficult of attainment, as he was a pretty strong character in his own strange way. There's no denying that, from Arthur's death onwards, he did increasingly "own" Sylvia and her boys after his fashion. And Sylvia, a strong character herself, couldn't help dominating him. Later, I think, he achieved something of the same peculiar equilibrium with George, and much more so with Michael. . . . Life went on for a while, in a half-hearted way, at Egerton House. I recall, not in much detail, but with a vague sense of misery and discomfort which still survives, the return of Jack, Michael and Nico and myself with Mary Hodgson from Ramsgate, and the ineffably tragic figure of Sylvia in her despair. . . . Of the last phase at Berkhamsted I have one little recollection which, though not particularly edifying, is perhaps worth recording. One day George and I were larking about in an intolerable way, arguing and letting off steam . . . until poor Sylvia, exasperated beyond endurance, cried out "Oh stop, stop, stop! You *know* you would never *dare* behave like this if your father was still alive!" . . . I only put this horrid little memory in because it is an instance [of] the . . . heartlessness or thoughtlessness of small boys.'

It was a heartlessness perceived by Barrie, who wrote in *Peter and Wendy*: 'Peter had seen many tragedies, but he had forgotten them all. . . . "I forget [people] after I kill them." ' A casual remark from one of the boys (probably Michael) was also noted down about this time and used in *Peter and Wendy*, which he had started writing, but was not to finish until 1910: 'Children have the strangest adventures without being troubled by them. For instance, they may remember to mention, a week after the event happened, that when they were in the wood they met their dead father and had a game with him.'

In order to remove Sylvia from the pain and sorrow of Egerton House, Barrie rented a rambling house in Scotland, Dhivach Lodge, set high in the wooded hills above Loch Ness, perched like a gull's nest over a ravine. It was a long and singularly damp holiday, from early June until mid-September. Peter Davies wrote:

'The whole pattern of the Dhivach holiday seems to me to have had something rather deplorable about it. . . . The boys did enjoy themselves, sometimes still chasing butterflies but fishing madly with worms most of the time in every burn within walking distance. Various people came to stay, including Crompton . . . and nice Madge Murray, J.M.B.'s niece, then in her very early twenties, the most normal and human member of the Barrie family, who sang songs at the piano and I think must have introduced a welcome note of natural gaiety into the household; and Captain Scott and Harley Granville Barker with Lillah [McCarthy] his then wife, a somewhat overwhelming person. . . . It would be fascinating to know what such guests as these thought of the Dhivach inmates. Plenty of scope for comment, one would say. And however thoroughly the boys enjoyed it, there must have been uncomfortable moments among the adults.'

Sylvia at Dhivach Lodge (JMB)

Mary Barrie was also at Dhivach, though she left in September to go on another of her motoring trips through France. Barrie wrote to Hilda Trevelyan on August 26th, 'I do nothing up here but fish & fish & fish, and we ought all to be fishes to feel at home in this weather.' In fact he was doing a good deal besides fishing. The remnants of his marriage were combining with his notes of A. E. W. Mason's political campaign and his flirtation with the Duchess of Sutherland

Notebook entry for 1907: '*Peter Pan* Ten years later – Wendy grown up & Peter still a boy. (one-act play?)'

Michael splashing, unable to swim (JMB)

to produce *What Every Woman Knows*, while Arthur's fatal illness and Barrie's troubled conscience about his own stupendous wealth were finding expression in a one-act play, 'The Accursed Thing'. Captain Scott's visit to Dhivach Lodge prompted an idea for yet another play, though it never progressed beyond the notebook stage:

—*North Pole* (or *South*) Play Tableau – Old man (leader) comes back when others gone – he must die. Ice – snow. We see his dream – succeeding ages represented by individuals getting nearer & nearer Pole, always having to turn back & die. At last he plants his staff or Union Jack at Pole & falls dying.

Barrie was also making numerous notes on Michael. Some of these appear to have been for a sequel to *Peter Pan* about Peter's brother, 'Michael Pan'. It never got much further than the title, perhaps because by this time Barrie had begun to incorporate elements of Michael's character into Peter Pan himself as he developed the book, *Peter and Wendy*:

'Sometimes . . . [Peter Pan] had dreams, and they were more painful than the dreams of other boys. For hours he could not be separated from these dreams, though he wailed piteously in them. They had to do, I think, with the riddle of his existence. At such times it had been Wendy's custom to take him out of bed and sit with him on her lap, soothing him in dear ways of her own invention, and when he grew calmer to put him back to bed before he quite woke up, so that he should not know of the indignity to which she had subjected him.'

In reality it was Barrie who fulfilled Wendy's role with Michael. He later wrote a short story about him, *Neil and Tintinnabulum*, which is as intimate as it is unknown, in which he elaborated on the nature of Michael's nightmares, referring to the boy as 'Neil':

'There was a horror looking for him in his childhood. Waking dreams we called them, and they lured Neil out of bed in the night. It was always the same nameless enemy he was seeking, and he stole about in various parts of the house in search of it, probing fiercely for it in cupboards, or standing at the top of the stairs pouring out invective and shouting challenges to it to come up. I have known the small white figure defend the stair-head thus for an hour, blazing rather than afraid, concentrated on some dreadful matter in which, tragically, none could aid him. I stood or sat by him, like a man in an adjoining world, waiting till he returned to me, for I had been advised, warned, that I must not wake him abruptly. Gradually I

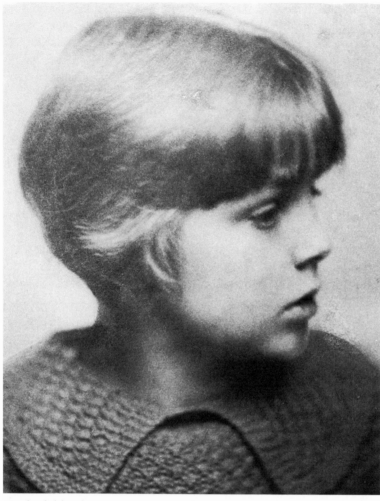

Michael in 1907, aged 7. Barrie alluded to Michael's dreams in a later version of *Peter Pan*: 'Peter is on the bed, asleep. . . . He is dreaming, and in his dreams he is always in pursuit of a boy who was never here, or anywhere: the only boy who could beat him.'

soothed him back to bed, and though my presence there in the morning told him, in the light language we then adopted, that he had been "at it again" he could remember nothing of who the enemy was. It had something to do with the number 7; that was all we ever knew. Once I slipped from the room, thinking it best that he should wake to normal surroundings, but that was a mistake. He was violently agitated by my absence. In some vague way he seemed on the stairs to have known that I was with him and to have got comfort from it; he said he had gone back to bed only because he knew I should be there when he woke up. I found that he liked, "after he had been an ass," to wake up seeing me "sitting there doing something frightfully ordinary, like reading the newspaper," and you may be sure that thereafter that was what I was doing. . . .

'What is the danger? What is it that he knows in times during which he is shut away and that he cannot remember to tell to himself or to me when he wakes? I am often disturbed when thinking of him (which is the real business of my life), regretting that, in spite of advice and warnings, I did not long ago risk waking him abruptly, when, before it could hide, he might have clapped seeing eyes upon it, and thus been able to warn me. Then, knowing the danger, I would for ever after be on the watch myself, so that when the moment came, I could envelop him as with wings.'

* * *

At the end of the summer holidays, George began his first term at Eton. He wrote regular letters to Sylvia (a compulsory school rule), and seems to have settled into his new life with surprising ease, picking up the Etonian dialect within a few days of his arrival. He wrote his first letter home on September 18th, 1907:

> Eton College,
> Windsor.
> Goodness knows the date!

Dearest Mother,

At last I am in my study ... It's not a bad den, and will be able to be fitted up jolly nicely. . . . There is a cup-board above my bed full of grub from the hamper, oh joy!

I have spoken to two or three chaps here already. They are jolly decent. One is called *Lord* Newton Butler. . . . The Matron came in just now and has taken care of all my chink. She is awfully decent, and she takes lots of chaps' chink. She saw my picture of you and said you were very pretty. . . . I'm afraid there's nothing else to say.

> Good-bye
> from your loving son
> George

George in 1907, aged 14

Egerton House was sold in October, and, with Barrie's financial help, Sylvia bought a new home in London, 23 Campden Hill Square, not far from Kensington Gardens and Leinster Corner. While the house was being renovated, she took Peter, Michael and Nico down to stay with her mother in Ramsgate, from where Michael wrote to Barrie on October 18th:

> DEAR MR BARRIE
> I hope you are quite well
> I HAVE SENT YOU A
> Picture of a Pirate he has
> GOT PLENTY OF WEAPONS
> and looks very fierce. Please
> COME SOON TO FISH
> from Michael with Love
> FROM NIK-O   THE END

In addition to supporting the Davies family, Barrie was helping a number of struggling writers, and had persuaded Frohman to invest money in several non-profit-making productions at the *avant-garde* Court Theatre in Sloane Square, run by Harley Granville-Barker and J. E. Vedrenne. All his life Barrie envied the rebellious, pioneering talents of writers such as Ibsen, though he himself seemed doomed to commercial success, and when Granville-Barker's play *Waste* was refused a licence by the Censor in October, Barrie rallied to the cause, lending his influence and support to the newly founded Committee seeking the abolition of the office of Censor. Soon he was hosting committee meetings at Leinster Corner, sending out circular letters requesting support from other writers, and drafting a petition to be laid before the Prime Minister. He wrote to Sylvia at Ramsgate on November 4th, 1907:

Harley Granville-Barker

> Dearest Jocelyn,
>   I am having a life of it over this censorship business. Receiving committees, telephones, telegrams, &c. all day and every day. I've done more business this last week or two than in all the rest of my life & it will go on till the 18th. It was stupid of me to get pushed into it but now that I am in I've got to do my best. There is just a shadow of a chance of its having any practical result.
>   When I can I'm working hard at my play [*What Every Woman Knows*], which is dull, with occasional bright moments. . . . I would have sent the boys fireworks but the

George's 'phiz', which he sent Sylvia from Eton: 'It is pretty opeless, but I don't care. It'll last 2 or 3 years & then I shall ave to be phizzed again in change clothes & *stick-ups*!'

post office won't pass them. . . . At least write and tell me how you are. I want to know so much that I think you might do this. I'm very tired.

Your
J.M.B.

In another letter to Sylvia, Barrie mentioned having received 'capital letters' from George, which must have provided a pleasant respite from his censorship work. None of these early Etonian epistles to Barrie have survived, but they were doubtless in a similar vein to those written by George to Sylvia:

Dearest Mother,

   I begin fagging tomorrow. My fagmaster is called Millington-Drake,* and is, I believe, awfully strict. . . . I am getting on rippingly at Eton footer, and shall probably be in my house Lower Boy team. . . . Yesterday was the Old Boy match. . . . At half past six came the sock supper! We had tons of sock, soup, and grouse and things. Towards the end a great silver challenge cup came round full of champagne. We all drank to the prosperity of the house. I was not TIGHT! . . . (Champagne is ripping stuff, and I wish I'd taken a longer booze!) Millington-Drake made some ripping speeches. . . . Mrs Millington-Drake came down to Eton yesterday. She had tea in the house and gave Lawrence major and me ten bob each! We were pretty bucked, I can tell you! . . . Millington-Drake has lent me a tremendous book to read, called 'The Letters of Queen Victoria (Vol. I)' It is a very instructive book, but I like it rather.

From your loving son
George

Barrie wrote to Sylvia on November 29th:

*Eugen Millington-Drake: George's fag-master, and head of Hugh Macnaghten's House, Captain of Boats, President of Pop, known at Eton as Millington-Drake K.C.M.G. (Kindly Call Me God), later became Sir Eugen Millington-Drake, K.C.M.G. Knight Commander of St Michael & St George).

Dearest Jocelyn,

   Tomorrow I am meaning to go to see George as they have a big 'footer' day, and I am a good deal agitated as to what hat Millington Drake would prefer me to wear. It will probably end (against my better judgement) in my donning the now somewhat *passée* bowler. I was lunching today with Bernard Shaw in his flat in Adelphi Terrace, a very pleasant place. . . . I hope you are all pretty well. When I don't hear I dread you may be ill, but I trust it is not so. . . . I am longing for you to be on Campden Hill. Love to all,

Your
J.M.B.

By Christmas 1907 the new house on Campden Hill was ready for occupation. Peter Davies described it in the *Morgue*:

'A more attractive house than the two earlier homes, so close by, in Kensington Park Gardens; and I expect a snob would have to admit that it was a better address. . . . Very early in the proceedings J.M.B. affixed to the dining-room ceiling, by means of a coin adroitly spun, the penny stamp with which he used to hallmark his acquaintances' houses, whether he effectually owned them or not. On the first floor, at the back, Sylvia had her lonely bedroom, next door to the schoolroom, whose most prominent feature was a new three-quarter-size billiard table presented by J.M.B. . . . On the second floor were nursery and night-nursery, where Mary Hodgson, Michael and Nico slept; and on the top floor were a two-bedded room for George and Jack when they came home, a single room at the back which I occupied, and another two-bedded room for slaves. . . . To 23 Campden Hill Square came, besides Mary Hodgson, Minnie the cook . . . and the pretty, buxom new house-parlourmaid, Amy, who stirred the young Adam in some of us, more or less obscurely.

23 Campden Hill Square

'And here, I think, Sylvia did succeed, gradually, in regaining something of the zest for life. The boys were a fond amusement and distraction for her, relatives came frequently, and the dog-like J.M.B. still living at Leinster Corner and constantly in attendance. . . . Everything must have been done, by all who had the care of us and above all by Sylvia herself, to shut out the imp of sorrow and self-pity from our young lives. In my own case, at any rate, it was not till a good deal later . . . that I began to look back with nostalgic yearnings on Egerton House and its garden and the three short years at Berkhamsted (long years, though, to a small boy), as on a sort of last paradise.'

Peter Pan had been once again revived for the holiday season – indeed its annual return was now taken as a matter of course, Frohman having pledged himself to revive it every Christmas for as long as the public cared to see it. At the request of the London Ambulance Service, Barrie had added a line 'about no one being able to fly until the fairy dust had been blown on him; so many children having gone home and tried it from their beds and needed surgical attention'.[1] On the last night of the run, the curtain came down at the end of Act V, followed by the usual deafening applause from the addicts in the front stalls. The curtain remained lowered for five, ten, fifteen minutes, the auditorium in darkness. The audience were bewildered, stamping their feet impatiently for the final tree-tops scene. Then Tessie Parke, the actress playing the baby mermaid, came on to the stage. 'My friends, I am the Baby Mermaid. We are now going to do a new act for the first and only time on any stage. Mr

Tessie Parke as the Baby Mermaid

Barrie told us a story one day about what happened to Peter when Wendy grew up and we made it into an act, and it will never be done again.'² The curtain rose to reveal Wendy as an old married lady, telling her daughter Jane the story of Peter Pan and her own adventures as a child in the Never Never Land. Barrie described the essence of the scene that followed in *Peter and Wendy*:

'Then . . . came the tragedy. . . . Jane was now asleep in her bed. Wendy was sitting on the floor, very close to the fire, . . . then the window blew open as of old, and Peter dropped on the floor.

'He was exactly the same as ever. . . . He was a little boy, and she was grown up. She huddled by the fire, not daring to move, helpless and guilty, a big woman.

'"Hullo, Wendy," he said, not noticing any difference, for he was thinking chiefly of himself. . . .

'"Hullo, Peter," she replied faintly, squeezing herself as small as possible. Something inside her was crying "Woman, woman, let go of me." . . .

'"Peter," she said, faltering, "are you expecting me to fly away with you?"

'"Of course, that is why I have come." . . .

'"I can't come," she said apologetically, "I have forgotten how to fly."

'"I'll soon teach you again."

'"O Peter, don't waste your fairy dust on me."

'She had risen; and now at last a fear assailed him. "What is it?" he cried, shrinking.

'"I will turn up the light," she said, "and then you can see for yourself."

'For almost the only time in his life that I know of, Peter was afraid. "Don't turn up the light," he cried.

'She let her hands play in the hair of the tragic boy. . . . Then she turned up the light and Peter saw. He gave a cry of pain. . . .

'"I am old, Peter. I am ever so much more than twenty. I grew up long ago."

'"You promised not to!"

'"I couldn't help it. I am a married woman, Peter."

'"No, you're not."

'"Yes, and the little girl in the bed is my baby."

'"No, she's not."

'But he supposed she was; and he took a step towards the sleeping child, with his dagger upraised. Of course he did not strike. He sat down on the floor instead and sobbed; and Wendy did not know how to comfort him, though she could have done it so easily once. She was only a woman now, and she ran out of the room to think.

'Peter continued to cry, and soon his sobs woke Jane. She sat up in bed, and was interested at once.

'"Boy," she said, "why are you crying?"'

Peter and Jane flew away, and in the stage version Wendy explained to the now ancient Nana: 'Don't be anxious, Nana. This is how I planned it if he ever came back, . . . and when Jane grows up I will hope *she* will have a little daughter, who will fly away with him in turn – and in this way may I go on for ever and ever, dear Nana, so long as children are young and innocent.' 'And heartless', added Barrie in the book – 'Gay and innocent and heartless.'

'When the curtain fell,' wrote Denis Mackail, 'there was another full quarter-of-an-hour's applause. And then something decidedly historical occurred. Mr J. M. Barrie actually showed himself on the stage. In his black overcoat, his scarf, and holding his bowler hat in his hand. He said nothing, the vision was distinctly brief, and he could still stick to [his claim] afterwards that never, since *Richard Savage*, had he taken a first-night author's call.' As they left the theatre, Barrie slipped Hilda Trevelyan his hand-written manuscript of 'Peter Pan: An Afterthought', on which he had inscribed: 'To Hilda Trevelyan – My incomparable Wendy'. The critic Ronald Jeans by chance saw the performance, and wrote in the *Liverpool Daily Post*: 'All those privileged to witness this never-to-be-forgotten and only performance of this striking act will acknowledge it to be the finest thing that Mr Barrie has done.'

*   *   *

Jack, aged 13

While Peter enrolled at Mr Wilkinson's celebrated institution in Orme Square, Michael and Nico started school at Norland Place in the New Year, escorted to and fro by Mary Hodgson. Sylvia's infrequent visits to the school were recalled by a former pupil, Betty Macleod, in the school's 1976 centenary magazine: 'On Visitors' day, twice, we noticed, watching drill, a lady with two really beautiful little boys. She had one of the saddest expressions on her face we had ever seen, and we wondered who she was. We were told that she was a friend of J. M. Barrie, and one of her boys was his model for . . . Peter Pan. Their name was Llewelyn Davies.' In contrast to George's evident happiness at Eton, Jack experienced nothing but misery at Osborne. He later told his wife that 'he hated it, he loathed it, he hated it with a deadly loathing. It was pretty awful – the ragging and the bullying that went on was intolerably horrible, and a little boy who had never been away from home was easy meat.'[3] Why did Jack not mention his unhappiness to Sylvia or Barrie? 'He was too proud. He adored his mother, and he didn't want to trouble her more than she was already troubled. He would never have told Barrie: he didn't confide in him as George, Michael and Nico did.' Denis Mackail alluded to Jack's growing resentment towards Barrie in *The Story of J.M.B.*: 'Jack, perhaps, with a touch already of inherited intolerance, had a deep-down notion that it was an interloper who was saving them all from ruin.' Jack's wife was more direct. 'He enormously disliked the idea of this silly little man presuming to take the place of his father. He wasn't the sort who bore malice, and I don't think that he *disliked* him – though, God knows, Barrie gave him cause enough in due course.' 'Jack's whole attitude towards J.M.B. is very difficult properly to understand', wrote Nico in 1976. 'Jack more than most could swing emotionally from plus to minus; fundamentally he was very fond of Uncle Jim, tho' there were numerous times when he swung against him, largely caused by his being the loner in the Navy with us other 4 being more constantly under J.M.B.'s eye. Much as Jack loved & worshipped our father, I can't believe for a moment that George would have been "second" in this. Had Jack been to Eton like the rest of us, his attitude to Uncle Jim might have been very different.'[4]

George returned to Macnaghten's House for his second term (or 'half', as it is called at Eton), and his letters continued to flow in high spirits to Sylvia and Barrie:

'[February 20th, 1908] Yesterday I was called "a baby who had grown out of his clothes". So I have, but it was meant because I'm not in tails. Some of my shirt always shows below my waistcoat, and if I tighten my braces, my trousers come up to my knees. I'm one of Eton's sights. Such is fame! . . . I have won two matches in Junior House Fives, and am consequently feeling rather bucked. [May 3rd] By a ghastly lie I got off going a walk with our dear Roger Woodhouse. I think it's excusable, because you can't say "No" when a chap asks you to go out for a walk with him. So I said a chap wanted to talk to me about something, and found a chap afterwards. On our walk we came across some chaps smoking away like anything, among them Viscount Carlton, who is about the biggest bounder out.* [May 14th] I saw Lady Cynthia Graheme today. She appeared wearing a hat 8 times the size of any ordinary hat. It was a sight for the gods! She came into Lower Chapel. I call it lip to Eton. . . . P.S. Love to the caterpillars.'

---

*Utilized by Barrie in his one-act play, *The Will*: 'Harry is at Eton, you know, the most fashionable school in the country. . . . We have the most gratifying letters from him. Last Saturday he was caught smoking cigarettes with a lord. (*With pardonable pride*) They were sick together.'

Frohman was once again staying in Paris, and in order to lure Barrie over, he announced the opening of *Peter Pan, ou le petit garçon qui ne voulait pas grandir*, at the fashionable Vaudeville Theatre. It was a gesture in the best tradition of Frohman's spectacular extravagance, since the two-week engagement barely met the cost of transporting the scenery from London, let alone paying the cast. The play was performed in English, though the audience were guided by a special 12-page synopsis, *L'Histoire de Peter Pan*, and the event received wide coverage in the Paris press, *Le Figaro* devoting three columns to a somewhat heavy-handed philosophical analysis of the play's symbolic meanings.

Michael's eighth birthday was on June 16th, and Barrie arranged for a redskin outfit, complete with bows, arrows, peace-pipe and wigwam, to be delivered to 23 Campden Hill Square in his absence. He wrote to Michael from Paris:

Pauline Chase in her third year as Peter Pan

> Hotel d'Albe,
> Avenue des Champs Elysées.
> 15 June 1908.
>
> My dear Michael,
>
> Paris is looking very excited today, and all the people think it is because there were races yesterday, but I know it is because tomorrow is your birthday. I wish I could be with you and your candles. You can look on me as one of your candles, the one that burns badly – the greasy one that is bent in the middle. But still, hurray, I am Michael's candle. I wish I could see you putting on the redskin's clothes for the first time. Won't your mother be frightened. Nick will hide beneath the bed, and Peter will cry for the police.
>
> Dear Michael, I am very fond of you, but don't tell anybody.
>
> The End.
> J. M. Barrie

Jack sent Michael two shillings for his birthday from Osborne, but George, at Eton, was feeling less flush: 'Many happy returns of the day! I hope you will get lots of presents, although I have not sent you one, owing to poverty and forgetfulness. . . . I hope you have been finding caterpillars. I have got about 40! . . . Now I must tidy up Millington-Drake's room.'

What Every Woman Knows began rehearsals at the beginning of July, with Gerald du Maurier and Hilda Trevelyan in the principal roles. It was Barrie's first full-length play for over three years, and he now devoted most of his time to rewrites and rehearsals. Sylvia and her boys therefore spent their summer holidays without him, renting

Nico being held aloft by Barrie's chauffeur, 'the splendid Alphonse' (JMB)

a farm-house in the heart of the New Forest. Peter Davies wrote:

'Butterflies were a principal lure this year. George still retained the bug-hunting enthusiasm of his very young days, and . . . I followed his lead in such things, and spent many happy days with him wandering in the woods and over the commons armed with net and killing-bottle and sandwiches for lunch, . . . while Jack was heartily bored by the whole business and thought it all tedious. In a word, he had outgrown it, maturing earlier than George. . . . Besides butterfly-hunting, I recall constructing a sort of encampment with George of old sacks over a hole in a sandy hillside, and spending hours crouched therein blissfully enough, eating plums and Mellin's Food biscuits; . . . [and] a grand motor expedition to Bournemouth – had J.M.B. come down? – involving the purchase of bows and arrows, banned since the dreadful day three or four years earlier at Black Lake when I had shot Jack in the lip. . . . I remember very little of Sylvia in the New Forest; only my own childish doings. I think that I, and probably George and Jack too, but perhaps Jack less than George, lived in the boy world to the exclusion of any other, and were little troubled by the disappearance of Arthur from our lives or by the misery which the bereft Sylvia no doubt did everything to hide from us. . . . I think she must have missed Arthur terribly indeed that summer. . . .

'One afternoon George and I, making for home towards the end of a day's pursuit of White Admirals and Fritillaries, encountered a company of Highlanders on the march along one of the dusty forest roads. . . . They halted and fell out for a few minutes, unbuckling their equipment and sprawling by the roadside in the relaxed attitudes of tired men, and George and I got into conversation with a sergeant and one or two of the privates at the rear of the little column. When they moved on again after their halt, we followed close behind them, enjoying the rhythm of the marching feet, and moved obscurely by a sense of unity with the sweating, swearing, back-chatting soldiers. . . . Somehow this scene has always remained vividly in my mind: rather like a piece of a silent film, for I have long forgotten what we talked about. It was a queer little romantic presage of the real marchings of six years later, for which the Highlanders were more or less consciously preparing themselves, [though] nothing could then have seemed more remote from the destiny of two small boys.'

After visiting Sylvia and the Five for their Bournemouth expedition, Barrie drove across country to Black Lake, calling in on Dolly Ponsonby at Shulbrede Priory:

'*Aug 12* [1908]. Mr Barrie arrived in the evening. He was quite talkative at dinner. Discussed Galsworthy whom he admires tremendously both as a man & a writer. . . . He says he thinks he is a man of very strong passions kept well under control. He was good about L[illah] Granville B[arker] too – said she had no sense of humour. . . . We talked a great deal of Sylvia's boys & it is extraordinary to see how they fill his life & supply all his human interest. Of course J.M.B. does alarm me. I feel he absolutely sees right through one & sees just *how* stupid I am – but I hope also that he sees my good intentions. The things he says about people so absolutely knock the right nail on the head that though they are not in the least unkind they are almost cruel.'

Captain Robert Falcon Scott

Captain Scott's mild flirtation with Pauline Chase had ended the previous year when he had met a young sculptress, Kathleen Bruce, at a luncheon party given by Aubrey Beardsley's sister, Mabel. 'I . . . sat between Max Beerbohm and J. M. Barrie', Kathleen later wrote in her *Autobiography*. 'Far down the other side of the table was a naval officer, Captain Scott . . . and I glowed rather foolishly and suddenly when I clearly saw him ask his neighbour who I was.' Kathleen was, at that time, being courted by an ardent admirer, a young law student with 'corn coloured hair and a crooked smile' named Gilbert Cannan. For the next twelve months she managed to string both men along, unbeknown to Barrie, who rather enjoyed choreographing other people's romances, and was decidedly piqued when he heard through A. E. W. Mason that she had accepted a proposal of marriage from Scott. Also wounded was Gilbert Cannan, who had, in the meantime, become secretary to Barrie's Committee campaigning for the abolition of the Censor. When Kathleen heard that Barrie had taken offence, she hurriedly wrote to Scott: 'We must not hurt so sensitive and dear a person. Please write [to him] *quite* by return of post. . . . As nice a letter as ever you can think of.' The apology evidently smoothed things over, and on August 5th, Barrie was passing on the information as one in the know to Pauline Chase: 'Capt. Scott wrote me that he is to be married to Miss Bruce shortly, so there!' Cannan, however, was less easily mollified, and looked to the Barries for comfort. Barrie liked the young man: he was impetuous and rather naïve, but he burned with ambition to become a writer, and Barrie was flattered by Cannan's admiration for him. Mary Barrie also responded to his outpourings of woe over his unrequited love for Kathleen Bruce. Cannan wrote to Kathleen: 'Yesterday Lillah [McCarthy] and Mrs Barrie came and had tea – Mrs Barrie suddenly began to talk to me like a mother. She really is a dear thing, and she seems to need a good deal of me – I feel the need and give – gladly.'[5]

On September 3rd, 1908, *What Every Woman Knows* opened at the Duke of York's Theatre in lavish, Frohmanesque style. In addition to the prodigious cast (the only unknown being Barrie's niece, Madge Murray), the election scene at the end of Act Two was amplified by a hundred extras crammed onto the stage. The play received unanimous praise from the critics: even Max Beerbohm enjoyed it, discerning that the characters 'are creatures of real flesh and blood, winged by Mr Barrie's whim; an immense relief from the sawdust-stuffed figures that the average playwright dresses up'.[6]

On September 2nd, the day before the opening of *What Every Woman Knows*, Captain Robert Falcon Scott married Miss Kathleen Bruce at Hampton Court Palace. Gilbert Cannan accepted defeat, and turned to Mary Barrie for consolation.

Gilbert Cannan

Barrie had seen little of Sylvia and the boys during the summer of 1908, but he now made amends by announcing his Christmas present to them: a three-week ski-ing holiday in Switzerland, staying at the Grand Hotel, Caux. George wrote to Sylvia from Eton on hearing the news:

> Sunday, December 13th, 1908.
>
> Dearest Mother,
>   I have asked my tutor about clothes for Switzerland. He said you have to have a knickerbocker change suit (a good warm one), sweaters and thick stockings. . . . From what he said about it it sounded topping fun to be in Switzerland. . . . The journey will be pretty exciting, I expect. I expect to be ill going from Dover to Calais, or wherever you cross the Channel. It will be rather funny travelling on Christmas Day. . . . Is Mrs Barrie coming? Perhaps she'll prefer to go Motor Touring or something else. We shall be a whacking party. It is kind of Uncle Jim to do it all. I hope Alphonse'll come! [Barrie's chauffeur]
>
>   Your loving son,
>   George

Mary was indeed included on the holiday; so was Gilbert Cannan, at Barrie's invitation. 'A rather odd party,' wrote Denis Mackail with a touch of understatement. 'Yet Cannan not only had an intense admiration for the host's genius and attainments, but was extremely popular with the boys.' Mackail went on to state that Barrie was too unobservant and preoccupied to notice his wife's growing infatuation with Cannan. Nico later remarked on 'how astonishingly simple/ignorant = un-knowing Barrie was about what went on around him in the so-to-speak dirty things of the world. . . . He frequently employed a safety-curtain which he would pull down between his own mind and the facts of life in the world around him.' Nico's argument seems at odds with Barrie's remarkable perception evidenced in so much of his writing, particularly in his notebook observations. That Mary Barrie and Gilbert Cannan were fond of each other's company was obvious enough to contemporaries. 'If Sylvia saw,' wrote Mackail evasively, 'then either it wasn't her business or else she also saw – one has to admit this – how the situation was playing into her hands. Temptation here, as well as elsewhere. The money again.' According to Diana Farr's *Gilbert Cannan: A Georgian Prodigy*, Cannan later alleged that 'Sylvia encouraged and abetted his affair with Mary Barrie, making it easy for them to meet and see each other unknown to Barrie'. Even Jack, at thirteen, was aware of their growing relationship, asking Barrie at Caux, 'Why is Mr Cannan always with Mrs Barrie?'[1] The reply is

George tobogganing at Caux. The faceless rider behind him is Gilbert Cannan: his face has been blotted out from the negative with paint (JMB)

Nico lugeing at Caux (JMB)

unrecorded. Perhaps he did not see; perhaps he did not see because, like many people in the same situation, he did not *want* to see; or perhaps he viewed what he saw as being no less innocent than his own flirtations with other women. While at Caux, he wrote to the Duchess of Sutherland:

January 9th, 1909.

My dear Milly,

   . . . The world here is given over to lugeing. I don't know if you have a luge, you have everything else. It's a little toboggan, and they glide down on it for ever and ever. And evidently man needs little here below except his little luge. Age annihilated. We are simply ants with luges. I say we, but by great good luck I hurt myself at once, and so I am debarred. . . .

   I hope . . . that I am to see you soon and explain you to yourself.

Yours always,
J. M. Barrie.

Your most esteemed virtue	Decency
Your highest characteristic in man	Fun.
Your highest characteristic in woman	Kindness
Your happiest employment	Redding
Your greatest misery	Nightmares
Your pet flower and colour	Rose, dark red.
Your favourite novelist	J. M. Barrie.
Your most admired poet	Longfellow
Your favourite opera and artist	Havn't seen any
Your favourite historical hero	Hereward the Wake
Your favourite historical heroine	Joan of Arc
Your favourite hero in fiction	Peter Pan
Your favourite heroine in fiction	Tiger Lily.
Your luxurious ambrosia and nectar	Lemonade & Chocolate pudding
Your most loveable name	Sylvia
Your pet antipathy	Castor Oil & Gregory Powder
What peculiarity can you most tolerate?	Asking Riddles
Your favourite amusement	Fishing.
At what age should a man marry?	26
At what age should a woman marry?	Whenever She likes
Do you believe in love at first sight?	No.
Do you believe in marrying for love and working for money?	Yes No NO
Were you ever in love? and if so, how often?	No Never
Your favourite proverb?	Birds of a feather flock to-gether
Your age next birthday	9
My confession	Michael Llewelyn Davies

Michael's 1909 entry in Barrie's Querist's Album

Nico's own memory of Caux was restricted to a tobogganing collision in which a pair of steel-pronged boots 'pranged my little bum'. Peter was equally oblivious to the soap–opera activities of Gilbert and Mary:

'One evening at dusk I was summoned to J.M.B.'s room, to find him sitting, in a somehow dejected attitude, at the far end of the room, in the half-light. As I entered he looked up, and, in a flat, lugubrious voice said: "Peter, something dreadful has happened to my feet," and glancing down I saw to my horror that his feet were bare and swollen to four or five times their natural size. For several seconds I was deceived, and have never since forgotten the terror that filled me, until I realised that the feet were artificial (bought at Hamley's), made of the waxed linen masks are made of, and that I had been most successfully hoaxed. . . . To that winter also belongs the story which J.M.B. used sometimes to tell in after years, of how Nico, then aged five, attracted the admiring attention of one of the lady guests at the hotel, who exclaimed: "My word, you *are* a lovely boy!" So he was, too, . . . but this was the last way to curry favour with a young Davies, and Nico duly retaliated with a face of fury and the comprehensive nursery repartee: "Oh, ditto!" . . .

'Near the end of the stay at Caux, Sylvia became alarmingly unwell, suffering great pain (I think close to the heart). . . . An English doctor who happened to be staying in the hotel was approached, and either refused outright to advise, or at any rate made himself as unhelpful as he could, on the grounds that he was on holiday. . . . From this time forward Sylvia, though sometimes better for shorter or longer periods, was never completely well.'

On his return to London, Barrie gave Gerald considerable help in producing a play written by Sylvia's brother Guy under the pseudonym of 'A Patriot'. Entitled *An Englishman's Home*, the play warned Britain of the threat posed by the expansion of Germany's navy, predicted an invasion, highlighted the average Englishman's indifference to the situation, and suggested that in all probability he would not respond to a call to arms until the invading Germans were trampling over his prized garden blooms and battering down his own back door. It was hailed by Lord Roberts as being the finest piece of propaganda he had ever seen, and the play's phenomenal success brought a measure of comfort to the ailing Sylvia. 'My beloved Guy,' she wrote from Campden Hill Square, 'the world is writing and talking of nothing else but your play. I am, alas, in bed, and cannot go, but I think of you all day. . . . Mummie tells people the author's name is a profound secret, but in my heart I know she tells everyone she meets!' George wrote to Sylvia on his return to Eton: 'The chap

Guy and Gerald du Maurier in their youth

in my carriage had been to "An Englishman's Home" on Saturday night. He thought all but the ending* very good. Of course the ending does rather spoil the lesson – it makes one think that even if the Germans did have a high old time for a bit, England would win in the end all right. I suppose it had to be put in to please the average public.' A fortnight later George himself was playing at war games with the Eton school corps: 'The Field Day on Thursday was rather fun. . . . I shouldn't think my firing would be very dangerous in actual warfare! It's rather fun seeing an enemy skulking along about 500 yds off, and potting at him. After about 30 minutes' engagement we retired at a double until we fell in with the rest of our company and marched back to Aldershot Station where we had lunch (rather a good one). We had a topping rag in the train coming back to Eton.'

The Eton College O.T.C. on a field Day exercise in 1909. George is in the front line, extreme right

In April 1909, Barrie revisited Edinburgh University, the scene of so much loneliness in his youth, to receive his second honorary LL.D. (St Andrews University had given him an honorary degree in 1898). The function lasted for over six hours, with Barrie dressed in an elaborate ceremonial gown – 'the gayest affair,' he wrote to Sylvia, 'all red and blue, and if Michael had met me in a wood he would have tried to net me as a Scarlet Emperor. . . . The five missed the chance of their lives in not encountering me in the streets arrayed in my glory.'[2] By Easter, Sylvia had recovered enough to take the boys down to Ramsgate to stay with their grandmother. Nico wrote impatiently to

---

*Guy's original ending gave triumph to the Germans (thinly disguised as the 'Nearlanders'), but Barrie and Gerald, catering for the box-office, replaced it with a last-minute British victory.

Barrie: 'Dear James . . . You are a big swank not to come sooner Come hurry up the train is coming From NICO THE END.' Doubtless Barrie was eager to join them, but he was working at Black Lake with Gilbert Cannan, who had recently been appointed to the newly formed Dramatic League, of which Barrie was a founder member, dedicated to the setting up of a National Theatre in England. Cannan was also still performing his duties as Secretary to the Committee seeking the abolition of the Censor, and Mary Barrie, after years of exclusion from her husband's work, had learnt to use a typewriter and was proving an invaluable help to both men.

Barrie's plans for a Peter Pan statue had also been making progress; he had commissioned the sculptor Sir George Frampton, R.A., to carry out the work, and had given him the photographs of Michael taken at Rustington to serve as a model. Barrie wrote to Sylvia from Black Lake on April 11th: 'Frampton was very taken with Mick's pictures & I had to leave them with him. He prefers the Peter clothes to a nude child. It will take him at least two years. George's wife can unveil it. I don't feel gay, so no more at present, dear Jocelyn.' Barrie's dejection persisted throughout the early summer; he was offered a knighthood, but, despite Sylvia's urgings to accept, he turned it down. He wrote to her again at Ramsgate on June 17th, the day after Michael's ninth birthday:

Nico, aged 4 and (*below*) birthday card from Nico to Barrie

> Dearest Jocelyn,
> . . . How I wish I were going down to see Michael and Nicholas. All the donkey boys and the fishermen and sailors see them but I don't. I feel they are growing up without my looking on, when I grudge any blank day without them. I can't picture a summer day that does not have Michael skipping on in front. That is summer to me. And all the five know me as nobody else does. The bland indifference with which they accept my tantrums is the most engaging thing in the world to me. They are quite sure that despite appearances I am all right. To be able to help them and you, that is my dear ambition, to do the best I can always and always, and my greatest pride is that you let me do it. I wish I did it so much better. . . . I am so sorry about those pains in your head.
> Your affectionate
> J.M.B.

The only heartening piece of news received by Barrie this month was that George had been given his 'Sixpenny' – colours awarded to the best eleven cricketers under sixteen. 'Perhaps no one who has never got a colour of some sort at Eton can comprehend the satisfaction it gives,' wrote Peter later; 'a successful love affair is possibly the only comparable triumph in after life.'

Peter Pan was revived for a second season in Paris at the beginning of July, and Barrie went over to spend two weeks with Frohman, then returned to London for another series of Censorship Committee meetings. By July 25th he was back at Black Lake Cottage, writing in low spirits to his old friend Quiller-Couch, who had written congratulating him on *What Every Woman Knows* and giving him news of his son, the Pippa:

'I'm glad you got some entertainment out of *What Every Woman Knows*. The first act I always thought really good . . . [but] the rest is rather of the theatre somehow, ingenious enough but not dug out of myself. It isn't really the sort of man I am. I fancy I try to create an artificial world to myself because the one I really inhabit, the only one I could do any good in, becomes too sombre. How doggedly my pen searches for gaiety. . . .

'The Boy! To think he is leaving Winchester instead of putting on his pinafore. To-morrow he will be leaving Oxford. An English boy has almost too good a time. Who would grudge him it, and yet he knows too well that the best is past by the time he is three and twenty.'

Barrie continued to work alone at Black Lake, preparing a speech he was due to give before a Government Committee set up to investigate the censorship issue. Mary Barrie was in London, and intended travelling down to the cottage on the afternoon of Wednesday, July 28th – the last day of the run of *What Every Woman Knows*. On Wednesday morning, however, the Black Lake gardener, Mr Hunt, chose to cripple Barrie's life by exposing him to the reality of Mary's relationship with Gilbert Cannan. The cottage staff had known about it since the previous November, when Gilbert and Mary had stayed at Black Lake in Barrie's absence; Hunt had held his tongue for eight months, and might well have remained silent altogether had Mary not irritated him by criticizing his gardening skills. The essence of Hunt's revelation and its inevitable result were later recounted by Barrie in the Divorce Court, in answer to questions from his barrister, Mr Barnard, K.C.:

Mary Barrie with Luath at Black Lake

BARNARD. Towards the end of July this year Mr Hunt made a communication to you as to what happened the previous November?

BARRIE. Yes.

BARNARD. What did he tell you?

BARRIE. He said his wife took up tea in the morning to Mr Cannan, and he was not in his room. She then went with tea to my wife's room and knocked and heard my wife saying, 'Gilbert, Gilbert!' She then returned to Mr Cannan's room and entered it. He was not there and the bed had not been slept in.

BARNARD. What did you do [after hearing Hunt's communication]?

BARRIE. On the same day I went to London and telegraphed my wife to meet me. She was going to come down that afternoon, but I telegraphed her to wait until she had seen me.

BARNARD. Did you tell your wife what Mr Hunt had said?

BARRIE. I told her and she said, 'It is all quite true.' I said, 'If it is all quite true, we must go and see Sir George Lewis about it.'

BARNARD. Sir George was not only your solicitor, but the friend of both of you?

BARRIE. Yes. . . .

BARNARD. What took place at the interview?

BARRIE. My wife said it was the only time it had ever taken place, and they had both been in a state about it. I said, 'If you will come back I will forgive you. No one would ever know anything about it.' She said it would all be pretence. I should be thinking of her all the time, but he was the only person in the world——[*Here Barrie hesitated, and was prompted by the President of the Court, Sir John Bigham*]

PRESIDENT. That she loved?

BARRIE. Yes. That he was the only person in the world to her.

PRESIDENT. She meant that she was in love with him?

BARRIE. Yes. She said that it would be a much more ignoble thing to go back to me in those circumstances.

BARNARD. Did you then offer to separate by deed if she would promise to have nothing more to do with him?

BARRIE. Yes.

BARNARD. And she refused.

BARRIE. Yes.[3]

The court transcript indicated little of the anguish suffered by all concerned in the two-month period between Hunt's revelation and the divorce case in October. Divorce was a scandalous business, but Mary was determined to cling to her one glimpse of happiness and marry Cannan. A number of Barrie's friends supported her, including H. G. Wells. Mary wrote to him in early August:

Postscript doodle from H. G. Wells to Mary Barrie

'He seems to have developed the most ardent passion for me now that he has lost me; that frightens me. . . . Poor thing, he is distracted and I am dreadfully sorry; he says he knows I would be happier with G.C. and that we ought to marry, one moment, and the next clamours for me. Anyhow I am to have money and that will help things somewhat, but I have no fear for my happiness, none at all.'

Cannan himself was well aware of the damaging effect that his involvement as co-respondent in a divorce case would have on his literary career, particularly when the petitioner happened to be the most successful writer in the country. He hoped, somewhat naïvely, that Barrie would see his way to allowing him to 'share' Mary, thus avoiding an actual divorce. Even Maurice Hewlett, one of Barrie's oldest friends, seemed to think that Barrie was being unreasonable in insisting that Mary should put aside Cannan altogether as an alternative to divorce. He wrote to her in August:

'I think J. is behaving very badly – *impossibly*, according to my way of looking at things. He must have been talked over by old [Sir George] Lewis – a loathsome Jew. . . . I envy Cannan the chance he has of making life good for you. I don't see how I can meet J. after all this. It amazes me that Mason hasn't made him more of a gentleman.'

Barrie took refuge in A. E. W. Mason's London flat shortly after the storm broke, where, Mason later told Peter Davies, 'he would walk up and down, up and down all night in his heavy boots until the sound of it drove everyone within hearing almost as frantic as the miserable little figure itself'.

Sir George Lewis doubtless advised Barrie to restrain his friendship with Sylvia until the divorce was over, since there was a not unreasonable chance that her name might be dragged into the proceedings by Mary Barrie. To Mary's credit, she never once cited her husband's long association with Sylvia, and made no public defence of her infidelity. Nevertheless, Barrie acted on Lewis's advice and went with Mason to Switzerland, while Sylvia took the boys away for a summer holiday at Postbridge in Devon. Sylvia's own reaction to the collapse in Barrie's marriage is unrecorded. Peter Davies wrote:

'Whether Sylvia regarded the divorce as, ultimately, a simplification of the relation in which she stood to him, or the exact reverse, who can say? . . . That [she] found him a comforter of infinite sympathy and tact, and a mighty convenient slave, and that she thankfully accepted his money as a gift from the gods to herself and her children – all that is clear enough. I think that she laughed at him a little, too, and was a little sorry for him, with all his success, as anyone who knew him well and liked him was more or less bound to be. I mean sorry for him in a general way, quite apart from the pity which his misery over the fact and machinery and publicity of divorce must have stirred in any generous breast.'

Barrie wrote to Sylvia from Switzerland, asking her to send him news of the boys and her own health. Sylvia replied evasively, 'I wish I could walk more, . . . but the hills try me now', then added that 'Michael (Saint) is going to Wilkinson's with Peter [next term] – you will think of me when I have to cut his hair – he is longing and longing for the moment'. Peter Davies commented:

Sylvia fishing the River Dart near Postbridge, Devon

'I can't clearly remember Michael's hair unshorn; but photographs show that he had the most entrancing curls, so that Sylvia's anguish and his own delight at the idea of losing them are equally understandable. . . . I have pretty clear recollections of the Postbridge holiday, . . . George and I worm-fished insatiably in the Dart. . . . Jack, I think, was less easily amused (more adult, perhaps), and occasionally sought the company of a neighbouring farmer's daughter. . . . It must have been dreadfully boring for Sylvia, but no doubt it was very healthy for all of us. To counteract that we stole an occasional Egyptian cigarette (Nestor) from the pink cardboard packets which Sylvia used, and smoked it surreptitiously behind the hedge that bounded the garden. . . . I think it was this summer, too, that George began to shock me to the core by strange locutions picked up at Eton. Obscenity and profanity would mingle horrifically and fortissimo in impassioned oaths when a big quarter-pound trout escaped after being hauled out of the water, wriggling irresistibly. Many public school boys acquire a certain eloquence in this kind of language, though by no means all; and George, in no sense a dissolute or ill-living boy, had unquestionably a marked talent for it, which he was from the age of sixteen at all times ready to display in suitable surroundings. . . . I may record that I soon discarded the youthful blush of shame, and became my brother's apt pupil. Of Sylvia herself at Postbridge I remember very little. I think she rarely went more than a few hundred yards from the house.'

Barrie continued to write to Sylvia from Switzerland, but his letters made no mention of his impending divorce. 'I can't write of it,'[4] he wrote to Pauline Chase, and Peter Davies commented: 'I doubt if he exposed his wounds much to anyone, being in most ways an exceedingly reserved character himself.' There remained one outlet for his anguish, however. While in Switzerland he wrote a one-act play, *The Twelve-Pound Look*, in which he portrayed himself as Harry Sims, a successful 'what-you-will' who is about to receive the honour of a knighthood. He engages a typist to answer his letters of congratulation, but when she arrives, he finds that she is none other than his ex-wife, Kate. Recovering from his surprise, Harry ('strictly speaking, you know, I am not Sir Harry until Thursday') is intrigued to learn the identity of the lover who caused the break-up of their marriage, and is crushed at the discovery that there was no such glamorous person:

KATE. There was no one, Harry; no one at all. . . . You were a good husband according to your lights. . . .

SIR HARRY (*stoutly*). *I* think so. . . . I swaddled you in luxury.

KATE (*making her great revelation*). That was it. . . . How you beamed at me when I sat at the head of your fat dinners in my fat jewellery, surrounded by our fat friends. . . .

SIR HARRY. . . . We had all the most interesting society of the day. . . . There were politicians, painters, writers——

KATE. Only the glorious, dazzling successes. Oh, the fat talk while we ate too much – about who had made a hit and who was slipping back, and what the noo house cost and the noo motor and the gold soup-plates, and who was to be the noo knight. . . . One's religion is whatever he is most interested in, and yours is Success. . . . I couldn't endure it. If a failure had come now and then – but your success was suffocating me. . . . The passionate craving I had to be done with it, to find myself among people who had not got on.

SIR HARRY (*with proper spirit*). There are plenty of them.

KATE. There were none in our set. When they began to go downhill they rolled out of our sight.

SIR HARRY (*clinching it*). I tell you I am worth a quarter of a million.

KATE (*unabashed*). That is what you are worth to yourself. I'll tell you what you are worth to me: exactly twelve pounds. . . . (*She presses her hand on the typewriter as lovingly as many a woman has pressed a rose.*) I learned this. I hired it and taught myself. . . . and with my first twelve pounds I paid for my machine. Then I considered I was free to go, and I went.

The critic W. A. Darlington wrote: 'Just as in *Tommy and Grizel* [Barrie] made the worst of himself into a sentimentalist, so now he made the worst of himself into Sir Harry Sims, the successful man in every worldly respect and yet a failure in his private life.'[5] The play is not, however, as autobiographical as it might seem, for Mary, unlike Kate, relished her husband's success to the full. The real cause of the break-up of their marriage was perceived by Meredith's son, Will, who wrote to Charles Scribner, Barrie's American publisher, in an effort to 'contradict false rumours':

'The whole truth is that Mrs B is a woman – with a woman's desires – which for many years she had controlled (& she had no children, which made it harder). Barrie is a son born to a mother – long after the rest of her family – & as so often is the case – with genius but with little virility. Now – people are now saying that Mrs Barrie had many lovers. This is false – I am certain of it – I have good authority.* . . .

*Diana Farr states that Mary later told Cannan's sister, in a moment of bitterness, that 'he had not been the only lover, but simply the one who was "unlucky enough to be caught."'

She was, as it happens, overcome by this man for whom she has left Barrie. She loves the man, as a young woman loves a man – & still loves Barrie as a mother loves a helpless child. Barrie urged her to return to him & give up the other – she, having at length after long battling against it, given in to the longing of her heart after a virile man, & no doubt the secret woman's longing for the birth of a child, would not.'[6]

Barrie's impotence was much rumoured in his lifetime, some wag dubbing him 'the boy who couldn't go up', but it remains a matter of speculation. Mary later confided to Hilda Trevelyan that she had enjoyed 'normal marital relations'[7] with her husband in the early days of their marriage, but Diana Farr, in her 1978 biography of Cannan, quotes an entry from John Middleton Murry's journal, written in 1955: 'What we were given to understand by Gilbert and Mary was that Barrie was guilty of unmentionable sex behaviour towards Mary. Knowing Mary I should say that *any* sexual approach towards her would have come into such a category for her. And I am pretty certain that Gilbert had no sex-relation with Mary at any time.' Diana Farr qualifies this provocative statement by pointing out that Middleton Murry was a surprisingly poor judge of character, and that he did not know either Mary or Cannan until many years later.

Barrie returned from Switzerland towards the end of September, in time to escort Michael to his first day at Wilkinson's preparatory school:

'When he was nine I took him to his preparatory, he prancing in the glories of the unknown until the hour came for me to go, "the hour between the dog and the wolf", and then he was afraid. I said that in the holidays all would be just as it had been before, but the newly-wise one shook his head; and on my return home, when I wandered out unmanned to his tool-shed, I found these smashing words in his writing pinned to the door:

THIS ESTABLISHMENT IS NOW PERMANENTLY CLOSED

'I went white as I saw that [he] already understood life better than I did.'[8]

Michael, aged 9 (JMB)

Another boy being jostled forward for Barrie's attention was Captain Scott's son, who was to be christened Peter, after Peter Pan. Scott had written to Barrie while the latter was in Switzerland, asking him if he would be Peter's godfather, and Barrie readily

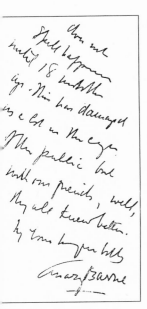

End of Mary's letter to H. G. Wells: . . .'does not spell happiness until 18 months ago. This has damaged us a lot in the eyes of the public but with our friends, well, they all knew better. My love to you both, Mary Barrie'

Barrie and Henry James on their way to the Censorship Committee hearings on August 6th, 1909 – nine days after Hunt's revelation about Mary Barrie's affair with Cannan

accepted. However, the date of the christening, October 13th, conflicted with another appointment – Barrie's own divorce case. A number of fellow writers had banded together and written a private letter to every editor in Fleet Street, reminding them that Barrie himself had been a journalist, and requesting them, 'as a mark of respect and gratitude to a writer of genius',[9] to abstain from exploiting the news value of the case since he is 'a man for whom the inevitable pain of these proceedings would be greatly increased by publicity'. Among the signatories to the letter were Henry James, A. E. W. Mason, Maurice Hewlett, Arthur Wing Pinero, William Archer, H. G. Wells and Beerbohm Tree. The Press responded generously, with only *The Daily Telegraph*, the *Daily Mail* and the *Daily Mirror* covering it in any detail. The undefended suit was soon over, Mrs Hunt's rambling evidence about taking cups of tea in and out of bedrooms at Black Lake being interrupted by the Court President with a curt 'That is quite enough.' Mary Barrie claimed in a letter to H. G. Wells that Barrie 'came out badly in court. 3 lies. First, never said it was the only time. 2nd. It is *my cottage*, lease is in my name and I bought it with my money. 3rd.* It is seven years since we separated and that does not spell happiness until 18 months ago'.[10] The matter of the ownership of Black Lake was academic: Barrie had no further desire to visit it. 'Never go back on happy footsteps,' he told the Duchess of Sutherland; 'be brave in your farewell – as you were brave in your crucifixion.'[11] Nor did he wish to go on living at Leinster Corner. At present he was installed in A. E. W. Mason's flat, but presently Sir George Lewis's wife found him one of his own in Adelphi Terrace House, between the Strand and the Thames. The flat was on the third floor, overlooking Bernard Shaw's residence, but this was more than compensated by a fine view of the river. Lady Lewis and E. V. Lucas's wife, Elizabeth, set to work on Barrie's behalf, organizing the move, while Barrie turned to the only life that was now left to him: Sylvia and her boys – 'my boys'.

Two days after the divorce case was over, Sylvia collapsed on the stairs at Campden Hill Square. Peter was in the house at the time: 'I happened to be about . . . and Mary Hodgson, red-faced and agitated, tended her and shooed me away, not before I had received an impression of direness and fatality, and a sense of shocked misery and half-comprehending desolation, which has remained with me ever since.' Doctor Rendel, who had been the family doctor for many years, was called and gave Sylvia an examination. Mary Hodgson

*The 3rd 'lie' refers to Barrie's 'Yes' in answer to the question, 'Did you live happily with your wife?' Mary's point that 'it is seven years since we separated' would seem to indicate some sort of marital happiness prior to the autumn of 1902 (the publication of *The Little White Bird* and Barrie's trip to Paris with Sylvia).

asked if she could do anything, and he replied, '*It is a grave matter –* say *nothing* to the family.' A specialist was consulted, who diagnosed cancer – 'too close to the heart to operate' – but once again, Mary Hodgson was sworn to secrecy. She later wrote to Peter Davies:

'*It was impressed on me that your Mother –* on *no* account – was to talk about her illness to me & that at all costs she must *not know how* ill she was. Life was to go on as usual and the Boys were just to be told Mother had to stay in bed and rest for a long time. . . . Nurse Loosemore came, an excellent nurse – who not unnaturally resented my presence in her domain. Occasionally there was a duel of words – your mother insisting that her children should come into her bedroom at all times and that their noise & chatter cheered her.'

The secret was well kept for a time: Sylvia's elder sister Trixie wrote to her sister May a few days later, still giving Barrie's divorce precedence as the main topic of interest:

> Felden, Boxmoor.
> [October 17th, 1909]

Darling May,

   . . . I am so distressed about Sylvia & shall go and see her soon. But I am not surprised, she never seemed to rest at all, & I expect when holidays come is quite tired out – at her age and after all she went through with Arthur it was bound to come to something, but I hope a rest will show improvement. As regards Mrs Barrie I think you have endlessly mistaken what I said to you, & what has now happened is only after all a perfectly natural sequence. It is a pity the man is so young, but those things do happen & I hear from Sylvia that he is very much in love with her & I sincerely hope there may be a baby or two. I do think she deserves something to make up for what she has probably suffered in seeing J. entirely wrapped up in someone else's children when it was very obviously his fault that she had none – Human nature is human nature after all & will out. . . . I was surprised that my most straight-laced friend Mabel wrote & said she was so glad that Mrs B. had someone to be fond of her now – & that if J. was unhappy he deserved it – tho' poor little man one knows well he is simply the victim of circumstance & of his own kindness.

   I have by the bye often heard you & Coley [May's husband] say she might be forgiven if she did seek consolation. Well well.

> Yr loving
> Trixie

George, at Eton, was seemingly unaware of his mother's illness:

Thursday, November 18th [1909]

Dearest Mother,

... It was topping having Mr Barrie down here on Sunday. I have grown a lot, as now I simply tower above him. I'm reaching the goal of my ambition – six feet of height! We went for a walk and then had tea with my tutor [Hugh Macnaghten]. He [Barrie] was very sad, of course, but he seemed to buck up a bit at times. Mr Mason does seem to be kind to him, getting all his clothes at blood tailors and things. The flat seems rather jolly too. We shall have to go and see him a lot next holidays, and cheer him up. I'm hoping he'll be able to come down here on St Andrew's Day with Mr Mason.

I suppose I'd better be getting some blue serge pattern to send you. ... Pray remember that one has to be rather à la mode in London! My taste in socks is settling down from loudness to real good taste. My last pair is quite a dream! Such an exquisite blue, you know, a trifle dark and subdued. I always rather liked blue! I've also got a lovely dark green Jaeger pair, which I feel certain you'll adore. I think I'm rather a coming man!

Your loving son,
George

Adelphi Terrace House in Robert Street, off the Strand. Barrie's flat was on the third floor; he later moved to the top-floor flat with the angled window

At the end of November, Barrie moved into his new flat in Adelphi Terrace, decorated for him by Elizabeth Lucas and Lady Lewis, who had also found him an indispensable manservant in the shape of 'the inimitable' Harry Brown, as Peter called him, 'who was to do so much for his comfort in the years that followed, and would soon be on intimate terms with all of us, calling Nico "Tuppence" and generally brightening the atmosphere'.

George and Jack returned at Christmas to find their mother more or less permanently confined to her bedroom, attended by Nurse Loosemore. A consultation with a third specialist had produced further anxiety. Mary Hodgson told Peter later, 'By this time your Mother was worried and restless. I had gone down stairs out of the way – returning – Dr R[endel] ... shook his head sadly. At this moment your Mother's bell rang gently. The rest of the gathering were in the School Room. Your Mother said, "Shut the door, Mary. You are the only one I trust – what did Dr Rendel say?" I replied, "Nothing," and she lay back bitterly disappointed.' By early spring, Sylvia was obliged to use a Bath-chair, lifted by two carrier men. Barrie was in constant attendance, resuming the role he had performed only three years before at the bedside of the dying Arthur.

Sylvia's illness was less intense – a gradual winding down of the body and spirit rather than a series of operations, but no less harrowing to witness. Some days she was able to go outside and watch Michael and Nico playing cricket with 'Uncle Jim' in Campden Hill Square, but for most of the time she remained in her room. Barrie paid for an 'Electrophone' to be installed by her bed – an ingenious device which enabled her to dial any theatre of her choice and listen to the performance on a pair of headphones. George wrote to her from Eton:

'How are you? You never say anything about how you're getting on. What rot it is to think you've never even seen this room. . . . How soon shall you go out in your bath-chair? I do hope I'll be able to wheel you on leave. . . . How I envy you being able to listen on the electrophone at night. I feel just like it myself. "Ah! now listen." "What is it?" "Um–um–um–la, la, la, la, etc." "Divine!" Or again: "Let's have 'The Arcadians' Electrophone?" "Yes." "Put us on to the Shaftesbury, please." "Oh yes, they're just finishing that decent song – 'Oh, what very charming wea-ther.'" "Perfect!"'

George may have been aware of Sylvia's condition, and have felt that frequent happy letters from Eton were the best possible tonic for her. Michael, although only nine, certainly had intuitive forebodings: Gerald du Maurier later told his daughter Daphne how, on one of his visits to see Sylvia, he noticed Michael sitting at a small desk in the corner of her bedroom, doing his homework, the tears rolling down his cheeks and splashing onto the paper.

At Easter 1910, Nico went to stay with Mary Hodgson for a short holiday in Morecambe. Sylvia wrote to him from her sick-bed:

Sylvia's sketch of Nico

23 C.H.S.
22nd [April, 1910]

Darling,

    Today Peter & Michael & Nurse & I went twice to Kensington Gardens. Michael sometimes sits at the end of the bath chair & guides it while the man pushes it behind. Will you guide it sometimes when I get back? It is very hot & I must get you a thin coat. I wish I could sit on the sands with you & throw stones into the sea! Dear darling Nico, I have got to be carried to bed now. I wish I could run upstairs instead! What would nurse say!

Goodnight my dear little boy.
Loving & loving,
Mother

Captain Scott was now busily preparing for his second expedition to the Antarctic, but did not disdain to join Barrie, Michael and Nico in games of exploration in Kensington Gardens. In his Dedication to *Peter Pan*, Barrie described them as 'our Antarctic exploits when we reached the Pole in advance of our friend Captain Scott and cut our initials on it for him to find, a strange foreshadowing of what was really to happen'. With Barrie acting as one of his financial sponsors, Scott left England in early June, setting out on his attempt to become the first man to reach the South Pole. There appears to have been some argument between the two men shortly before Scott sailed, but, whatever the cause, Barrie remained a fervent supporter of the expedition throughout the three years of its duration.

By the end of June, Sylvia appeared to be making a slight recovery, but was still not strong enough to travel down to Eton. This was left to Barrie, who had grown particularly fond of Arthur's old colleague and George's housemaster and tutor, Hugh Macnaghten. 'Hugh was a queer one,' wrote Peter in his *Morgue*, 'as queer in his own way as J.M.B. in his, and the two ways had something in common. Hugh was too good to be wise.' Macnaghten's House was considered to be the best at Eton, and George was, at sixteen, a major asset to it in the realm of sport. His tremendous popularity among the other boys was evidenced by his early election to Pop – Eton's élitist social club, membership of which is normally restricted to boys in their final year. As a full-blown Eton blood, George was a known figure to every boy in the school, yet it never went to his head. 'He had absolutely no vanity,' recalled a contemporary, 'no conceit whatsoever. It was quite extraordinary – almost unique in my experience – for someone quite so successful. He was a tremendous blood at Eton, but you'd never have known it. He wasn't a great talker, but he had great charm. He was rather shy, rather reserved, but his sense of humour was exquisite.'[12] Barrie was, not unnaturally, overwhelmed with pride in this boy who was making such a graceful transition from the child in the red tam-o'-shanter to the gay young Etonian who still retained so much of the bright boy-knight about his looks and personality. Little wonder that he availed himself of every opportunity to visit him, taking him out for the day, or watching him play cricket from the side of the field. Many boys of George's age might have found the constant companionship of a strange little man something of an embarrassment among their peers; it would seem that George felt quite the reverse. On July 1st he wrote to Sylvia, 'I've written to Uncle Jim to fulfil his telephone promise and come down tomorrow. I do hope he'll be able to do so. I'm feeling very keen to see his best silk socks! I hope it isn't going to rain to stop him coming or anything of that sort.' Peter later commented on George's use of the term 'Uncle Jim', which Michael and Nico had been using for some time, 'symbolizing

George with his housemaster and tutor, Hugh Macnaghten

the intimacy which had so rapidly increased since 1907, until he was closer by far to us, as well as directing our destinies, than any of our real uncles. . . . J.M.B. is now clearly seen in the role of leading uncle, if not step-father; perhaps guardian angel best describes him.' It was a role that Sylvia utilized with increasing frequency. Peter was in his last term at Wilkinson's, and was due to join George at Eton in the Christmas half. He had taken a scholarship exam, but since Barrie had already guaranteed all the boys' fees, there was no anxiety over the result. Sylvia wrote to Barrie on July 6th as he was about to set off for Eton and collect Peter after his exam:

> 23 Campden Hill Square,
> Kensington.
>
> Dear J,
> . . .Will you do something for me? I want 1½ doz. white collars (George wears the shape) for Peter & 2 doz. white ties (also like George), as they are best bought at Eton. The shop is called New & Lingwood. Ask for collars for tails & Peter will know what size & can try one on if wanted. He must bring them home with him.
> I so liked your letter about G & P! I have thought so much of Peter & am wondering how he has done. . . . I suppose George can't be let off camp for his delicate mother's sake.
> Affec:
> S.

A few days later, Wilkinson interrupted Peter in a game of 'corridor cricket' to announce with some surprise that he had brought off his Eton scholarship, albeit twelfth on the list. In recording his 'puny triumph' in the family *Morgue*, Peter apologized for 'dwelling a little on this, the solitary distinction, such as it was, that I ever attained in my mostly mis-spent life. That it gave pleasure to Sylvia in her last sad weeks has always been to me a source of secret satisfaction.'

By July, Sylvia was convinced that she was seriously ill, despite the assurance of her family and doctors to the contrary. In an effort to elicit the truth, she proposed taking her five boys on holiday into the wilds of Devon – a scheme that met with Barrie's approval, but filled Emma du Maurier with horror. Mary Hodgson later explained to Peter, 'Your mother *insisted* on going out of town *with her family*, thinking it would finally decide matters if they would *not* let her go. Dr R[endel] said, "If Sylvia wishes to go, she should have what she wishes." Nurse L[oosemore] said Dr R and J.M.B. were quite *mad* & eventually told me to make myself & the boys scarce on the journey "as *anything* might happen".' The house selected for the holidays was

Ashton Farm, a lonely farm-house in the valley of the River Oare, miles from the nearest doctor, but selected by Sylvia because it would provide excellent fishing for her boys.

Dolly Ponsonby visited her shortly before she left London. 'I think she was in a black gown, and lying on the sofa. I realized then that she was not going to live, and I remember going back and telling my husband, and weeping.'[13]

The journey to Ashton made an exhausting day for Sylvia: five hours by rail to Minehead, then fifteen miles across Exmoor by car. 'At Minehead there was a climax', wrote Mary Hodgson to Peter. 'Your Mother insisted that the two youngest and myself [instead of Nurse Loosemore] should travel in the car. . . . Nurse Loosemore barely spoke to me thereafter. At Ashton, I only saw your mother at odd times. I think the powers-that-be thought I was not to be trusted, and were probably wise in that view.' Barrie was obliged to stay not at the farm-house but in rooms in the neighbouring village, since Emma du Maurier had announced her intention of coming down to be with her daughter and sleep in the only spare room. Nevertheless he was in daily attendance, sitting with Sylvia as he had sat with Arthur, revising his manuscript of *Peter and Wendy*, or recording his thoughts in his notebook:

Emma du Maurier in 1910 – a widow for the past 14 years

—*Peter Pan. Revise.* What time of year, summer winter autumn? Peter doesn't understand – 'There's only spring.'
—Michael saying 'If good in heaven will God sometimes let me go down to Hell to play?'
—The dying. Friends around talk of other things. Wonder about dying, when silent really making preparations for dying – for the journey.
—*Death.* One thinks of the dead as a bird taking lonely flight. If saw we would realise it is always one of a great flock of birds.
—*Play.* Man who brings up 4 girls as guardian (better than boys?).
—*The Second Chance*: 'Beware, or you may get what you want.'

Emma du Maurier arrived at the farm-house at the beginning of August, and wrote regular accounts of Sylvia's condition to her daughter, May:

'[August 1st, 1910] . . . It is terrible to think dear Sylvia is so far from doctors. . . . It is a nice house but hill all round, even from the lawn to the garden is quite a hill. This ought never to have been taken. Today Sylvia is staying in bed, she seems quite to wish to. She seems glad I have come and hopes I can stay and of course I shall, but you can imagine what I feel. [August 5th] . . . Dr Spicer came this morning. . . . When Sylvia heard the doctor was to sleep here (for we all think it a great mistake if he didn't) she was angry and then began to cry, and said "I believe I am very ill", so you can imagine how dreadful that was. . . . Dear Sylvia has such bad nights, even with trional, and she looks so wan and thin, it breaks my heart to look at her. . . . She doesn't wish the boys ever to be kept away from her; of course they are out all day until tea time, and when they are in the garden she can see them. [August 24th] . . . Dear Sylvia had a bad night and seems very languid and weak this morning. Yesterday afternoon she seemed more comfortable and wished to hear the gramophone and the boys came in. However too many of them soon tire her. Dear little Nicholas is very good but of course he is lively and wants to jump about and climb on the backs of the others and all that is too much in her room. After tea they play games in the garden and it amuses her to watch them.'

Sylvia (JMB)

Peter Davies recalled how George and Jack, both wearing new suits, went into the room where Sylvia lay on a sofa, and 'how she greatly enjoyed their stylish appearance and exclaimed with delight: "What a pair of young rakes!" Crompton visited the farm-house for a few days, our only other visitor being Maude Adams, whom Barrie brought down for a night or two that she might see and be seen by Sylvia and "her boys (my boys)". For the rest of the time we went our ways blithely enough, I seem to remember. The remote and beautiful Doone valley, a few miles from Ashton, was among our regular fishing-places . . . and we made almost daily expeditions, sandwiches in pocket, up the valleys of the Lynn and the Oare. . . . In the evenings we would take the day's catch of small trout in to show Sylvia, as she lay, so much frailer than we knew, on a sofa or in her bed. . . . From now onwards, while we fished and golfed and walked furiously, or made expeditions to Lynton and ate huge teas with bilberry jam and Devonshire cream, or on idle days watched the buzzards circling slowly, high above the valley of the Lynn – while, in fact, we went our boyish ways – Sylvia weakened rapidly, and I think she never again left her room.'

Faced with the inevitable, Sylvia once again attempted to draft a Will, though it was not found until several months after her death:

'Sylvia's Will.

'I would like everything to go on as far as possible as it has been lately. Twenty-three [Campden Hill Square] to be kept up for the dear boys with Mary (whom I trust with my whole heart) looking after them.

'At any time I know friends who love them will come & stay sometimes – one at a time – & see them & be with them for a little just as if I was there. What I wd like wd be if Jenny* wd come to Mary & that the two together would be looking after the boys & the house & helping each other. And it would be so nice for Mary.

'I would like Mama & J.M.B. & Guy & Crompton to be trustees & guardians to the boys & that May & Margaret would give their dear advice & care. ... I would also like the advice of dear Hugh Macnaghten. ... J.M.B. I know will do everything in his power to help our boys – to advise, to comfort, to sympathise in all their joys & sorrows.

'At present my Jack is going into the Navy – if he should grow to dislike it and if there was anything else, I know he (J.M.B.) would do all that was best. I want all the boys to treat him (& their uncles) with absolute confidence & straightforwardness & to talk to him about everything. I know he will understand always & be loving & patient. I hope from my soul that they will be happy & lead good lives & be as much as possible like their most beloved father & I also hope that if they marry they will be good & tender husbands & fathers & be with their wives as happy as he & I were. ... They have all been the most splendid & beloved & affectionate & open sons & I know they will go on being affectionate brothers & help each other all they can in the years to come. I do not want my Michael to be pressed at all at work – he is at present not very strong† but very keen & intelligent: *great care* must be taken not to overwork him. Mary understands & of course J.M.B. knows & will be careful & watch.

'I do not wish any of my dear boys to look at me when I am dead – it is a great mistake I think – let them remember me at my best & when I could look at them – that must have been the best time always because I love them so utterly.

'I will be cremated & buried with my Arthur at Hampstead next to beloved Papa. Perhaps Mama or May will keep my trinkets & give them to the wives of my five boys when the time comes. ... I would like Mama to go over my letters in case anything has to be kept – otherwise I would like *everything* burnt.

'I do not want any of my boys to go to my funeral, nor do I want it made into a long gloomy day for them.'

Sylvia (JMB)

Peter wrote in his *Morgue*: 'On the morning of the day Sylvia died, ... Nurse Loosemore told us she was not well enough to see us, as she usually did before we went off on our various activities, but that she sent us all her love and would see us in the evening. Jack went off in the car to Minehead with Lloyd [a golfing friend] to play golf, George and I set out on our usual all-day fishing expedition. I

*Mary Hodgson's sister.
†A reference to the fear that Michael might be suffering from tuberculosis.

question whether any of us, even George, the eldest and much the most intimate with J.M.B., felt more than a vague sense of oppression – certainly no clear forebodings.' Denis Mackail related how Sylvia, 'as she lay there in bed, . . . asked for a hand-mirror. She looked in it, and laid it down. "Don't let the boys see me again," she said.'[14] Sylvia's last moments were recounted by Emma du Maurier in a letter to her daughter May, written on the afternoon of August 27th, 1910:

'At $\frac{1}{4}$ to 2 [Nurse Loosemore] called me, and the doctor was holding dear Sylvia's hands and asked me to fan her, but I didn't know the end was so near. She was breathing with great difficulty and I couldn't bear to look at her, then they called in Mr Barrie and I saw what it was and it was all over in about a $\frac{1}{4}$ of an hour. It was her breathing that was exhausted, not heart failure. The doctor, nurse, Mr Barrie and I were the only ones in the room. . . . Darling Sylvia looked perfectly lovely – so calm and happy, and those who love her can only be thankful she is at peace.'

After spending that morning fishing with George, Peter decided to walk home alone:

'It was a grey, lowering, drizzly sort of day, and I walked fast, and was pretty blown, I remember, by the time I reached the top of the steep footpath which led from the river-valley up to the house. As I went in at the gate, it struck me that there was something peculiar in the aspect of the house: in every window the blinds had been drawn. Somehow or other the dreadful significance of this sombre convention conveyed itself to my shocked understanding, and with heart in boots and unsteady knees I covered the remaining thirty or forty yards to the front door. There J.M.B. awaited me: a distraught figure, arms hanging limp, hair dishevelled, wild-eyed.

'In what exact words he told me what I had no need to be told, I forget; but it was brokenly, despairingly, without any pretence of philosophy or resignation or the stiff upper lip. He must have been sunk in depths far below all that, poor Jimmy; I think it was I that propelled him, as much as he me, into the room on the left of the little entrance hall, where we sat and blubbered together. Good cause for blubbering too, for both of us; but I remember, and wish I didn't, sobbing out "Mother! Mother!" at intervals during the sad and painful scene, and realising, even as I did so, that this wasn't altogether natural in me – that, though half involuntary, it was also a half-deliberate playing-up to the situation. I can forgive myself now, after thirty-five years, for this rather shameful bit of nervous reaction: the rest of it, the tears and misery and desolation, were genuine enough. . . . I am almost sure . . . that I went in to look my last on Sylvia as she lay dead in the room on the ground floor which had been made into her bedroom. . . . All I retain . . . is a dream-like, cloudy sense of going in and standing for a matter of seconds, confused, unhappy, frightened, looking and yet not looking at the pale, lifeless features, and then of escaping to I know not what limbo in some remote corner of the house . . . Nico, then aged six and three quarters, has a memory of approaching the door of Sylvia's room, meaning to go in as had been his habit after tea each day, and of being shooed away with significant gruffness by one of his kind brothers, probably Michael. . . . He very well remembers Mary Hodgson trying to explain things to him, and how she laid the responsibility on God, adding hopelessly enough, to soften the blow, that sometimes people who were so spirited away were brought back, and it might be that she would come back at Christmas. And he remembers, thereupon, crying out in misery, half hysterically, "Cruel God! Cruel God!"

'Of how the word of death was spoken to George, when he came back that evening from his day's fishing, I know nothing; or to Michael, then a little over ten years old, and the most highly strung and impressionable of us.'*

Jack recalled his own memories in 1952:

'When the car fetched . . . me back from Minehead, I was taken into a room where [Barrie] was alone and he told me she was dead. He also told me, which angered me even then, that Mother had promised to marry him and wore his ring. Even then I thought if it was true it must be because she knew she was dying. I was then taken in to see her and left with her for a bit. She looked quite natural, as she'd always been so pale, very lovely and asleep.'[16]

Sylvia's 'engagement' ring

When Nico married in 1926, Barrie gave his wife some of Sylvia's jewellery, including a diamond and sapphire ring which, he told Nico, he had given to Sylvia 'as we would have been married had your mother lived'. The abortive betrothal, if true, was never made known to Sylvia's family in her lifetime, and there is no mention of it in any surviving correspondence. Peter was sceptical that such an engagement had ever taken place:

'J.M.B. was quite capable of imagining, and of coming in the end to believe, such a might-have-been. . . . No doubt there must have been

---

*Barrie told a later friend, Mrs Hugh Lewis, that Michael had 'broken into a rage and stamped his feet in a fury of words' upon hearing the news of his mother's death.[15]

conversations between them during those [last] months about the future, and about what they were to be to each other; and she may well have given him the thought of marriage – if it could be called that – to play with. But by then . . . he already had reason to suspect that her disease might prove fatal, and I guess that she too, though never told, suspected it also. At any rate that's how I see it. Others may well say, and doubtless did, that it would have been the most natural thing in the world: that she was already more intimate with him than with any other living being, that he had adored her for years and loved her children, that she was taking so much from him that she could scarcely refuse if that was what he wished, and in fact it was much the best solution. All this is true enough. But I think that to Jack . . . the thought was intolerable and even monstrous; so much so that he could not refrain from expressing himself in the most forcible manner to that effect when J.M.B. in an unguarded moment spoke to him of it. To me too, I confess, the idea of such a marriage is repugnant. Up to a point, perhaps, this is mere sentimentality. The two sublime creatures of one's childhood die when one is too young to have much sense of reality, and the naïve impression remains, so that in after life no one who survives to meet the more calculating glance of one's maturity can ever move in the same dimension as the enchanted dead. . . . But it does seem to me that a marriage between Sylvia, the widow, still so beautiful in her forty-fourth year, of the splendid Arthur, and the strange little creature who adored her and dreamed, as he surely must have dreamed, of stepping into Arthur's shoes, would have been an affront, really, to any reasonable person's sense of the fitness of things. And I do not believe that Sylvia seriously contemplated it. . . . Let me not be thought unmindful, in writing what I have written, of the innumerable benefits and kindnesses I have received, at one time and another, from the aforesaid strange little creature, to whom, in the end, his connection with our family brought so much more sorrow than happiness.'

The morning after Sylvia's death, George and Peter were dispatched to the nearest village with a sheaf of telegrams addressed to relatives and friends:

'As we walked down the hill on this gloomy errand, . . . George remarked to me, perhaps merely speaking his thoughts aloud, . . . that in spite of the tragedy that had come upon us, we seemed to have got up and washed and tied our ties and put on our boots and eaten our breakfast all right: that it wasn't, in fact, the end of the world. Life went on. Physically speaking, we were much as before. . . . For an instant I was shocked, . . . but further reflection persuaded me that there was something in what he said. . . . It was not indifference or resignation or fatalism that George, aged seventeen, was expressing, but a sort of rough-and-ready working philosophy, based on an instinctive sense of proportion. . . . I knew quite well that he was feeling things at least as deeply as I was myself. But he was the eldest brother, and felt his responsibility.'

As there were still another three weeks of the summer holidays left to the boys, it was decided that Michael, Nico and Mary Hodgson should remain at Ashton Farm while George, Jack and Peter accompanied Barrie and their mother's coffin back to London for her funeral. Jack later told his wife of the 'hideous five-hour train journey, and how every time the train stopped at a station, Barrie got out of the carriage and stood with bowed head in front of the guard's van where the coffin was, draped in purple cloth, as if he was on sentry-duty'.[17] Peter remembered virtually nothing of the funeral, writing in his *Morgue*:

Michael fishing (JMB)

'Grotesque that one should retain so little of all that, and yet that one should clearly remember going with J.M.B. and George, presumably the morning after the funeral, to an old-fashioned . . . shop in the Haymarket . . . to purchase exciting, slender 8-ft fly-rods, and fine casts and flies, with which to divert ourselves during the remainder of the holidays! For it had been decided, by those who took charge of our destinies, that George and I should go back with J.M.B. [to Devon], there to fish till Eton and Wilkinson's claimed us. . . . And I dare say it worked well enough, and that the new rods helped, as no doubt J.M.B. with generous cunning knew that they would, to do the trick. At any rate one seems to remember quite enjoying oneself, flogging the little upland streams and hauling out the little trout, and putting the lowly worm behind one for ever.'

'Sylvia . . . leaves with us an image of such extraordinary loveliness, nobleness and charm – ever unforgettable and touching', wrote Henry James to Emma du Maurier on hearing the news of her death.

'Mrs Darling was now dead and forgotten', wrote J. M. Barrie in *Peter and Wendy*, watching her boys fishing the summer streams.

When Sylvia's second Will was found several months after her death, Barrie made a careful, hand-written copy and sent it to Emma du Maurier, adding: 'The above is an exact copy, including the words "Sylvia's Will", of paper found by me at 23 Campden Hill Square. . . . It is undated, but I do not doubt it to be the will written by her at Ashton, Exmoor, a few days before her death, of which all she told me was "I thought I was dying and I began to write a will."' Part of the second paragraph, as transcribed by Barrie, read: 'What I would like would be if Jimmy would come to Mary, and that the two together would be looking after the boys and the house and helping each other. And it would be so nice for Mary.' In fact Sylvia had not written 'Jimmy' but 'Jenny' – Mary Hodgson's sister. The mistranscription was no doubt unintentional, although the word 'Jenny' is clear enough, and Barrie can have had no illusions that his presence at Campden Hill Square would be 'nice for Mary'. In the event, Jenny's services were not called upon, and Mary was obliged to tolerate Barrie's omnipresence at Campden Hill Square, in accordance with Sylvia's supposed last wishes. Even before the discovery of the will, it was clear to all concerned that only Barrie had both the time and the means to assume full responsibility for the boys. The alternative was to divide them up among relatives, but Sylvia had expressly stated to Emma du Maurier that she wanted

13

Sylvia's 2nd Will and (*below*) Barrie's transcription for Emma du Maurier, in which 'Jenny' has become 'Jimmy'. The error, if noted at the time, would have changed little. Emma du Maurier had written to Henry James in September 1910: 'I, & Crompton Davies & Mr Barrie are guardians & think it is pretty certain that Mr Barrie will live with them. I am too old to really be of any use to them. He is unattached & his one wish is to look after them in the way Sylvia would have wished. His devotion to Arthur during his illness & his friendship & affection ever since to all the family makes us all feel that he has a good claim' them to remain together as a family. Any lingering objections to Barrie's official adoption of the Five were overruled when he produced Sylvia's Will, confirming 'Jimmy's' right to look after the boys with Mary.

It was an imperfect solution to all but Barrie and the boys themselves. George, at seventeen, regarded him as a close and intimate friend. Jack, a year younger, was showing signs of resentment, but nevertheless preferred the relative independence of Campden Hill Square in the holidays to any of the other alternatives. Peter, at thirteen, had confused emotions: he shared a degree of Jack's resentment, but worshipped George, and allowed himself to be led by George's trust in Barrie. Michael, 'the mysterious boy of the so open countenance . . . with the carelessness of genius'[1], was now ten. His love for 'Uncle Jim' amounted to adoration, and the complexity of their relationship far exceeded that of Barrie's with George in the days of *The Boy Castaways*. Denis Mackail, who knew both Barrie and Michael at this time, wrote:

'Michael . . . looks like his mother, and hasn't escaped her charm. . . . Not wax for Barrie by any means – but you can steer or lead little boys of ten in a way that you can't do afterwards. [Barrie's] spell is still irresistible when it chooses, and here is the boy – quick, sensitive, attractive, and gifted – who is to be everything else that the magician most admires. There is no cloud between them. From Barrie . . . Michael has no secrets. You can call him the favourite . . . He and Barrie draw closer and closer, and perhaps it isn't always Barrie who leads or steers. He has given his heart to Michael . . . and has transferred an enormous part of his ambition. Is it dangerous? No answer.'

Sylvia's 'darling doodle Nico' would be seven in November. Being so young, he was the least affected by the early deaths of his parents, and his demonstrative, extrovert personality was a great asset in lifting occasional periods of gloom in the household. Like Michael, Nico regarded Barrie not as a father, nor as a brother, 'just the person I always hoped most would be coming in to see me'. As for Barrie, all five boys were 'my boys', though even he must have perceived the irony of his guardianship as he continued his labours on *Peter and Wendy*:

icture-letter from Nico to Barrie

'Then [the lost boys] went on their knees, and holding out their arms cried, "O Wendy lady, be our mother."

'"Ought I?" Wendy said, all shining. "Of course it's frightfully fascinating, but you see . . . I have no real experience."

'"That doesn't matter," said Peter, . . . "What we need is just a nice motherly person."

' "Oh dear!" Wendy said, "you see I feel that is exactly what I am. . . . Very well, . . . I will do my best." '

Unfortunately there were two contenders for the role of the 'nice motherly person' to the five orphans at Campden Hill Square. Mary Hodgson, by now a confirmed spinster, looked upon herself as the boys' substitute mother. Barrie, however, considered that he was *in loco parentis* to the boys, as both father and mother. The inevitable conflict that arose from their rivalry was only held in check by the boys themselves, particularly Michael and Nico, whose devotion to Mary was unshakeable.

Peter at Eton

The bizarre story of 'Barrie and his Lost Boys', and their inevitable parallel with *Peter Pan*, made excellent fodder for society gossip and speculation. It was all fairly harmless, except to Peter, who had begun his first term at Eton a few weeks after Sylvia's death, and was mercilessly ragged as 'the real Peter Pan'. Being a scholar, Peter slept in 'College' – a special house reserved for scholarship boys – and he saw little of George, so much his senior, and living in Macnaghten's House. The teasing he received at Eton led to a phobia so passionate that in after life he came to loathe his association with the play, referring to it only as 'that terrible masterpiece'. He revealed his feelings briefly in the *Morgue*: 'What's in a name? My God, what isn't? If that perennially juvenile lead, if that boy so fatally committed to an arrestation of his development, had only been dubbed George, or Jack, or Michael, or Nicholas, what miseries would have been spared me.' Barrie made frequent visits to Eton, but Peter lacked George's intimacy with him, and confided little of his unhappiness.

Barrie had always harboured a curious fascination for the English public school system, perhaps because his own education at Dumfries Academy was so entirely of another world. In a later speech he told his audience, 'Your great English public schools! I never feel myself a foreigner in England except when trying to understand them. I have a great affection for one at least of them, but they will bewilder me to the end; I am like a dog looking up wistfully at its owner wondering what that noble face means, or if it does have a meaning. To look at, these schools are among the fairest things in England; they draw from their sons a devotion that is deeper, more lasting than almost any other love.'[2] Eton became a source of romance for him, like the aristocracy – an institution which he could tease and flirt with, but never fully embrace – and it was not long before the stage Captain Hook was proclaiming 'Floreat Etona!' as he projected himself into the mouth of the crocodile.

Dolly Ponsonby and her husband Arthur, who was now a leading

A 'Record of Breaks' between Barrie and Michael. Barrie had presented the boys with their first billiards table in 1907: 'Ask Nico not to break the billiard table absolutely until next half!' implored George from Eton

M.P. in Asquith's Liberal Government, visited Barrie in February 1911:

'*Thurs. 23rd Feb. 1911.* A[rthur] & I to lunch with Barrie in his little flat in Adelphi Terrace. He was so dear & wonderful. He is really profound & every word he speaks is full of pure gold & so human & kind & true. He always a little frightens me because his insight is so acute. He told us much of the boys & their characters & of George [who] though at Eton is still a strong Liberal. He says they write one another long letters on politics. The little ones too he says are Violent Radicals & at one moment would hardly consent to a Tory entering the house. When I asked him what they really understood about it, he explained so charmingly & simply his method. "I tell them that the dirty little raggamuffins are as good as they, & why shouldn't they have the same advantages" – or words to that effect. He talked of the differences between Lloyd George & Winston, how L.G. lost his head & said rash things, & how Winston never did but made his mistakes on purpose. . . . I had tea with him too at Campden Hill Sqre & the children with Michael & Nicholas. Margaret [Llewelyn Davies] came in & was rather depressed & unnatural. . . . J.M.B. described much to the children's amusement how he flew on the stage at "Peter Pan". The Company, hearing he was going to fly, all rushed round to the front to see him – & J.M.B. had the safety curtain let down as promptly!'

On March 7th, Barrie was writing to his old friend Quiller-Couch from Adelphi Terrace:

'I have not much concern now with literature and the drama, which both have flowed me by. I have in a sense a larger family than you now. Five boys whose father died four years ago and now their mother last summer, and I look after them, and it is my main reason for going on. The Llewelyn Davies boys. However, I do a little writing also and do it here, tho' mostly I am with them.'

The boys went down to stay with Emma du Maurier at Ramsgate for Easter while Barrie remained in London, making his final revisions on *Peter and Wendy*. Nico wrote to him from Ramsgate on April 22nd:

Dear Mr Barrie thanks for the letter you sent me yesterday   Buck up buck up what are you doing   having your dinner   then push it away and read my letter

FROM NIC-O

With the boys' summer holiday already on his mind, Barrie wrote to the Duchess of Sutherland: 'I wonder whether you would in the goodness of your heart set some factor in Sutherland searching for a house for me up there for August and September. I bring four boys with me; what they yearn for is to be remote from Man and plenty of burn trout fishing, of which they never tire from the rising to the setting of the sun. The rate would not so much matter but there should be space for about ten of us including maids.' The Duchess duly responded with Scourie Lodge, a small manor house on the north-west coast of Scotland. Barrie wrote to his cricketing friend Charles Turley Smith on July 10th: 'We are going for seven weeks or so beginning of August to Scourie in the west of Sutherland. 630 miles rail, then a drive 44 miles. The nearest small town is farther than from here to Paris in time. Nothing to do but fish, which however is what they want. . . . I have been teaching Michael to bicycle, running up and down the quieter thoroughfares of Campden Hill and feeling what it must be like at the end of a Marathon race. Have also taken him to a garden in St John's Wood where an expert teaches him fly fishing on a lawn. . . . I have nearly finished my P. Pan book.' Barrie's extravagance on the boys' behalf was beginning to cause concern among their relatives, particularly Margaret Llewelyn Davies, who had strong socialist principles, and spent much of her time working in London's slums. Dolly Ponsonby's diary records a visit from her while Barrie was in Scotland with the boys:

'*Monday Aug 7th, Bank Holiday* [1911] M[argaret] & I talked all morning of Sylvia & Arthur's boys – & Jimmy Barrie. M is very desperate at moments about them & I too have felt the pity of their easy luxurious lives. In fact it has been on my tongue to say to J.M.B. does he want George to be a fashionable gentleman? Of course in principle he doesn't. In principle he is all for the ragged raggamuffins & says he wants the boys to be for them too. But in his desire to make up to the boys for all they have lost, he gives them every material pleasure. Nothing is denied them in the way of amusement, clothes, toys, etc. It is very, *very* disheartening, & when one thinks of Arthur their father – almost unbearable. . . . J.M.B. takes the boys to very grand restaurants in their best evening clothes & they go on to stalls or box at the theatre. They buy socks costing 12/6 a pair & Michael, aged 11, is given very expensive lessons in fly fishing.'

Barrie wrote to Nurse Loosemore from Scourie Lodge on September 17th:

rrie with the Duchess of
therland and four of 'my boys'
Scourie Lodge in 1911. Back
w, l to r: George (aged 18), the
uchess of Sutherland, Peter
4); front row: Nico (7), Barrie
1), Michael (11)

Dear Miss Loosemore,

. . . We have been here since the last week of July, and return
to London in about a week's time. It is a remote place,
nearly 50 miles from a railway, and when you want food you
have to kill a sheep. It is very beautiful with sea & lochs, all
as blue as the Mediterranean, and in the course of their
wanderings the boys see eagles, otters, whales, seals, &c. The
wanderings are all in search of fish, and it is a great place for
fishing. Michael has caught a salmon & nearly a hundred
sea-trout. . . . His first sea-trout had a tragic history. It
weighed $2\frac{1}{2}$ lbs & he went to bed with it on a chair by his
side. Next day it was sent to England to be stuffed & arrived
on Bank Holiday. The shop was closed so it was taken to the
gardener's cottage of one of the firm. The gardener's wife
thought it was a gift from some anonymous friend and ate it.
I didn't dare tell Michael until he got the salmon.

Jack of course is not with us as he is still on his cruise in
Canadian waters. But he writes very interesting letters and
seems to be very well. They are all happy I think. It is
already a year since their mother died. I took Nicholas out to
fish that day, and it was a happy day for him as she would
have wished. . . .

Yours always,
J. M. Barrie

Your greatest misery	Early School
Your pet flower and colour	Wood Sorrel. Mauve.
Your favourite novelist	Robert Louis Stevenson.

Your greatest misery	Being able
Your pet flower and colour	Cornflower . Dark Blue .
Your favourite novelist	Rider Haggard

Your greatest misery	Nightmares (or) Impositions.
Your pet flower and colour	Rose , dark. red.
Your favourite novelist	J. M. Barrie.

Your greatest misery	Crying
Your pet flower and colour	Rose purple
Your favourite novelist	J M Barrie

Michael and Nico were accompanied on their fishing expeditions by a local Scots gillie, Johnny Mackay, who, according to Barrie, taught Michael 'everything that is worth knowing (which is largely a matter of flies)'. A few months before he died in 1977, Johnny recounted with pleasure how Barrie, while fishing with the humbler worm, 'looked so scruffy that when the Duchess of Westminster saw him she thought he was a poacher and ordered him off her land; and he was too shy to say who he was, so he went'.

In the spring of 1912, Nico left Norland Place and joined Michael at Wilkinson's. 'Michael was always the cleverest of us five, he couldn't help coming top in every class. I was not bad at this and that, but Michael was always 10 times better.' Nico may not have reached Michael's academic heights, but he made a lasting impression on a number of his contemporaries at Wilkinson's, including the future Poet Laureate, Cecil Day Lewis:

'The most remarkable boy at Wilkie's, as I remember it, was Nicholas Llewelyn Davies, . . . not for exceptional intelligence or prowess at games, . . . but because he possessed the magnetism which very occasionally distinguishes one small boy from the crowd of his fellows. . . . To analyse such magnetism is impossible. Nico had great charm, certainly, and poise, and a not unpleasing touch of arrogance,

Four 1911 entries in Barrie's Querist's Album. From top: George, Jack, Michael and Nico

Nico in Wilkinson's uniform

and a lively face with two prominent front teeth; but other boys possessed these qualifications. Nico's magnetism, however undefinable its source, was visible in its effect, for we used to follow him around like the tail following a comet. . . . My own incipient hero-worship, hitherto largely nourished on books, was now turned upon Nico. We had arrived at Wilkie's in the same term, but he seemed to me to be an altogether superior kind of being. . . . Before very long, however, we became friends, sharing our bottles of ice-cream soda on the cricket ground and lording it over the retainers whom Nico's magnetic personality attracted, myself as a sort of Grand Vizier to him. On one occasion he took me back to his guardian's house in Campden Hill Square, and introduced me to him. I remember a large, dark room, and a small dark man sitting in it: he was not smoking a pipe, nor did he receive us little boys with any perceptible enthusiasm – indeed, I don't think he uttered a single word – which was a bit out of character on his part, since the small dark man, Nico's guardian, was the author of *Peter Pan*. After this negative encounter, we went up to an attic and fired with an air-gun at pedestrians in the Square.'[3]

If Day Lewis had known Barrie better, he would have realized that his silence was not in the least out of character. Many of the boys' friends encountered the same apparent indifference. 'The most self-confident people in the world became as if they had a raw lemon in their mouths when they met Barrie' was how one of Michael's friends remembered him. 'I was terrified, and didn't dare speak in his presence. He never said a word, just sat like a tombstone. I viewed him with the utmost dislike, and I think that went for most of Michael's friends, though they would never have told Michael.'[4] Sylvia's sister May had a similar response to Barrie: 'He paralyses me as much as ever', she wrote to Emma du Maurier at about this time. The boys, of course, experienced none of these barriers. Nico wrote of him, 'He was the most wonderful of all companions, and the wittiest man I shall ever know, and all the usual talk about his being obsessed with thoughts of his mother and with general gloom is largely distortion (I cannot recall his once talking about his mother in all the years I knew him). . . . A creature of moods, yes indeed: maybe to be expected of a man of genius; hours of silence, but many many more hours of humour.'

George was now in his last half at Eton: 'In the 1st XI, Treasurer of Pop, Fives Choices, Essay Prize – a splendid performance indeed', observed Peter. Barrie wrote to George on May 29th, 1912:

Sir George Frampton's statue of Peter Pan in Kensington Gardens. The statue, commissioned and paid for by Barrie, was erected in secrecy during the night of April 30, 1912, so that May morning strollers might conceive that it had appeared by magic. The response was not altogether favourable, and questions were asked in the House of Commons about an author's right to advertise his wares in such unorthodox fashion. Although Barrie's 1906 photographs of Michael had been the inspiration for the statue, Frampton had used another boy, James W. Shaw, as a model, and Barrie was dissatisfied with the results. 'It doesn't show the Devil in Peter', he complained

George in Pop at Eton

'This confounded excitement about the XI has rather caught me and I have begun to dream about it. Mix them, curve them, swerve them, break them, and if he still hits it, kick him. I can't think of any better tip. . . . I wish I was as good at bowling as at the idiotic thing of flinging rings onto watches. . . . Do you remember how we plugged at the baskets of oranges at Olympia one Christmas? Only a few years ago, but you were no older than Michael is now.'

He wrote to George again on June 3rd:

'Floreat Etona! I hope the weather is to be propitious and that you will have a perfect day . . . without a cloud in the sky for your last 4th of June. It is four years since the day when your mother and I were there and you made us stay on for the fireworks and were really just a small boy, impaling yourself by the waterside on railings. I did not then know even that there was such a thing as Pop. It has swum into my ken like some celestial young lady. . . . The great thing for me at all events is the feeling that if your father and mother were here on this 4th of June they would be well pleased on the whole with their eldest born. . . . Just off to 23 to cricket in the square.'

A month later, George distinguished himself in the Eton v. Harrow match at Lord's by knocking up the second highest Etonian score, bowling out Harrow's top batsman, and pulling off a sensational high left-handed catch which featured in several newspapers. 'I am greatly delighted and rayther [*sic*] proud', Barrie wrote to him on July 8th. 'Your mother used to speak of the possibility [of playing at Lord's] with shining eyes.' Michael, too, was showing himself to be a promising athlete at Wilkinson's: Captain of Football, in his cricket 1st XI; the only sport that defeated him was swimming – he had always been terrified of water, and was unable to swim a stroke. He was now twelve years old, enjoying the golden year between childhood and adolescence, his last summer as a boy. After recounting how 'the dazzling creature' had scored 26 runs in his final prep-school match against Juddy's, Barrie wrote of Michael in *Neil and Tintinnabulum*:

George's spectacular catch at Lord's

'A rural cricket match in buttercup time with boys at play, seen and heard through the trees; it is surely the loveliest scene in England and the most disarming sound. From the ranks of the unseen dead, forever passing along our country lanes on their eternal journey, the Englishman falls out for a moment to look over the gate of the cricket field and smile. Let Neil's 26 against Juddy's . . . be our last sight of him as a child. He is walking back bat in hand to the pavilion, an old railway carriage. An unearthly glory has swept over the cricket ground. He tries to look unaware of it; you know the expression and the bursting heart. . . . [He] gathers up the glory and tacks it over his bed. "The End," as he used to say in his letters. I never know him quite so well again. He seems henceforth to be running to me on a road that is moving still more rapidly in the opposite direction.'

Barrie treated his boys to an even greater extravagance for the summer of 1912: Amhuinnsuidh Castle, a vast baronial mansion in the Outer Hebrides. 'The cost must have been fabulous', wrote Peter. 'The fishing was to match.' In his Dedication to *Peter Pan*, Barrie recounted how he arranged for Johnny Mackay, Michael's gillie at Scourie, to spend the holidays with them in the Outer Hebrides:

'Nothing that happens after we are twelve matters very much' – Michael, aged 12, with Barrie in July 1912

'The rebuffs I got from all of you! They were especially crushing in those early days when one by one you came out of your belief in fairies and lowered on me as the deceiver. My grandest triumph, the best thing in the play of *Peter Pan* (though it is not in it), is that long after Michael had ceased to believe, I brought him back to the faith for at least two minutes. We were on our way in a boat to fish the Outer Hebrides (where we caught *Mary Rose*), and though it was a journey of days he wore his fishing basket on his back all the time, so as to be able to begin at once. His one pain was the absence of Johnny Mackay, for Johnny was the loved gillie of the previous summer . . . but could not be with us this time as he would have had to cross and re-cross Scotland to reach us. As the boat drew near the Kyle of Lochalsh pier I told Michael and Nico it was such a famous wishing pier that they had now but to wish and they should have. Nico believed at once and expressed a wish to meet himself (I afterwards found him on the pier searching faces confidently), but Michael thought it more of my untimely nonsense and doggedly declined to humour me. "Whom do you want to see most, Michael?" "Of course I would like most to see Johnny Mackay." "Well, then, wish for him." "Oh, rot." "It can't do any harm to wish." Contemptuously he wished, and as the ropes were thrown on the pier he saw Johnny waiting for him, loaded with angling paraphernalia. I know no one less like a fairy than Johnny Mackay, but for two minutes Michael was quivering in another world than ours. When he came to he gave me a smile which meant that we understood each other, and thereafter neglected me for a month, being always with Johnny. As I have said, this episode is not in the play; so though I dedicate *Peter Pan* to you I keep the smile, with the few other broken fragments of immortality that have come my way.'

'Where we caught *Mary Rose*' – the Ghost Mother, who had first appeared in Barrie's notebook for 1886, was still a long way from being named; but it was here in the Outer Hebrides, while fishing near the Castle on Loch Voshimid, that he pointed out to Nico a tiny island in the middle as being 'the island that likes to be visited'. People had been known to vanish on such islands, he told Nico. Years went by, and then suddenly they came back; the rest of the world had grown old, but they were as young as the day they disappeared. The story began to combine with his earlier notion about ghosts, which he had written in *The Little White Bird*: 'The only ghosts, I believe, who creep into this world, are dead young mothers, returned to see how their children fare.' Perhaps it was the thought of Sylvia returning one day to find Michael so changed that she fails to recognize him that led Barrie to conclude, in a letter to Quiller-Couch: 'No-one should come back, however much he was loved.'[5]

These thoughts were not restricted to the fantasy of stories and plays: he was actually writing to Sylvia once a year, 'telling her how things now were with her children',[6] though he later destroyed these letters.

'The island that likes to be visited' – Mary Rose's island (left) on Loch Voshimid

Barrie's concern for Michael seemed more pronounced this summer. Nico remembered several occasions when 'Uncle Jim turned round and found Michael had disappeared – he'd probably wandered off to fish somewhere else. And then we heard this haunting, banshee wail, "Mi-i-ichael-l-l!" It was an extraordinary sound as it echoed through the hills. And of course Michael was always perfectly all right, and wondered what all the fuss was about.'

Numerous guests came to stay at Amhuinnsuidh throughout August and September: A. E. W. Mason, Anthony Hope (Hawkins), his American wife and their children; E. V. Lucas, his wife Elizabeth and their daughter Audrey; and another Lucas, though no relation – Lord Lucas, better known as Bron Herbert, who had lost his leg in the Boer War. 'Before Lord Lucas reached Amhuinnsuidh,' recalled Nico, 'everyone said, "Nico's bound to ask him about his wooden leg," and I was most strictly told *not* even to be aware of it. We all gathered to meet him outside the castle when he arrived, and my very first words were "Can I see your wooden leg?" To which he immediately said "Yes. Where's my bedroom? Come upstairs and I'll take it off and show you—" And up we went and he did.'

Amhuinnsuidh Castle in the Outer Hebrides, overlooking the Atlantic Ocean

Peter wrote in his *Morgue*:

'George (aged 19) was much intrigued by Betty Hawkins, and I think this was his first . . . experience of the delights of a flirtation with an attractive *femme du monde*. I also doubt whether Betty Hawkins ever had a more attractive adolescent to play around with. They enjoyed themselves quite a lot, sheltering from the eternal rain in the fishing-huts by the side of those lonely romantic lochs. She was very easy on the eye, and American, which perhaps accounts for the circumstance, rare enough in those far off days, that occasional nips of whisky fed the flames of dalliance. On these occasions George forcibly taught me the elements of tact, i.e. the necessity of making myself scarce, and I envied from afar, being just at the stage when poor J.M.B. had had to give me, by the banks of the burn, a small talking to for indulging at Eton in what my tutor euphemistically termed water-closet talk. He very nearly penetrated my juvenile defences by telling me it had always been his view that a man without some element of coarseness in his nature was not a whole man, which must have disconcerted me, coming from him. But I don't think he knew what was afoot between George and Betty: not that it amounted to anything.'

If Barrie did suspect Betty's 'little tendresse' for George, then he doubtless looked upon it as Anthony Hope's just desert for having made his celebrated *cri de cœur* at the first night of *Peter Pan*, 'Oh, for an hour of Herod!'

Mary Hodgson gave a characteristically prosaic account of the Scottish holiday in a letter to her sister Nancy:

Amhuinnsuidh Castle
1st September 1912.

Michael in Wilkinson's uniform

My dear Nancy,

    I trust you received the salmon & served it up with mayonnaise sauce. It was one of Michael's catches. . . . Minnie* also sent fish to her home, also Lilian* also Bessie* also Mr Brown (J.M.B.'s butler), also Michael's ghillie – the man who accompanies him in his travels & whom I implore not to bring him back in pieces. . . . E. V. Lucas & his family have departed after a month's stay. A. E. W. Mason also, after 10 days. Anthony Hope Hawkins, wife, son & daughter & governess have been here five weeks & are still hanging on. Nurse Loosemore, who nursed Mrs Arthur, is also here for an indefinite period. . . . We have had (to use slang) the pick of the literary genius's of England, but alas – either my liver is out of order, or my ideals too high, for at close quarters they are but mortal – & very ordinary at that.

    The weather has been very good for *Scotland*, & the fishing splendid. They (the boys) generally go on ponies & are getting quite expert at riding. Jack is not with us – his

*Members of the staff at 23 Campden Hill Square.

holidays do not come convenient. J.M.B. is well, & much better than I have seen him for some years. Did you realise how well George played at Lord's Cricket Ground? You would have thought someone had given Nico sixpence that day, his spirits were so high. . . . The school is 2 miles away. The mistress has a *strap* – Nicholas has seen it. We leave here about the 17th, if all goes well. Then Peter goes to Eton alone, & George to Cambridge. Michael is now top of his school, & Nico is top but one of his class. I trust mother is keeping well, my love to you all,

Dadge.*

On Barrie's return to Adelphi Terrace, he found, among the pile of mail awaiting him, a letter from an anonymous woman enclosing a drawing of Peter Pan by her four-year-old son, Peter, which he had made after listening to *The Little White Bird*. Numerous people sent such letters, usually as bait for an autograph, but this letter was unsigned. The boy had written his name, Peter Lewis, at the foot of the drawing, and with the aid of the postmark, Barrie tracked him down to Glan Hafren in Wales. He sent him a copy of *Peter Pan in Kensington Gardens*, with an accompanying letter:

22 September '12.

My dear Peter,

Your mother rote me a letter but she did not tell me her name (which makes me like her better . . .), but she sent me some fine ~~pictyours~~ pikturs (dash it all) u drew about P. Pan, and they are just like the picters P.P. would draw himself. . . . Peter's mother thinks Mr. Barrie has a lot of people admiring him, but oh, Peter's mother, u are mistaken and he is a lonely dreary person and is *very* pleased to hear that some one thinks him nicer than he is . . .

Your friend,

J. M. Barrie

The correspondence might have ended here, had it not turned out that Peter Lewis's godfather was one of Barrie's own literary heroes, George Meredith. This was their only connection with the literary world, but Barrie liked the sound of their Welsh home and family life: Peter had three sisters, contemporaries of Michael and Nico, and he saw that a friendship with the Lewises might provide the boys with friends of their own age in the land of their Llewelyn ancestors.

In February, 1913, the news reached England that Captain Scott and his fellow explorers had perished in the frozen wastes of the

---

*A family nickname.

Antarctic. 'Had we lived, I should have had a tale to tell of the hardihood, endurance, and courage of my companions which would have stirred the heart of every Englishman', wrote Scott in his *Message to the Public*, found in his tent. 'These rough notes and our dead bodies must tell the tale, but surely, surely, a great rich country like ours will see that those who are dependent on us are properly provided for.' The news of Scott's heroism did indeed stir the hearts of Englishmen, but not their pockets, and the Mansion House Fund set up for the benefit of 'those who are dependent on us' met with a poor response. Barrie set pen to paper and wrote a letter which appeared in *The Times* of February 19th, 1913, under the heading MR. J. M. BARRIE'S APPEAL:

'Mr. J. M. Barrie, who is the godfather of the late Captain Scott's son Peter, has addressed the following letter to the Press:–

The Athenæum, S.W., Feb. 18.

Sir, – As a friend of Captain Scott, may I say what is in the minds of many others, that despite the fine help of the Press, things are not going too well with the various schemes started to do honour to the men who have done so much honour to us. Almost every Briton alive has been prouder these last days because a message from a tent has shown him how the breed lives on; but it seems almost time to remind him of that more practical Englishman who said of a friend in need, "I am sorry for him £5; how much are you sorry?" Of every 100 who are proud of those men in the tent some 99 have not yet said how proud they are.'

Other newspapers published his appeal, and the public responded by swelling the Mansion House Fund to almost twice its original target. At the beginning of April, Kathleen Scott sent Barrie a letter addressed to him from her husband, written while he lay dying in his tent:

Part of Scott's last letter to Barrie

My dear Barrie

We are pegging out in a very comfortless spot – Hoping this letter may be found & sent to you I write a word of farewell – It hurt me grievously when you partially withdrew your friendship or seemed so to do – I want to tell you that I never gave you cause – If you thought or heard ill of me it was unjust – Calumny is ever to the fore. My attitude towards you and everyone connected with you was always one of respect and admiration – Under these circumstances I want you to think well of me and my end and more practically I want you to help my widow and my boy your godson – We are showing that Englishmen can still die with a bold spirit fighting it out to the end. It will be known that we have accomplished our object in reaching the Pole and that we have done everything possible even to sacrificing ourselves in order to save sick companions. I think this makes an example for Englishmen of the future and that the country ought to help those who are left behind to mourn us – I leave my poor girl and your godson. . . . Do what you can to get their claims recognised.

Goodbye. I am not at all afraid of the end but sad to miss many a simple pleasure which I had planned for the future on our long marches – I may not have proved a great explorer, but we have done the greatest march ever made and come very near to great success. Goodbye my dear friend.

> Yours ever,
> R. Scott

We are in a desperate state feet frozen &c, no fuel and a long way from food, but it would do your heart good to be in our tent, to hear our songs and the cheery conversation as to what we will do when we get to Hut Point.

Later. – We are very near the end but have not and will not lose our good cheer – we have four days of storm in our tent and now have no food or fuel – We did intend to finish ourselves when things proved like this but we have decided to die naturally in the track.

As a dying man my dear friend be good to my wife & child – Give the boy a chance in life if the State won't do it – He ought to have good stuff in him – and give my memory back the friendship which you inspired. I never met a man in my life whom I admired and loved more than you but I never could show you how much your friendship meant to me – for you had much to give and I nothing.

Everything about Scott appealed to Barrie, and nothing more so than the manner of his death. For years he carried Scott's letter around in his pocket, producing it at every opportunity, but never allowing the more personal references to be published. In the end he came to regard the explorer as another variation on the Peter Pan theme. 'When I think of Scott,' he later told an audience, 'I remember the strange Alpine story of the youth who fell down a glacier and was lost, and of how a scientific companion, one of several who accompanied him, all young, computed that the body would again appear at a certain date and place many years afterwards. When that time came round some of the survivors returned to the glacier to see if the

Peter Scott with his mother

Michael in 1913

prediction would be fulfilled; all old men now; and the body reappeared as young as on the day he left them. So Scott and his comrades emerge out of the white immensities, always young.'[7]

It was ironic that Scott's request to Barrie to help his widow and son should have arrived on the eve of Michael's adolescence and departure to Eton. Barrie wrote to Kathleen Scott on April 11th, 1913: 'I have been hoping all this time that there was some such letter for me from your husband, and the joy with which I receive it is far greater than the pain. I am very proud of the wishes expressed in it. . . . I know a hundred things he would like me to do for Peter, and I want out of love for his father to do them all. And I want to be such a friend to you as he wished. I should have wanted to be that had there been no such letter, and now I feel I have a right to ask you to give me the chance.' Kathleen, however, was not to be pressurized into any hasty decisions; she did not wish to become another Sylvia, with Barrie acting as a guardian to her boy, and although she skilfully retained his friendship and help, she never allowed him to take over the reins of her life.

At the end of April, Michael began his first half at Hugh Macnaghten's House. Unlike George, who had adapted to Eton within the first few days, Michael was utterly miserable, crying himself to sleep every night and refusing to make friends. Barrie wrote to George, who was up at Cambridge: 'Michael is so far very lonely and unhappy at Eton, and I am depressed thereby', and to Charles Turley Smith: 'Many thanks for the bluebells and a squeeze of the hand . . . for the affection that made you know how sad I would be about Michael gone to school. He is very lonely there at present, and I am foolishly taken up about it. It rather broke me up seeing him crying and trying to whistle at the same time.' The cause of Michael's unhappiness was homesickness. He missed Mary Hodgson; he missed Uncle Jim; most of all, he missed his mother. For three years, Barrie had tried to take her place; hardly a day had gone by when he had not walked him home from school, played billiards or cricket with him, or helped him through his nightmares, 'sitting there doing something frightfully ordinary, like reading the newspaper'.[8] But now that Michael was alone, with no Barrie to fill his mind with other thoughts, he began to pine for 'the touch of vanished hands'. He had, in Peter's words, 'the true stuff of the poet in him from birth', and his extreme sensibility only added to the awareness of his loss. He fought hard to disguise his emotions, hiding behind a shield of reserve, or trying to mask his depressions with a dry, laconic sense of humour that owed much to his guardian. Barrie wrote later, 'I think few have suffered from the loss of a mother as he has done.'[9] In an effort to ease Michael's loneliness, he offered to write to him every day, instead of once a week as he had done to George. Michael responded

by writing back to him, every single day. By the time he came to leave
Eton, there were over 2,000 letters between them. These letters
survived until 1952, when Peter, overcome with depression himself,
decided to burn them. 'They were too much,'[10] he told Mary
Hodgson. Doubtless he felt that they might be misinterpreted in a
Freudian age prone to dissection and analysis. Something of Barrie's
relationship with Michael may be glimpsed in the wandering pages of
Neil and Tintinnabulum. In a chapter entitled 'The First Half',
Barrie wrote:

'The scene is changed. Stilled is the crow of Neil, for he is now but
one of the lowliest at a great public school, where he reverberates but
little. The scug Neil fearfully running errands for his fag-master is
another melancholy reminder of the brevity of human greatness.
Lately a Colossus [at his prep-school], he was now infinitely less than
nothing. What shook him was not the bump as he fell, but the general
indifference to his having fallen. He lay there like a bird in the grass
winded by a blunt-headed arrow, and was cold to his own touch. . . .
In that dreadful month or more I am dug up by his needs and come
again into prominence, gloating because he calls for me, sometimes
unable to do more than stand afar off on the playing field, so that he
may at least see me nigh though we cannot touch. The thrill of being
the one needed, which I had never thought to know again. I have
leant over a bridge, and enviously watching the gaiety of two
attractive boys, now broken to the ways of school, have wished he was
one of them, till I hear their language and wondered whether this was
part of the necessary cost.'

In another chapter, Barrie recalled one of Michael's nightmares at
Eton:

'On this occasion his dame [matron] had remained with him all night,
as he had been slightly unwell, and she was amused, but nothing
more, to see him, without observing her, rise and search the room in a
fury of words for something that was not there. The only word she
caught was "seven". He asked her not to tell me of this incident, as he
knew it would trouble me. I was told, and, indeed, almost expected
the news, for I had sprung out of bed that night thinking I heard
[him] once again defending the stair. By the time I reached [him] it
had ceased to worry him. "But when I woke I missed the newspaper,"
he said with his adorable smile, and again putting . . . his hand
deliciously on my shoulder (that kindest gesture of man to man). . . .
How I wished the newspaper could have been there. There are times
when a boy can be as lonely as God.'

The last of the Allahakbarrie teams, matched against E. V. Lucas's team at Downe House in July 1913. Back row, l to r: George, Thomas Gilmour, Will Meredith, George Meredith Jnr, Denis Mackail, Harry Graham, Dr Goffe. Centre: A. A. Milne, Maurice Hewlett, Barrie, George Morrow, E. V. Lucas, Walter Frith. Front row: Percy Lucas, Audrey Lucas, T. Wrigley, Charles Tennyson, Willie Winter

Nico was now the only boy left as a permanent resident at Campden Hill Square. On the night of June 13th, Barrie told him to look in the papers the next morning for surprising news. Nico was up betimes, and by the time Barrie came down to breakfast, had searched the cricket pages from end to end, but could find nothing of interest. What he had failed to notice was that his guardian's name was among the new baronets in the Birthday Honours List. He was no longer Mr Barrie, but Sir James Barrie, Bart. – 'TO HAVE and TO HOLD the said name dignity state degree style and title of Baronet aforesaid on to him ... and the heirs male of his body lawfully begotten.' Barrie had rejected a simple knighthood in 1909, but was unable to resist a baronetcy – an hereditary title that none of the Five could inherit. The boys greeted the news with a mixture of pride and derision – both of which delighted Sir James enormously. Michael and Nico started calling him Sir Jazz Band Barrie, or simply Sir Jazz, but soon drifted back to plain Uncle Jim. Jack, however, picked up on 'the Bart' and 'the little Baronet', depending on his mood, though he too, somewhat reluctantly, resorted to Uncle Jim as an alternative to Sir James.

As well as writing to Michael every day, Barrie continued to keep in frequent contact with George at Cambridge, putting him in touch with young actresses who might amuse him – 'if you have the pluck to approach' – taking a keen interest in his work – 'There was an essay prize your father got at Trinity that I am keen you should go in for' – or encouraging his efforts in the Cambridge Amateur Dramatic Club – 'I'm avid to know how you felt as well as how others thought you felt at the first A.D.C. – "Stage" fright!' He wrote to him for his twentieth birthday on July 19th, 1913:

George in the Cambridge A.D.C.

> My dear George,
>   Only the other day – and now you have come to twenty years. When I saw you first, I said you were a gorgeous boy, and long afterwards I discovered that your mother thought I had been singularly happy in my choice of adjectives. 20 years with nothing very heinous on your soul I think, and many hopeful traits. May all turn out as your father and mother would have wished. It rests mainly with you, but I like to try to help. . . .
>   Affectionately,
>   J.M.B.

Peter wrote of George in the *Morgue*: 'He had turned from a boy into a young man, and must have spread his wings a little in the vacations. . . . He had a devoted and in many ways invaluable mentor in J.M.B., but the way cannot have been made altogether easy for him, as the first of the family to grow up against so peculiar a background.' In the summer of 1912, George and Jack had met three sisters, the Mitchell-Innes girls, at a dance given by Sylvia's sister, May, at her house in Cheyne Walk. All three girls were 'swept off their feet' by the two boys, but it was Josephine, the eldest, who succeeded in winning George to herself. She was, according to her sister Norma:

Josephine Mitchell-Innes. Barrie later wrote to her (28 June 1915): 'I knew there was one matter on which George could make no mistake.'

'terribly gay, and absolutely the right sort of person for George. He wasn't a great talker – he was rather shy, rather reserved. He had a vein of sadness in him – we all recognised it – whereas Dophine [Josephine's pet-name] was all fun and laughter, a tremendous mimic, and full of courage if anything went wrong. . . . George stayed with us several times in Scotland during his Cambridge life, and a great many times at our home, Churchill, in Hertfordshire. . . . George never took any credit for *Peter Pan* whatsoever, absolutely none – he was far too modest. He always said he was George Darling in the play – climbing in and out of kennels. But I remember he gave *The Little White Bird* to Dophine – rather shyly – he just wrote "Josephine's" inside it – just like George to write that. . . . I think one or two people were rather disturbed about Barrie, though of course it was never talked about openly. There was something very sinister about him, rather shivery. But of course George was deeply fond of him, and understood him so well – saw through him a little, I think – but never said anything unkind about him. George had extraordinary understanding, which is perhaps what gave him his sadness. It was almost what the Germans call *Weltschmerz* – a sadness of the world, not a personal sadness about himself. He had a very clear vision of people and life, and yet a beautiful sense of humour and *sans-souci* charm.'[11]

As eldest son, George was required to sign various documents relating to Sylvia's estate, which evidently distressed him. Barrie wrote to him at Cambridge on November 18th, 1913:

'Yes, it was all very sad, and I knew how you were feeling it. Many things besides this will remind you now of the last days at Ashton, and they will take on a new meaning to you. Your mother did not want your minds to dwell on sadness even for a moment when you were younger. She grudged every second of happiness you were deprived of. I don't know if I told you that in the paper of directions she wrote at the end, but which was not found till long afterwards, she said she did not wish her funeral day to be made long and wearisome for you, and also that she did not wish any of you to go to the funeral. It can only be afterwards that a boy realises the unselfishness of a mother's love. It is a pain as well as a glory to him.'

Noël Coward as one of the Lost Boys in the 1913/14 *Peter Pan* revival

The boys might be growing up, but a part of their childhood would always remain the same age: *Peter Pan*, now in its ninth annual revival, and as firmly rooted in the Christmas tradition as Santa Claus. But if Peter grew no older, Pauline Chase, who had played him every year since 1906, was beginning to feel her age, and this was to be her final season. 'When [the lost boys] seem to be growing up, which is against the rules, Peter thins them out,' warned Barrie in *Peter and Wendy*. The actors playing the Lost Boys found that the system also applied to them. Pauline Chase wrote in *Peter Pan's Postbag*: 'Every December a terrifying ceremony takes place before *Peter Pan* is produced, and this is the measuring of the children who play in it. They are measured to see whether they have grown too tall, and they can all squeeze down into about two inches less than they really are, but this does not deceive the management. . . . "It won't do, my lad. . . . We are sorry for you, but – farewell!" Measuring day is one of the many tragedies of *Peter Pan*.' A new recruit to the Lost Boys this year was the young Noël Coward, aged fourteen, who was given the part of Slightly. Barrie made a point of attending the rehearsals of each *Peter Pan* revival, adding the occasional new line from the store of children's remarks jotted down in his notebook during the course of the year. Sometimes one or more of the Davies boys accompanied him, and Michael's opinion was now beginning to play an increasingly important part in his decisions.

This year, however, Barrie's mind was on a new project, as bizarre as anything he had yet attempted. *Hullo, Ragtime!* had been playing for over a year to packed houses, and Barrie had taken the Five to see it some dozen or more times. In November 1913, they went to see another revue at the Palace Theatre, featuring the French music-hall star, Gaby Deslys. Gaby was a phenomenon of the decade, the first of the modern sex-symbols, whose fantastic head-dresses, semi-nudity on stage, provocative dancing and scandalous private life more than compensated for her limited acting talent. She was a discredit to the theatrical profession, and Barrie was spellbound by her. Since the boys were equally enraptured, he took immediate steps to make her acquaintance and invited her round for tea in his flat at Adelphi Terrace. She could speak very little English, but he found her to be entrancing, and determined there and then that she should become his next star. He would write her a revue. Gaby could scarcely believe her good fortune; she knew well enough that she was little more than a glorified chorus-girl, and the prospect of having England's leading dramatist at her feet was flattery indeed. Cecil Beaton wrote, 'Out of sheer *joie de vivre*, on leaving [his Adelphi flat] she ran down the many circles of staircases ringing the doorbells of each flat as she passed.' [12] When the news leaked out that Sir James Barrie was proposing to write Mam'selle Gaby Deslys a revue, a number of his peers were shocked and appalled; others, who knew him better, sensed that it was just another of his unpredictable flirtations, and prayed that the infatuation would pass before he made a fool of himself in public. A few, perhaps, perceived that in tackling a ragtime revue, Barrie was attempting to keep pace with the younger generation, and in particular his boys. Certainly they gave the enterprise their full support, and Barrie began to fill Michael's Christmas present – a new notebook – with a wild assortment of ideas: 'Combine theatre with cinematography – Cinema way of kissing. Burlesque of American titles, "Nope" & "Yep" – Gaby a chorus-girl, flirts with conductor in pit.' Tucked away at the foot of the same page is a glimpse of the other Barrie: '*Father & Son* (Me & Michael). Mutually fond of each other – His avoidance of my sentiment – I feign hurt, hide my pride. . . . Michael coming to me cried one tear at Dhivach – I picture it remorsefully alone among hills & streams – Send his laugh to be friends with it & gay together. Embarrassed when I tell it of him at Eton (has long forgotten it).' More notes on Michael were followed by a long glossary of Eton slang: '*Tanning* is by a boy, *Swiped* by a master (*not* swished) –

Gaby Deslys

A letter from Barrie to Peter Scott

3, ADELPHI TERRACE HOUSE,
STRAND, W.C.

January 18
1914.

MY dear Peter
HALLO i
am so glad too
get your ripp
ing letter it
is a lovly let
ter the reaso
n i have not
wrote writ
rot before
is becaus i
have been in
SWITSERSLA
ND WITH NI
KOLAS AND MI
KAL AND THEM
UTHER BOYS.
IT IS TIME U
SAWED PETE
R PAN i AM
TOO RING YOURE
MOTHER UP
ABOUT IT TOMO
RROW. HE IS BR
AVE HE CAN
FLY
i AM
YURE LOVIN
g
GODFATHER

Scrawled across the fly-leaf of a novel in the producer's celebrated blue pencil: 'Dear Michael, This will admit two to the Duke of York's Theater. Charles Frohman'

George aged 21 in July 1914

Tug = Colleger, Scug = Dirty small boy'.

When Frohman arrived at Easter, he found that his playwright had apparently abandoned the theatre in favour of the new medium of cinematography. Barrie was fascinated by it: it was a new toy, like his early cameras and the steam-car. He was now devising an entertainment even more fantastic than Gaby's revue, though in due course it would become a part of it. His scheme was to host a 'Cinema Supper': half a dozen all-star sketches written by himself and performed before an invited audience at the Savoy Theatre, followed by a banquet at the Savoy Hotel. Unbeknown to the guests, who were to include the Prime Minister and members of the Government, Barrie planned to have cameras throughout the auditorium and banquet-hall, filming their candid reactions. He then intended to edit the film into short sequences, to be projected at various points throughout Gaby's revue on a huge screen at the back of the stage. A thirty-foot close-up of Prime Minister Asquith would, Barrie felt, make an original back-drop to one of Gaby's erotic dance routines. Frohman listened to the Baronet's proposal with a sense of *déjà vu*: he seemed to recall a similar madness of ten years ago, when the same writer had proposed a play in which people flew about the stage and crocodiles swallowed alarm-clocks. He was, however, no longer the Napoleon of Broadway: a series of box-office flops (including a recent effort from Barrie's own pen, *The Adored One*) had somewhat depleted his funds; moreover his health was poor, and he now had to move about with the aid of a stick. But his sense of adventure, like Hook's brain, was as gigantic as ever. He suggested that they should repair to Paris for further discussions, taking George, Peter and Michael with them. Peter Davies described the visit in his *Morgue*:

'We stayed at the Meurice in the Rue de Rivoli, and . . . wore in the evenings tail coats and white ties. This was George's first . . . glimpse not only of Paris but of what might be called the cosmopolitan hotel and restaurant *vie de luxe*, as it existed before the First Great War. A morning wandering round the Louvre or the Latin Quarter – lunch at Armenouville – afternoon looking through the bookstalls by the river . . . or flinging rings over hooks with the rest of the party . . . or (once) placating the goddess in the Rue Pasquier* – tea at Rumpelmayer's while the band played *Je sais que vous êtes jolie*, followed by a game of L'Attaque with Michael – dinner at Fouquet or Larue . . . – a revue or a French play which none of us understood, least of all Frohman, who probably bought the English rights nevertheless – and finally supper at the Café de Paris with Irene [and] Vernon Castle dancing. George took to all this like a duck to water . . .

*A well-known red-light district.

and it was then that George and I first clearly saw what Jack had missed by being sent into the Navy instead of to Eton.'

Barrie widened George's horizon still further by sending him off to Italy for two weeks in the summer. He wrote to him at Massa Carrara on June 29th, 1914:

'It seems to be a little heaven below, and your first introduction to Italy something you won't forget. London is very close just now, and when evening comes I envy your roof garden and the fireflies. . . . Peter sends me orders to take him to the opera at Long Leave. . . . My [Cinema] Supper is on Friday & I have written half a dozen plays for it. I'll send you a programme.'

The Cinema Supper went according to plan, with Lillah McCarthy, Henry Ainley, Marie Löhr, Irene Vanbrugh, Marie Tempest, Gerald du Maurier and Granville-Barker taking part in Barrie's sketches. However, the Prime Minister, upon learning that his unguarded gestures and grimaces had been recorded on cellulose, hurriedly wrote a letter from 10 Downing Street, forbidding the exhibition of his likeness in a music-hall revue. A number of other guests shared Asquith's indignation and Barrie was obliged to think up alternative material for his cinematic sequences. His solution was to hire a team of film technicians, persuade Bernard Shaw, G. K. Chesterton and William Archer to dress up as cowboys, then film them in the wilds of Hertfordshire doing a Western burlesque. This too fell flat, since Barrie had omitted to tell Shaw that he intended projecting his performance on stage while another actor did a simultaneous impersonation of him. Shaw was unamused, and confiscated the film.

Barrie wrote again to George on July 13th:

'Peter and I set out on Saturday to wire you the result of the Eton & Harrow match and forgot about it in the stress of going to the opera. Both nights of Long Leave did he drag me to the opera. . . . Another piece of news just arrived tonight is that Michael who went in for the College Scholarship exam came out seventh. He will stay on at Macnaghten's, but I am glad he went in and some other boy can be made happy with the scholarship. . . . Very near your birthday now! . . . I hope all is still very happy in your romantic home. It is an experience you won't forget. Write soon.'

The mention of Peter dragging his guardian to the opera prompted him to comment in the *Morgue*:

Barrie in his favourite fishing hat

'Being himself totally unmusical, [Barrie] not only did not en- courage such leanings, but in one way and another could not help discouraging them. . . . I felt obscurely then, and feel strongly now, that a little more encouragement in the artistic way would have been very good for us all; would have filled a real need in our sprouting natures. . . . The lighter side of life was thoroughly catered for, and for that I am duly and deeply grateful. *Hullo, Ragtime!* and its successors, with which J.M.B. was so oddly and closely connected, was one of our major preoccupations, and delights, and what we didn't know about revue was scarcely worth knowing. . . . I don't forget that Rupert Brooke went to *Hullo, Ragtime!* ten – or was it twenty? – times; or that Michael wrote two wonderful sonnets; or that George was good enough for anyone's money as he was, . . . [but] the fact is that music and painting and poetry, and the part that they may be supposed to play in making a civilized being, had a curiously small place in J.M.B.'s view of things. I think it was of far more interest to him that George and all of us should excel in games and fishing . . . than that we should acquire any real culture in Matthew Arnold's sense of the word.'

At the end of July 1914, Barrie took George, Michael and Nico up to Scotland for their summer holidays. Jack, now a Sub-Lieutenant in the Royal Navy, was with his ship in the North Atlantic, but Peter, who was finishing his Eton O.T.C. summer Camp, would be joining them in a few days. Barrie had rented a large shooting lodge, Auch Lodge, near the Bridge of Orchy in Argyllshire, with fishing rights to the Orchy and Kinglass rivers, and once again had arranged for Johnny Mackay to be on hand as a gillie to Michael and Nico. He wrote to Lord Lucas (of the wooden leg) from Auch Lodge on July 31st, 1914:

'Nicholas is riding about on an absurdly fat pony which necessitates his legs being at right-angles to his body. The others are fishing. The waters are a-crawl with salmon, but they will look at nothing till the rain comes. The really big event is that Johnny Mackay (Michael's gillie) has a new set of artificial teeth. He wears them and joins in the talk with a simple dignity, not boastful, but aware that he is the owner of a good thing – rather like the lady who passes round her necklace.'

Auch Lodge, near the Bridge of Orchy in Argyllshire

He wrote again on Tuesday, August 4th, 1914:

'We are so isolated from news here, that when I wrote last I was quite ignorant that Europe was in a blaze. . . . It seems awful to be up here at such a time catching fish, or not catching them, for it has rained four days and nights and is still at it, and all the world is spate

Form 1 (top left)

1. The best place to hang a bunch of mistletoe? 'The gallows
2. Your favourite motto? I know a motto
3. Your greatest ambition? To be some one else
4. Your ideal man? The: Other one
5. Your ideal woman? Jenny Geddes
6. Your opinion of motor cars in general? Horrible
7. Do you believe in spiritualism? No
8. Your ideal way of spending Xmas day? Amberscinital
9. Your idea of absolute misery? Hotel life
10. Your favourite picture? Mona Lisa
11. The most suitable place for a flirtation? Royal academy
12. Your favourite play? Hell & Hamlet
13. Your favourite song? I dont think
14. Your favourite musician? Max Pemberton
15. Your favourite magazine? Ponder magazine
16. The most unselfish thing you could do? Fill up this page
17. When did you feel at your worst? At Mürren

Autograph JM Barrie   Date 20 Jan 1864

Form 2 (top right)

1. The best place to hang a bunch of mistletoe? Up the chimney.
2. Your favourite motto? There's always worse in Egypt.
3. Your greatest ambition? To be of use.
4. Your ideal man? Captain Scott
5. Your ideal woman? Mrs Tragetis
6. Your opinion of motor cars in general? good
7. Do you believe in spiritualism? No
8. Your ideal way of spending Xmas day? with a house full of youngsters.
9. Your idea of absolute misery? Cold feet.
10. Your favourite picture? Whistler's Mother.
11. The most suitable place for a flirtation? North Pole
12. Your favourite play? Quality Street.
13. Your favourite song? Trilby's
14. Your favourite musician? M. L. D.
15. Your favourite magazine? G. O. Paper.
16. The most unselfish thing you could do? To eat a very sour orange.
17. When did you feel at your worst? at my worst!

Autograph Mary Hodgson   Date 25.1.14.

Form 3 (bottom left)

1. The best place to hang a bunch of mistletoe? In the dark.
2. Your favourite motto? Per mare per terram
3. Your greatest ambition? To grow a moustache.
4. Your ideal man? The Kaiser
5. Your ideal woman? Non-existent.
6. Your opinion of motor cars in general? Have'nt got one.
7. Do you believe in spiritualism? Yes
8. Your ideal way of spending Xmas day? Being drunk
9. Your idea of absolute misery? Being sober
10. Your favourite picture? Two lips & a kiss.
11. The most suitable place for a flirtation? A lunatic asylum.
12. Your favourite play? Anna Karenina
13. Your favourite song? The girl I've left behind me (thank g—)
14. Your favourite musician? Nicholas
15. Your favourite magazine? The B.O.P of course.
16. The most unselfish thing you could do? Suicide.
17. When did you feel at your worst? I always do.

Autograph Santa Claus   Date Xmas.

Form 4 (bottom right)

1. The best place to hang a bunch of mistletoe? In the coal-cellar
2. Your favourite motto? Honi soit qui mal y pense
3. Your greatest ambition? Pavement artist
4. Your ideal man? See 'Puck' for Prof Rade
5. Your ideal woman? Mary-Ann Smith
6. Your opinion of motor cars in general? Oh' So-So! Rather!
7. Do you believe in spiritualism? Rather!
8. Your ideal way of spending Xmas day? Indoors
9. Your idea of absolute misery? Jolly Joe Jinks
10. Your favourite picture? 'Il Giocondo' by BP
11. The most suitable place for a flirtation? 'The Tube'
12. Your favourite play? 'Babes in the Wood'
13. Your favourite song? 'The great American Railway'
14. Your favourite musician? Handel
15. Your favourite magazine? 'Home-chat'
16. The most unselfish thing you could do? Tear this book up
17. When did you feel at your worst? At 12 o'ck, 1st April, 1899

Autograph Michael L Davies   Date Feb 1914

'My Confession Book', Nico's
successor to the Querist's Album,
with 1914 confessions from
Barrie, Mary Hodgson, George
(signed 'Santa Claus') and
Michael

and bog. . . . We occasionally get the morning paper in the evening,
and there may be big news to-day.'

There was indeed big news, of which Barrie and the boys were
blissfully unaware. At midnight on August 4th, Great Britain
declared war on Germany. George wrote in his diary:

> *Tuesday, Aug 4.*
> A vilely wet & windy day. After lunch I
> went to the bottom of the Kinglass &
> fished up, but caught nothing. The
> burn was too big.

Wednesday, August 5th, the first day of war, proved to be more favourable for George's fishing: 'Still rather wet, but the burns have gone down. I fished the Kinglass . . . getting 5 trout.' Even when Peter arrived from London next day with news of the war, George took it in his stride: '*Aug 6*. Peter arrived for breakfast, bringing with him a letter to me about joining the Special Reserve or Territorials. We took lunch out up the burn that runs into the Kinglass under the railway bridge & each got 10 trout weighing 30 oz. Pouring rain. We went to London in the evening.' Peter Davies wrote in his *Morgue*:

'The letter proved to be a circular from the Adjutant of the Cambridge O.T.C., pointing out that it was the obvious duty of all undergraduates to offer their services forthwith. . . . This slightly disconcerting document – for great wars were a novelty then – was taken to apply to me also, as I had left Eton and was due to go to Trinity next term. Accordingly George and I travelled back to London the same night, in a carriage full of reservists rejoining the colours, who by their boozy geniality did a good deal to reconcile us to the dark fate which seemed to have descended on us so unexpectedly. Next day we went down to Cambridge, where the Corps Adjutant, a major in the Rifle Brigade, recommended the Rifle Depôt at Winchester as a suitable gambit. The "Pack up your troubles" philosophy caught from the reservists was by now beginning to recede from us, and I think George as well as I had odd sensations in the pit of the stomach as we emerged from Winchester Station and climbed the hill to the Depôt. At any rate George had one of those queer turns, something between a fainting fit and a sick headache, to which he had been prone since childhood, and had to sit for a few minutes on a seat outside the barracks. I would willingly have turned tail and gone back to London humiliated but free. George however, the moment he recovered, marched me in with him through those dark portals: and somehow or other . . . we found ourselves inside the office of Lt. Col. the Hon. J. R. Brownlow, D.S.O., commanding the 6th (Special Reserve) Battalion of the King's Royal Rifles. . . . [He] was busy writing, and looked up to ask rather gruffly what we wanted.

'"Well – er – Sir, we were advised by Major Thornton to come here to ask about getting a commission – Sir," said George.

'"Oh, Bulger Thornton at Cambridge, eh? What's your name?"

'"Davies, sir."

'"Where were you at school?"

'"Eton, sir."

'"In the Corps?"

'"Yes, sir, Sergeant."

'"Play any games? Cricket?"

'"Well sir, actually, I managed to get my eleven."

'The burn that runs into the Kinglass under the railway bridge'

George in 1914

‘ "Oh, you did, did you?"

'The Colonel, who had played for Eton himself in his day, now became noticeably more genial, and by the time he had ascertained that George was the Davies who had knocked up a valuable 59 at Lord's (which knock he had himself witnessed with due appreciation) it was evident that little more need be said.

‘ "And what about you, young man?" he asked, turning to me.

‘ "Please, sir, I'm his brother" was the best I could offer in the way of a reference.

‘ "Oh, well, that's all right, then. Just take these forms and fill them in and get them signed by your father and post them back to me. Then all you have to do is to get your uniforms . . . and wait till you see your names in the London Gazette. I'm pretty busy just now, so good-bye." And the Colonel dismissed his smile, waved dismissal to two slightly bewildered Second-Lieutenants designate, and went on with his writing.

'So easy it was, in August 1914, to obtain the King's commission in the Special Reserve of the 60th Rifles.'

Meanwhile Barrie, at fifty-four, was feeling decidedly useless. He returned to London a few days after George and Peter and offered his financial aid to Lord Lucas, who had turned his family home, Wrest Park in Bedfordshire, into a hospital (henceforth known as Wrest in Beds). His money, as always, was gratefully received, but there was little else he could do, so he returned to Auch, where Michael and Nico had remained with Mary Hodgson. George and Peter were still waiting to be gazetted, and they too travelled to Scotland for a few more weeks of fishing. '*Aug. 21.* A slack day fishing Michael's burn. One trout of 6 oz. . . . Let me not be daunted.' A few days later, Barrie received an indirect summons from Prime Minister Asquith requesting him to put aside his plans for a ragtime revue and write a stirring propaganda play extolling the cause of the allies. Thomas Hardy, H. G. Wells, and several other authors had been asked to conjure up similar odes to patriotism, though few approached the task with any measure of enthusiasm. Barrie agreed to have a go, but needed time to think about it. He wrote to George in Scotland at the end of August: 'I hope all is going well at Auch. You will have seen that the opening of the first real battle [Mons] has not gone too well for the allies tho' of course it is only a rebuff. It all goes to show that the war will be a long one. . . . Nothing in men's minds & faces here but the seriousness of the war. . . . Fish as much as you can just now. Loving, J.M.B.' This was the first instance of Barrie using the signature 'loving' as opposed to 'your affec^te' in his (surviving) letters to George, and it perhaps indicated both premonition and a maternal urge to protect him from the inevitable, to 'envelop him as with

George's fishing diary for 1914

wings'.[1] George took his guardian's advice, fishing every day in the remote Highland rivers and lochs with his brothers. He was now unofficially engaged to Josephine Mitchell-Innes, and wrote to her frequently, confiding his fears of the future. Her sister Norma recalled, 'Our brother Gilbert thought the war was going to be one long cavalry charge, everyone waving their swords – smash the Kaiser! – terrific! But George had absolutely no illusions whatsoever. He knew what he was in for from the word go.' On September 9th, George and Peter received their orders to proceed to Sheerness for training. George wrote in his little fishing diary:

> *Sept 9.*
> In the morning I threw a farewell Jock
> Scott, Blue Doctor, & Silver Doctor
> over the Orchy. Not a rise. The fish were
> very lively, evidently owing to the rain
> that came after lunch.
> *Finis.*

On the same day, Barrie wrote to Mrs Hugh Lewis at Glan Hafren, who had now become a firm friend: 'Jack is in the North Sea, he is scarcely allowed to tell me that much, and George and Peter are waiting for their commissions. So the world suddenly alters and we must hope for the better. But it has all at once passed into the hands of our young men, and for what they may be we are responsible. I believe they are to be as right as rain. . . . I am probably going to America on Saturday: we must all try to do something.'

The American visit was an impulsive attempt on Barrie's part to raise support for the allies. He persuaded A. E. W. Mason and his business manager, Gilmour, to go with him. Their journey was to be shrouded in mystery: nothing must leak out until they arrived, but when the *Lusitania* docked in New York, Barrie found letters awaiting him from the Consul-General and the British Ambassador, both urging him to call the mission off lest he offend American neutrality and embarrass the British Government. On September 20th, the *New York Tribune* published a front-page article:

SIR J. M. BARRIE CAUGHT TRYING TO SURPRISE NEW YORK:
*Would Slip Into City Like Peter Pan to Look Around, but
Reporters Catch Him and Make Him Talk –*
'It has been seventeen years since Sir James has been in America, and his arrival this time has been looked forward to with the utmost interest. There were stories that his trip . . . was made to further our interest in the cause of England. But this was all upset by Sir James.

'"I've been coming for a long time," he said, "and since we're out of the fighting – and writing – for some time, we came to look around." . . .

'It was a severe examination that he underwent before an ever growing audience, and when it was all over and he had again declared that his trip had nothing to do with the war in England, he said:–

' "I had only one boast left. I was never interviewed. Now you have taken that away from me." '

Barrie locked himself away in the Plaza Hotel, but was cornered by a persevering reporter from the *New York Herald*, who managed to penetrate his suite and obtain a rare interview with the playwright:

'Sir James found the ordeal of being interviewed a difficult one, so he fell to talking about children. . . .

' "It's funny," he said, "that the real Peter Pan – I called him that – is off to the war now. He grew tired of the stories I told him, and his younger brother became interested. It was such fun telling those two about themselves. I would say, 'Then you came along and killed the pirate' and they would accept every word as the truth. That's how *Peter Pan* came to be written. It is made up of only a few stories I told them."

'Once engrossed in the subject of children Sir James underwent a transformation that was remarkable.

' "Do you know," he said, "I like the moving pictures? In them I can see cowboys. I have always wanted to be a cowboy." '

With the reporter out of the way, Barrie sat down and wrote to George, who had begun training at Sheerness:

c/o Messrs Scribner, New York.
24 Sept. 1914

My dear George,
  A letter from M. & N. y'day tells me in a casual sort of way (as if it were not about the most important news in the world to me) that you have been summoned to Sheerness. I am looking forward so much to getting some details. . . .
  Mason went off today to Canada to speak. Gilmour has been to Washington staying at the Legation . . . & I am mostly in hiding. Great placards outside, 'BARRIE EXONERATES THE KAISER' &c. &c. 'BARRIE SAYS WAR WILL BE LONG' varied with more social ones, such as 'BARRIE LIKES OUR VIRGINIA HAM'.
  Last night I had a Gin Whizz with a Long Tom in it. I slept well. Mason had two & slept better. . . .
      Your loving
      J.M.B.
  P.S. I am going to stay with Roosevelt.

On October 1st, a long interview appeared in the *New York Times*, in which the reporter stated that Sir James had escaped down an elevator shaft on seeing him approach, and that he was therefore obliged to content himself with interviewing Sir James's manservant, Brown. After much discussion about his master's pipe, in which Brown revealed, 'He does not smoke any pipe . . . he just puts that one in his mouth to help the interviewers', the intrepid reporter asked him about Barrie's views on the Kaiser. 'Sir James is a great admirer of the Kaiser, though he has not, like Mr. Carnegie, had the pleasure of meeting him in society. When he read in the papers on arriving here that the Kaiser had wept over the destruction of Louvain . . . he wondered which eye it was that the Kaiser wept with. . . . Sir James is of a very sympathetic nature.' Barrie had evidently instructed Brown to maintain strict neutrality while he was in America, in accordance with the President's wish: 'To express no preference on matter of food, for instance, and always to . . . walk in the middle of the street lest he should seem to be favoring either sidewalk.' Sir James had further instructed him, 'When we reach New York, . . . we shall be met by reporters who will pretend that America is eager to be instructed by us as to the causes and progress of the war; then, if we are fools enough to think that America cannot make up its mind for itself, we shall fall into the trap and preach to them, and all the time they are taking down our observations, they will be saying to themselves, "Pompous asses." . . . Above all, oh, Brown, if you write to the papers giving your views of why we are at war – and if you don't you will be the only person who hasn't – don't be lured into slinging vulgar abuse at our opponents, lest America takes you for another university professor.' The interviewer concluded his article, 'A disquieting feeling has since come to me that perhaps it was Sir James I had been interviewing all the time, and Brown who had escaped down the elevator.' Barrie wrote to George the following day:

My dear George,
   . . . I must get hold of an interview – 'Barrie at Bay –
Which was Brown?' – that appeared in the *New York Times*
y'day & is being a good deal talked of. It is all about Brown's
views of the war, the President, the German Ambassador &c.
including his 'Sir James's pipe', & they are trying to find out
who the interviewer was. I flatter myself you will be able to
guess! Brown has no suspicions & says 'tut tut tut' & 'Did
you ever!' to which I reply that I never.
   I am picturing you both as having very hard and laborious
work with a tremendous lot of stiff marching. . . .
             Your loving
             J.M.B.

Peter described his training at Sheerness with George in the *Morgue*:

'The afternoon we arrived, eight young officers (children, I should call them now) who had only joined a week or two earlier, with little or no more previous training than ourselves, had just received their orders from France, to replace casualties in the Battalions on the Marne and the Aisne. This somewhat abrupt confrontation with the exigencies of the service had, temporarily, a depressing effect, and I remember George, as we undressed in our tent that night, breaking a rather long silence with the words, "Well, young Peter, for the first time in our lives we're up against something really serious, **** me if we aren't."

'In a day or two his usual gaiety reasserted itself, and I believe our time "on the square" was a regimental record for light-heartedness of a most unmilitary kind, entirely due to George's unorthodox attitude. . . . [He] had quite made up his mind by now that life was going to be too short for much seriousness to enter into it. . . . The "young officers" of that Reserve Battalion, in those very early days of the war, were mostly from Oxford and Cambridge, with a few younger, straight from school. . . . Hardly any had thought of the army as a career. Looking back, I can see that they were what would nowadays be called a "cross-section" of the élite and cream of the nation. Average age about twenty-one; on the whole a devoted, laughing, fatalistic, take-it-as-it-comes company, often coarse of tongue, too young to have been coarsened in body or soul by the asperities of adult life – the bloom of youth on them still. . . . Among them George was unquestionably conspicuous; few that survive would recall anyone whose image serves better as the flower and type of that doomed generation.'

George, shortly before leaving for the Western Front

Barrie arrived back in London on October 22nd, and immediately wrote to George: 'Here I am again and thirsting nightly to see you. . . . I thought of rushing out to Sheerness, . . . but I also wonder whether there is any possibility of you & Peter being able to run up to town. Reply, reply, reply!' He wrote again on November 15th:

My dear George,
    Very glad to get your letter and to hear there is some chance of your getting a couple of nights soon. I shall be your humble servant for the occasion. It is very strange to me to read of your being at your musketry practice, for it seems to me but the other day your mother was taking bows and arrows out of your hands and pressing on me the danger of giving you penny pistols. Last week or so darts to fling against a target were considered too risky. In some other

ways it all seems longer than it is, however. . . . We seem farther away from July of this year than that July was from the days of crinolines. There is certainly some gain – a stirring of manhood, but at a terrible cost. I enclose you the Eton Chronicle, from which I see that 8 per cent of Etonians have been killed. In the Army all over the percentage of killed is under 2 per cent. . . . I dined at Asquith's the other day, and he was certainly hopeful and K. of K.* is also encouraging. Once they are back on German soil it mightn't take so long, but to get them back! . . . I've written a short play with the Kaiser as chief figure which has its points I think but unfolds a tragic tale. When I have copies I'll want your opinion. . . .

My love
J.M.B.

The short play was Barrie's attempt at dramatic propaganda, *Der Tag* – the German toast to victory. It took the form of a duologue between the German Emperor and the Spirit of Culture, reminiscent of Bernard Partridge's patriotic cartoons in *Punch*, but proved to be too sympathetic to Germany for the average Briton's taste. It is also among the very few examples of Barrie's writing in which there is none of his redeeming humour:

EMPEROR. . . . Britain has grown dull and sluggish: a belly of land, she lies overfed, no dreams within her such as keep Powers alive. . . . Britain's part in the world's making is done: 'I was,' her epitaph . . .

CULTURE. She fought you where Crecy was and Agincourt and Waterloo, with all her dead to help her. The dead became quick in their ancient graves, stirred by the tread of the island feet, and they cried out, 'How is England doing?' The living answered the dead upon their bugles with the 'All's well.' England, O Emperor, was grown degenerate, but you have made her great again. . . .

EMPEROR. God cannot let my Germany be utterly destroyed.

CULTURE. If God is with the Allies, Germany will not be destroyed. Farewell!

November 25th, 1914, would have been Sylvia's forty-eighth birthday; five days later Barrie wrote to George:

* Kitchener of Khartoum.

My dear George,

I was very gratified by your writing me for your mother's birthday. I would rather have you do so than any one alive; you can understand how I yearn to have you sitting with me now and at all times. What you don't know in the least is the help you have been to me and have become more and far more as these few years have passed. There is nothing I would not confide in you or trust to you. . . .

I was amused by a letter from your tutor [Hugh Macnaghten] in which he bewailed my having the son in *The Will* sent to Eton. He would undoubtedly, he says, have been sent by such a father to Harrow! But it was a werry nice letter indeed. . . . I was in Lord Lucas's hospital 'Wrest in Beds' the other day – 100 wounded. One of them told me (he had a broken leg) that he thought the French officers were better than the English. His explanation was thus – 'They wouldn't have sent me here 'cos I had this bad leg. There was a Frenchy near me what had the top of his head blown off & his officer said to him "You run up to the tent & get your head bandaged & come back slippy." He didn't come back slippy, so the officer went & fetched him. Yes, I think their officers are better than ours.' Amazing, isn't it?

I've done *Der Tag*, my war play, and will get you a copy. It's also possible I'll turn the [Granville-]Barker revue into a shorter thing for Gaby. Jack wires he may get up tomorrow tho' whether only for the day he doesn't say.

Your loving
J.M.B

In early December, George was posted to the 4th Battalion of the Rifle Brigade, prior to his departure for the Western Front. He wrote to Barrie, telling him he would be allowed a short leave – his first since joining. Barrie replied, 'Your news is great, and . . . I'll keep the time as clear as the deck of one of H.M. ships!' Peter Davies later speculated:

Gaby

'Did George, during those last few hours of freedom, have anything more than just a mild flirtation with Gaby? I like to think so. Both were charmers, and it would have been a good finale. It is my belief that J.M.B., though so insulated himself . . . from the flesh and the Devil, had the perception and imagination and tolerance and sense of the fitness of things to smile on such a little piece of naughtiness, . . . and even pave the way for it. I have no evidence one way or the other, . . . but I will leave the theory in, because I think it a charming one, which George would have appreciated. And you never know. J.M.B.

had his moments of profound insight and wisdom as well as his practically limitless generosity. And he loved George with an exceeding great love.'

A. E. W. Mason once referred to 'the emotional frankness with which Barrie could always write but never speak'.[2] In saying good-bye to George, Barrie doubtless had to exercise considerable self-control not to reveal his emotions and the premonition already in his notebook:

— *The Last Cricket Match*. One or two days before war declared – my anxiety & premonition – boys gaily playing cricket at Auch, seen from my window – I know they're to suffer – I see them dropping out one by one, fewer & fewer.

This theme later became *Barbara's Wedding*, written in 1917, but not produced until 1927. However, the departure of Second Lieutenant George Llewelyn Davies from Campden Hill Square provided Barrie with an idea for a more immediate play, *The New Word*. Its theme embodied his own periodic dilemma: the embarrassment which afflicts two males, both undemonstrative, who want to communicate their fondness for each other, but cannot. The two males in question are a father, Mr Torrance, and his son, Roger, a Second Lieutenant about to leave for the Front:

MR TORRANCE. Do you remember, Roger, my saying that I didn't want you to smoke till you were twenty?
ROGER. Oh, it's that, is it? . . . I never promised.
MR TORRANCE (*almost with a shout*). It's not that. (*Kindly*) Have a cigar, my boy?
ROGER. Me?
(*A rather shaky hand passes him a cigar-case.* ROGER *selects from it and lights up nervously. He is now prepared for the worst.*)
MR TORRANCE. . . . My boy, be ready; I hate to hit you without warning. I'm going to cast a grenade into the middle of you. It's this, I'm fond of you, my boy.
ROGER (*squirming*). Father, if any one were to hear you!
MR TORRANCE. They won't. The door is shut, Amy is gone to bed, and all is quiet in our street. Won't you – won't you say something civil to me in return, Roger?
(ROGER *looks at him, and away from him*) . . .
ROGER. Hum. What would you like me to call you?
MR TORRANCE (*severely*). It isn't what would *I* like. But I dare say your mother would beam if you called me 'dear father'.
ROGER. I don't think so. . . . It's so effeminate.

MR TORRANCE. Not if you say it casually.

ROGER (*with something very like a snort*). How does one say a thing like that casually?

MR TORRANCE. Well, for instance, you could whistle while you said it – or anything of that sort.

ROGER. Hum. Of course you – if we were to – to be like that, you wouldn't *do* anything.

MR TORRANCE. How do you mean?

ROGER. You wouldn't paw me?

MR TORRANCE. . . . Roger! you forget yourself. (*But apparently it is for him to continue.*) That reminds me of a story I heard the other day of a French general. He had asked for volunteers from his airmen for some specially dangerous job – and they all stepped forward. Pretty good that. Then three were chosen and got their orders and saluted, and were starting off when he stopped them. 'Since when,' he said, 'have brave boys departing to the post of danger omitted to embrace their father?' They did it then. Good story?

ROGER (*lowering*). They were French.

MR TORRANCE. Yes, I said so. Don't you think it's good?

ROGER. Why do you tell it to me?

MR TORRANCE. Because it's a good story.

ROGER (*sternly*). You are sure that there is no other reason? (MR TORRANCE *tries to brazen it out, but he looks guilty.*) You know, father, that is barred. . . .

(. . . MR TORRANCE *snaps angrily*)

MR TORRANCE. What is barred?

ROGER. You know.

When George left London for Winchester, prior to his embarkation for France, he took with him in his kit-bag a somewhat incongruous book to read in the trenches. It was not given to him by Barrie; he had bought it himself, a few days before his departure: *The Little White Bird*.

Barrie wrote to him on December 21st, 1914:

My dear George,

When your things arrived at 23, I thought it meant you were on the eve of starting, but I admit I hoped I was wrong, and now your letter comes and I know. You are off. It is still a shock to me. I shall have many anxious days and nights too, but I only fall into line with so many mothers. The Orea cigarettes will be sent weekly and anything else I can think of, to cheer you in a foreign land, tho' France and Belgium can scarcely seem that to us any more. I shudder over the weight of your pack, and know that for my part I

Madge Titheradge as Peter Pan
in the 1914/15 revival

would be down under it. . . . Michael was with me at *Der Tag* today. It was received with much applause, but it struck me that in their hearts the Coliseum audience thought it heavy food. In the programme were performing pigs, and immediately in front of it a man sang a war-song about the Kaiser saying he was 'in a funk' and the Crown Prince advising him 'to do a bunk'. Good company!

I'll write often and will be so glad of any line from you.

Your loving,
J.M.B.

The following night, *Peter Pan* opened for its tenth revival, with Madge Titheradge as the new Peter, and Barrie's niece, Madge Murray, as Mrs Darling. Barrie wrote to his god-daughter, Pauline Chase, who had married Alec Drummond in October: 'To wish you both a very happy Christmas. In a sense it is pretty grim to send Christmas greetings this year, but tho' we cannot forget the war, it makes us think still more of the home, and I wish you much of the truest happiness in yours. . . . I am going to the P. Pan performance today, and hope all will be well, but you needn't be afraid, I shan't forget the Peter of the Past. I expect the fairies have their knuckles in their eyes today.'[3] Barrie took his godson, Peter Scott, to see the play; at the end, he asked the five-year-old boy what he had liked best, and was particularly gratified by his answer: 'What I think I liked best was tearing up the programme and dropping the bits on people's heads.'[4] Peter gave him an empty box as a Christmas present, and Barrie duly acknowledged it:

> Adelphi Terrace House,
> Strand, W.C.
> Dec. 30, 1914.

Dear Peter,
> When I look upon my Box,
> With pride and joy I rocks,
> From my head to my socks,
> And everybody knocks
> At my door, and flocks
> To see my box.

> Signed by The Author.
> The writes of translation are reserved.

> Your Loving
> Godfather,
> J.M.B.

On the same day, George wrote to his brother Peter from France:

'How goes it in Sheerness? I expect it's getting bloodier and bloodier. I invent little prayers of thanksgiving that I'm not there still. . . . We have been here for five days now, with no immediate prospect of moving. . . . I am becoming a most accomplished linguist. Next time we advance on Rue Pasquier I shall be irresistible! I have two reasons for writing to you. (1) Will you send me a pair of those things you put inside gum-boots? . . . (2) In the event of my being killed, wounded or missing, you might communicate with Josephine. A loathsome job for you, but otherwise she won't know till it's in the papers. . . . I did very well in the interval between Sheerness and Winchester (oh! Winchester was loathsome). I told you about meeting G. Deslys, didn't I? Of course, that was the great show, but I had a good time all round.'

Peter replied on January 10th, 1915:

'I haven't got those gum-boot sock things yet but as soon as I can I will send them. The other duty I will try to perform if it becomes necessary, though it wouldn't be a particularly easy letter to compose, would it? . . . Perhaps by the time this reaches you you will have been "in the trenches", receiving your baptism of fire, and all that sort of thing. I wish you would write and tell me exactly what your sensations are, and whether you experience any more of that jolly old depression which descended upon us during the first week at [Sheerness]. I still get it sometimes, and if I thought the war was bound to last more than a year from now, I believe I should commit suicide.'

George wrote to Barrie on January 13th:

One of George's letters from France. The 'Passed by Censor' stamp was a particular source of pride to Barrie

Dear Uncle Jim,
    I have got some spare time now that is not occupied with sleeping, & I'll try & see how much news I can give you.
    The fear of death doesn't enter so much as I expected into this show. The hardships are the things that count, and one gets very soon into the way of taking them as they come. . . .
    [*After a long account of trench routine*] Don't you get worried about me. I take every precaution I can, & shall do very well. It is an amazing show, & I am unable to look forward more than two or three hours. Also don't get anxious about letters. I'll send them whenever there's a chance, but there are less chances than I expected.
                              Your affec.
                              George

Jack in 1914

Barrie meanwhile was writing to George:

'Hoping for another letter as soon as you have the time. You should see how I plunge thro' my letter-bag looking for one from you. It is almost too exciting, and I have some bad nights, I can tell you. I have an idea your Uncle Guy goes out this week. Jack is now on the *Harpy*, a destroyer as big as the *Brazen*, and I hope a bit more comfortable. . . . Peter is still signalling at Chatham, and I hope to have him up for Saturday night. Today Mick, Nick and I were at *David Copperfield*, a big [audience] of school girls largely, and every time Owen Nares came on as David there were loud gasps of 'Oh how sweet!' Almost too sweet I shd have thought. . . . There is what I believe to be a well grounded idea that we shall be visited in this isle, and probably in this metropolis very soon, by Zeppelins & other air craft. Have been making enquiries as to where the coal-cellar is at 23. . . . Johnstone said he thought you were near Ypres. Wherever you are, I hope you see near your bed the flowers I want to place there in a nice vase, and the illustrated papers, and a new work by Compton Mackenzie which I read aloud to you! I shall be so anxious till I get another line from you.'

Peter Davies wrote, 'I think this letter well illustrates . . . the peculiar and characteristic form which J.M.B.'s affection for George and Michael took: a dash of the paternal, a lot of the maternal, and much, too, of the lover – at this stage Sylvia's lover still imperfectly merged into the lover of her son. To criticise would be easy; yet I don't think it did, or would have done, George any harm.'

Barrie's letter crossed in the post with George's news of the 22nd:

Guy du Maurier, a professional soldier too sensitive for his job. During the Boer War he saw a man killed next to him; the shock was so profound that within a few days his hair had turned completely white

'The malady that laid me low has been successfully vanquished, & I am now a young bull once again, & ready for our next show. We shall be in the trenches again either tomorrow night or the night after. . . . I don't think there's very much danger to expect, except from sickness, which is always ready in this weather to show its face. . . . But I take every care that can be taken, I can promise you. . . . I suppose Uncle Guy is somewhere about by now. I should like to come across him, but there isn't much chance. . . . I dare bet he won't have much to say for this game. Picturesqueness is distinctly lacking.'

Guy du Maurier, now a Lieutenant-Colonel in the Royal Fusiliers, was fighting four miles farther down the line from George. He too was sending home regular accounts of life in the trenches, to his wife Gwen. Unlike George, who clearly took great pains to shield Barrie from the reality of the trenches, Guy – a professional soldier and a veteran of the Boer War – gave his wife as accurate a picture as the Army Censor would allow him to paint:

'The trenches are full of dead Frenchmen. When one is killed they let him lie in the squelching mud and water at the bottom; and when you try and drain or dig you unearth them in an advanced state of decomposition. . . . All the filth of an Army lies around rotting. . . . The stink is awful. There are many dead Highlanders just in front – killed in December I think – and they aren't pleasant. One gets used to smells. . . . Two hundred of my men went to hospital today – mostly frost-bitten feet; bad cases are called gangrene and very bad cases the toes drop off. . . . When we've done our four days I'll try and go over and see George who I think is only two miles off. I haven't seen anyone I know lately. I fancy most of the Army I know are killed or wounded.'

George wrote to Barrie on January 27th, telling him that 'I have recovered entirely from my late sickness, and have never been better in my life. . . . On the whole then, my dear Uncle Jim, there's nothing for you to be anxious about. Of course, there's always the chance of stopping an unaimed bullet, but you can see it's a very small one. And I am far too timorous a man (I am a man now, I think) to run any more risk than I must. . . . Are you rehearsing with Gaby yet?'

Barrie had finished writing his revue for Gaby, entitled *Rosy Rapture, or The Pride of the Beauty Chorus*, and was out filming new sequences which had to be edited before rehearsals could begin. He wrote to George on February 8th: 'I have not heard from you since the postcard sent Jan 31, which of course is not very long, and you warned me there might necessarily be these pauses. So I grin and bear it. Not much grinning. . . . How I wish I knew what you are doing at this moment. I wish I was your ghillie.'

George was also writing frequent letters to his four brothers, his girl Josephine, and Mary Hodgson:

Feb. 11 [1915]

Dear Mary,

The veteran is off to the trenches again soon, after a fine rest, & finds himself with terrible holes in his pants. Do send me out two pairs of long ones, new, you know the kind. Also some soap, or I must go unwashen.

By Jove, Mary, when I get home I shall never get up in the mornings at all. I shall be frightfully idle. That is one advantage of the firing-line trenches. As an officer I don't sleep at all in the night, so there is no getting up in the morning. But sheets! And a proper bed! Oh, I hope the war isn't going on for ten years.

Meanwhile life is very bearable here. And when I get back I shall be more conceited than ever. You'll all shudder.

Yours affec.

George

When George had been at Eton, Barrie had treated him to the occasional hamper from Fortnum & Mason in response to his claims that he was on the verge of starvation. The trenches were no different:

23 Campden Hill Square,
Kensington, W.
14 Feb. 1915.

My dear George,

Practical affairs first. The eatables were sent off *instanter* from Fortnum & Mason, and shd arrive to-day or tomorrow according to their calculation, but I can see that you are probably already back in the trenches. Besides the usual things in their hampers there is a tongue, ham & turkey, and if you find that those keep, we shall repeat. Mary is also sending you some new underwear. . . .

I can understand that getting ready to go back [into the trenches] is uncommonly like 'putting on your pads', but what I should feel worst . . . is that cutting across in the moonlight. Certainly it must be a bit creepy, and I don't feel as friendly to the moon as I once did. My own feeling about the moon is that it is at its best at Rustington, because we had many lovely moons there in the days when we were all so happy together. However I trust your best moons are still to come. . . .

I am always at Nico about writing to you, and he is always deciding to do it tomorrow, with results known to you. He seems to have got to a stage when letter-writing assumes the appearance of a Frankenstein to him. . . .

Loving
J.M.B.

Nico's confession for Charlie Chaplin. It was an enthusiasm shared by Barrie, who harboured an ambition that Chaplin should play Peter Pan on screen

Nico summoned up the requisite concentration a week later:

A postscript doodle from Nico to George

Sunday 21st [Feb. 1915]

Dear George,

Excusez-vous moi s'il vous plait for not writing before. . . .
I am going to tea with Aunt Gwen to day and I shall see
Angela and Daphne. Uncle Jim is at present laid up with a
cold. Uncle Guy is having an awful time I believe. He went
out with 900 men. He has only 200 left. The other 700 are
laid up with their toes nearly off. . . . Jack wears a *ring* now.
Have you fallen in love with any French girls yet? I *guess so*
Eh! What!!? . . . I went to Peter Pan a few weeks ago and
the new Peter is quite good. . . . Mary hopes you've got the
underclothing. . . .

Love from your affectionate
Nico.

George received a slight leg-wound on the night of February 14th,
but he made no mention of it to Barrie (the information was given in a
letter from Guy to Gwen), and his next letter was as cheerful as ever:

'We had an awful walk up to [the] trench, through a sea of mud, & it
was a pitch dark night. . . . Oh, Lord it was muddy! I did badly that
night. I had to go along behind, & by mistake I got into the
communication-trench behind, which is full of liquid mud above the
knees. Here, being a bit unsteady on my pins, I elected to fall over
backwards. Behold me sitting with exceedingly cold water trickling
into me everywhere, unable to move, & shouting for help! . . . Is
Gaby still ill? How I long to see the revue.'

Barrie replied on February 19th:

'Gaby is back so I expect the burlesque shd be on in about three
weeks. I'm writing a little one-act thing [*The New Word*] to go with
it, and as all my thoughts are with 2nd Lieutenants, it has to be about
one. It is just a family talk between one & his people, chiefly his
father, on his first appearance in uniform. I fancy "2nd Lieut" is the
most popular word in the language today, tho' a short time ago it
didn't exist to us. . . . Tomorrow is your father's birthday, and I feel
he would be very pleased with you all, which was always the best
birthday to him.'

The New Word was to be a short curtain-raiser to *Rosy Rapture*,
now in rehearsal at the Duke of York's. Although it had been
motivated by George's departure for the Front, an older theme had

found its way into the play – a memory that had been in the author's mind since the age of six:

MRS TORRANCE. . . . . Rogie dear, . . . I'll tell you something. You know your brother Harry died when he was seven. To you, I suppose, it is as if he had never been. You were barely five.

ROGER. I don't remember him, mater.

MRS TORRANCE. No – no. But I do, Rogie. He would be twenty-one now; but though you and Emma grew up I have always gone on seeing him as just seven. Always till the war broke out. And now I see him a man of twenty-one, dressed in khaki, fighting for his country, same as you. . . .

George wrote to Barrie on February 20th:

'Fortnum & Mason's goods have just arrived – boxes & boxes of them. We are a grateful party of officers, & shall be in clover for the six days' rest that is coming. It is good of you. I shall probably ask for more in a fortnight or three weeks. This time I ask you for a new novel. I ask for the devil of a lot, but everything I get here is worth thirty times what it was in the piping times of peace. . . . P.S. Cash is running short. Could you get me 100 francs from the bureau de change at Charing Cross in notes?'

Barrie replied on February 28th:

Peter

My dear George,

Your letter dated 20th Feb arrived yesterday and made me happy for the moment at all events. I had hardly finished reading and re-reading it (quite as if I was a young lady) when there arrives, unexpected, a gent of the name of Peter. He had managed at last to get two days by bearding his colonel, and in he walked, larger than ever, and between you and me a d–v–l–shly handsome fellow in my opinion and I guess in that of any candid person. Peter, whom a few years ago we chuckled over as rather a comic, is a werry fine youth indeed. . . . Life, sir, is odd, as you have been seeing this last two months, but it is even odder than that. Such a queer comedy of tears and grimness and the inexplicable – as your du Maurier blood will make you understand sooner than most. It will teach you that the nice people are the nastiest and the nastiest the nicest, and on the whole leave you smiling.

A few things to note from your last. For one thing I enclose four pounds in French money, and for another it is always a blessed thing for me when you want something. So if you don't want, go on inventing. I'll send you a book or two tomorrow (this is Sunday). Then I'll also send tomorrow a hamper similar to the last from Fortnum & Mason as it, thank goodness, seems to have been a success. . . . The one great doing for me is when we are all together again.

                    Loving
                    J.M.B.

Although Guy and George gave widely differing accounts of the miseries of trench warfare, both shared a similar response to the stark beauty of ruins. Guy had written to Gwen of 'a lone and much-shelled chateau, looking picturesque in the rising moonlight'. George came across the same chateau a month later, writing to Barrie:

'It was a bright moonlit night, & the chateau looked wonderful. It was all white with four great pillars in front, one of them broken. I walked up to it feeling, in spite of mud & dirt, like a Roman Emperor. It is the best sight I've seen yet. And then of course romance was a bit spoiled by an N.C.O. just behind me making some low remark about spotted fever (alluding to the shrapnel marks that covered the walls). . . . Next day I prowled round the chateau. It was really nothing but a shell, with whole rooms battered to bits. There was a little shrine out in the garden, practically untouched by gunfire. On the altar, just in front of the figure of Christ, there was a charger of four cartridges. To a sentimental civilian like me, not yet hardened into a proper mercenary, this had rather a striking effect. Perhaps it sounds a bit cheap, but the chateau, which was rather beautiful, had made me feel romantic.'

Peter Davies commented, 'No word could be more aptly applied to George than romantic. He was romantically minded . . . and romantic in appearance. He had a nice "dirty" mind, too, and that makes a delightful combination, particularly when it is seasoned with a gay and at times extravagant sense of humour.'

Michael was now fourteen, still unhappy at Eton, but, according to Hugh Macnaghten, 'resolved to face every event with absolute self-possession, however much it costs him. . . . Very full of anxieties, a boy of a tender heart and delightful feelings, full of promise. . . . Very anxious not to give himself away or show any excitement.'[5] Michael's only surviving letter to George is distinctly lacking in the usual Etonian slang adopted by boys of his age:

George. 'It is impossible to do justice to the charm of his modesty or to his character,' recorded the *Eton College Chronicle* in March 1915; 'the Greek epithets σώφρων [wise] χαρίεις [elegant], καλός κἀγαθός [honourable and good] express him best.'

Eton College
Windsor.
3rd March 1915.
X A.M.

Dear George,

As I am at the present moment afflicted with a belly-ache, and ∴ staying out, I seize the chance to write this news letter. Leave is passed, last week-end I found Peter at 23, having got leave from Friday to Sunday evening. And Uncle Jim rehearsing plays with a bad cold. I went to the Coliseum, which was not at its best. . . . The evening [of returning to Eton] passed in the usual way: – Tea: then wait, wait, wait, with futile attempts to play Rat-tat etc: books for Mary to pack: taxi comes early: wait: bag in taxi: hurried farewells, and station: crowds of boys: greetings which freeze on sight of Sir James: shouts of Good Lord here's Davies! on finding a carriage: walk up to tutor's [i.e. Macnaghten's House] on arriving, to feel you haven't been to leave at all, except for the atmosphere of purses replenished and change suits: supper & prayers after which [Macnaghten] comes in & asks all about George & Peter & Leave in general, while doing his best to obliterate the foot of the bed. Then lights suddenly go out at ten when a new book by Wells or Bierce becomes very interesting. Wake in morning to the refrain of 'Nearly a quarter to seven, Mr Davies. Are you awake, sir?' To which the only possible reply is a grunt. A superhuman effort drags you to the shower-bath, etc. . . .

My dame has just come in, and on my suggestion asks me to give you her best regards. . . . Again enters [my dame] with castor-oil in Brandy, which now reposes in my belly. . . . I had a letter from Jack this morning, in which he says he has done over 3,000 miles in the last twelve days, which seems rather a lot. . . . My source of information is now beginning to diminish rapidly and I feel that you will have to be satisfied with nine pages or thereabouts. . . . I cudgel my brains, but I can find nothing more to say, so I fear I must finish. J'ai fini.* Now for a letter to Jack, and then the night only.

Michael.

*An expression taught to the boys as children by Mary Hodgson to indicate that they needed assistance in the lavatory.

George wrote to Barrie on March 7th:

'There is nothing to chronicle, except the gruesome fact that I've seen violent death within a yard of me. I was quite safe myself, Uncle Jim, as I was right down underneath the parapet. The poor chap wasn't one of my fellows, & put his head up in a place where at that time he could scarcely fail to stop a bullet. The top of his head was shot off, so he didn't feel it. But it was a dreadful sight. I oughtn't to write about these things, but it made an impression. Good luck with the burlesque. I am longing to see it. . . . Fortnum & Mason has again rolled up in abundance. It is so good of you.'

On the evening of Thursday, March 11th, Barrie wrote the last letter to reach George alive:

Envelope containing Barrie's last letter to George

My dear George,
    I don't know when news from quite near you may reach you – perhaps later than we get it – but we have just heard that your Uncle Guy has been killed. He was a soldier by profession, and had reached a time of life when the best things have come to one if they are to come at all, and he had no children, which is the best reason for caring to live on after the sun has set; and these are things to remember now. He certainly had the du Maurier charm at its best – the light heart with the sad smile, & it might be the sad heart with the bright smile. There was always something pathetic about him to me. He had lots of stern stuff in him, and yet always the mournful smile of one who could pretend that life was gay but knew it wasn't. One of the most attractive personalities I have ever known.
    Of course I don't need this to bring home to me the danger you are always in more or less, but I do seem to be sadder to-day than ever, and more and more wishing you were a girl of 21 instead of a boy, so that I could say the things to you that are now always in my heart. For four years I have been waiting for you to become 21 & a little more, so that we could get closer & closer to each other, without any words needed. I don't have any little iota of desire for you to get military glory. I do not care a farthing for anything of the kind, but I have the one passionate desire that we may all be together again once at least. You would not mean a feather-weight more to me tho' you came back a General. I just want yourself. There may be some moments when a knowledge of all you are to me will make you a little more careful, and so I can't help going on saying these things.
    It was terrible that man being killed next to you, but don't

be afraid to tell me of such things. You see it at night I fear with painful vividness. I have lost all sense I ever had of war being glorious, it is just unspeakably monstrous to me now.
                    Loving
                    J.M.B

Peter Davies wrote, 'Surely no soldier in France or Flanders ever had more moving words from home than those in this tragic, desperately apprehensive letter. . . . Plenty of other people, no doubt, were thinking and writing much the same sort of thing, but not in such perfection. Indeed, taking all the circumstances into consideration, I think it must be one of the great letters of the world. Its poignancy is so dreadfully enhanced, too, by the realisation that, whatever of the pathetic there may have been in Guy du M., . . . far, far the most pathetic figure in all the world was the poor little genius who wrote these words, and afterwards, no doubt, walked up and down, up and down his lonely room, smoking pipe after pipe, thinking his dire thoughts.'

On the following Monday, March 15th, Nico and Mary Hodgson were asleep in the night nursery at Campden Hill Square. 'Suddenly there came a banging on the front door, and the door-bell ringing and ringing. Mary got out of bed and went downstairs, while I sat up with ears pricked. Voices soon came up the stairs, but stopped just short of the landing. Then I heard Uncle Jim's voice, an eerie Banshee wail – "Ah-h-h! They'll all go, Mary – Jack, Peter, Michael – even little Nico – This dreadful war will get them all in the end!" A little later, realising I was awake, he came and sat on my bed for a while. I don't think he spoke, but I knew that George was dead.'

George had been killed in the early hours of March 15th. Lord Tennyson's son, Aubrey, wrote to Peter from Flanders a few days later, giving him as many details as he could gather:

'The battalion was advancing to drive the Germans out of St. Eloi. . . . Stopford Sackville was marching alongside of George part of the way up, & he says he fancied George had a sort of premonition that he was going to be killed & said he hoped that they would not take him back into one of the villages behind but would bury him outside his own trench, & that he considered it was the finest death one could die & he wished to be buried where he fell. He was the first officer to be shot that night. The Colonel was talking to all C Company officers before the attack was made, & George was sitting on a bank with the others, when he was shot through the head, & died almost immediately, so that he can have felt nothing. It was impossible to comply with his wishes & bury him there, [so] they took him back and buried him in a field on the left of the road ... outside Voormezeele ... and they took a lot of trouble making the grave look nice, & planting it with violets. .... I do not stand alone in this battalion in my affection for George. When I first asked about him when I got here, I was told by an officer who has been in the battalion for some years that he had never known any officer come into the battalion, who after so short a time had won the love of everyone, so much so that all his brother officers felt when he was killed that even though they had only known him such a short time, they had lost one of their best friends. As regards myself I don't think anyone can ever take his place, as there is no one whom I have ever loved more.'

Peter Davies wrote in his *Morgue*:

'I remember getting a telegram at Sheerness from J.M.B. – GEORGE IS KILLED, HOPE YOU CAN COME TO ME. – And I remember arriving at the flat in Adelphi Terrace, ... and that it was all very painful. .... The effect on J.M.B. was dire indeed, poor little devil. Oh, miserable Jimmie. Famous, rich, loved by a vast public, but at what a frightful private cost. Shaken to the core – whatever dark fancies may have lurked at the back of his queer fond mind – by the death of Arthur; tortured a year or two later by the ordeal of his own divorce; then so soon afterwards prostrated, ravaged and utterly undone when Sylvia pursued Arthur to the grave; and after only four and a half years, George; George, whom he had loved with such a deep, strange, complicated, increasing love, and who as he knew well would have been such a pillar for him to lean on in the difficult job of guiding the destinies of Sylvia & Arthur Llewelyn Davies's boys – "my boys".'

A telegram from the King and Queen conveying their sympathies arrived later in the day, followed by other telegrams and letters of condolence as the news spread that one of Sir James Barrie's adopted sons had been killed. Among them was a small white envelope, addressed in pencil, and stamped 'PASSED BY CENSOR':

March 14 [1915]

Dear Uncle Jim,
    I have just got your letter about Uncle Guy. You say it hasn't made you think any more about the danger I am in. But I know it has. Do try not to let it. I take every care of myself that can be decently taken. And if I am going to stop a bullet, why should it be with a vital place? But arguments aren't any good. Keep your heart up, Uncle Jim, & remember how good an experience like this is for a chap who's been very idle before. Lord, I shall be proud when I'm

home again, & talking to you about all this. That old dinner at the Savoy will be pretty grand. . . .

The ground is drying up fast now, and the weather far better. Soon the spring will be on us, & the birds nesting right up in the firing line. Cats are the only other thing left there. I wonder what spring will bring for us in this part of the line. Something a little different from the forty-eight hours routine in the trenches, I daresay. . . .

Meanwhile, dear Uncle Jim, you must carry on with your job of keeping up your courage. I will write every time I come out of action. We go up to the trenches in a few days again.

Your affec.
George

By the week-end, the four surviving brothers had forgathered at Campden Hill Square. Nico, aged eleven, remembered 'seeing Jack standing by the dining-room window looking down the square, with big tears running down his cheeks. For myself, I'm afraid, my chief feeling was the thrill at seeing Jack and Peter in their uniforms.'

Peter concluded his *Morgue* with his own retrospective thoughts on George, and the effect of his death on their lives:

'For his brothers, George's death was, with no exaggeration, a bad business. . . . The fortunes of war brought me pretty close to him for a short time within a few months of his death, and I had in the preceding five or six years been with him a great deal, fishing latterly, and bug-hunting in the more childish days before that; but it would be untrue to say that there existed tremendous intimacy between us, or that we were bound together by that ineffable love of brother for brother which one has occasionally read of. On the other hand it is not in the least untrue to say that I have gone on missing him possibly ever since I last saw him, leaning out of the window as his train steamed away from Sheerness station and calling out, "Till our next merry meeting!" He had so much that was really good without being in the least goody-goody, and was such fun, and so tolerant, and would have been such value always; and blood and background and memories are a mighty strong bond; and how few, after all, are those in all one's life with whom one can be completely at ease. That he had his fair share of the celebrated du Maurier charm or temperament, is certain; there was also a good leavening of sound, kind, sterling Davies in him too. I think he had that simplicity which J.M.B. and [Hugh] Macnaghten saw in Arthur, and which, though I only partly understand it, I dimly perceive to be perhaps the best of all characteristics. In fact I think he had in him a very great

George's last letter. At the foot of the page, Barrie has written: 'This is the last letter, and was written a few hours before his death. I knew he was killed before I got it.'

deal of all the best and finest qualities of both Arthur & Sylvia. But it was all thirty years ago, and he was only twenty-one, and what do I know about him really?

'This much is certain, that when he died, some essential virtue went out of us as a family. The combination of George, who as eldest brother exercised a sort of constitutional, tacitly accepted authority over us, who was of our blood, and on whom still lingered more than a little of our own good family tradition, with the infinitely generous, fanciful solicitous, hopelessly unauthoritative J.M.B., was a good one and would have kept us together as a unit of some worth; as it was, circumstances were too much for J.M.B. left solitary, as well as for us, and we became gradually, but much sooner than would or should have been the case, individuals with little of the invaluable, cohesive strength of the united family. . . .

'Oh well, bugger it. To make an end of this penultimate chapter of the family morgue, the epitaph which a poet wrote for George and his kind seems as appropriate as anything I know of:

Here dead lie we because we did not choose
To live and shame the land from which we sprung;
Life, to be sure, is nothing much to lose,
But young men think it is, and we were young.

George's grave in the British War Cemetery at Voormezeele. Peter visited the cemetery in 1946. 'I had the place to myself, and never remember feeling more alone. It was a grey, lowering, dismal sort of day, shivery too, in spite of the month. All sorts of vague thoughts came and went in my head, of dust and skeletons and the conqueror worm, and old, unhappy, far-off things, and older days that were happier. What with one thing and another I am not ashamed to admit that I piped an eye.'

On March 22nd, 1915, seven days after George's death, *Rosy Rapture, or the Pride of the Beauty Chorus* opened at the Duke of York's Theatre, preceded by *The New Word*. Nico thought Gaby's revue the most glittering piece of entertainment he had ever witnessed in his life: 'I must have seen it over twenty times, and knew every song off by heart – particularly "Some Sort of Mother", which must be the best tune Jerome Kern ever wrote. Of course I was only eleven, but to me it was just about the most wonderful thing Uncle Jim had ever done. Unfortunately no one else agreed with me, and it was a more or less total disaster.'

Frohman was due in London at the end of May, but Barrie begged him to come earlier in the hope that he might have ideas on how to salvage *Rosy Rapture*. The 'Beaming Buddha' agreed, and booked himself a passage on the *Lusitania*, despite the threat of attacks by German U-boats. When he boarded the liner on May 1st, he was asked, 'Aren't you afraid of U-boats?' 'No,' he replied, 'only I.O.U.-boats.'[1] Ethel Barrymore sent him a last-minute cable, imploring him not to sail. But Frohman had made up his mind. Barrie needed his help, and he would go. On May 7th, 1915, the *Lusitania* was torpedoed off the Irish coast, and sank within twenty minutes. When Frohman was offered a place in one of the lifeboats, he refused. 'Why fear death?' he is reputed to have said. 'It is the greatest adventure in life.'[2] His body was later washed up below the Old Head of Kinsale and taken back to America for burial.

Frohman on board the *Lusitania*

Frohman was once asked what he would like to have written about him after his death. He replied, 'All I would ask is this: "He gave *Peter Pan* to the world." . . . It is enough for any man.'[3] His claim was fully justified: had it not been for Frohman's daring and vision, there would have been no *Peter Pan*, and for Barrie his death meant not merely the loss of one of his greatest friends (in Peter Davies's opinion, 'the only non-Davies whom he knew how to love'), but the end of a unique theatrical partnership. Frohman's faith in Barrie had been absolute; his biographers wrote: 'It was often said in jest in London that if Barrie had asked Frohman to produce a dramatization of the Telephone Directory, he would smile and say with enthusiasm: "Fine! Who shall we have in the cast?" ' Barrie's grief at the news of Frohman's drowning was genuine enough; but, as with Captain Scott, he took a characteristic pride in his association with another 'heroic' death, particularly as Frohman had chosen to echo Peter Pan's 'To die will be an awfully big adventure' as his last words. They were attested by the actress Rita Jolivet, who survived the disaster and publicized them in an interview. Barrie, however, could not resist changing them to a closer approximation of the text. He wrote to Pauline Chase, 'His last words . . . were really, I feel sure, "Death will be an awfully big adventure." '[4]

At the end of May, Lord Lucas joined the Flying Corps, despite the handicap of his wooden leg, and Barrie assumed much of the responsibility for the maintenance of 'Wrest in Beds'. The work was rewarding, but it lacked glamour; he hankered after the opportunity to play a larger role – something that would bring him into contact with the fighting at the Front. There had been various reports in the press of starving, homeless children wandering around the French countryside near Reims. The image appealed to Barrie's imagination: he talked it over with his friend Elizabeth Lucas, and suggested that she might like to set up a temporary orphanage for them. Elizabeth responded to the idea, and Barrie gave her an initial £2,000 with which to set the scheme in progress. She managed to acquire the loan of Bettancourt, a large château to the south-east of Reims, and transformed it into a home for the orphaned children. Barrie now had the ideal excuse to visit the war zone for himself, albeit not the Front Line. He wrote to Gilmour from the Château de Bettancourt on July 26th:

Barrie and orphan at Bettancourt

'I had very easy travelling all the way, indeed semi-regal, owing to the good graces of the Scotland Yard people. We are about 18 miles from the Front & 120 from Paris. . . . You can hear the guns from Rheims direction in the north. . . . Aeroplanes make a great stir over our heads. . . . The Germans occupied the Chateau in their rush for Paris & it is now becoming a child's hospital. One boy had a leg blown off by a shell at Rheims. His parents wept to see him but they bored him – so he wandered off to play. A significant note – The drummer went round the other night to warn the villagers all dogs must be chained up at nights. This because the dogs have developed a grim hunt for bodies which they scrape up in the night. I'll be back in a week.'

Barrie returned to England at the beginning of August and took Michael and Nico up to Scotland for their annual fishing holiday. As there were only three of them this year, they moved from hotel to hotel instead of renting a house. Barrie spent most of his time writing letters, in which he gave vivid accounts of his visit to France, illustrated with more macabre details of the wounded children and starving dogs. Nico chronicled the Scottish holiday in a letter to Mary Hodgson:

Tomdoun Hotel,
Glengarry,
Invernessshire.
Sunday 15th August 1915.

Dear Mary,

Thank you very much for your 2 letters. We went to Dhivach last Monday. We saw the fall in the burn and the place where Uncle Jim and George and Jack played cricket. . . . In the arbour we found the initials of all our names still there. . . . Was the flicker-show any good? Did you like Charlie Chaplin? I had a long letter from Jack. He went ashore on Gallipoli with a letter to the French Headquarters. . . . I miss you here very much. I have caught five trout here and Michael 15. But then Michael — — — — —!!

Well love from
NICHOLAS LLEWELYN DAVIES

Barrie's friendship with the 'Welsh Lewises' had been largely confined to a lengthy correspondence with Mrs Hugh Lewis – the mother of the boy who had sent him a drawing of Peter Pan in 1912 – but earlier this summer he had taken Peter to spend a few days at the Lewises' home, Glan Hafren, in Wales. Barrie wrote to her from Scotland on September 1st:

Dear Mrs Lewis,

I wish there were a few more like you, but it is perhaps better that you should remain unique. . . . It has been rather grim in Scotland this year. The highlands in many glens are as bare of population owing to the war as if this were the month before Creation. I have just Michael and Nicholas with me and they feel it too, but they climb about, fishing mostly, and if you were to search the bogs you would find me in one of them loaded with waterproofs and ginger beer. . . . I wish we could hurl ourselves straight upon Glan Hafren, but we shall be here till the 8th and that only gives us an exact week before Michael returns to school, and we need that time in London. It shows how much we must have talked of you that he (the dark and dour and impenetrable) has announced to me that he wants to go to see you. I was never so staggered.

Glan Hafren, 1915: Peter Lewis, Barrie, and Peter Davies

'The dark and dour and impenetrable' was a description that Barrie was fond of using when referring to Michael. It was, of course, only one aspect of his character, but Barrie took a curious pride in it: he liked to boast that Michael had grown out of him, was beyond his reach. It was a form of self-mockery, born of self-defence, and is poignantly evident in the closing pages of *Neil and Tintinnabulum*, in which Michael is no longer the boy Neil, but the adolescent Tintinnabulum:

Michael and Nico playing clock-golf

'Tintinnabulum's opinion of himself . . . is lowlier than was Neil's; sometimes in dark moods it is lowlier than makes for happiness. He has hardened a little since he was Neil, coarsened but strengthened. I comfort myself with the curious reflection that the best men I have known have had a touch of coarseness in them. . . . He had to refashion himself on a harsher model, and he set his teeth and won, blaming me a little for not having broken to him the ugly world we can make it. . . . By that time my visits [to Eton] were being suffered rather than acclaimed. It was done with an exquisite politeness certainly, but before I was out of sight he had dived into some hilarious rumpus. Gladly for his sake I knew my place. . . . His letters from school tend at all times to be more full of instruction for my guidance than of information about where he stands in his form. . . . On important occasions he even writes my letters for me, requesting me to copy them carefully and not to put in any words of my own, as when for some reason they have to be shown to his tutor. He then writes, "Begin 'Dear T.' (not 'Dearest T.'), and end 'Yours affec.' (not 'Yours affectionately')." . . .

'You readers may smile when I tell you why I have indited these memories and fancies. It was not done for you but for me, being a foolish attempt to determine, by writing the things down (playing over by myself some of the past moves in the game), whether Tintinnabulum really does like me still. That he should do so is very important to me as he recedes farther from my ken down that road which hurries him from me. . . .

'On the whole, I think he is still partial to me. Corroboration, I consider, was provided at our parting, when he so skilfully turned what began as a tear into a wink and gazed at me from the disappearing train with what I swear was a loving scowl. . . . He no longer needs me, of course, as Neil did, and he will go on needing me less. When I think of Neil I know that those were the last days in which I was alive.'

Michael's unhappiness at Eton had lasted nearly two years, but by the autumn of 1915 he had begun to assume a nonchalant façade that masked his inner feelings. Sebastian Earl, a contemporary at Eton, remembered him as having 'a quite remarkable lightness of touch, lightness of imagination. He had tremendous charm – a romantic charm, never sentimental. I think his greatest gift was his wit. . . . He was wholly un-Etonian – it didn't seem to rub off on him at all.'[5] Another Etonian friend, Clive Burt, described him as 'a cat that walked alone. He was always very reserved – not a seeker after popularity or great friendships, though both were open to him. He was, of course, quite brilliant – I believe Hugh Macnaghten, his tutor, thought he was the most remarkable boy he had ever taught in all his years at Eton.'[6]

While still only fourteen, Michael wrote an essay on 'What makes a Gentleman', in which Macnaghten perceived 'a kinship in spirit to his guardian'. Part of the essay read:

'I believe I am right in saying that John Ball made use of the following couplet in his discourses:
            "When Adam delved and Eve span,
            "Who was then the gentleman?"
'Doubtless Ball used the word gentleman in the more degrading sense, denoting one of the upper classes – I think he was wrong. Adam was no gentleman, not because he was not Lord Adam, but because he gave away his wife in the matter of the apple. . . .

'Laurence Oates, a very gallant gentleman, went out into the blizzard because he knew he could not live and wished to give his friends a better chance. He was a gentleman because when he knew he was being brave he did not say "I'm a hero and I'm going to die for you," but merely remarked he was going out for a bit, and left the rest to their imagination.'

One of Michael's greatest admirers at Eton was another boy in Macnaghten's House, Roger Senhouse. Roger was a year older than Michael, and, in view of his later relationship with Lytton Strachey, clearly had a crush on him. Towards the end of his life, Roger kept a desultory form of Journal in which he recorded occasional scraps of autobiography. In 1967 he wrote:

Roger Senhouse and Michael at Eton

'Michael Ll. D. . . . was the one profound influence in my life, from the moment of our first meeting in his room. . . . I became so wrapped up in Michael that I faltered, soon I began to fail in concentration on my work, believing things would come as easily to me as to Michael, concentrating my energies in trying to please him, my mentor, tho' one year younger than me. . . . Hugh Macnaghten had been quick to observe the fantastic influence that genius had over me. . . . He even told J.M.B., who came so regularly to visit Michael, bringing him the most delicious home-made chocolate cakes, how obsessed I was with him. . . . This led to my taking Extra Books in Trials in a futile attempt to keep some sort of pace with Michael. . . . Macnaghten was slightly jealous of our friendship, almost worshipping Michael himself & always encouraging me to prevail upon him when depressed "because I know how very close you are to him".'

Michael wrote to Mary Hodgson from Eton for her (37th) birthday, enclosing a pen-knife:

> H. Macnaghten's.
> Thursday. [October 14th, 1915]
>
> Dear Mary,
>   I am writing this on Thursday because I shall be so busy tomorrow, to beg your acceptance of this little votive offering, a trivial little token of my regard for you, I assure you, etc etc etc. It is not very pretty, but it is the best Eton & I could do. . . . Have you seen much of Peter? I expect we shall yet be reduced to calling him, respectfully of course, the Social Subaltern. I've not heard from Jack, tho' I write every Sunday. Tears come to me eyes as I think of this pathetic instance of brotherly loyalty. . . . Miss J. Mitchell-Innes was kind enough to motor over & have tea with me. I fear alas she was not impressed. . . . Talking of TEA, I'd like one of those chocolate cakes. You can stick a Belgian flag in it if you think cakes are an extravagance. Now I must work.
>   Yrs
>   Michael

December 1915: the second Christmas of the war. *Peter Pan* was again revived, though only George Shelton as Smee remained from the original 1904 cast. This year it was decided to drop the Lagoon Scene: partly for economy, partly because Peter's curtain line, 'To die will be an awfully big adventure', was felt to be somewhat inappropriate under the circumstances. Barrie spent New Year's Eve alone in his Adelphi Terrace flat, where he had begun work on a new play, *A Kiss for Cinderella*. He wrote to Mrs Hugh Lewis at Glan Hafren: 'Here I am all alone as M. and N. are in bed and I've come back to the flat for tonight. Christmas evening was even gayer as I had to come in to town and Brown and his wife were away, so I had to make my own fire and dinner (eggs) and bed. The fire was worst, as there were no sticks, but I found a straw basket Mrs Brown goes to market with – or rather went, for it will accompany her no more.' His notebook entry took a less frivolous turn:

—Dream. That in own bed & awakened by unknown horror – dark, know something cautiously moving bed clothes – I move body slightly – movement of thing stops. Long pause. Then it resumes,

Unity Moore as Peter Pan in the 1915/16 and 1916/17 revivals

gentlest possible pushing of me – I resist without pushing back. Pause. Pushing resumed. Elec[tric] lamp near me, I set teeth for courage to turn on light – queer idea I won't be able to do it – I push out hand to – hand is stopped by something limp which doesn't push but just prevents – later it makes my hand always miss lamp – I feel being pushed now – no sound of breathing. Then feel stronger attempt evidently to push me out of bed. At last I rushed from darkness to mother's room (she has been dead many years) & cried to her abt my degenerate self – thing I have evolved into was trying to push me out of bed & take my place. Till that moment of telling I had no idea what the thing was.

Glan Hafren, 1916. Standing, l to r: Michael, Eiluned Lewis, Medina Lewis. Sitting: Nico, May Lewis, Barrie

Michael had been intrigued to meet the 'Welsh Lewises' ever since the previous summer, when Barrie and Peter had returned from Glan Hafren with glowing reports. Mrs Lewis invited them to pay another visit at Easter, and this time Michael and Nico went too. Peter Lewis's three sisters, Eiluned (variously called Jane or Bittie), Medina and May were home on holiday from boarding school, and Michael was entranced by them: 'they are so utterly a family out of a book', he wrote to Mary Hodgson. For Barrie, Glan Hafren provided a regular retreat such as he had not enjoyed since Black Lake. Medina recalled in 1977:

'J.M.B. found *The Vicar of Wakefield* atmosphere a welcome change to London. He was very nervous that this first Easter holiday with us might be a failure – he was so anxious to give the boys pleasure; but after the visit he told my mother how much they had enjoyed it, and that even Michael "the dour and impenetrable" (I distinctly remember those adjectives) had said he wanted to come again. I'm sure their visits meant far more to us than to them; and yet I think we made an amusing change for the boys from the sophisticated, theatrical life they were so used to living in London. I feel they looked on us as sisters, which of course they'd never known before. We were girls who were friends rather than girl-friends. Watching us playing on the lawn, J.M.B. once said to my mother, "They're so innocent, it almost hurts." '[7]

Michael, Medina and Peter Lewis

In September 1916, Nico left Wilkinson's and joined Michael in Hugh Macnaghten's House at Eton. Now that Michael was happier, Barrie alternated his daily letters between the two boys:

September 24th, 1916.

Dearest Nico,
    It is great and good and splendidiferous your liking
Eton from the start. Michael is to let me know a good day

for coming down to see you. . . . Think of Michael having a
fag! I think when I come down we shall have to sit on his
head so as to prevent his becoming too uppish. He will be
calling out 'Boy!' just to show off. . . . I miss you awfully.
Loving,
J.M.B.

In addition to his daily letters to
Barrie, Michael wrote frequently
to Mary Hodgson

Nico was allowed to share a room with Michael, thus forestalling the
homesickness that Michael had endured, and Barrie began writing
Nico a serial story entitled 'The Room with 2 Beds':

14 Nov 1916.

The Room with 2 Beds
(cont'd)
(Have you read the grand new serial?
The best place to begin is the middle.
Synopsis of preceding chapters – Sherlock and What Ho go
down to Eton.
Principal characters –
Sherlock, aged 91.
What Ho, aged 5.
Davies Bros, and other kids.)

'Have you a plan?' I enquired anxiously.
'Have I a plan!' he repeated with a lick of disdain. In short,
he had no plan. The Eton Case baffled him.
Sherlock H was baffled!
But not for long.
'Our first step, What Ho,' he said, . . . 'is to get you
entered for a pupil at My Tutor's house.'
'Me!' I astounded.
'There will be no difficulty,' he clapped, 'your intelligence
is of such a juvenile character that you will easily be
mistaken for a scug.'
He was right. He was always right. . . .
'Next,' Sherlock fluttered, 'you must be made fag to
Davies major.'
'I can't,' I said, 'Bowman is his fag.'
'You must get rid of Bowman,' he annunciated. . . .
At that moment the unsuspecting Bowman passed,
chewing a banana mess, which ran down his person.

Sherlock lifted him like a puppy by the collar & dropped him over the bridge into the river.

'Your way is now clear,' he said, wiping his hands. . . .

Loving

J.M.B.

With Michael and Nico both at Eton, Barrie spent most of his time at Adelphi Terrace, developing his *Dream* notes into a one-act play entitled 'The Fight for Mr. Lapraik'.* Mr Lapraik is two men: the young man he used to be, and the worldly success he has now become (just as Neil and Tintinnabulum represent two sides of Michael's character). The young Mr Lapraik returns, ghost-like, to inform the now ageing Mrs Lapraik that he is her husband. She asks who is the older Mr Lapraik – the man she believes to be her husband:

LAPRAIK. He is what I have grown into, my dear. I am what he used to be. . . . Look at me, Nora, what do you see?

MRS LAPRAIK. I see the man who married me so many years ago. My lover! A boy he seems to me now. You are somehow that boy come back. . . .

Michael with his house cricket cup

LAPRAIK. I am that boy come back to look for his fine ideas and conduct and aspirations of twenty-five years ago – to see what the man I became has made of them.

Lapraik then tells his wife how he had lain asleep, to be awakened by 'something bending over me, pushing me stealthily. . . . *I knew that the degenerate thing I had become was trying to push me out of this shell that is called me, and to take my place*' [Barrie's italics].

Work on 'The Fight for Mr. Lapraik' alternated with the continuing saga of Sherlock H., What Ho, and Michael and Nico's twin-bedded room at Eton:

16 Nov 1916.

The Room with 2 Beds
(cont'd)
Chap 10 – Fags & the Fag System.

I was a fag!
I was Major Davies's fag!

*The play, variously entitled 'The Fight for Mr. Lapraik', 'The Fight for Mr. Lapraille', and 'The House of Fear', never progressed beyond the typedraft stage.

In passing I ought to mention that quite a number of boys have this melting title. . . . The honour is naturally much coveted, and it amused me to notice that the small brother of Davies always referred to him proudly as 'my Major.'. . .

I find it will be impossible to convey any adequate account of the strange happenings at Eton . . . without first saying a few words about Fags and the Fag system. . . .

The origin of the word *Fag* is interesting: Anglo-Saxon *F*, Sanscrit *A*, Rumanian *G*. To be fagged = To be tired out – 'that tired feeling which comes if you don't use our lotion.'

One of the oldest traditions of Eton is that no senior . . . must let himself get tired or, in the *vox populum*, fagged. He therefore hires a scug (Anglo-Saxon S C Є 9, meaning a cheese-paring, or, more accurately, an infinitesimal piece of the rind) to get tired for him. . . . The senior lies in bed reading O. Henry while his fag does all the tiring things for him, such as attending chapel. . . .

Endless tales have been written of the bullying of fags. At Eton the 'bully' is an institution, [and] it is his duty to kick the little ones. This makes them hardy. . . .

    (To be cont'd)
    J.M.B.

Nico, aged twelve, responded to Barrie's serial with a saga of his own that moved at a decidedly faster pace:

                               'The Room' etc.
My dear Uncle Jim,   17th November 1916.

               The Dynamite King
                 CHAPTER II
             The Deadman's Rock

'Let us dine out to-night Smith' I cried.

'No' he rapped 'I want to stay here in order to tug the lobe of my left ear.'

'Shall I leave you?' I queried.

'No, something may happen.' . . .

Suddenly to my horror I saw a ghost come up from the sea! Ah! How I struggled to get loose. Then the ghost advanced and touched me. I shivered! Then, to my relief & astonishment it said 'Rise up Petrie'

I knew the voice so well.

      IT WAS NAYLAND SMITH.

'My Aunt Sempronia's whiskers!' he said, you're as

white as——Good Lord! That creature's moving, he said, pointing to the dead man. It was alive!
IT WAS THE DYNAMITE KING=FU-MANCHU!
Order your next week's copy!
Much love,
Nicholas
Llewelyn
Davies.

Barrie and Hugh Macnaghten at Eton

Michael wrote to Mary Hodgson on December 10th: 'My tutor [Hugh Macnaghten] told me he wished I was like Nico; he says he's the heart & soul of the house, so you can see Nico's firmly settled in that quarter. The point is that he's far far heartier than I ever was or shall be.'

There was little to brighten Barrie's world during the term-time, apart from his weekly instalments of 'The Dynamite King' and his letters from Michael. The last months of 1916 were particularly savage: Lord Lucas shot down over German lines and killed; both his nephews killed; 'Wrest in Beds' burnt down; and the hospital at Bettancourt closed as Elizabeth Lucas was too exhausted and ill to continue its organization.

At nineteen Peter Davies had become eligible for the trenches, but scarcely had he arrived on the Western Front than he found himself in the thick of the bloodiest conflict of the war: the Battle of the Somme. After two months he was invalided home, suffering from eczema and shell-shock, from which he recovered by the following Easter; the mental wounds, however, left their scars for life. Of the four surviving brothers, Peter's desolation at the death of George had been the greatest; Barrie had written to Charles Turley Smith, 'I feel painfully for Peter between whom and George there was a devotion not perhaps very common among brothers.' With George dead, his parents dead, and no real communication with Barrie, Peter had lived for two years in a void, now filled with little but the memory of mud, and bodies, and bits of bodies. In later life he took meticulous care to suppress all evidence of his own past: his *Morgue* consists almost entirely of letters relating to his ancestors, his parents, his brothers, Barrie – everyone but himself. Since he also published Denis Mackail's official biography, he was able to censor his role to a minimum. One letter that survived this suppression was written by Crompton's wife, Moya, at the time of Crompton's death in December 1935:

'Crompton mentioned your name, Peter, in his second or third last letter to me. . . . He said you were always a very special person to him, that he felt a loving intimacy with you beyond what he felt for almost anyone else, and I remember him telling me in the early years of our marriage more than once "Peter is the One". You were certainly his favourite of the five sons of your beautiful mother, of whom he never spoke without a break in his voice.'

Davies major and minor returned to London for the Christmas holidays, spending much of their time in the Adelphi flat as Peter was being nursed by Mary Hodgson at Campden Hill Square. Barrie wrote to Mrs Thomas Hardy on December 29th: 'I have my boys home now for the holidays . . . and the flat is for the nonce a noisy spot. Just listen for a moment and you will hear another plate go smash.' While Nico pursued his hectic social life of Christmas parties, Michael gratified Barrie by reading the various manuscripts awaiting his inspection. It was Barrie's proudest boast that Michael, while still a school-boy, had jumped 'from being astride my shoulders fishing, I knee-deep in the stream, to [becoming] . . . the sternest of my literary critics. Anything he shook his head over I abandoned. There was for instance that little tragedy *Mr Lapraik*, which I liked until I foolishly told Michael its subject, when he frowned and said he had better have a look at it. He read it, and then, patting me on the back, as only he and George could touch me, said, "You know you can't do this sort of thing." End of *Mr Lapraik*.'[8]

Michael wrote to Eiluned Lewis at Glan Hafren on January 15th:

An Etonian letter from Nico to Eiluned Lewis

MONDAY
the ? January
in the year 1917 of grace.

Dear Jane,
   I choose the prettiest in your bright constellation of names; . . . Sir James, Davies minor, & yr humble servant have just returned from Brighton, with its poisonous people piers post-cards picture-palaces & penny in the slots. Have you ever been there? I trow not, else you would not be the purre & innocent maiden that you appearrr. . . . Peter D. is now at Sheerness, preparatory to France again, & Jack D. in the North Sea. Nico D. is entirely the young Etonian that you w'd expect. He grows in all directions. Believe me, madam, I am, hoping this finds you as it leaves me etc –
               Yr ob^dt serv^t
               Michael Ll. Davies

At the end of the month, Michael and Nico returned to 'the Room with 2 Beds' and Barrie to the loneliness of his Adelphi flat. Having

Gary Cooper in the 1930 film version of *The Old Lady Shows Her Medals*, re-titled *Medals*, in which Cooper plays the Old Lady's 'son', loosely based on George. Barrie lived to see fourteen screen adaptations of his works, including Cecil B. De Mille's 1919 epic, *Male and Female* (below, with Gloria Swanson), thinly based on *The Admirable Crichton*

abandoned 'Mr Lapraik', he started work on a new one-act play, *The Old Lady Shows Her Medals*: 'Three nice old ladies and a criminal, who is even nicer, are discussing the war over a cup of tea.' The criminal is the Old Lady of the title; her medals are the regular letters she receives from her son, fighting for King and Country; her crime is that she has no son: the envelopes, 'all addressed in pencil . . . with the proud words "Opened by Censor" on them' – contain blank pieces of paper.

Early in 1917, Barrie learned that all was not well between Mary and Gilbert Cannan, whom she had married in 1910. There were rumours that Cannan had seduced Mary's maid and made her pregnant, though Mary herself was still childless; now, it seemed, he had taken up with another woman, leaving his wife in reduced circumstances. Kathleen Scott, who had retained her friendship with the Cannans, told Barrie that Gilbert was losing his reason and had already been admitted to several mental homes for short durations. Barrie never liked to discuss his own broken marriage; he knew where the fault lay, and if ever a word was raised against Mary, he would contradict it with a flat statement: 'She was *perfection*.'[9] Nor did he blame Cannan. 'I always held that he had many fine qualities,' he wrote to Kathleen, 'and I hope they will yet bring him to port.'[10] Mary's pride did not allow her to approach her former husband for money: instead, Barrie wrote to her on March 5th:

My dear Mary,
    It would be silly of us not to meet, and indeed I wanted to go to you all day yesterday. I thought perhaps you would rather come here, and of course which ever you prefer is what I prefer, but that is your only option as I mean to see you whether the idea scares you or not. Painful in a way the first time but surely it need not be so afterwards. How about coming here on Wednesday to lunch at 1.30? If you are feeling well enough I wish you were doing war work. There must be posts you are so particularly fitted for. We could have some talk about that. All personal troubles outside the war seem so small nowadays. But just one thing I should like to say, because no one can know it so well as I, that never in this world could a young literary man have started with better chances than Mr Cannan when he had you at the helm.
                    Yours affectionately,
                    J.M.B.

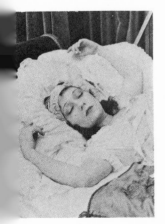

Prompted by a suggestion from A. E. W. Mason, Barrie had exhumed his notes on *The Second Chance* (see page 150) and was turning them into a full-length play under the title *Dear Brutus*. The idea sprang from Old Solomon Caw's warning to Peter Pan in *The Little White Bird*: 'In this world there are no second chances.' Evidently Mary Cannan thought otherwise, for, according to Elizabeth Lucas, she took Barrie's offer of help to mean a second chance of marriage. But Barrie stood by the moral of his play: that people who are given a second chance invariably make the same mistakes again. He offered to pay her an annual allowance, and to see her once a year, but further than that he would not go.

Jack in 1917

Meanwhile Jack Davies was pursuing his first chance of marital bliss. His ship was based in the Firth of Forth, and while on shore-leave in Edinburgh he had met and fallen a victim to an 'extraordinarily pretty' nineteen-year-old daughter of a Scots banker, Miss Geraldine Gibb. Without consulting Barrie, Jack proposed to her, and Geraldine – or Gerrie, as she was known – accepted. Jack wrote to her from H.M.S. *Octavia* on March 25th:

'I can honestly hardly believe my stupendous luck. Fancy being engaged to you! . . . I cannot see the point in being engaged for years & years can you? It seems such unutterable waste of very good time. Perhaps (your word is law) you think otherwise, in which case yours so very humbly has only to be told. But, bien aimée, & these loathsome details have to be faced, my Guardian has to be talked to gently on the everlasting question of dibs. Lord but it's unseemly to mix up filthy lucre in a question of any sort, but it has to be done, doesn't it, & knowing the dear little man as well as I do this sort of question has somewhat naturally never cropped up before & I'm hanged if I know what he'll say. He's infernally wealthy himself but knows me – or rather knew me before I met you – & so knows my wonderful incapacity for keeping money. Still, I shall see him this next visit to town & as I know so well he's one of God's own, I have the highest hopes. . . . We've a house in London that no one lives in now as we're all away. It's quite small but my mother did it all & it's most wonderful inside. . . . I wonder, will it be OURS one day? As a sailor one has such a mighty small use for a house in London – still, it's for one of the family Davies, so why not us? . . . The family will fight for you if I know anything of them. My particular pal is Nicholas – the youngest, whose smile you liked [on the photograph] in my cabin. He's a bird & will ask to take you straight to his heart. George, John,* Peter, Michael & Nicholas – we're all saints! Poor old George was killed in France. He was a wonderful person. That really was a case of "they whom the Gods love die young." Peter is one of God's own. Michael is at present rather trying, but he'll get over it.

*Jack preferred Gerrie to call him by his proper name, John.

Just 16 & full of Eton you know, but withal a good fellow. And Nico. He'll never be trying. . . . Mother you really would have adored. Everyone did. Father died when I was 12 & Mother never really got over it. They were wonderful people, I suppose really rather too perfect to go on. But I should so have loved to go to Mother & say, "Here's a daughter for you at last." She always longed for a daughter but never had one. She was so lovely herself that it seems a great pity she hadn't a daughter like her. There are so very few people I can ever talk to about this sort of thing that I know you'll forgive me. . . . Are you happy to know that someday you'll be Mrs John Llewelyn Davies herself? To me it's so wonderful I'm beaten all of a heap!'

Jack went to London at the beginning of April to put his case to Barrie. He wrote to Gerrie on April 4th:

'I haven't seen the little Baronet yet, but am lunching with him today. . . . My pay's about £230 & I also have about £180 & with your £100 that's £510. Wonderful mathematician. Now if I can only persuade Guardy to add £200 – which is such an utter flea-bite to him – I really don't see why the deed shouldn't be done. But I have a grizly feeling he'll be "un peu difficile" to put it mildly. He's the dearest fellow in the world, but he knows me!'

Jack wrote again the following day:

Michael's only surviving Eton
etter to Barrie. He rarely signed
is letters with anything less
ormal than 'Yours', even to
Mary Hodgson

'You'll have to take a big pull on yourself to bear this news bravely. I spoke to my Guardian about you & he says that to gain his consent & help we are to wait a year. It's a grizly thought I know, but when you think what his help means to us, I think we can do it, don't you? . . . Cause if we go against him & get married he'll never help us. I know him well enough to be sure of that. . . . One thing, if by any chance I got shifted from [Edinburgh] . . . I think the little Baronet could probably get me shifted back again all right. He has untold influence if only he'd use it & not have some silly idea about seeing if separation would make any difference to us. Of course it *does* make a filthy difference, but not in the way he means! . . . Damn all hard-headed & so-called level headed Guardians. No, I don't mean that because he's been so almighty good to us. I'm an ungrateful beast, but it's so infernally hard to wait. . . . Michael and Nico are having tea in here now, & pulling my leg hard about you. One has just said, "Don't put crosses at the end, it isn't done." He got a matchbox in the chest!'

At the end of the Easter holidays, Michael and Nico returned to the playing fields of Eton, while Peter was dispatched back to the chaos of the Somme. Barrie had long planned to visit George's grave behind the Western Front, and in June he received the necessary permissions from the War Office, together with directions on how to locate it. He had hoped that Thomas Hardy would accompany him, but Hardy declined: 'I have had to come to the conclusion that old men cannot be young men, and that I must content myself with the past battles of our country if I want to feel military.'[11] Barrie therefore set out alone, though under military escort. Although he wrote to a number of friends telling them that 'the only time I was in any danger was searching for George's grave, which I found',[12] he gave no indication of his emotions. Doubtless Housman expressed them for him (and countless others) in *A Shropshire Lad*, which Barrie had read 'year in, year out – over and over again'[13] since its publication in 1896, when he spoke of the 'lads that will die in their glory and never be old'.

When Michael and Nico came back to London for the summer holidays, they found that their guardian had moved to the top floor of Adelphi Terrace House. The new flat was considerably more spacious than its predecessor, the largest room commanding a spectacular view of the River Thames from four panoramic windows. Barrie turned it into his work study – not so much on account of the view, but because of its vast fireplace, or ingle-nook, wherein he could curl himself up on a wooden settle. There was an added attraction: being only five foot three, he could clear the chimney beam without lowering his head, while most other mortals sustained mild concussion every time they penetrated the ingle-nook.

Barrie in his ingle-nook. The sofa had the reputation of being the most uncomfortable in London. The photograph on the far right is of George at Eton; his cricket cap hangs below it

The annual fishing holiday was reduced to a fortnight in August as Michael and Nico had to go off to the Public Schools camp on Salisbury Plain – no longer the 'bit of a spree' that it had been in George's day: most of the boys would be putting their training into practice in the near future. Despite his nonchalance, the prospect of the trenches was beginning to weigh on Michael: he would be eligible within a matter of months. Macnaghten wrote in his report that he had been 'strangely difficult' during the past term. 'He never means to be rude, but he is too clever not to see the weak points in his Tutor [i.e. Macnaghten himself] and others, yet his judgement is unerring: the cleverest boy I have had in my house.'[14]

In the middle of August, Barrie, Michael and Nico went up to Scotland to fish, travelling by way of Edinburgh for their first glimpse of Jack's inamorata, Gerrie. Barrie gave a fanciful account of the prologue to the meeting in a letter to Lady Juliet Duff on August 14th:

Jack

'We were all outwardly calm, but internally white to the gills; Nicholas kept wetting his lips, Michael was a granite column, inscrutable, terrible; I kept bursting into inane laughter, and changing my waistcoats. So the time of waiting passed, the sun sank in the west and the stars came out with less assurance than usual. What is that? It is the rumble of wheels. Nico slips his hand into mine. I notice that it is damp. Michael's pose becomes more Napoleonic, but he is breathing hard. The chaise comes into view. I have a happy thought. They are probably more nervous than we are.'

In 1976 Gerrie recalled:

'I was – well, yes – nervous, I knew he'd come up to vet me, but I don't think I was in awe of him. My mother was horrified that I should marry someone who was mixed up with Barrie – she said, "I don't trust that man." He didn't cut that much ice in Scotland – he was certainly no prophet in his own country. The only reason my mother tolerated the idea of our marriage was that she adored Gerald du Maurier. Barrie and the two boys came up on the train from London – we met them at the station, had dinner at the North British Hotel next to the station, then they caught the next train to go and fish up in the Highlands. It was an extraordinary dinner: I don't think the Bart said a single word throughout the meal – certainly not to me. Michael talked to me – he was very considerate, tried to make me feel relaxed. He was very attractive, very charming, and had the most wonderful smile. All the boys made feverish conversation, but the Bart never said anything. Nor did I.'

Barrie's letter to Lady Juliet Duff concluded with a transcript of an imaginary conversation between Jack and Gerrie after the first meeting:

Gerrie

Jack.   Buck up, Gerrie, that's the worst over.

Gerrie. Oh dear, I was so nervous and they were all so calm. . . . I took to Nicholas at once. I feel I can get round him.

Jack.   Rather. What about Michael?

Gerrie. He alarms me. Did anybody ever get round Michael?

Jack.   I can't say I ever did. . . . The third chappie [i.e. Barrie] is the important one.

Gerrie. (*gasping*). I know. Oh, Jack!

Jack.   Yes, he's a bit like that. His heart's all right.

Gerrie. His face is so expressionless. . . . He never smiled once.

Jack.   I bet you he thought he was smiling all the time. That's the way he smiles. . . . He's really rather soft. We can all twist him round our little fingers. . . . You see he is essentially a man's man. He doesn't know what to say to women. They don't interest him. I think he's a woman-hater. . . . What are you to wear for dinner?

Gerrie. Does it matter? He won't notice.

Jack.   No, but Michael will. He takes Michael's opinion on everything. All depends on Michael. If Michael says 'Let them marry next week' . . . Uncle Jim will fix it up. If on the other hand Michael says 'Delay for three years,' it will be fixed that way.

Gerrie. Oh, if he should say that!

Jack.   He won't.

Gerrie. How can you be sure?

Jack.   I should kick him.

Jack and Gerrie were married on September 4th, 1917 – less than three weeks after their ordeal at the North British Hotel.

16 In his Dedication to *Peter Pan*, Barrie wrote, 'Sometimes . . . Michael liked my literary efforts, and I walked in the azure that day when he returned *Dear Brutus* to me with the comment "Not so bad."' The play went into rehearsal in September 1917, with Gerald du Maurier directing as well as giving the performance of his career as the jaded, lonely Will Dearth. Each of the eight characters who yearn for a second chance reflects an element of the author's own personality – particularly Mr Purdie, a solitary soul who must always be wooing some woman other than his wife. Psychoanalysis was beginning to sweep into fashion, and Barrie was one of its earliest victims; *Dear Brutus*, however, makes it clear enough that he himself was his own best analyst, and was under no illusion that a second chance to live his life over again would be any different from the first. He rejected Hardy's theory that people are governed by fate, and drew instead on a maxim from Shakespeare's *Julius Caesar*, as well as on his own theme of the black spot, or 'Accursed Thing', in *The Will*:

PURDIE. . . . It isn't accident that shapes our lives.

JOANNA. No, it's Fate.

PURDIE. . . . It's not Fate, Joanna. Fate is something outside us. What really plays the dickens with us is something in ourselves. Something that makes us go on doing the same sort of fool things, however many chances we get. . . . Something we are born with. . . . Shakespeare knew what he was talking about –

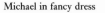

Michael in fancy dress

> The fault, dear Brutus, is not in our stars,
> But in ourselves, that we are underlings.

The only character to benefit from his second chance is Dearth, who sighs to his wife in the first Act, 'Perhaps if we had had children –Pity!' The magic wood of the second Act grants him his wish and he is given a dream-child, Margaret. In an echo from *The New Word* and Barrie's last letter to George – 'more and more wishing you were a girl of 21 instead of a boy, so that I could say the things to you that are now always in my heart' – Dearth tells Margaret in passing that sons are 'not a patch on daughters. The awful thing about a son is that never, never – at least, from the day he goes to school – can you tell him that you rather like him. By the time he is ten you can't even take him on your knee.' The scene also contained an exchange for Mary Hodgson's benefit:

DEARTH. . . . I do wish I could leave you to do things a little more for yourself. I suppose it's owing to my having had to be father and mother both. I knew nothing practically about the bringing up of children, and of course I couldn't trust you to a nurse.

MARGARET (*severely*). Not you; so sure you could do it better yourself. That's you all over.

In his review of *Dear Brutus* in *The Times*, A. B. Walkley wrote:

'When Mr. Dearth "comes to" and, suddenly realizing the loss of his dream-child, breaks into a sob, you catch your breath. . . . What Barrie can do with children and the love of them we all know. But surely he has never touched the theme with such tender and delicate felicity as he gives it here?'

Dear Brutus opened on October 17th; the following day Barrie was writing to Kathleen (now Lady) Scott, trying to persuade her to allow him to become guardian to her son Peter, aged nine. Lord Knutsford had advised Lady Scott that she should appoint a guardian in the event of her death, and had offered himself for the post. Barrie wrote to Kathleen:

'The only change in Lord Knutsford's advice that I should like you to make is to substitute my name for his. If you have sufficient faith in me it is my earnest wish that you should do so. . . . He can't possibly love Peter more than I do, but he has the advantage of having [a] daughter, while I have no woman to work with me or to fall back upon should my end come before too long. Experience teaches me that the one drawback in my tending my boys is that I have no female influence for them; the loss to them is very great and I must tell you this bluntly, as I think its value increases as the boy grows into a man.'

Peter Scott, aged 10

Barrie wrote again to Kathleen a week later:

'If it were just between [Lord Knutsford] and me I would beg you to risk making it me, but it would not be wise to make it either of us without further arrangements in case of our death. . . . This is so important to Peter that I think I am quite out-weighed. But I should like you to say in your will, or whatever the paper is, that it would be a pleasure to you to think that I was looked upon as an uncle to Peter to whom he would come whenever he wanted. I should try to be a good uncle to him.'

Kathleen took Barrie's advice, and neither man became guardian. However, Peter paid his godfather frequent visits at Adelphi Terrace House, writing in his autobiography, *The Eye of the Wind*:

Barrie in the doorway of his Adelphi study. Relics of the Five are scattered about the room: Sylvia, George and Jack in the oval frame (see p. 54), George's catch at Lord's on the piano (p. 203) next to a drawing of Sylvia, and photographs of George, Michael (p. 296) and Nico (p. 200), hanging on the wall to the left

'The room in which he wrote was dominated by a huge open hearth piled high with wood ash, and with a high-backed settle in the inglenook on one side of it. . . . It was full of pipe smoke and books. As a very small boy I used to go there for tea, sometimes with my mother, sometimes alone and feeling very independent. . . . Barrie knew all about how to get on with children. Although there were often long silences I cannot ever remember feeling shy in his company.'

Jack's wife, Gerrie, was now staying with Barrie at Adelphi Terrace as Jack had been transferred to Portsmouth:

'I used to sit in a corner of that huge study, as quiet as a mouse. Sometimes Barrie would talk a lot; at other times he'd be wrapped in silence, except for his cough. Most of the time he paced up and down the room, as if I wasn't there, and then suddenly he'd say something. I can't now recall the context, but I remember him asking me if I knew how Guy du Maurier had been killed. I said something like, "Yes, wasn't he shot?" And Barrie said, "Yes. He was shot. And he wandered about the battlefield for half-an-hour with his stomach hanging out, begging somebody to finish him off." I was quite horrified. Why did he tell me? Was he deliberately trying

267

to shock me? I never told my husband, I never told anybody because it struck me as being so queer, so cruel. Perhaps he had something on his mind, I don't know. He just told it to me point-blank, then went on with whatever he was doing.'

Another unpleasant surprise was in store for Gerrie. Although Mary Hodgson had been at Jack's wedding, she had stood at the back of the church, and had avoided meeting his new wife:

'While I was staying at the flat, Barrie took me to meet Mary Hodgson at Campden Hill Square. We waited in a room for her, and then she came in and Barrie said, "Mary, this is Gerrie, Jack's wife –" She gave me a paralysing look but didn't say anything, so I tried to be pleasant and said, "Oh, Mary, do look at this something-or-other we've been sent as a wedding present", whereupon she wheeled round and walked out of the room. Barrie didn't say a word to her; I think he was absolutely terrified of her. He knew how Michael and Nico loved her, and he wasn't prepared to put a foot wrong in their books.'

Peter had been expected back on short leave from France in the second week of October, but had failed to materialize at either Campden Hill Square or Adelphi Terrace. Barrie was just beginning to get anxious when he received word from him that he was staying with a married woman and her daughter at their home in Epping Forest. Knowing Barrie's 'safety-curtain' to the ways of the flesh, it would have been easy for Peter to have left it at that. Instead, he chose to acquaint his guardian with the truth. He was having an affair, not with the daughter, but with her mother, Vera Willoughby, a professional artist who was almost twice his age.

Barrie was 'shocked to the core'.[1] Apart from the moral considerations, he felt that such a relationship could only lead to unhappiness: Gilbert and Mary were proof of that. Peter, however, had made up his mind. He wrote to Mary Hodgson from Flanders on October 27th:

Peter in 1917

My dear Mary,
    I don't know whether you have heard anything about my fall from the path of righteousness, but I presume you have. If it is so, I'd like you to know that I don't myself look upon it as a fall at all – that I know I'm doing right, in fact, and that though you will never be anything but very distressed about it, you will be wrong to be so. I'd sooner have had your approval than anyone else's, and that not only because you know me better than anyone

else. But I'm afraid I never shall. Please don't worry about me more than you can help – I'm more pleased with the prospect of life than ever before, and rightly so, believe me. I seem to have made rather a mistake in being so open about it, but I really do believe you'll agree with me there. In any case, this is a sincere apology for not coming to see you when I was on leave. I think you will be able to understand that.

Yrs,
Peter.

Mary's disapproval of Peter's affair was about all that she and Barrie had in common. They had known each other for a quarter of a century, but despite all they had gone through, she no more approved of him now than she had during the boys' childhood days in Kensington Gardens. She admired him as a writer, respected him as a Baronet, but her disapproval of him as an influence in the boys' lives was as firmly rooted as ever. Her niece, Mrs Mary Hill, wrote in 1976:

'When it was made known that J.M.B. had been made the children's Guardian, she was extremely upset. She only agreed to continue the running of the Campden Hill Square household because she had promised to do so to Mrs Arthur, and her motto in life was "A promise is a sacred thing." This task she did not enjoy since she was responsible to J.M.B. . . . He indulged their every wish, and this she considered detrimental to their upbringing. Eventually the time arrived when she considered she had fulfilled her obligation to Mrs Arthur, and that the boys should be handed over to the sole charge of J.M.B. However, her resignation was not accepted, and for the sake of the two youngest, whom she always spoke of as "my babies" or "my boys", she stayed on for as long as she could tolerate the situation. Her main concern was that her presence would become more of a hindrance than a help to the boys when they found their loyalties being continually divided between herself and J.M.B., particularly in the case of Michael.'[2]

Mary Hodgson

Mary Hodgson had offered her resignation in December 1916, but it had taken Barrie by surprise; Jack was still unmarried, Peter was one of the family, and Barrie did not relish the prospect of finding a replacement to run Campden Hill Square. The alternative was for the boys to move into Adelphi Terrace, but at that time he was still living in his comparatively small flat on the second floor. It is probable that this was the motivating factor in his acquiring the spacious top-floor flat – in readiness for Mary's next offer of resignation. But the offer was not forthcoming. Mary seemed to have readjusted to the situation, and looked set for a long sojourn at Campden Hill Square. Naturally any suggestion of her going would have to come from Mary herself: Michael and Nico would never forgive him if they felt he had compelled her to leave against her wishes.

Whether by accident or design, Barrie now put into motion a scheme that could not fail to sting her into action. He proposed that the unsuspecting Gerrie should assume full responsibility for the running of 23 Campden Hill Square: she would be the new mistress, with Mary acting on her instructions. The arrangement was to begin shortly after Michael and Nico arrived back from Eton for the Christmas holidays. Gerrie herself had no suspicions that she was being used as a pawn: 'He simply said, "You'd better go and live at 23." My husband was due home on sick-leave over Christmas, so the idea was that we should move our things in when he got back.'

Michael, Nico and Mary formed a reception committee for Jack and Gerrie on the top step of 23 Campden Hill Square, Nico recalling in 1975:

An Etonian letter from Nico to Barrie

'We were standing outside the front door of 23, waiting to greet Gerrie and Jack, who were getting out of a cab. As they started to climb up the steps, Mary just turned her back on them and walked inside the house. Jack was furious, understandably, but Michael and I wouldn't hear a word against her. Don't forget she was *the* person in our lives – she was the mother. She terrified pretty well everybody else in the family, but to Michael and me she was wholly unique and wholly irreplaceable.'

Gerrie now found herself in 'a quite impossible situation. Mary absolutely refused to speak to me. Everything was communicated via Michael or Nico, or written down as messages on bits of paper.' Jack and Gerrie awoke on their first morning at Campden Hill Square to find one such message had been slipped under the bedroom door during the night. It was from Mary Hodgson to Jack: 'Things have been going on in this room of which your father would not have approved.' Gerrie was unable to discuss her predicament with the boys:

'It was a completely taboo subject – besides, I was too shy, or maybe my pride got in the way. J.M.B. had told me I was in charge, and so I had to try my best. But I was completely outside my orbit – I was far too young and inexperienced, only a year or so older than Michael, though he was far, far more sophisticated than me. I tried on one or two occasions to be pleasant to Mary, to try and coax her into conversation, but she adamantly refused to address one word to my face. If I was standing next to Michael, she would convey her answers to him, always referring to me in the third person. She was completely demented.'

Barrie spent most of Christmas 1917 at Campden Hill Square, but naturally turned a blind eye to the tension. He wrote blithely to Peter Scott from Campden Hill to thank the boy for his Christmas present:

> 22 December, 1917.
> My dear Scott
> I am sitting here smoking the tobacco out of your pouch. It is a lovely pouch and I watch people in case they try to steal it. Who steals my purse steals trash, but if anyone tries to steal my pouch he had better watch out.
> I am hoping to see you soon. I am with my boys and they are as rowdy as ever.
> My love to your mother and you.
> I am
> My dear Scott
> Your humble servant
> Barrie.

The domestic imbroglio came to a head in early January. Barrie and the boys had gone out before breakfast, and Gerrie was alone in the house. She went downstairs and found a note from Mary Hodgson propped up against a frozen water-jug – 'Either you leave this house or I do.' Gerrie's reaction was immediate:

'I started packing there and then, telephoned my husband who had gone to see a friend, he came back to help with the luggage, and by night-fall we were staying in a hotel off Knightsbridge. That evening I began feeling exceedingly ill. Jack phoned Barrie's doctor and said, "I think my wife's having a miscarriage." The doctor said "Why?" My husband, poor young man, hadn't got a clue. So then he called another doctor, and they shovelled me on to a stretcher and removed me to a nursing home. It was a miscarriage, and I spent the rest of the time weeping and weeping – I couldn't stop – Sheer nerves. I never saw Mary Hodgson again. I think Barrie was absolutely delighted when Mary handed in her notice as a result of it all. Everything could be blamed on me, and he didn't lose face with the boys. I suppose Mary Hodgson stayed long enough until the flat was ready for them, and then he moved them in.'

Barrie responded to Mary's written letter of resignation with a letter of his own:

23 Campden Hill Square.
10 Jan 1918.

My dear Mary,

As I think you find it easier I am answering your note by another. I suppose I must accept your resignation very sorrowfully as the wisest step in circumstances that are very difficult. No need for me to repeat of what inestimable service to me have been your love and devotion to the boys, particularly to Michael and Nicholas who came into our hands when they were so young.

I earnestly hope that you will continue to see much of them in the future and be their friend thro' life. If you care to consult me about your own future I shall be very glad. I also hope you will now let me make the arrangement Mrs Davies asked me to make in the last weeks of her life and which I told you of a day or two after her death. It is entirely a matter between her and you, and I trust you will allow her earnest wish to be carried out.

Always your most sincere friend,
J. M. Barrie.

Nico and Michael at Glan Hafren

The 'arrangement' was a sum of £500, left to her by Sylvia, to which Barrie offered to add a further £500 of his own. Mary refused to accept either amount. She was mortified at the news of Gerrie's miscarriage, and suffered such guilt over her behaviour towards her that in later life she steadfastly refused to meet any of the boys' wives in case her innate jealousy once again mastered her better self.

Barrie took Michael and Nico down to Tillington, near Petworth in Sussex, to stay with E. V. Lucas, who had separated from Elizabeth and was living alone with Audrey. Lucas later remarked on the 'minute thoughtfulness for others'[3] that had begun to creep into Michael's character, an empathy evident in his handling of the current domestic crisis. Michael wrote to Mary from Tillington on January 20th, 1918:

Barrie and Michael

My dear Mary,

Do you mind if I try to reduce the painfulness of things by putting them down here in writing? I believe I can do it.

I am assuming that matters have gone too far to turn back now, through whose fault I will not say, tho' I shrewdly suspect it had a little to do with everybody.

Before going any further, let me assure you with the utmost assurance that it will not be at all possible for Nico and me to continue living at 23 with Jack & his wife – as

A locket given to Mary Hodgson.
Top to bottom: Michael, Peter,
George, Jack and Nico

you suggested. The proof lies in the last three weeks, whatever you say. This may be hard luck on Jack, but the fact remains, & when a man marries, his family is the one he is setting up for himself. You yourself said that Jack is having too much done for him. That is so, so why sh'd he be allowed to go on in this easy way, undisturbed and disturbing?

It w'd be hardly possible for us to go on living at 23 even without Jack and Gerrie, unless you came back. As to this last it rests with your 'pride', & with your opinion as to the importance of maintaining 23 as a home for Nico.

(I hope all this doesn't sound callous. You know me too well to make that mistake.)

The present scheme I believe is to let things remain undecided for a month or two, so as to see which way to turn. As to whether going and living at the flat will be worse for Nico and me, that rests with our own strength of mind, don't it – and particularly with mine I believe.

And of course the chief reason of 23's importance was that you were there – & – do not say I am wrong – I am sure we shall see very nearly if not as much of you as before.

Let us weigh the past with the (??) future:
Past. We have seen you only in the holidays, which has not been very much. We have written about once a week or so (when old Nico could be roused).
Future. Of course we shall write as much if not more (when I can rouse old Nico). And in the holidays – mind you! – you're to come with your gingham & take up your quarters in the attic we'll have ready for you – if only to see my mustache grow! And besides that you will overcome yr dislike of travelling, & be dragged off in the summer holidays, or whenever we do disappear in the wilds. And – mind you! – this is absolutely serious – none of your absurd ideas of pride or absurd ideas of Uncle Jim not wanting you! That's what I call false pride, & harmful at that. Think how glad he'll be to get us off his hands for a time!

This frivolousness of pen really hides the most serious inwardness I've ever had. I'm going to draw up a form for you to sign.

The chief sadness this week then is the leaving of 23, & that was bound to come, so don't let *us* be cowards.

Also – & I know this is not my business at all – do take that paltry thousand to please Nico & me, if only to start a social revolution! We'd have made it a billion only that's not a billionth part enough. I know it's twice as hard for you as it is for us, and that's precious hard. Nico is unaware of the state of affairs, so please Mary don't make it harder by refusing anything.

AU REVOIR.

MICHAEL.

Peter wrote to Mary from Flanders two days later:

My dear Mary,

    I've heard one or two disquieting rumours lately about 23. Will you please tell me what's really happened, please? Because whatever I am or am not, or am thought to be or am not thought to be, I will always do anything in my power to help you. It seems to me from what I've heard – which is very little – that things are happening otherwise than they might have happened had I been at home; Nico would be heart-broken if you were to go – Michael too, I think. But I know so little – I wish you'd write.

Yrs,

Peter.

By the time Mary received Peter's letter, the deed had been done. Campden Hill Square – 'Little Old New Babylon' as Michael used to call it – was to be closed down as a home for the boys, and by the Easter holidays Michael and Nico would be living with Barrie in his Adelphi Terrace flat. Mary appears to have faced up to her departure in good grace, judging by Barrie's letter to her of January 25th:

My dear Mary,

    Thank you heartily for your letter, and for what you say about myself also, for I deeply appreciate it. No one knows, no one could know, so well as myself, what you have been to the boys, except indeed the boys themselves. What you say of the future is a great relief to me, for the uncertainty of life is before us all more than ever in these days, and the knowledge that if the need arose 'The trust continues' is the best that could be said to me. The practical matters we can talk over.

Yours very sincerely,

J. M. Barrie.

Barrie wrote to Elizabeth Lucas four days later, bringing her up to date with the domestic situation:

Audrey, Elizabeth and E. V.
Lucas

'Michael's letter to Audrey has told you of our adventures at Tillington where we had a very happy time, and Michael discovered an old shop at Petworth and triumphantly bought a soap-dish for his room here [at Adelphi Terrace]. That room is not finished yet, indeed three rooms are still in confusion which will give you some idea of the difficulties with workmen nowadays. . . . I had begun to feel in my bones tho' that it was all too fine a flat for me and that for my lonely purposes all I really needed was this room and the bedroom. . . . However the way has been cleared by trouble at Campden Hill. Mary is going sometime in February. This means Michael and Nicholas making this their home, as my idea is to put caretakers into Campden Hill for a little and then store the furniture and dispose of the lease. Of course it is a great thing to me to look to having Michael and Nico here tho' they are so much away. A sad thing is that Michael is now $17\frac{1}{2}$ and in a year or less is eligible for the army. The depression of it all! I shy at thinking of it but it has no doubt a great deal to do with the gloom in which one seems to get enveloped.'

Barrie wrote to Elizabeth again on February 20th:

'I emerge out of my big chimney to write to you. I was sitting there with a Charlotte Brontë in my hands (when I read her I think mostly of Emily) and there was a gale on the roof; it is probably not windy at all down below, but with the slightest provocation the chimneys overhead in their whirring cowls go as devilish as the witches in Macbeth, whom they also rather resemble in appearance. . . . As I had to do without you this time, and scorned to put anyone in your place, the decoration of this room is perforce all my own. . . . The floor is matting, with rugs by Michael Llewelyn Davies, Esq. . . . There are no pictures beyond tiny ones, the books and wood crying out against our experiments therewith. . . . Naught else but in the fireplace two old settles and piles of firewood. . . .

Barrie curled up on his wooden settle, from the painting by Sir John Lavery

'I had an odd thought today about the war that might come to something, but it seems to call for a poet. That in the dead quietness that comes after the carnage, the one thing those lying on the ground must be wondering is whether they are alive or dead. Out there the veil that separates the survivors and the killed must be getting very thin, and those on the one side of it very much jumbled up with those on the other. . . . Perhaps it is of this stuff that ghosts are made. These be rather headachy thoughts. I expect the lot on the other side of the veil have as many Germans as British, and that they all went off together quite unconscious that they had ever been enemies. To avenge the fallen! That is the stupidest cry of the war. What must the fallen think of us if they hear it.'

Gripped by the idea of the veil, Barrie set to work at once on another one-act play inspired by George, *A Well-Remembered Voice*. It concerns a mother, still grieving the death of her son, Dick. Her mourning is for all the world to see: she wears black, leaves Dick's 'sacred' fishing-rods lying around the study, and holds futile seances in an effort to get in touch with him 'on the other side'. Her husband, Mr Don, is an extension of the father in *The New Word*: outwardly unemotional, he seems to be more interested in his newspaper than his wife's seance. She does not resent his apparent indifference; she knows that 'a son is so much more to a mother than a father'. After the seance is over, Mrs Don goes to bed, leaving her husband alone in the study.

Barrie, standing by his study windows, where he would gaze for hours at the seven bridges visible across the Thames. 'Charing Cross Bridge is the ugliest of them all,' he once commented, 'but I never want to see it pulled down. It was across that bridge that the troop-trains took our boys to France.' The framed photograph on the sill is of Michael (p. 113)

> *He stands fingering the fishing-rods, then wanders back into the ingle-nook. . . . Through the greyness we see him . . . in the glow of the fire. He sits on the settle and tries to read his paper. He breaks down. He is a pitiful lonely man.*
>
> *In the silence something happens. A well-remembered voice says, 'Father'.* MR DON *looks into the greyness from which this voice comes, and he sees his son. We see no one, but we are to understand that, to* MR DON, DICK *is standing there in his habit as he lived. He goes to his boy.*

MR DON. Dick!

DICK. I have come to sit with you a bit, father.

(*It is the gay, young, careless voice.*)

MR DON. It's you, Dick; it's you!

DICK. It's me all right, father. I say, don't be startled, or anything of that kind. We don't like that.

Peter Scott's painting of Barrie in his ingle-nook

MR DON. My boy!

>   (*Evidently* DICK *is the taller, for* MR DON *has to look up to him. He puts his hands on the boy's shoulders.*) . . .

DICK. I say, father, let's get away from that sort of thing.

MR DON. That is so like you, Dick! I'll do anything you ask.

DICK. Then keep a bright face.

They talk matter-of-factly about the old days, Eton and cricket and fishing; although Dick talks in the manner of George, his character is closer to Peter Pan – indeed the whole scene is reminiscent of Peter's last meeting with Wendy. The 'crafty boy' roams about the room, always changing the subject when Mr Don looks as though he is in danger of becoming too emotional. The sight of his old fishing-rods prompts a memory:

DICK. . . . Do you remember, father, how I got the seven-pounder on a burn-trout cast? . . . It was really only six and three-quarters. I put a stone in its mouth the second time we weighed it! . . . When I went a-soldiering I used to pray – just standing up, you know – that I shouldn't lose my right arm, because it would be so awkward for casting. (*He cogitates as he returns to the ingle-nook.*) Somehow I never thought I should be killed. . . .

MR DON. Oh, Dick!

DICK. What's the matter? Oh, I forgot. . . . Haven't you got over it yet, father? I got over it so long ago. I wish you people would understand what a little thing [death] is. . . .

MR DON. Tell me, Dick, about the – the veil. . . . I suppose the veil is like a mist?

DICK. The veil's a rummy thing, father. Yes, like a mist. But when one has been at the Front for a bit, you can't think how thin the veil seems to get; just one layer of it. . . . We sometimes mix up those who have gone through with those who haven't. . . . I don't remember being hit, you know. I don't remember anything till the quietness came. When you have been killed it suddenly becomes very quiet; quieter even than you have ever known it at home. Sunday used to be a pretty quiet day at my tutor's, when Trotter and I flattened out on the first shady spot up the river; but it is quieter than that. I am not boring you, am I? . . . I wish I could remember something funny to tell you. . . . Father, do you remember little Wantage who was at my private* and came on to Ridley's house in my third half? . . .

MR DON. Emily Wantage's boy?

DICK. That's the card. . . .

*i.e. Prep-School.

MR DON. She was very fond of him.

DICK. Oh, I expect no end. Tell her he's killed.

MR DON. She knows.

DICK. . . . That isn't the joke, though. You see he got into a hopeless muddle about which side of the veil he had come out on . . . and he got lost . . . (*He chuckles*) I expect he has become a ghost! . . . Best not to tell his mother that. . . . Ockley's name still sticks to him. . . . He was a frightful swell you know. Keeper of the field, and played at Lord's the same year. . . .

MR DON. What did you nickname him, Dick?

DICK. It was his fags that did it! . . . His fags called him K.C.M.G.

MR DON. Meaning, Dick?

DICK. Meaning 'Kindly Call Me God!' . . . Father, don't feel hurt though I dodge the good-bye business when I leave you. . . . I'll just slip away.

MR DON. What I'm afraid of is that you won't come back. . . . When will you come again?

DICK. There's no saying.

As at the end of *Peter Pan*, Dick returns to the Neverland beyond the veil. The critic W. A. Darlington observed that in *A Well-Remembered Voice* 'for once in Barrie's writings there is an admission that the feeling between father and son can be deeper and truer even than that between a son and his mother'.[4] Or, perhaps, a boy and his nurse.

Michael was now in Pop, VI Form, Football XI, and co-editor of the *Eton College Chronicle* – 'writing leaders and poems galore',[5] boasted Barrie with pride to Charles Turley Smith. To enter more fully into his life, Barrie took out a regular subscription to the *Chronicle*, which enabled him to follow the boys' activities. Michael had implied to Mary Hodgson that the Easter holidays at Barrie's flat were being looked upon as a 'trial period'. In his only surviving letter to Michael, Barrie was clearly at pains to make the flat as attractive as possible for their return:

Michael in Pop at Eton

29 March 1918

Dearest Michael,

Pretty lonely here for this week-end, 'Bank holidays' are always loneliness personified to me, but I think that you & Nico are almost on the way [home] and rejoice with great joy. Nico said you might get off on Monday after all, but I'm not counting on it, too good to be true. I got your dressing-table out [of Campden Hill] all right & have been trying various plans to make the rooms nice. I have brought a few – very few – things from 23, but of course everything I've done is very open to re-arrangement – in

Michael and (*below*)
Nico in the Eton
O.T.C.

fact it is wanted. . . . Your account of the boys' musical in the *Chronicle* makes me want to see the M.S. thereof. Would it be possible for you to get the loan of it?

> Loving,
> J.M.B.

Nico was now fourteen, and the last of the Five to overtake Barrie in height, reaching five foot four in May, which allowed him the distinction of wearing tails at Eton instead of a bum-freezer. Barrie wrote to him from Adelphi Terrace:

'I must say it is pretty awful to think of you in tails. "Bringing his tails behind him" doesn't Mary say about her lamb? I would really rather you grow down instead of up, back into the blue suit & the red cap, heigho! You will have to be more of a comfort than ever to me in my old age, especially when I give at the knee permanently. . . . I want to come down as soon as M & you fix a good time. Could you wear only one tail the first time so that I can get used to the idea gradually?'[6]

Barrie communicated the 'painful news' of Nico's tails to various friends, adding to Elizabeth Lucas: 'Seems so little time since he was in blue and red, and we were all flying about in Kensington Gardens.'[7]

Michael was due to enlist on November 12th, 1918. On November 11th, Germany capitulated with a suddenness that caught the world unawares – not least Barrie, who was in France on an official tour, and spent Armistice night in Paris. He wrote to Mrs Hugh Lewis on November 22nd:

'So it actually is ended! . . . "It is finished" rather than "we have won". . . . It was dear of Peter [Lewis] to say that about Michael. You can guess how thankful I am. I don't think he will be wanted for the army now, and I'm going to Eton on Sunday . . . to "go into his future". He writes "I'll do anything you like. P.S. How about my going round the world?" They marched at Eton with their bath-tubs as drums and the night ended with Michael getting 500 lines (for standing on his head on a roof when he should have been in bed!).'

Michael's suggestion of going round the world was indicative of his mood: he had no desire to break away from Barrie, whom he still loved as few sons love their father, but he had a not unnatural desire to roam before deciding on a future. E. V. Lucas later wrote, 'He seemed to have everything at his feet, and one used to look at him and wonder what walk of life he would choose; but he gave few signs, being, for all his vivid interest in the moment, more in the world than

of it, an elvish spectator rather than a participant.'[8] Eiluned Lewis
recalled that Michael wanted to go to Paris, as his grandfather,
George du Maurier, had done, living the Bohemian life in an artist's
studio and developing his passion for drawing. Macnaghten and
Barrie did not agree. They felt he should first go to Oxford and secure
a degree; to please Barrie – always Michael's priority – he conceded
defeat, matriculating at Christ Church in January 1919. In return,
Barrie gave him a motor car and a country cottage as a token of
independence, though the cottage was rarely used.

Barrie and Cynthia Asquith

During the summer of 1918, Barrie had engaged a secretary. That
she could neither take shorthand nor type was of small account, since
the woman in question was Lady Cynthia Asquith, the daughter-in-
law of the former Prime Minister, whom Barrie had met at a dinner
party. Lady Cynthia was aged thirty – the same age as Sylvia had been
when Barrie met her at Sir George Lewis's dinner party in 1897. Like
Sylvia, Cynthia had an elusive beauty that artists strove to capture
but rarely achieved; like Sylvia, she had, at that time, two boys – the
younger, Michael, being the same age as George had been when his
red tam-o'-shanter first caught Barrie's eye in 1897; unlike Sylvia,
she had tremendous ambition: to write, to paint, to act – to do
virtually anything that would bring her in enough money to maintain
her expensive family. She had been married seven years to
Herbert ('Beb') Asquith, the eldest surviving son of H. H. Asquith.
Like Arthur, he had studied for the Bar; unlike Arthur, he had failed,
and had turned to more artistic pursuits, none of which brought in
much money. He had enlisted in 1914, and was now serving as a
gunner in the army, fighting in France.

The entry of Cynthia Asquith into the scheme of Barrie's life was a
gradual process,* which at present held decidedly less significance
for Barrie than for his new secretary. His life still revolved around
'my boys'.

Peter was demobilized early in 1919. He had won the Military
Cross in the previous year, but it was little compensation for his
three-year ordeal. Mackail wrote, 'He had been through something
more than a furnace, and what was left of him was for a long while
little more than a ghost; a shattered remnant that even Barrie
couldn't help.' Peter continued to live with Vera Willoughby,
helping her to run an antique shop in Soho. Barrie wrote to Nico at
Eton:

'Michael has told you of the trouble connected with Peter, but I

---

*Janet Dunbar gives a much fuller account of Cynthia Asquith's role in Barrie's life in her 1970
biography, *J. M. Barrie: The Man Behind the Image*. Cynthia herself wrote *Portrait of Barrie* in
1954.

Michael

want you to know that tho' it is a real trouble which has caused me much pain for a long time, I hope it will all vanish by and by. Also I love him just as much as ever, and he has all his old dear ways and he comes here a good deal & will come more, and I look forward to us all being all together again. He is as fond of you as in the old days. . . . He speaks a lot about you to me, and I tell him you are a joy and a pride to me, but of course I never mention such things to you. No, no, I keep it dark. . . . Michael speaks of learning to swim when he comes back [from Oxford], as he is to have a punt at Christ Church next term. He rode his machine to Berkhampstead on Sat^y and was escorted over Egerton by the lady now there. . . . Alas once more the Savoy looms without my favourite company. I think I shall ask for potatoes with a Nico in them and a half bottle of Michael 1900 vintage.'⁹

Nico, like Michael, shared most of his adolescent problems with Barrie. He wrote to him from Eton on March 23rd:

Dear Uncle Jim,
. . . I am afraid this has not been a very happy half for me.
I expect my tutor will tell you in my report, which I
expect will be bad. Otherwise I will tell you everything. It
is a long affair. My tutor is very sick about it but I don't
think you would mind. I hope to heaven you won't. It is
about me going about with a smaller boy named
Wright. He is under 2 years younger and a good
bit lower in the school. My tutor says it does both him
and me harm, which I will never believe. He jaws about
Sentimentality also, which is rot. Wright's people don't
object in the slightest and I don't think you will. . . . I can
quite see there would be a lot of harm if I led him into
bad ways and used bad language, but as I do neither of
them in any way and nor does he, where's the harm? It
enfuriates me. In these sort of cases I feel quite helpless
without Michael here. . . . The chief reason why I go
about with him so often, and is the only reason, is that I
like him better than anyone else in my tutor's. He is good
looking, and because of that my tutor says I am so to
speak in love with him, whereas it is just perfectly natural
friendship. I have been in despair about everything lately.

Loving
Nico

Nico recalled that Barrie's response to such problems was invariably calming and sympathetic:

'He was never harsh or critical – he always tried to offer advice as a friend, not as a parent, even when I was very young (which, incidentally, is one reason why he got on so well with children – he always treated them as equals). From the time Michael left Eton, I wrote to Uncle Jim every day, which led to my pouring out my thoughts and problems to him – not to a father, not to a brother, rather to a very intimate friend. I think Michael looked on him in much the same way. He was always extraordinarily easy to talk to – I never remember thinking, "Oh, Lor – what's Uncle Jim going to say when he finds out?" On the other hand, we never talked about the so-called "facts of life", and when, a year or so later, I did go through a more or less bi-sexual stage, I never mentioned it to him. But then how many boys would mention such things to their parents?'

Oxford had one great consolation for Michael – a renewal of his friendship with Roger Senhouse. Another Eton contemporary who had joined him was Robert (later Lord) Boothby:

'Michael was the most remarkable person I ever met, and the only one of my generation to be touched by genius. He was very sensitive and emotional, but he concealed both to a large extent. He had a profound effect on virtually everyone who came into contact with him – particularly Roger Senhouse, who was also a great friend of mine. I don't think Michael had any girl-friends, but our friendship wasn't homosexual; I believe it was – fleetingly – between him and Senhouse, yet I think Michael would have come out of it. Michael took me back to Barrie's flat a number of times, but I always felt uncomfortable there. There was a morbid atmosphere about it. I remember going there one day and it almost overwhelmed me, and I was glad to get away. We were going back to Oxford in Michael's car, and I said, "It's a relief to get away from that flat", and he said, "Yes it is." But next day he'd be writing to Barrie as usual. . . . It was an extraordinary relationship between them – an unhealthy relationship. I don't mean homosexual, I mean in a mental sense. It was morbid, and it went beyond the bounds of ordinary affection. Barrie was always charming to me, but I thought there was something twisted about him. Michael was very prone to melancholy, and when Barrie was in a dark mood, he tended to pull Michael down with him. . . . I remember once coming back to the flat with Michael and going into the study, which was empty. We stood around talking for about five minutes, and then I heard someone cough: I turned round and saw Barrie sitting in the ingle-nook,

Michael and Barrie at Glan Hafren

almost out of sight. He'd been there all the time, just watching us. . . . He was an unhealthy little man, Barrie; and when all is said and done, I think Michael and his brothers would have been better off living in poverty than with that odd, morbid little genius.* Yet there's no doubt that Michael loved him; he was grateful to him, but he also had an affinity with him that ran very deep.'[10]

In the early summer of 1919, Cynthia Asquith took a temporary respite in her secretarial duties as she was expecting a third child. She and her husband had been lent a house at Thorpe, in Suffolk; she wrote to Barrie, inviting him to stay. Barrie replied on June 20th:

> Dear Lady Cynthia,
>   I don't suppose I shall be able to get down. I want to come but I shd have done it before Michael got back. They shrink, these boys, from going anywhere, the death of their parents is really at the root of it, and down in my soul I know myself to be so poor a substitute that I try to make some sort of amends by hanging on here when there is any chance of my being a little use to them. Even in admitting this I am saying more to you than I do to most.
> Yours
J.M.B.

Barrie on the roof of Adelphi Terrace House, photographed by Jack

The excuse was both for Michael's sake, and for his own. Michael was due to set off for Paris at the end of the month, and Barrie liked to be with him when he was in London. A fortnight later he wrote to Nico at Eton (2 July 1919): 'Michael, [Clive] Burt, Senhouse and Boothby are actually off to France! They are at this moment dining together early at Waterloo. I can't conceive easily a more delightful prospect for four happy undergrads.' Boothby recalled, 'We had tremendous fun. We climbed a tree in the Champs Elysées and sat in it all night and waited until the peace procession marched by. . . . Michael loved Paris: he could speak fluent French, and I think he had a romantic idea of setting up his easel on the left bank and becoming an artist.'[11] 'Paris was choc-a-bloc, you couldn't get a room anywhere', remembered Clive Burt. 'Then Michael suggested we try the Hotel Meurice as Barrie always used to stay there, and Bob Boothby thought he too could pull a few strings as his Uncle was "well-known" at the Meurice. We went along, presented our

---

*Nico disagreed with this view. He wrote, 'I am quite unable to admit that J.M.B.'s influence was "unhealthy": oppressive maybe and over-constant – and I can believe that Michael was relieved to get away from the flat, as many many undergraduates have felt as they were speeding from their home with a friend back to Oxford. But so far as I am concerned, speaking as the fifth brother, I'm glad I lived with that odd little man rather than living in poverty, or, for that matter, with virtually any other person I have ever known.'

credentials, and were summarily ejected; retired to a turkish-bath, and eventually ended up in one of those rooms favoured by prostitutes where two could sleep while the other two roamed the streets, then changed over.'[12]

When Michael returned from his Parisian exploits, he found Barrie absorbed in writing a new play. The first notes had been made in 1892: '*Play: The Haunted House* – on all ghosts really mothers come back to see their children.' The theme had recurred at regular intervals throughout Barrie's notebooks and works during the intervening twenty-seven years, and he was now distilling them into *Mary Rose*, the story of a young mother who disappears on an island in the Outer Hebrides, returning years later to search for her son. Like Peter Pan, she has remained the same age as on the day she vanished, but her son has grown into a man, whom she no longer recognizes. Although Barrie was gripped by the subject, he found the writing physically painful as he had developed a form of writer's cramp in his right hand. He had been naturally left-handed as a child, and therefore found little difficulty in the switch. For the first time since his school days, his handwriting became legible, though he liked to claim that he thought more darkly down his left arm.

The Paris visit had whetted Michael's appetite for freedom, and throughout his next year at Oxford he was restless and dissatisfied. Senhouse introduced him to some of his Bloomsbury friends, taking him to Ottoline Morrell's home, Garsington Manor, for week-ends. Lytton Strachey found Michael 'a charming creature – and what is rarer, an intelligent one ... the only young man at Oxford or Cambridge with real brains'.[13] But Michael shied away from becoming part of a set. Dora Carrington later wrote to Strachey of another boy who 'reminded me of Michael Davies. He had a strange character: he hardly expanded even when the whole party became wild and tipsy. He was very anxious to be thought a man and put on a charming expression trying to look severe and unconcerned.'[14] In the spring of 1920 Dora Carrington wrote to Strachey from Oxford observing that Michael was 'unhappy and moody. Perhaps that is just the gloom of finding Barrie one's keeper for life.'[15]

Mary Rose began rehearsals at the beginning of April 1920, with Nico, now aged sixteen, in constant attendance. Michael, however, had set off on a forty-mile hike with a new Oxford friend, Rupert Buxton. Buxton had been head boy at Harrow, with as many academic distinctions to his credit as Michael had acquired at Eton. Clive Burt remembered him as having 'a kindred spirit to Michael: very musical, very poetic'.[16] Robert Boothby had a different opinion:

'Buxton was exceptionally clever, but he had a morbid influence on Michael: he was dark, gloomy, saturnine, with an almost suicidal

Barrie's first left-handed letter

Michael at Garsington Manor with (left) Dora Carrington and Julian Morrell

Fay Compton as Mary Rose

Evan Talbot, Audrey Lucas,
Michael and Barrie on the shore
facing Eilean Shona

streak in him. I remember Michael asked me, "Why don't you like my being friends with Rupert Buxton?" And I said, "The answer to that is doom – I have a feeling of doom about him." My friendship with Michael and Senhouse was almost perfection, and those Oxford days were the happiest of my life. We were gay together, always gay; but when Buxton came along, the gaiety left.'[17]

Meanwhile *Mary Rose* had opened at the Haymarket, with Fay Compton in the title role giving the performance of her career, and many of the critics hailing the play as Barrie's finest work. He had also started work on a murder play, which he was writing to please Michael, who had first suggested it. But Michael appeared to have lost interest; or rather, was preoccupied with establishing his own independence. 'Barrie tried not to see it,' wrote Mackail, 'and was wretched and miserable when he did. . . . He needed this boy's love also, more than anything on earth, and had known for years that he had it. But now, though [Michael] still only wanted to help him, he seemed to be shying away. . . . Poor Barrie again. And this time poor Michael. Seven when his father died; an orphan at under ten. So quick, and clever, and so extraordinarily attractive. But now so unhappy too.' At the end of June, Michael took matters into his own hands: he informed the authorities that he would be leaving Oxford and going to the University of Paris in the autumn. Barrie's reaction is unrecorded, but he can hardly have welcomed the thought of Michael spending most of the year in France. Perhaps he would change his mind, as he had done over a similar impulse to leave Eton. Barrie determined to make this year's summer holiday an outstanding success. He rented an entire island for August and September: Eilean Shona, off the west coast of Scotland. 'A wild rocky romantic island it is too', he wrote enthusiastically to Cynthia Asquith on August 13th, 'it almost taketh the breath away to find so perfectly appointed a retreat on these wild shores. . . . Superb as is the scene from the door, Michael, who has already been to the top of things, says it's nought to what is revealed there – all the western isles of Scotland lying at our feet. A good spying-ground for discovering what really became of Mary Rose.'

To make the holiday the more attractive, Barrie had suggested that Michael and Nico might like to bring along a few of their friends. Roger Senhouse came, somewhat apprehensively, since, on a previous visit to Adelphi Terrace, Barrie had not addressed a single word to him. Nico brought two Eton friends, and Elizabeth and Audrey Lucas were also included in the house party. However, Barrie's enthusiasm for the holiday soon began to wane, and by August 17th he was writing to Cynthia:

'This island has changed from sun to rain, and we have now had about 60 hours of it so wet that you get soaked if you dart across the lawn. It's dry for the moment and anon I will be observed – or rather, I won't be, for there is no one to observe me – playing clock-golf by my lonely self. I am mostly by my lonely self. . . . The others are out sea-fishing . . . and the party is merrier without me. . . . Michael has been drawing more sketches of me, and they are more than enough. He has a diabolical aptitude for finding my worst attributes, so bad that I indignantly deny them, then I furtively examine myself in the privacy of my chamber, and lo, they are there.'

Barrie wrote again to Cynthia on September 7th:

'We are a very Etonian household, and there is endless shop talked, during which I am expected to be merely the ladler out of food. If I speak to the owner of the puppy [Roger Senhouse] he shudders but answers politely and then edges away. Our longest conversation will be when he goes –
'*He:* (with dry lips but facing the situation in the bull-dog way)
   "Thank you very much for having me. Awfully good of you."
'*I:* "Nice to have you here."
            '(Exeunt in opposite directions)
'Do my letters seem aged? I certainly feel so here. I have a conviction that they secretly think it indecent of me to play tennis, which however I am only suffered to do as a rare treat. They run about and gather the balls for me, and in their politeness almost offer to hold me up when it is my turn to serve. By the way, what an extraordinarily polite game tennis is. The chief word in it seems to be "sorry" and admiration of each other's play crosses the net as frequently as the ball. I fancy this is all part of the "something" you get at public schools and can't get anywhere else. I feel sure that when any English public school boy shot a Boche he called out "Sorry". If he was hit himself he cried, "Oh, well shot".'

In November of the previous year Barrie had been elected Rector of St Andrews University: a three-year appointment, which required him to make an address to the students at some point during the three years. He had not yet decided on a subject, but hours of arguing and debate with Michael and his student friends on Eilean Shona helped to formulate his ideas. Barrie was fond of a pretence towards the old accepted values, but his notebook shows that the views of a younger generation were not wasted on him:

—Age & Youth the two great enemies. . . . Age (wisdom) failed – Now let us see what youth (audacity) can do. The 2 great partners in state shdn't be Tory, Liberal or Labour – but Age & Youth. . . .

Barrie 'playing clock-golf by my lonely self' on Eilean Shona, photographed by Nico

Michael at Eilean Shona

Barrie at work on Eilean Shona

Rectors all advise work, labour sublime outlook, &c. This really not in touch with young men they used to be. No one can bridge that gulf (boys at Eton cheered General but said 'Silly Ass'). Youth already knows nearly as much as Old & feel far more. Old advising young with advice rather a mockery just after War which young men died for. . . . They shd put statesmen who make war in front line. They shd be convicting me in dock (instead of my addressing) & condemning.

—*Present Day – War Result – The Young – Plays – Lit*^{re} *&c*. Might be speech or play with scene laid a few years hence. Present discussions of immorality of plays &c is all muddled ∵ the two sides (really old & young – i.e. Before & After War) don't understand (admit) that they have different views of what constitutes immorality. As dif[ferent] as ours from, say, an African tribe (This really the great result of war which at first didn't seem to show itself. It isn't those who fought agst their elders, but those who have been growing up *since* the war agst outlook of others (the soldiers are merely discontented). In short, there has arisen a new morality which seeks to go its own way agst the fierce protests (or despair) of the old morality. No argument can exist between the two till this is admitted. In present controversy it isn't admitted – the Old screams at the New as . . . vile ∵ not Old's way – and New despises Old as played out and false sentiment. When they admit that the other has a case to state, then . . . they can argue – not before.

—This sentimentality is deep in it and is the flag of the Old (at least in New's opinion). From Art the two seek different things. In the Old's plays, novels &c, what public wanted was to be made to like characters so much that the work *had* to have happy endings – to be *sympathetic* was the one aim of the artist. Undoubtedly this often led to sloppiness & insincerity in the works of great writers – all must end happily at any cost. We were brought up to this.

—The *New* no longer ask for this. They don't care tho' characters end miserably or not – they don't want to be sympathetic with them, they enjoy seeing them stripped of their qualities as much as the Old liked them to be emphasized. It may be a mood (but it is perhaps something better), but they are out for dissection, exposure, they have lost simple faith – probably the War is main cause of it – they query everything. Perhaps they accept too little & we accepted too much.

—In a *play* they cd be shown in action as things will be a few years hence, when by the passing away of the old (or a revolution) they have established their new morality and new laws of the land. The Sentimental-Sympathetic may be illegal – the old put out of way & little statuettes of them kept instead. There may be Class A, Class B people, &c. A love scene might be under accepted conditions that to

Throned on a cliff, serene, Man saw the sun
hold a red torch above the farthest seas,
and the fierce island pinnacles put on
in his defence their sombre panoplies;
Foremost the white mists eddied, trailed, & spun
like seekers, emulous to clasp his knees,
till all the duty of the scene seemed one
led by the secret whispers of the breeze.

The sun's torch suddenly flashed upon his face
and died; and he sat content in subject night
and dreamed of an old dead foe that had
sought & found him;
a beast stirred wildly in his resting-place;
and the cold came; Man arose to his master-height
shivered, & turned away; but the mists were round him
                                            Eilean Shona.

propose marriage is Class B and 'living together' Class A – and more honoured because more difficult to go on with. The end of it shd not be satire but leaving the idea open that New may be better than Old. We can't be sure that they are wrong & we right – *we who seem to have made the greatest mess of things that has ever been made in the history of the world.*

Sonnet written by Michael on the summit of Eilean Shona, and (*right*) Barrie's transcription (with proof corrections) as it appeared in his St Andrews Address, *Courage*, with 'secure' and 'duty' changed to 'serene' and 'beauty'

Michael on Eilean Shona

At the end of the holiday, Michael decided to return to Oxford instead of going to Paris. The reasons for his last-minute change of heart are unclear: in all probability it was his own decision, though Elizabeth Lucas may have had a hand in the matter. Barrie wrote to her on October 17th:

'It was nice of you to have that talk with Michael and I have no doubt that for the time at least it had a steadying effect. All sorts of things do set him "furiously to think" and they seem to burn out like a piece of paper. He is at present I think really working well at Oxford and has at any rate spasms of happiness out of it, but one never knows of the

288

> ' Throned on a cliff serene Man saw the sun
> Hold a red torch above the farthest seas,
> And the fierce island pinnacles put on
> In his defence their sombre panoplies ;
> Foremost the white mists eddied, trailed, and spun
> Like seekers, emulous to clasp his knees,
> Till all the beauty of the scene seemed one,
> Led by the secret whispers of the breeze.
>
> ' The sun's torch suddenly flashed upon his face
> And died ; and he sat content in subject night,
> And dreamed of an old dead foe that had sought
> and found him,
> A beast stirred boldly in its resting-place,
> And the cold came ; Man rose to his master-height,
> Shivered, and turned away ; but the mists were
> round him.'

morrow. I think few have suffered from the loss of a mother as he has done.'

December 1920, and Barrie was again attending rehearsals for *Peter Pan* – its sixteenth consecutive annual revival. More lines were being added from his notebook, jotted down in curious juxtaposition with notes for his St Andrews address:

—*P. Pan*. Child: 'Mother, what hour was I born?' '$\frac{1}{2}$ past 2 in the morning.' 'Oh, mother, I hope I didn't wake you.'

—*Patriotism*. As world grows smaller, views of P[atriotism] shd be more world-wide. The men out there were realising this on both sides as they faced each other.

—*Hook*. Eton & Magdalen. . . . Studied for Mods. Took to drink in 1881, elected M.P. following year, &c.

—T. Hardy great when political swells are dead, rotten & forgotten.

—So far as self is concerned, neither school nor university of any importance to me. . . . Nothing disgusts me more than people beslavering me with praise, but I think an individual may have done me harm by thinking too little of me.

—Good subject for Rectorial address might be the mess the Rector himself has made of life. . . . First piece of advice, don't copy me.

—Great thing to form own opinion, don't accept hearsay. Try to get at what you really see in it all. Question authority. Question accepted views, values, reputations. Don't be afraid to be among the rebels. . . . Speak scornfully of the Victorian age. Of Edwardian age. Of last year. Of old-fashioned writers like Barrie, who accept old-fangled ideas. Don't be greybeards before your time – too much advice is to make you so.

—Youth shd demand its share in running of the country (tho' we have no intention of giving it them). Look around & see how much share Youth has now that the war is over – they got a handsome share while it lasted.

—*P. Pan.* 'I thought it was only flowers that died.'

—*Play Title* – 'The Man Who ~~Didn't~~ *Couldn't* Grow Up' or 'The Old Age of Peter Pan.'

After spending Christmas in Paris with Nico and Elizabeth Lucas, Michael returned to Oxford. Barrie wrote to Elizabeth Lucas on February 27th, 1921:

Barrie at his desk in Adelphi Terrace House

'Michael will be back soon, but contemplates a reading-party with another undergrad in Dorset, and that will be much better for him than London. He is working hard and really enjoying his life at Oxford for the present at least. He has the oddest way of alternating between extraordinary reserve and surprising intimacy. No medium. In his rooms at Oxford lately he suddenly unbosomed himself marvellously. One has to wait for those times, but they are worth while when they come.'

Barrie spent Easter with Cynthia Asquith and her family at Stanway, the home of her parents, Lord and Lady Wemyss, then moved on to Dorset, where Michael was staying in a little inn at Corfe Castle, reading for his finals with Rupert Buxton. The rest of the holiday was spent in London, with only Nico and his gramophone for company: 'You and your Jazz! I heard the Jazz Band at the Coliseum one night & thought it so abominable that I nearly got up in my seat and yelled!'[18] Nevertheless, like Peterkin's hammer, Barrie missed the blare when Nico returned to Eton: 'Once again I take up the pen at the beginning of a new half and thus indite thee. With melancholy heart I saw the iron horse glide away with you from Paddington, but must be must be, and at any rate we had a grand time.'[19]

Michael's last letter to Nico: 'Be mild'

Work was Barrie's constant hedge against loneliness during the term-time, and with Michael also back at Oxford, he now concentrated his energies on rehearsing the murder play he had written for him, *Shall We Join the Ladies?* The play was to be performed at the opening of the Royal Academy of Dramatic Art's new theatre on May 27th with a glittering cast: Irene Vanbrugh, Marie Löhr, Fay Compton, Dion Boucicault, Charles Hawtrey, Sybil Thorndike, Cyril Maude, Leon Quatermaine, Lady Tree, Lillah McCarthy, Nelson Keys, Madge Titheradge, Norman Forbes, Hilda Trevelyan, Sir Johnston Forbes-Robertson and Gerald du Maurier. Even Frohman had never gathered such an assembly; and all for the sake of a one-act play written to please

Michael. Twenty-one in a few weeks' time, the first night would be as much a tribute to his coming of age as to the opening of R.A.D.A.'s theatre.

On Thursday, May 19th, Cynthia Asquith worked at the flat until six o'clock, then went to have dinner with a friend, leaving Barrie alone to write his nightly letter to Michael. Despite their occasional differences, the daily exchange of correspondence between Barrie and Michael had continued without interruption, and recently Cynthia had arranged a 'great cave' of Michael's letters into chronological order, starting with his first effort, written as a child of five.

At about eleven o'clock Barrie put on his hat and coat, took the letter and went down in the lift to post it. He was about to leave the building when a stranger came up to him. He introduced himself as a reporter from a London newspaper, and wondered whether Sir James could oblige him with a few more facts about the drowning. Barrie looked blankly at him. What drowning? The reporter then realized that Barrie was unaware of the news received from Oxford less than an hour before: that two undergraduates, Rupert Buxton and Michael Llewelyn Davies, had been drowned while bathing in the River Thames at Sandford Pool. Their bodies had not yet been recovered, but the tragedy had been witnessed by two men working at a near-by paper mill.

Barrie needed no further details. He knew that Michael could barely swim a stroke, knew that none the less he had gone on trying, knew that Buxton was his closest friend. There could be no mistake. He walked back to the lift, returned to his flat and shut the door. Some time later he telephoned Peter and Gerald du Maurier. Later still he rang Cynthia Asquith, telling her, in a voice she scarcely recognized: 'I have had the most terrible news. Michael has been drowned at Oxford.'[20] When she arrived at the flat, she found him in a state of complete shock. Peter and Gerald were also there, but Barrie was inconsolable: he simply did not hear them. He refused to go to bed, and when Cynthia returned early next morning, she found that he had spent the entire night pacing up and down the study. Peter went down to Eton to break the news to Nico and bring him back to the flat. When Barrie saw him, he cried out, 'Oh, take him away, take him away!'[21] Nico wrote in 1975:

'Strangely, I don't remember feeling hurt by this, rather did I understand in some way how my very closeness to Michael made his more or less uncontrollable grief even more uncontrollable. . . . My first duty was to go and break the news to Mary Hodgson, who was working as a midwife for Queen Charlotte's Hospital. I was riding on the top of the bus when I saw her, walking along the street. I ran back

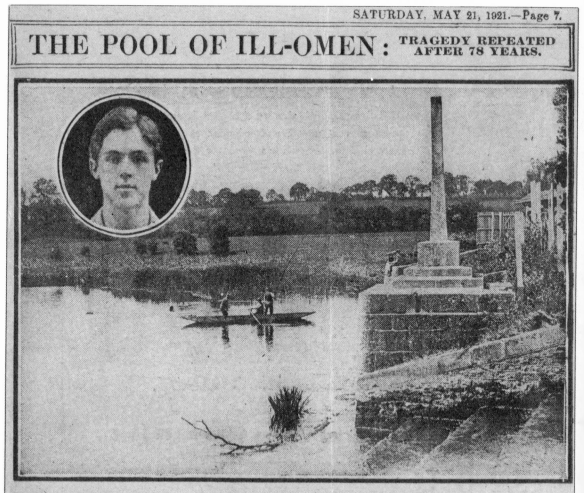

THE POOL OF ILL-OMEN: TRAGEDY REPEATED AFTER 78 YEARS.

Sandford Pool, Oxford, where Mr. Michael Llewellyn Davies (inset) and Mr. Rupert Buxton, both undergraduates, were drowned while bathing. The bodies were recovered yesterday. Mr. Davies was one of Sir James Barrie's adopted sons; the other, believed to be the original of "Peter Pan," was killed in action. The monument in the picture commemorates two other Oxford men drowned there in 1843.

to her, and she immediately knew what had happened by the look on my face. We stood in a doorway and sobbed together.'

Most of London's newspapers carried the story on their front pages. The *Evening Standard*'s coverage was typical:

THE TRAGEDY OF PETER PAN

SIR J. M. BARRIE'S LOSS OF AN ADOPTED SON

'There is something of the wistful pathos of some of his own imaginings in the tragedy which has darkened the home of Sir James Barrie. Almost the first remark of friends, on hearing of the death of the adopted son of the dramatist to-day . . . was: "What a terrible blow for Sir James!" The young men, Mr Michael Llewelyn Davies

292

and Mr Rupert E. V. Buxton ... were drowned near Sandford bathing pool, Oxford, yesterday. The two undergraduates were almost inseparable companions. Mr Davies was only 20 and Mr Buxton 22.... The "original" of Peter Pan was named George, [who] was killed in action in March 1915.... Now both boys who are most closely associated with the fashioning of *Peter Pan* are dead. One recalls the words of Peter himself: "To die would be an awfully big adventure." '

The two bodies were not recovered until Friday afternoon, and an inquest was held at Oxford the following day. It was established that the pool, or weir, was a known danger spot: a large memorial overlooked it, commemorating two students who had been drowned there in 1843. The men who had witnessed Michael's death testified that the pool was 'as still as a mill-pond' at the time of the tragedy. 'I heard a shout', stated one. 'I looked in the direction and saw two men bathing in the pool in difficulties. ... Their heads were close together: they were sort of standing in the water and not struggling.' 'Did you form the impression that they were clasped?' 'Yes, that was my impression.'[22] Since it was known that Michael could not swim, the jury returned a verdict of accidental drowning and 'expressed the opinion that Mr Buxton lost his life in his endeavour to save his friend. The Dean [of Michael's College] in making this communication to the Coroner completely broke down with emotion.'[23] It was rumoured among some that the accident had been suicide. Boothby was 'convinced that it was a mutual suicide pact'. 'Perfectly possible,' wrote Peter in his notes for the family *Morgue*, 'but entirely unproven.' Nico commented, 'I've always had something of a hunch that Michael's death was suicide. He was in a way the "type" – exceptionally clever, subject to long fits of depression. I'm apt to think – stressing think – that he was going through something of a homosexual phase and maybe let this get a bigger hold on his thinking than it need: I have no knowledge of Rupert's leanings in this direction, but I would guess they preferred each other's company to anyone else's.' Barrie himself mentioned suicide in later years to Josephine Mitchell-Innes as the possible cause of Michael's death; yet a part of him refused to accept any such notion. Had not Sylvia entrusted him to his care? 'I do not want my Michael to be pressed at all at work – he is at present not very strong but very keen and intelligent: *great care* must be taken not to overwork him. Mary understands and of course J.M.B. knows & will be careful & watch.'

Following the inquest, Michael's body was brought back to Adelphi Terrace, where it remained until the funeral. Barrie had not slept for two days and nights: he 'looked like a man in a nightmare', wrote Cynthia in her diary. She called in his doctor, Sir Douglas

Shields, who persuaded him to take a sleeping draught. For the rest of the time he remained shut away in his bedroom, refusing to see anyone. 'No praise or gratitude can possibly be too great for Cynthia during these days', wrote Denis Mackail. 'It may be said . . . that it was she who preserved his reason, for throughout that almost unimaginable week-end there were moments of terrible danger.' The 'terrible danger' was Barrie's overwhelming desire to end his own life – a life rendered utterly pointless without Michael.

On Monday, May 23rd, 1921, Michael was buried in Hampstead Churchyard, close to the graves of his mother and father. A few weeks before, Barrie had written in his notebook:

> *Death.* One who died is only a little ahead of procession all moving that way. When we round the corner we'll see him again. We have only lost him for a moment because we fell behind, stopping to tie a shoe-lace.

Barrie after Michael's death. 'For ever and ever I am thinking about him.'

Michael's death had a profound effect on virtually everyone who had known him. 'I am sure if he had lived he would have been one of the remarkable people of his generation', wrote Lytton Strachey to Ottoline Morrell on hearing of his death. 'The uselessness of things is hideous and intolerable.'[1] Lord Boothby recalled in 1976, 'When Michael died, I received a number of hysterical letters from friends, the most hysterical being from Edward Marjoribanks, the brilliant half-brother of Quintin Hailsham. I'm convinced that Edward's own suicide a few years later was motivated by Michael's death. I remember, too, the devastating effect it had on Roger Senhouse: I can see him now, being led away from Michael's funeral, sobbing. I don't think Roger would have ever taken up his unhealthy life with Lytton Strachey had Michael lived. As for myself, I've made a pretty good mess of my life, which would have been very different if Michael had lived. He had a great influence over me, more than anyone else I've ever known. He would have stopped me doing many foolish things. He would have kept me on the rails.'

But the grief of Michael's friends was all but eclipsed by the intensity of Barrie's despair. 'All the world is different to me now' he wrote to Elizabeth Lucas in December 1921; 'Michael was pretty much my world.' To Michael's Oxford tutor, Robin Dundas, Barrie wrote a year later, 'It may seem strange to you that I did not write to you long ago, but what happened was in a way the end of me, and practically anything may be forgiven me now. He had been the one great thing in my life for many years, and though there are little things to do, they are very trivial.'[2] On the eve of the anniversary of Michael's death, Barrie wrote to Elizabeth Lucas, 'Do you know that this day a year ago Michael was alive and as well as any of us and that next day he was dead. That is really why I am writing to you to-day. I feel that he is at Oxford to-day in his rooms and that tomorrow he is

Barrie being carried aloft by the students of St Andrews University after delivering his address, *Courage*, in May 1922. He later wrote to Michael's Oxford tutor, Robin Dundas, 'It was not St Andrew's students I was seeing on that occasion, but an Oxford one'

going out to be drowned, and doesn't know it.' A similar theme occurred in other letters: in November 1922 he was corresponding with Robin Dundas about putting up a memorial to overlook 'that terrible place' which, he told him, 'I see every night of my life'; on November 7th he wrote to another friend, F. S. Oliver, 'I go looking for him there . . . pretty well every night of my life.' That night Barrie had a dream, which he recorded in his notebook:

Memorial to Michael and Rupert Buxton overlooking 'that terrible place', Sandford Pool

—*Michael*. On 7th Nov 1922 I dreamt that he came back to me, not knowing that he was drowned and that I kept this knowledge from him, and we went on for another year in old way till the fatal 19th approached again & he became very sad not knowing why, and I feared what was to happen but never let on – and as day drew nearer he understood more & thought I didn't – and gradually each knew the other knew but still we didn't speak of it – and when the day came I had devised schemes to make it impossible for him to leave me yet doubted they could help – and he rose in the night and put on the old clothes and came to look at me as he thought asleep. I tried to prevent him going but he had to go and I knew it and he said he thought it would be harder if I didn't let him go alone, but I went with him, holding his hand and he liked it and when we came to the place – that pool – he said goodbye to me and went into it and sank just as before. At this point I think I woke but feeling that he had walked cheerily into my room as if another year had again begun for us.

—The above was all the dream and the notes to follow come out of thinking about it, all except this that I knew from the moment of his return I must never let him know that anything had happened to him – that this so to speak was vital to his life. All must go on as if he had returned from some ordinary outing.

—If I write about this I should picture the old life going on so precisely as before that often for a length of time I cease to have uneasiness. I have no idea till the fatal day is approaching that he will again be taken from me then.

—I give details of ~~his~~ our time together during the extra year, lived quite ordinarily tho' strangely close to each other.

—I do some things that he had wanted before and tht then I had not done.

—Fears of spoiling him, and fight not to do it.

—How in agony I had to let him go away sometimes to live ordinary life of ~~young~~ youth.

—It is not necessary to make him nearly 21 – He could be younger if I like.

—Perhaps sinister hostile powers like clouds in M. James's fairy book.

—His gallant fear of water which he confides to me in the extra year.

Michael, aged 12, standing against an idyllic Scottish landscape. The picture was the most prominent of those hanging in Barrie's flat. 'It is as familiar an expression to me as if he himself had come into this room to quiz me, not at all conscious of what was to befall, . . . while some photographs seem to foretell the whole tragic story,' wrote Barrie to Robert Boothby. 'We know that because such have been there will be such again, though not for us.'

Notebook entry on Michael

(How this affects me.

—He might write from school of fear of water when learning to swim, so tht this vague shadow haunts the story.

—It might be called 'Water' – (or The Silent Pool) or 'The 19th'.

—Mary Hodgson coming back?

—He can't get past the fatal date.

—Our real letters in it?

—In some strange ways his tastes – disposition – are different. Also he seems to know vaguely some new strange things and to have forgotten other things.

—Fatal night coming to me light pressed lips says going to bathe – must go – must.

—In dream did he return like one so much older or just as had left me – or a year younger? – In last case it would mean he can't get past a certain age as well as a certain day. In the other cases it is only the day tht is the obstacle.

—Trying to lock in, guarded by others – he is in such agony of mind tht I have to let him out. He goes to pool.

—To go with him on the fatal day is as sad as Ch[arles] Lamb 'crossing fields' with his sister taking her to asylum.

—His hand on my shoulder.

—Must be clear tht there is nothing suicidal about it.

—I make him become an accomplished swimmer to help him fight the fatal day. (Day better than night?)

—When he reappears it is as suddenly as from the next room, and in as matter-of-fact way. He never knows he has been away.

—Effect on my own life. Give up ordinary work – he chides me for laziness – His joy of living greater than ever – ecstasy of childhood comes back.

—It is as if long after writing 'P. Pan' its true meaning came to me – Desperate attempt to grow up but can't.

—Enquiring back I find he had always had great difficulty to pass the 19th Illness – once lost, &c.

—I dry the pool – water comes back. Or build high wall yet he is found drowned in it. (We try going far away – a similar pond is there. Terrible when he vaguely knows it is, must be a dreadful day for him.

—This as if pond followed.

—A love affair? (How would I treat it seeing I think he will go again?

Although the story suggested in these notes never emerged, the 'true meaning' of *Peter Pan* found its way into the stage directions of the play when it was finally printed in 1928:

PETER (*passionately*) I don't want to go to school and learn solemn things. No one is going to catch me, lady, and make me a man. I want always to be a little boy and to have fun.

(*So perhaps he thinks, but it is only his greatest pretend.*)

The death of Michael was a considerable blow to Jack and Peter; for Nico, it was devastating. 'Nicholas is sometimes overwhelmed by what he has lost' Barrie wrote to Elizabeth Lucas, 'and is a touching boy at such times'.[3] When Nico went up to Oxford in 1922, Barrie wrote to Michael's former tutor, Robin Dundas:

Stanway, 1922: l to r—Michael Asquith, Barrie, Simon Asquith, Queen Mary

'I heard from Nicholas with uncommon pleasure of how you have had him out, and I may add that he wrote so enthusiastically about you that I feel confident you will get more out of him as he settles down more to Oxford. He is not of course a Michael, life has so far presented no problems to him, nothing terrible and nothing thrillingly joyous such as Michael saw. He is thoroughly the Eton child as yet, to whom Eton standards and ways are the sum of his outlook. Apparently it is not easy to step out of that last year at Eton into the world – and least easy to those who have been conspicuous in the athletic circle. He will never probably be 'intellectual' in any prominent way, but he is able I think in the sense that he has a powerful brain, and he is very lovable and a true admirer of the fine things. . . . He has not read greatly but has good taste in poetry especially and likes to hear it talked of by those who care for it. Most of his reticence is owing to his passionate regard for Michael. He has a sort of childish fear of breaking down when that name is mentioned. Nevertheless the more it is mentioned to him the better I am pleased. He is very emotional and frightened thereat.'[4]

Barrie with a new generation of Davieses: Nico's daughter, Laura

Nico continued to live with his guardian in the holidays, but he knew he could not replace Michael. 'Uncle Jim told me that I understood him better than anyone else alive, yet I realized I could never be a substitute for all that he had lost. When Michael died, the light of his life went out.' Nico 'left the nest' in 1926 to marry Mary James, and in 1931 Peter announced his engagement to one of the Ruthven twins, Margaret. 'The event is one I have long hoped for', Barrie wrote to Mrs Oliver, 'and when it is accomplished I suppose I shall feel that my task is over and, as Henley wrote, the long day done.'[5] Apart from the occasional visits of 'my boys', and his friendship with Cynthia Asquith, Barrie lived alone, the 'Hermit of the Adelphi', roosting high in his eyrie above the Thames. Like Margaret Ogilvy, he gradually emerged from his grief. He entertained again: Charlie Chaplin, Mary Pickford, the Archbishop of Canterbury; dabbled in politics again, befriending Michael Collins, speaking out against Hitler, hosting luncheon parties for Ramsay MacDonald, Stanley Baldwin and Winston Churchill. He made numerous speeches –

Barrie with Elisabeth Bergner, for whom he wrote *The Boy David*, the last play of his life. Ostensibly about the young King David of the Bible, the play was an echo of an old, old theme: the boy David who had died in childhood, the boy David of *The Little White Bird*, the eternal lost boy: Peter Pan. Barrie remembered Elisabeth Bergner's performance as David in his Will as being 'the best performance ever given in a play by me.'

despite his maxim that there is 'no surer sign of mediocrity than being accepted as a successful after-dinner speaker',[6] became Chancellor of Edinburgh University, received the Freedom of half a dozen cities, and was awarded the Order of Merit. His friendships with children continued unabated, from Cynthia Asquith's two sons, Michael and Simon, to the young Princess Margaret, who, at the age of three, proclaimed that Sir James 'is my greatest friend, and I am *his* greatest friend'.[7] Barrie went so far as to draw up a contract with the Princess, an echo of his Agreement with Jack a quarter of a century before, awarding her a penny a night for two lines contributed by her to his last play, *The Boy David*. In March 1937, King George VI sent Barrie a message informing him that if the debt was not paid in full, he would be hearing from His Majesty's solicitors. Barrie, delighted, prepared a large sack of pennies with the intention of taking them to Buckingham Palace in person; but on June 21st, at the age of seventy-seven, he died, the pennies undelivered. Peter and Nico were with him. 'He was tired', said Nico. 'He wanted to go.'

Michael's death had, in Mackail's phrase, 'altered and darkened everything for the rest of his life'. Yet there remained for him one unfailing consolation. When he delivered his address to the students of

St Andrews University in 1922, he read them the sonnet Michael had written during his last summer on Eilean Shona. Barrie did not mention Michael by name. He spoke of him simply as 'the lad that will never be old'.

Sources UNPUBLISHED SOURCES

1. *Some Davies Letters and Papers, 1874–1915*, compiled in six volumes by Peter Llewelyn Davies between 1945 and 1951. Peter outlined the purpose of what he referred to as the family *Morgue* in a series of notes found after his death: 'Intention: To show, by extracts from letters & diaries, with short notes, the sort of Davies and du Maurier people we are sprung from. . . . To "lay a ghost" in my own case, and free myself to either destroying all documents or dispersing them between Jack & Nico'. In a letter sent to his two surviving brothers to accompany the first instalment of the *Morgue*, Peter wrote: 'If you think the whole thing is a mistake, you can always tear it up and throw it away, as I shall now proceed to tear up and throw away the letters, some of which are here copied'. Peter's original plan had been to take his compilation up to the death of Michael in 1921, but his process of destruction overtook the speed of his transcription, and by 1952 he had abandoned the task at George's death, consigning all further material in his possession to the incinerator. In every sense the *Morgue* is a tragic document, since its compilation was, in Nico's opinion, a contributory factor towards Peter's suicide.

2. *The Walter Beinecke Jnr Collection*, housed at Yale University as part of the Beinecke Rare Book and Manuscript Library. The collection contains the major part of Barrie's letters and manuscripts extant (including much Davies material not transcribed in the *Morgue*), as well as the surviving copy of *The Boy Castaways of Black Lake Island*, and Barrie's forty-eight notebooks. These notebooks were made available to me on microfilm, and some of my transcriptions differ from the same extracts printed in earlier biographies; similar discrepancies occur with many of Barrie's letters in the Beinecke Collection, particularly when compared with those in *The Letters of J. M. Barrie* (Peter Davies Ltd, 1942). While making no claim to infallibility, I believe my transcriptions to be accurate, thanks to Nico's help in deciphering the more illegible passages of Barrie's handwriting.

3. *The Barrie Birthplace Collection*, administered by the National Trust for Scotland, which contains unpublished drafts of Barrie's works, as well as a number of early photographs.

4. *Material owned by Nicholas Llewelyn Davies*, including the majority of photographs reproduced here. Many of the letters and documents in his possession do not appear in Peter's *Morgue*.

5. *The Margaret Ogilvy Sweeten Collection*, which includes letters and photographs associated with Barrie's childhood, and with the Barrie and Ogilvy families.

6. *The Mary Hodgson Collection*, made available by her niece, Mrs Mary Hill. It contains various photographs, mementoes and letters from the Davies boys, particularly Peter and Nico, who wrote to her frequently until her death in 1962.

7. *The Pauline Chase letters* in the Victoria and Albert Museum.

8. *The Roger Lancelyn Green Collection*. As author of *Fifty Years of Peter Pan* (Peter Davies Ltd, 1954), Roger Lancelyn Green has amassed a wealth of Barrie knowledge and material. His collection includes Nina Boucicault's 1904 rehearsal script of *Peter Pan*.

9. *The Lillie Library Collection, University of Indiana*. In his Dedication to *Peter Pan*, Barrie implied that the original draft of the play had been lost. In fact he had given it to Maude Adams, who in turn presented it to the Lillie Library.

10. *Dolly Ponsonby's unpublished Diaries, 1890–1914*, made available by the Dowager Lady Ponsonby.

11. *Material owned by Geraldine Llewelyn Davies*, including several hundred letters from Barrie to Jack and herself, as well as personal correspondence with her husband.

A number of smaller collections have also been consulted, their owners being acknowledged in the Introduction. In addition I have drawn extensively from my own taped interviews, and correspondence carried out between 1975 and 1978 by Sharon Goode and myself.

Sources

PUBLISHED SOURCES

Barrie's own works:

The majority of Barrie's books and plays were published in Great Britain by Hodder & Stoughton Ltd, the exceptions being *Better Dead* (Swan Sonnenschein); *The Little Minister* [novel], *Sentimental Tommy, Tommy and Grizel* (Cassell); *Neil and Tintinnabulum* (privately printed 1925, subsequently included in Cynthia Asquith's *The Flying Carpet*, Partridge, 1925); *The Greenwood Hat, The Boy David, McConnachie and J.M.B.: Speeches by J. M. Barrie, The Letters of J. M.Barrie* (Peter Davies). An incomplete list of Barrie's numerous contributions to newspapers and periodicals appears in *A Bibliography of the Writings of Sir James Matthew Barrie Bart., O.M.* by Herbert Garland (The Bookman's Journal, 1928) and *Sir James Matthew Barrie: A Bibliography* by B. D. Cutler (Greenberg, New York, 1931). My extracts have been taken from photo-copies of the original articles supplied by the Colindale Newspaper Library. A useful 'Barrie Book List' is given by Roger Lancelyn Green in his brief but excellent monograph *J. M. Barrie* (Bodley Head, 1960). There is no single 'authorized' version of Barrie's plays, since the author delighted in revising his texts after they had appeared in print. The majority are available in three different versions: an acting edition, published by Samuel French Ltd.; a semi-novelized version, published individually as part of the 23-volume *Uniform Edition of the Works and Plays of J. M. Barrie* between 1913 and 1937 by Hodder & Stoughton, Cassell, and Peter Davies Ltd.; and, thirdly, in script format in *The Definitive Edition of the Plays of J. M. Barrie* (Hodder & Stoughton, 1942). Excerpts quoted in this book have been taken from the last, unless otherwise stated. Barrie's speeches, with the exceptions of *Courage* and *The Entrancing Life*, were gathered together in 1938 as *M'Connachie and J.M.B.: Speeches by J. M. Barrie* (Peter Davies); the texts often differ from contemporary transcriptions in *The Times* and other newspapers, which in turn deviate from the actual words spoken – evidenced by certain speeches recorded on Movietone and Pathé newsreels. My excerpts have been taken from the Peter Davies compilation. Similar problems of consistency occur with Barrie's novels, where the US and British texts often differ: my extracts are from the latter. The novelization of *Peter Pan*, first published as *Peter and Wendy* (Hodder & Stoughton, 1911), has been re-titled *Peter Pan* (currently in Puffin paperback), but should not be confused with 're-told' – i.e. simplified – versions masquerading under the same title.

Select Bibliography:

The following books and articles have also been consulted. In particular, Denis Mackail's encyclopaedic biography, *The Story of J.M.B.*, has been of inestimable help. The only other biographies of similar standing are W. A. Darlington's highly perceptive *J. M. Barrie*, and Janet Dunbar's more recent *J. M. Barrie: The Man Behind the Image*. An asterisk indicates those works from which I have quoted, and I am grateful to their respective publishers for permission to do so. Publication dates are for Great Britain, unless otherwise stated.

ADLARD, ELEANOR (ED): **Dear Turley* (Muller, 1942)
AGATE, JAMES: *Those Were the Nights* (Hutchinson, 1946)
ANSELL, MARY: *Happy Houses* (Cassell, 1912)
—**The Happy Garden* (Cassell, 1912)
—**Dogs and Men* (Duckworth, 1923)
ASQUITH, CYNTHIA: *Haply I May Remember* (Barrie, 1950)
—**Portrait of Barrie* (Barrie, 1954)
—*Diaries: 1915–1918* (Hutchinson, 1968)
BEATON, CECIL: **Contribution to *The Rise and Fall of the Matinée Idol*, edited by Anthony Curtis (Weidenfeld 1974)
BEERBOHM, MAX: **Last Theatres* (Hart-Davis, 1970)
BLAKE, GEORGE: **Barrie and the Kailyard School* (Barker, 1951)
BLOW, SYDNEY: **Through Stage Doors* (Chambers, 1958)
BOOTHBY, LORD: **My Yesterday, Your Tomorrow* (Hutchinson, 1962)

—*My Oxford* (Contribution) Edited by Ann Thwaite (Robson Books, 1977)

BRAYBROOKE, PATRICK: *Barrie: A Study in Fairies and Mortals* (Dranes, 1924)

CARDUS, NEVILLE: *Autobiography* (Collins, 1947)

CARRINGTON, DORA: **Letters and Diaries*, edited by David Garnett (Cape, 1975)

CHALMERS, PATRICK: *The Barrie Inspiration* (Peter Davies, 1938)

CHASE, PAULINE: **Peter Pan's Postbag* (Heinemann, 1909)

—*My Reminiscences of Peter Pan* (Strand Magazine, Jan. 1913)

COCHRAN, CHARLES: *Cock-a-Doodle-Do* (Dent, 1941)

COMPTON, FAY: *Rosemary: Some Remembrances* (Rivers, 1926)

COVENEY, PETER: *The Image of Childhood* (Peregrine, 1967)

DARLINGTON, W. A.: **J. M. Barrie* (Blackie, 1938)

DARTON, F. J. HARVEY: *J. M. Barrie* (Nisbet, 1929)

DU MAURIER, ANGELA: *I'm Only the Sister* (Peter Davies, 1949)

DU MAURIER, DAPHNE: **Gerald: A Portrait* (Gollancz, 1934)

—*The Du Mauriers* (Gollancz, 1937)

—*Growing Pains* (Gollancz, 1977)

DU MAURIER, GUY: **Letters from Lieut.-Col. G. L. B. Du Maurier, D.S.O., 3rd Battalion Royal Fusiliers, To His Wife* (Bumpus, 1915)

DUNBAR, JANET: **J. M. Barrie: The Man Behind the Image* (Collins, 1970)

ELDER, MICHAEL: *The Young James Barrie* (Macdonald, 1968)

FARR, DIANA: **Gilbert Cannan: A Georgian Prodigy* (Chatto, 1978)

FRASER, MORRIS: *The Death of Narcissus* (Secker & Warburg, 1976)

GEDULD, HARRY M.: *Sir James M. Barrie* (Twayne, New York, 1971)

GREEN, ROGER LANCELYN: **Fifty Years of Peter Pan* (Peter Davies, 1954)

—*J. M. Barrie* (Bodley Head, 1960)

HAMMERTON, J. A.: *J. M. Barrie and His Books* (Marshall, 1900)

—**Barrie: The Story of a Genius* (Sampson Low, 1929)

—*Barrieland: A Thrums Pilgrimage* (Sampson Low, 1931)

HICKS, SEYMOUR: *Between Ourselves* (Cassell, 1930)

HOLROYD, MICHAEL: **Lytton Strachey: A Biography* (Penguin, 1971)

KENNEDY, JOHN: *Thrums and the Barrie Country* (Cranton, 1930)

KENNETT, LADY: **Self Portrait of an Artist* (Murray, 1949)

LEWIS, C. DAY: **The Buried Day* (Chatto, 1960)

LOWNDES, MARIE B.: **Diaries and Letters*, edited by Susan Lowndes (Chatto, 1971)

LUCAS, AUDREY: **E. V. Lucas: A Portrait* (Methuen, 1939)

LURIE, ALISON: *The Boy Who Couldn't Grow Up* (*New York Review*, Feb 1975)

LYTTON, THE EARL OF: *Anthony* (Peter Davies, 1935)

MACCARTHY, DESMOND: *Theatre* (Kee, 1954)

MACKAIL, DENIS: **The Story of J.M.B.* (Peter Davies, 1941)

MACLEOD, BETTY: **Contribution to Norland Place School, 1876–1976*, edited by Joan Keene (Old Norlanders Association, 1976)

MARCOSSIN, I. & DANIEL FROHMAN: **Charles Frohman: Manager and Man* (Bodley Head, New York, 1915)

MASON, A. E. W.: **'James Barrie'* (Article in *Dictionary of National Biography*, O.U.P. 1949)

MAUDE, CYRIL: *Behind the Scenes with Cyril Maude* (Murray, 1927)

MAUDE, PAMELA: **Worlds Away* (Heinemann, 1964)

MEREDITH, GEORGE: *Letters of George Meredith*, edited by His Son (Constable, 1912)

MILLINGTON-DRAKE, EUGEN: *Hugh Macnaghten's House Record, Eton: 1899–1920* (Ballantyne, 1930)

MORRELL, OTTOLINE: *Ottoline: The Early Memoirs of Lady Ottoline Morrell 1873–1915*, edited by Robert Gathorne-Hardy (Faber, 1963)

MOULT, THOMAS: *Barrie* (Cape, 1928)

ORMOND, LEONEE: *George du Maurier* (Routledge, 1969)

ROBBINS, PHYLLIS: **Maude Adams: An Intimate Portrait* (Putnam, New York, 1956)

ROY, JAMES A.: **James Matthew Barrie: An Appreciation* (Jarrolds, 1937)

Sources

RUSSELL, BERTRAND: *The Autobiography of Bertrand Russell, 1872–1914 (Unwin, 1967)

SCOTT, PETER: *The Eye of the Wind (Hodder & Stoughton, 1961)

SHELTON, GEORGE: It's Smee (Ernest Benn, 1928)

STEVENSON, ROBERT LOUIS: *The Letters of Robert Louis Stevenson, edited by Sir Sidney Colvin, 5 vol. (Heinemann, 1924)

TERRISS, ELLALINE: Just a Little Bit of String (Hutchinson, 1955)

TERRY, ELLEN: Memoirs (Gollancz, 1933)

THOMAS, GWENDOLEN: 'Barrie and Hanny' (John o'London, Jun.–Nov. 1953)

TREWIN, J. C.: The Edwardian Theatre (Blackwell, 1966)

—The Theatre since 1900 (Dakers, 1968)

VANBRUGH, IRENE: *To Tell My Story (Hutchinson, 1948)

WALBROOK, H. M.: *J. M. Barrie and the Theatre (F. V. White, 1922)

WALKLEY, A. B.: *Drama and Life (Methuen, 1922)

Source notes

Chapter 1 (1860–1885)

1. All quoted extracts in this chapter are from *Margaret Ogilvy* (Hodder & Stoughton, 1896) unless otherwise indicated below.
2. Barrie, *The Greenwood Hat* (privately printed, 1930), pp. 1–2.
3. Barrie, *Sentimental Tommy* (Cassell, 1896), p. 335.
4. Barrie, *Peter and Wendy* (Hodder & Stoughton, 1911), p. 10.
5. Speech at the Prize-Giving at Dumfries Academy, 30 June 1893: *M'Connachie and J.M.B.: Speeches by J. M. Barrie* (Peter Davies, 1938), p. 4. Hereafter referred to as *Speeches*.
6. Speech on being awarded the Freedom of Dumfries, 11 December 1924. *Speeches*, pp. 83–4.
7. *The Greenwood Hat*, pp. 64, 67.
8. *Dumfries Herald*, 24 January 1877.
9. Prize-Giving at Dumfries Academy, *Speeches*, pp. 5–6.
10. See *Sources*: Unpublished Sources, 2.
11. Freedom of Dumfries, *Speeches*, p. 88.
12. ibid., pp. 88–9.
13. Mackail, *The Story of J.M.B.*, p. 44.
14. ibid.
15. Hammerton, *Barrie: The Story of a Genius*, p. 74.
16. *The Greenwood Hat*, pp. 132, 134, 214.
17. *Nottingham Journal*, 28 January 1884.
18. *The Greenwood Hat*, p. 7.

Chapter 2 (1885–1894)

1. Speech at the Authors' Club Dinner, 12 December 1932. *Speeches*, pp. 248–9.
2. *The Greenwood Hat*, p. 178.
3. Blake, *Barrie and the Kailyard School*, p. 64.
4. *Letters of Robert Louis Stevenson*, IV, p. 273.
5. ibid., p. 274.
6. Speech to the Incorporated Society of Authors, Playwrights and Composers, 28 November 1928. *Speeches*, p. 156.
7. *Peter and Wendy*, p. 267.
8. *Edinburgh Evening Dispatch*, 6 November 1889.
9. Letter to Mrs Fred Oliver, 21 December 1931.
10. Jerome, *My Life and Times*, p. 133.
11. Letter to Maarten Maartens, 20 November 1893.
12. *British Weekly*, 19 May 1892.
13. *Edinburgh Evening Dispatch*, 21 September 1887.

Chapter 3 (1894–1897)

1. *Sketch*, 4 July 1894.
2. Ansell, *Dogs and Men*, p. 26.
3. Letter to Cynthia Asquith, 10 November 1935.
4. Unpublished, in the possession of the Quiller-Couch family.
5. *Margaret Ogilvy*, pp. 193–4.
6. ibid., pp. 201–2.
7. Letter to Maarten Maartens, 17 December 1893.
8. Letter to Quiller-Couch, 26 March 1895.
9. Marcossin and Frohman, *Charles Frohman*, pp. i–iv, 255.
10. ibid., p. iii.
11. *Tommy and Grizel*: reproduced as a frontispiece to Vol. IV of the American Peter Pan Edition of *The Works of J. M. Barrie* (Scribner, 1929).
12. Maude, *Worlds Away*, pp. 137–45.
13. Robbins, *Maude Adams*, p. 41.
14. Told by Barrie to Peter Llewelyn Davies's wife, Margaret.

Chapter 4 (The Davies Family)
1. Quoted by Peter Davies in his *Morgue*. See *Sources*: Unpublished Sources, 1.
2. Millar, *George du Maurier*, p. 34.
3. Letter from du Maurier to Tom Armstrong, 25 March 1890.
4. Letter from Dolly Ponsonby (*née* Parry) to Peter Davies, December 1946.
5. Entry in Dolly Ponsonby's diary, see *Sources*: Unpublished Sources, 10.
6. Daphne du Maurier, *Gerald*, p. 71.
7. Dolly Ponsonby to Peter Davies, op, cit.
8. *Peter Pan*, Act I.

Chapter 5 (1898–1900)
1. Letter to Quiller-Couch, 12 February 1899.
2. ibid., 11 December 1896.

Chapter 6 (1900–1901)
1. Mackail, *The Story of J.M.B.*, p. 300.
2. Maude, *Worlds Away*, pp. 144–5.
3. Mackail, *The Story of J.M.B.*, p. 306. All further extracts and quotations by Denis Mackail come from this source.
4. Barrie, *The Little White Bird* (Hodder & Stoughton, 1902), p. 110.

Chapter 7 (1901–1904)
1. Ansell, *Dogs and Men*, p. 42.
2. Dedication to *Peter Pan*.
3. ibid.
4. Letter from Mary Hodgson to Nico Davies, November 1946.

Chapter 8 (1904–1905)
1. Robbins, *Maude Adams*, p. 90.
2. Marcossin and Frohman, *Charles Frohman*, p. 362.
3. Blow, *Through Stage Doors*, p. 162.
4. Green, *Fifty Years of Peter Pan*, p. 73.
5. Blow, op. cit., p. 162.
6. Dedication to *Peter Pan*.
7. *Anon: A Play*. See *Sources*: Unpublished Sources, 9.
8. Mackail, *The Story of J.M.B.*, p. 368.
9. Green, op. cit., p. 89.
10. Daphne du Maurier, *Gerald*, p. 110.
11. Lucas, *E. V. Lucas*, pp. 76–7.
12. *Peter and Wendy*, pp. 202–3.
13. Unpublished draft of the Dedication to *Peter Pan*.

Chapter 9 (1905–1906)
1. Letter from Dolly Ponsonby to Peter Davies, December 1946.
2. Taped interview with Geraldine Llewelyn Davies, March 1976.
3. Dolly Ponsonby to Peter Davies, op. cit.
4. The *Morgue*. All other comments by Peter Davies are from the same source, unless otherwise indicated.
5. Daphne du Maurier, to the author, March 1976.
6. Robbins, *Maude Adams*, pp. 90–1.
7. Mackail, *The Story of J.M.B.*, p. 379.
8. Daphne du Maurier, *Gerald*, p. 111.
9. Unpublished draft of the Dedication to *Peter Pan*.
10. Robbins, op. cit., p. 93.
11. *The Times*, 1 June 1906.

Chapter 10 (1906–1907)
1. Daphne du Maurier, to the author, March 1976.

2. Chase, *Peter Pan's Postbag*, p. 19.

Chapter 11 (1907–1908)
1. Dedication to *Peter Pan*.
2. Blow, *Through Stage Doors*, p. 166.
3. Taped interview with Geraldine Llewelyn Davies, March 1976. All other comments by Gerrie are from this source.
4. Letter from Nico Llewelyn Davies to the author, 1976. All other comments by Nico are from letters written by him to the author or his co-researcher between 1975 and 1978.
5. Diana Farr, *Gilbert Cannan*, p. 30.
6. Beerbohm, *Last Theatres*, p. 387.

Chapter 12 (1908–1910)
1. Taped interview with Geraldine Llewelyn Davies, March 1976.
2. Letter to Sylvia, 3 April 1909.
3. *The Daily Telegraph* and *Daily Mail*, 14 October 1909.
4. Letter to Pauline Chase, 8 October 1909.
5. Darlington, *J. M. Barrie*, p. 109.
6. Will Meredith to Scribner, 9 November 1909.
7. Roger Lancelyn Green, to the author, December 1975.
8. Barrie, *Neil and Tintinnabulum*, p. 65.
9. Dunbar, *J. M. Barrie: The Man Behind the Image*, p. 181.
10. Mary Barrie to H. G. Wells, 21 October 1909.
11. Interview in *Homes & Gardens*, Aug–Nov 1942.
12. Taped interview with Mrs Norma Douglas Henry, March 1978.
13. Letter from Dolly Ponsonby to Peter Davies, December 1946.
14. Mackail, *The Story of J.M.B.*, p. 426.
15. Letter from Medina Lewis to the author, June 1977.
16. Letter to Peter Davies, 1952.
17. Interview with Geraldine Llewelyn Davies, op. cit.

Chapter 13 (1910–1914)
1. *Neil and Tintinnabulum*, pp. 77–8.
2. Speech to Wallasey High School for Girls, 26 February 1924. *Speeches*, p. 64.
3. Day Lewis, *The Buried Day*, pp. 72–4.
4. Taped interview with Sebastian Earl, May 1976.
5. Letter to Quiller-Couch, 7 March 1911.
6. Barrie's Notebook dated 6 October 1926.
7. Address to St Andrews University, 3 May 1922. *Courage*, p. 32.
8. *Neil and Tintinnabulum*, p. 93
9. Letter to Elizabeth Lucas, 17 October 1920.
10. Letter from Peter Davies to Mary Hodgson, 11 June 1953.
11. Taped interview with Norma Douglas Henry, March 1978.
12. Beaton, *The Rise and Fall of the Matinée Idol*, p. 55.

Chapter 14 (1914–1915)
1. *Neil and Tintinnabulum*, p. 95.
2. *Dictionary of National Biography*, article on Barrie.
3. Letter to Pauline Chase, 24 December 1914.
4. Dedication to *Peter Pan*.
5. Macnaghten, *Fifty Years of Eton*, p. 84.

Chapter 15 (1915–1917)
1. Marcossin and Frohman, *Charles Frohman*, p. 384.
2. ibid., p. 386.
3. ibid., p. 182.
4. Letter to Pauline Chase, 12 May 1915.

Source notes

5. Taped interview, April 1976.
6. Taped interview, May 1976.
7. Letter from Medina Lewis to the author, September 1977.
8. Unpublished draft of the Dedication to *Peter Pan*.
9. Letter from Medina Lewis to the author, November 1977.
10. Letter to Kathleen Scott, 2 April 1917.
11. Thomas Hardy to Barrie, 24 June 1917.
12. Letter to Charles Turley Smith, 15 July 1917.
13. Asquith, *Portrait of Barrie*, p. 59.
14. Macnaghten, *Fifty Years of Eton*, p. 86.

Chapter 16 (1917–1921)
1. Letter from Nico to the author, January 1976.
2. Letter from Mary Hill to the author, January 1977.
3. Article in *The Times*, 21 May 1921.
4. Darlington, *J. M. Barrie*, p. 119.
5. Letter to Charles Turley Smith, 11 March 1918.
6. Letter to Nico, 9 May 1918.
7. Letter to Elizabeth Lucas, 12 May 1918.
8. Article in *The Times*, 21 May 1921.
9. Letters to Nico, 2, 23, 25 February, 10 March 1919.
10. Taped interview with Lord Boothby, December 1976.
11. ibid.
12. Taped interview with Clive Burt, May 1976.
13. Holroyd, *Lytton Strachey*, p. 1125.
14. Carrington, *Letters and Diaries*, p. 268.
15. ibid., p. 154.
16. Interview, op. cit.
17. Interview, op. cit.
18. Letter to Nico, 27 February 1919.
19. Letter to Nico, 29 April 1921.
20. Cynthia Asquith's diary, quoted by Janet Dunbar in *J. M. Barrie: The Man Behind the Image*, p. 256.
21. Letter from Nico to the author, December 1975.
22. *Oxford Times*, 27 May 1921.
23. ibid.

Epilogue
1. Holroyd, *Lytton Strachey*, p. 1125.
2. Letter to Robin Dundas, 16 June 1922.
3. Letter to Elizabeth Lucas, 15 September 1921.
4. Letter to Robin Dundas, 15 November 1922.
5. Letter to Mrs F. S. Oliver, 21 December 1931.
6. Letter to Cynthia Asquith, 14 November 1924.
7. Mackail, *The Story of J.M.B.*, p. 711.

Illustration sources and acknowledgements

The majority of photographs have been reproduced direct from original prints, or new prints from original nitrate negatives. The author gratefully acknowledges the following sources for supplying the illustrations reproduced on the pages indicated:

Academy of Motion Picture Arts and Sciences (Los Angeles): 259 (bottom); Beinecke Rare Book and Manuscript Library, Yale University: 13, 31 (bottom), 57 (bottom), 58, 59, 73 (bottom), 80 (bottom), 81 (top), 84 (bottom), 85, 86, 87, 88, 89, 90, 91, 92, 94 (top), 96 (bottom), 103, 104, 107 (top), 120, 125 (bottom right), 157 (top), 261 (bottom), 297; Elisabeth Bergner: 299; Lord Boothby: 255; British Film Institute: 39 (bottom), 259 (top); Theodora Calvert: 46, 133, 135 (top), 145; Centre du Rearmament Morale, Caux: 170 (top); Jeremy Clutterbuck: 251; Colindale Newspaper Library: 292; Norma Douglas Henry: 214 (bottom); Daphne du Maurier: 172 (bottom), 207; Dumfries Museum: 9; Janet Dunbar: 176; EMI-Pathé News: 1; Eton College: 239; Diana Farr: 23 (top), 169, 177; Roger Lancelyn Green: frontispiece, 19, 65, 110, 114, 115 (top), 118, 215, 233, 252; Mary Hill: 53 (bottom), 62 (top), 83 (top), 193, 219 (top), 254, 269; Lavinia Hinton: 275 (top); University of Illinois: 181 (top); *Illustrated London News*: 181 (bottom); Dorothy E. Jackson: 131 (top left & bottom); Eiluned and Medina Lewis: 249, 253, 258, 265, 272, 282; Lillie Library, University of Indiana: 100; Geraldine Llewelyn Davies: 60 (top), 97, 99 (bottom), 164, 235 (top), 260, 261 (top), 263, 264, 283; Nicholas Llewelyn Davies: 11, 23 (bottom), 41, 42, 44 (bottom), 45, 47, 50, 51, 52, 53 (top), 54, 55, 56, 57 (top), 66, 67, 68, 69 (bottom), 71, 72 (bottom), 74, 75, 76, 77, 78 (top), 79, 81 (bottom), 83 (bottom), 94 (bottom), 95 (top), 96 (top), 98, 101, 102, 108, 111 (right), 113, 115 (bottom), 117, 121, 122, 123, 124, 125 (top), 126 (top), 128, 129, 130 (top right), 132, 134, 135 (bottom), 136, 138, 139, 140, 141, 142, 143, 144, 146 (top), 147, 148, 149, 151, 154, 156, 157 (bottom), 159, 161, 167, 171, 173, 174, 178, 184, 185, 187, 188, 189, 191, 194, 195, 197, 199, 200, 202 (bottom), 203, 204, 211 (bottom), 213, 214 (top), 217, 220, 223, 228, 234, 235 (bottom), 237, 238, 240, 242, 245, 248 (top), 250, 257, 270, 273, 276 (top), 278, 279, 280, 281, 284 (top), 285 (bottom), 286, 287, 288, 290 (bottom), 296 (bottom), 298; Ruthven Llewelyn Davies: 73 (top), 78 (top), 82, 84 (top), 99 (top), 125 (bottom left), 152, 158, 170 (bottom), 180 (top), 196, 268; National Portrait Gallery of Scotland: 35, 107 (bottom), 275 (bottom); National Trust for Scotland (Barrie Birthplace, Kirriemuir): 15, 17, 28, 29, 116, 209, 262, 289, 294, 298 (top); *Punch*: 48; Foy Quiller-Couch: 31 (top), 33; the Estate of Arthur Rackham: 61 (top), 62 (bottom), 64, 69 (top), 70, 80 (top), 95 (bottom); Radio Times Hulton Picture Library: 43, 160, 202 (top), 216 (top), 230; Royal Borough of Kensington and Chelsea Photographic Archive: 34 (bottom); St Andrews University: 295; Sir Peter Scott: 168, 211 (top), 216 (bottom), 266, 276 (bottom); Margaret Ogilvy Sweeten: 4, 20, 27; Times Newspapers Ltd: 267, 290 (top); Julian Vinogradoff: 284 (bottom). Author's own collection: 3, 6, 7, 8, 14, 15, 16, 18, 22, 24, 34 (top), 36, 37, 38, 39 (top), 44 (top), 60 (bottom), 63, 72 (top), 93, 106, 109, 111 (left), 119 (top), 126 (bottom), 127, 146 (bottom), 162 (bottom), 166, 175, 183, 219 (bottom), 227, 247, 248, 285 (top).

Photographs taken by the author: 85 (bottom), 162 (top), 206, 222, 246, 296 (top), 300.

Photographic research by Bridget Holm and the author.